ANSWERS TO THE LABOUR QUESTION

Industrial Relations and the State in the Anglophone World, 1880–1945

Since the mid-nineteenth century, public officials, reformers, journalists, and other elites have referred to "the labour question." The labour question was rooted in the system of wage labour that spread throughout much of Europe and its colonies and produced contending classes as industrialization unfolded. *Answers to the Labour Question* explores how the liberal state responded to workers' demands that employers recognize trade unions as their legitimate representatives in their struggle for compensation and control over the workplace.

Gary Mucciaroni examines five Anglophone nations – Australia, Canada, Great Britain, New Zealand, and the United States – whose differences are often overlooked in the literature on political economy, which lumps them together as liberal, "market-led" economies. Despite their many shared characteristics and common historical origins, these nations' responses to the labour question diverged dramatically. Mucciaroni identifies the factors that explain why these nations developed such different industrial relations regimes and how the paths each nation took to the adoption of its regime reflected a different logic of institutional change. Drawing on newspaper accounts, parliamentary debates, and personal memoirs, among other sources, *Answers to the Labour Question* aims to understand the variety of state responses to industrial unrest and institutional change beyond the domain of industrial relations.

(Political Development: Comparative Perspectives)

GARY MUCCIARONI is a professor of political science and director of the Master of Public Policy program at Temple University.

Political Development: Comparative Perspectives

Editors: JACK LUCAS (University of Calgary) and
ROBERT C. VIPOND (University of Toronto)

Political Development: Comparative Perspectives publishes books that explore political development with a comparative lens, with a particular focus on studies of Canadian, American, or British political development. Books in this series use historical data and narratives to explain long-term patterns of institutional change, public policy, social movement politics, elections and party systems, and other key aspects of political authority and state power. They employ cross-country comparison, within-country comparison, or single-case analysis to illuminate important debates in comparative political science and history.

Editorial Advisory Board

Gerard Boychuk	*University of Waterloo*
Andrea Louise Campbell	*Massachusetts Institute of Technology*
Jean-François Godbout	*Université de Montréal*
Ursula Hackett	*Royal Holloway, University of London*
Richard Johnston	*University of British Columbia*
Desmond King	*Oxford University*
Robert Lieberman	*Johns Hopkins University*
Debra Thompson	*McGill University*
Carolyn Hughes Tuohy	*University of Toronto*
Richard Valelly	*Swarthmore College*
Margaret Weir	*Brown University*
Christina Wolbrecht	*Notre Dame University*

Books Published in This Series

Lost on Division: Party Unity in the Canadian Parliament / Jean-François Godbout

The Daily Plebiscite: Federalism, Nationalism, and Canada / David R. Cameron, edited by Robert C. Vipond

Faith, Rights, and Choice: The Politics of Religious Schools in Canada / James Farney and Clark Banack

Sleeping Dogs: Quebec and the Stabilization of Canadian Federalism after 1995 / Andrew McDougall

Answers to the Labour Question: Industrial Relations and the State in the Anglophone World, 1880–1945 / Gary Mucciaroni

Answers to the Labour Question

Industrial Relations and the State in the Anglophone World, 1880–1945

GARY MUCCIARONI

UNIVERSITY OF TORONTO PRESS
Toronto Buffalo London

© University of Toronto Press 2024
Toronto Buffalo London
utorontopress.com

ISBN 978-1-4875-5149-0 (cloth) ISBN 978-1-4875-5152-0 (EPUB)
ISBN 978-1-4875-5151-3 (paper) ISBN 978-1-4875-5153-7 (PDF)

___

Library and Archives Canada Cataloguing in Publication

Title: Answers to the labour question : industrial relations and the state in the anglophone world, 1880–1945 / Gary Mucciaroni.
Names: Mucciaroni, Gary, author.
Series: Political development: comparative perspectives.
Description: Series statement: Political development: comparative perspectives | Includes bibliographical references and index.
Identifiers: Canadiana (print) 20230468004 | Canadiana (ebook) 20230468047 | ISBN 9781487551490 (cloth) | ISBN 9781487551513 (paper) | ISBN 9781487551537 (PDF) | ISBN 9781487551520 (EPUB)
Subjects: LCSH: Industrial relations – English-speaking countries – History – 19th century. | LCSH: Industrial relations – English-speaking countries – History – 20th century. | LCSH: Industrial relations – Government policy – English-speaking countries – History – 19th century. | LCSH: Industrial relations – Government policy – English-speaking countries – History – 20th century.
Classification: LCC HD6971 .M83 2024 | DDC 331.0917/521 – dc23

___

Cover design: Will Brown
Cover images: Immigrant City Archives dba Lawrence History Center; Edin Photo; Library of Congress LC-USZ61-1200

We wish to acknowledge the land on which the University of Toronto Press operates. This land is the traditional territory of the Wendat, the Anishnaabeg, the Haudenosaunee, the Métis, and the Mississaugas of the Credit First Nation.

University of Toronto Press acknowledges the financial support of the Government of Canada, the Canada Council for the Arts, and the Ontario Arts Council, an agency of the Government of Ontario, for its publishing activities.

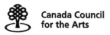

Contents

1 Answers to the Labour Question   3
2 Why the Anglophone Nations Diverged   21
3 How the Regimes Emerged   47
4 The Statist Answer: Australasia   58
5 The Voluntarist Answer: Great Britain   86
6 Elusive Answers: The United States before the 1930s   133
7 The Legalist Answer: The United States   171
8 Limited Statism: Canada's First Answer   197
9 Canada Capitulates to Legalism   228
10 Conclusions   246

Appendix   271
Notes   273
Works Cited   283
Index   303

ANSWERS TO THE LABOUR QUESTION

Industrial Relations and the State in the
Anglophone World, 1880–1945

1 Answers to the Labour Question

From Boston to New Orleans, from Mobile to Rochester, from Baltimore to St. Louis, we have now but one purpose; and that is, having driven all other political questions out of the arena, having abolished slavery, the only question left is labor – the relations of capital and labor.

(Wendell Phillips, *The Labor Question*, Boston:
Lee and Shepard, 1884, p. 33)

Organized labor now confronts organized capital ... and the burning question of modern times is how shall the ever-recurring controversies between them be adjusted and terminated?

(Richard Olney, *Legality and Propriety of Labor Organizations,
Some Suggestions Submitted by Richard Olney, esq.*, 1894)

For nations in the throes of industrialization in the mid-nineteenth century, public officials, reformers, and journalists began referring to "the labor question" or "the labor problem" (Zieger 1969, 279; Hyman 1989). The labour question was rooted in the system of wage labour that spread throughout much of Europe and its colonies and produced contending classes of employers and employees as industrialization unfolded. By the late nineteenth century class conflict had intensified in all industrial nations. When technological innovations increased productive capacities, capitalist economies experienced an "organizational revolution" as larger and more powerful aggregations of capital and labour rose to dominate markets (Marks 1989, 79–82). Swings between boom and bust became more acute, and the economy's disruptive effects rippled throughout society. Workers demanded not only higher wages, better working conditions, and control over craft production, but also that employers recognize their organizations as their legitimate representatives and that they enter into collective bargaining. Labour often resorted to strikes, boycotts, and similar actions to pressure employers; employers resorted to lockouts and frequently enlisted the state's coercive powers to maintain control.

Whether one viewed the labour question as a problem of social justice or of social order, industrial capitalism posed a great challenge for the state, particularly in countries with democratic forms of government. As actual or threatened disruptions to commerce and daily life became more acute, elites worried about the survival of the existing political and social order. The liberal state, unavoidably drawn into these conflicts, responded with a variety of answers to the labour question. The situation challenged two bedrock assumptions of liberalism – one, that capital and labour could coexist in harmony and, two, that the state could maintain a "neutral" role in class relations. Industrial capitalism made it very difficult, if not untenable, for the liberal state to maintain these assumptions. The more acute or frequent the conflicts became, the more class harmony appeared out of reach and the more likely it would impel the state to behave in ways that punctured the myth of neutrality. Thus, the labour question posed a great challenge to elites, especially in industrial nations where workers had developed some capacity to exert influence in the industrial and political realms. Particularly important was whether those segments of the working class that could organize to defend their interests believed that employers were satisfying their demands for just treatment and recognition. If they did not and threatened to foment disorder, then the state might have to choose between its own legitimacy in the eyes of workers and the need to maintain social order, especially if industrial unrest placed the community at risk.

Labour leaders, employers, public officials, and reformers sought answers to the labour question on the terrain of industrial relations.[1] Industrial relations consist of a set of institutional arrangements that prescribe how conflicts between capital and labour are prevented or resolved. Decisions about institutional design reflected how nations tried to reconcile and make trade-offs among social justice, workplace control and democracy, social order, and class harmony. The specific issues that constituted institutional design involved whether the state should regulate industrial relations by granting and enforcing rights and obligations to each side in the employment equation, what those should be and the proper balance between workers and employers' interests, and how disputes should be resolved when acute conflicts erupted between them.

Regardless of how much or little the state supported enlarging labour's rights and its ability to challenge employers, the state invariably had an interest in mitigating industrial unrest to avoid public inconvenience, disruptions to production, and physical harm if labour conflicts turned violent. The state faced a range of options, at least in theory, in seeking to maintain industrial peace. Those options had different implications for the relationship between labour and capital and for the role of the state. The state might attempt to maintain the existing balance of class relations or shift the balance in favour of capital or labour. It might insert itself into dispute resolution on an ad hoc or permanent basis and do so in ways that were more coercive or less so towards either one or both parties. This book is about why nations chose different answers to the labour question and how they came to make those choices.

The Anglophone Nations in Comparative-Historical Perspective

Very little comparative analysis exists of the important formative stage of the state's role in industrial relations,[2] and even less focuses on the Anglophone nations as a group.[3] The dominant focus of the comparative study of advanced political economies has been overwhelmingly on Europe and the United States. Whenever discussed as a group, the Anglophone nations typically get lumped together in the "varieties of capitalism" literature as "market-led" or "liberal market" economies (see, for example, Hamann and Kelly 2017). Yet, the Anglophone nations came up with a strikingly broad array of answers to the labour question. The differences in the role of the state among the Anglophone nations during the twentieth century were arguably as great as those between them and the continental European nations.

Table 1.1 presents the Anglophone cases that fit under three distinct industrial relations systems, or "regimes" as I shall label them. At one end of the spectrum, we find the statist regimes of Australia and New Zealand, which adopted compulsory arbitration or "wages boards." In these "Australasian" nations, tribunals, and boards virtually displaced collective bargaining. At the other end of the spectrum, Britain developed a voluntarist regime that provided maximum autonomy to labour and capital in the conduct of industrial relations. The state granted labour basic legal rights of organization, freeing them from prosecutions for criminal conspiracy, granting them immunity from civil liability and ending most judicial interference in their affairs. The decision of each to engage in collective bargaining and the content of agreements between employers and unions were left up to the two parties to decide.

The North American nations adopted regimes that occupied a distinct middle ground between the other two regime types, establishing a regulatory structure that guaranteed rights and placed obligations on labour organizations and employers, but did not displace collective bargaining.

As in the United States, the state's primary role was to provide an elaborate legal framework to supervise the procedures for workers to organize, certify unions as exclusive bargaining agents, and ensure that both sides bargain in good faith and uphold agreements. Thus, this regime goes much further than the minimal labour rights established under voluntarism but falls far short of displacing collective bargaining with state determination of wages, benefits, and conditions of employment. Finally, Canada represents a hybrid regime. It grafted Canada's version of the Wagner Act (legalism) on to a very limited form

Table 1.1. Industrial Relations Regimes of the Twentieth Century

	Regime Type		
Level of Regulation of Industrial Relations	Statism: High	Legalism: Moderate	Voluntarism: Low
Legal protections afforded trade unions	Very high (registered unions gain right to exclusive jurisdiction as the legally recognized bargaining agent for workers in an industry and right to refer disputes to conciliation and arbitration boards)	High (employers must recognize unions and bargain in good faith; body of law regulating union representation certification and "unfair labour practices")	Low. Basic legal rights to union organization, picketing, etc. (elimination of unions as criminal conspiracies in restraint of trade; immunity against employer civil suits)
Mode of determining wages, benefits, and working conditions in unionized industries	compulsory arbitration if collective bargaining fails (at request of one of the parties to a dispute, courts or boards determine contract provisions)	collective bargaining	collective bargaining
Cases	Australia, New Zealand	Canada*, United States	Great Britain**

* plus compulsory investigation and conciliation
** plus voluntary, ad hoc tripartite conflict resolution

of statism that included compulsory investigation and conciliation of disputes only in mining and public utilities.

Why did these countries end up with such different answers to the "labour question"? That these nations faced similar challenges and shared many common historical roots and yet went down such dramatically different paths makes these outcomes all the more puzzling. Second, *what does their experience with finding answers to the labour question tell us more generally about how institutional changes occur?* The chapters that follow seek to answer these questions.

The similarities among the Anglophone countries provide us with a good deal of analytical leverage to pinpoint causal factors (along with tracing out the impacts of earlier events, trends, and decisions upon later ones for each case separately). Australia, Canada, Great Britain, New Zealand, and the United States were industrial capitalist economies with private property ownership of the means of production and the wage system of labour. All faced serious industrial relations crises at approximately the same time – between the last decade of the nineteenth and first three decades of the twentieth centuries. All five established stable liberal democratic regimes under "the rule of law" before the twentieth century, followed English common law traditions, and were English-speaking (with the partial exception of Canada). Four were former British colonies that enjoyed a considerable degree of self-government during the colonial period.[4] Four were parliamentary systems and used royal commissions extensively to study issues and recommend new policies.

The dominant labour organizations of all five nations largely rejected socialism and revolutionary class politics during the reform period and sought reforms within existing capitalist and liberal democratic institutions. Though they differed in some important ways, the movements often used militant tactics but did not seek to replace the wage system and private control over the means of production with expropriation and central planning. Rather, in the main, they sought to enlarge labour's share of national income, improve its working conditions, raise its standard of living, and mitigate the risks and vulnerabilities that an unregulated market would create.[5] To the extent that some of these movements championed socialist ideas (e.g., nationalized industries), they did so after the period examined here when their industrial relations systems had become established. Although all of the labour organizations faced some degree of repression, relative to other nations on the European continent and elsewhere, most of them were not outlawed and driven underground. Most had gained or were in the process of gaining incorporation in liberal democratic processes, including the voting franchise and affiliation with political parties.

Finally, in all of these nations liberal progressives or "radical liberals" emerged who were generally oriented towards using the state in positive ways to regulate and reform (rather than overturn) capitalism, although some anticipated a gradual, peaceful transition to socialism. Most believed that reform could enhance the life of individual workers and promote class harmony. These educated, middle-class reformers recognized the need for labour to organize to protect its interests vis-à-vis large, powerful corporations and sought ways to reduce industrial unrest. The paramount concern with most reformers was to find practical ways to mitigate class conflict that, they argued, was destructive to all concerned, especially the public.

We should note that for the purposes of understanding why each nation made the choices that it did, all of these nations were independent sovereigns, including Canada and Australia. Canada gained independence from Great Britain in 1867 under the British North America Act, which formalized Canada's status as a self-governing nation, long before the period covered in this study. While the independence of the Australian Commonwealth and its six colonies did not occur until 1901 (just after many of the colonies had adopted their modern industrial relations regimes), British governments had afforded the settlers of these colonies many years earlier a considerable measure of self-government to pursue their own domestic policies (Quinlan 1989, 27–9).

Before learning about the key historical milestones that marked the emergence of new industrial relations regimes in each of the five Anglophone nations, let us first turn to a more in-depth discussion of different types of industrial relations regimes.

The Role of the State and Types of Industrial Relations Regimes

I label the answers to the labour question "industrial relations regimes" to denote the enduring set of formal institutional rules and informal expectations that nations established to deal with class conflict and specifically regarding how the state would (or would not) mediate the relationship between capital and labour over the terms of employment and workplace control.

When I refer to the state and industrial relations, we must not confuse the role of the state in *creating and maintaining industrial relations regimes* with its *assigned role within a regime* once it is established. As we will see, the state in all the Anglophone nations played important political roles in shaping the institutional regimes that emerged in their respective nations; however, the extent and nature of their role *within* those regimes varied dramatically. It is the latter that I seek to explain.

The role of the state in an industrial relations regime refers to its level of intervention in balancing employer–employee powers and resolving disputes, and what tools the state uses to perform those tasks. States have a wide variety of tools potentially at their disposal, including the conferral of legal rights and obligations enforced through regulations and court orders; conciliation and mediation services, which may be more institutionalized and elaborate or less so; and legal authority to make awards and enforce settlements. Although distinct, labour rights and industrial relations regulation are closely linked. Since much regulation of industrial relations involves establishing and enforcing labour's rights to organize and engage in collective bargaining; in general, the greater the level of legal protection, the greater the level of regulation of industrial relations. However, regulation of employer–employee relations can go far beyond implementing labour's rights; conversely, robust protections for union rights can coexist with keeping the state out of a host of matters that are left to employers and unions to negotiate on their own.

Industrial relations regimes include more than public policies and state institutions. They include the relations between labour and capital that exist *outside* of the state's actions, such as whether each side regards the other as a legitimate partner in the system of production and whether the two sides resolve differences through consensus-building or adversarial processes. Decisions about which parties to industrial relations enjoy which rights and what regulations each will be under, are secondary to fundamental decisions over whether the state ought to play *any* role in granting rights or policing industrial relations.

We can identify four distinct types of industrial relations regimes among the Anglophone nations of the nineteenth and twentieth centuries: *repression, voluntarism, legalism,* and *statism.*

Under **repression,** employers and the state use a variety of means to block labour's demands to organize, have their organizations recognized, and represent workers' interests. The degree of repression may vary substantially. Some regimes totally outlaw independent labour organizations, drive them underground, and impose harsh penalties, including incarceration, on labour leaders and activists who engage in collective action. Other regimes permit labour organizations to exist but place severe constraints on their ability to operate by allowing employers, for example, to refuse to recognize and work with unions. Under labour repression, employers usually enlist the power and resources of the state to make it difficult for labour to organize or operate effectively for their members. Courts may issue injunctions or other orders pre-empting or punishing unions for engaging in strikes or other actions, basing their decisions on legal doctrines that privilege the property rights of employers and the "right of contract" of individual employers and employees. Workers who undertake collective action may be found liable for damages or guilty of "conspiracies in restraint of trade" under anti-trust laws. The state often discourages and suppresses strikes, boycotts, and similar activities intended to exert economic pressure on employers by employing police and militias to intimidate, arrest, incarcerate, or use violence against trade unionists, or permit employers to hire their own private police forces.

While labour repression was generally less harsh and pervasive in the Anglophone world than in Germany and other continental European nations, it existed in one form or another in all of them (Marks 1989, 55).[6] Drawing upon an ideology that viewed markets as natural phenomena that depended upon freedom of choice for individuals, jurists invented a variety of common law doctrines and statutory interpretations that considered unions unlawful "combinations in restraint of trade" and thwarted their efforts to strike and engage in other actions. By the late nineteenth century, the state formally permitted trade unions to exist and passed laws exempting them from criminal liability, except in the United States where unions had always been legal. However, governments sometimes ignored these laws or they continued to criminalize the *actions* of trade unions, or unions remained subject to civil penalties. In many instances, employers and the state enlisted police and the military against strikers, often leading to violent confrontations.

One possible answer to the labour question was for organized labour and employers to reach a détente on their own accord, in which employers would accommodate labour's demands for trade union "recognition" and collective bargaining, with only minimal state intervention. ("Recognition" refers to when employers accept the idea that employees have the right to negotiate employment conditions as group rather than as individuals and that organizations of the workers' own choosing are legitimate agents for that purpose.) **Voluntarism** (or "self-regulation") may be distinguished from labour repression through "joint control" over wages and working conditions by employers and employee organizations and by the removal of legal obstacles to labour's ability to organize and negotiate wages and other conditions of employment.[7] As long as they do not engage in behaviour that would be otherwise illegal, labour and business enjoy considerable autonomy in pursuing their interests and in bringing economic pressure to bear upon one another. "Laissez faire" or "free enterprise for all" might be other names for this regime. The outcome of disputes is solely left up to the strength that each side can muster in competition with the other. Each side has greater latitude to engage in a variety of behaviours (e.g., strikes, yellow dog contracts), that would be forbidden or curtailed under other regimes. Neither party has a legal obligation to engage in collective bargaining. Their agreements have no legal force but are honoured informally as "gentlemen's agreements."

The willingness of employers and employees to recognize each other as legitimate partners and to engage in collective bargaining should not be confused with the absence of conflict. The existence of strong institutionalized collective bargaining arrangements does not necessarily preclude strikes, lockouts, and similar disruptions. Precisely because both sides in the conflict have considerable leeway to organize and exert pressure upon the other, the competitiveness may result in considerable conflict and unrest.

Thus, voluntarism is distinguished by the state guaranteeing few legally enforceable rights and the absence of state compulsion. The state does not compel employers and employees to recognize one another or engage in collective bargaining. As Kahn-Freund (1954, 54–5) puts it, "Employers are under no legal obligation to negotiate … [and] the law recognizes the desirability of collective bargaining, but it refuses to apply legal sanctions so as to enforce it." It scrupulously attempts to maintain a neutral, arms-length distance from industrial relations, intervening mainly to remove barriers to voluntary association and collective action. It bestows no official recognition upon unions, establishes a minimal legal framework to regulate the conduct of industrial relations, supplies little in the way of permanent agencies or procedures for facilitating voluntary agreements, and intervenes in disputes only under extraordinary circumstances.

The state's role is not inconsequential, however. The state's involvement extends, first, to the removal of legal and judicial impediments, such as injunctions, civil liability for damages so that labour organizations are free to organize and engage in picketing and other non-violent actions. Second, during periods of acute industrial unrest when disruption to vital interests is at stake, the state may intervene more actively to facilitate agreements between the parties through conciliation and arbitration. Except during wartime, the interventions are purely voluntary. Both parties must agree to enter such processes and are not bound by any decisions that mediators or arbitrators make (Kahn-Freund 1954, 91). Third, although voluntarism provides considerable freedom for each side to pursue its interests, the state counterbalances this impulse by stressing norms and processes that favour restraint, conciliation, and "responsible" behaviour (Fox 1985, 246–9).

Where voluntarism did not take hold, a deeper level of state involvement was virtually inevitable. Repression was one option, but this answer could prove difficult to sustain in the long run because the spread of mass democratic politics could enable labour to challenge the legitimacy of the industrial relations regime and of the government itself. But the more immediate problem with repression was that it risked igniting further unrest, particularly during times and in places when labour organization was easier and might have more disruptive potential. When that happened, the only way for the state to establish legitimacy in the eyes of labour *and* maintain industrial peace was to find an alternative to repression.

Virtually all the answers to the labour question that involved non-repressive state intervention posed potential risks for the labour movement. The state could simply act as a guarantor of labour rights and impose obligations upon employers. But state involvement also meant the possibility that the state would reduce trade unions' autonomy as well, compromise its bargaining strength, and undermine their organizational purpose to defend workers' interests. Labour would have to decide whether the protections would be worth the risks. And the options that labour had to consider were not necessarily under its control. The state faced a similar dilemma. Rebalancing class relations by guaranteeing labour rights could reduce labour unrest by forcing employers to accept unions and channel industrial conflict into non-violent processes of dispute resolution. But it could also embolden the unions in their conflicts with employers, setting the stage for further unrest. And of course, employers could resist incursions on their prerogatives by both labour and the state.

Like voluntarism, **legalism** reserves the resolution of labour disputes involving wages, working conditions, and similar matters up to negotiated settlements between employers and labour organizations. The state does not adjudicate disputes in order to determine wages, benefits, working conditions, and the like. The relative leverage of each party in the negotiations is the most immediate determinant of the terms of the settlements that arise out of the negotiations. Legalism is necessary where voluntarism is not possible; that is, where the enforcement of labour rights and employer obligations is necessary. Legalism, like statism, includes an important element of compulsion that is absent in voluntarism and a much larger, more positive, and continuous involvement of the law in policing industrial relations. Legalism goes beyond removing barriers to labour organizing and peaceful activities, to determining and enforcing the rights and responsibilities of employers and employees.

The legalist regime establishes an elaborate framework for industrial relations that includes defining rights, obligations, and processes that each side must follow. Under the auspices of a permanent, formally politically independent regulatory agency, the state supervises representation elections, certifies labour organizations as exclusive bargaining agents, specifies what actions by employers and unions constitute "unfair labour practices," and adjudicates whether one party or the other has violated the law (with courts acting as venues for appeals). While voluntarism has a permissive orientation, legalism has a promotional one. Legalist regimes inevitably and overtly reshape class relations within the sphere of industrial relations. Historically their launch has been associated with efforts to strengthen employee organizations vis-à-vis employers, for example, by prohibiting employers from refusing to recognize trade unions, trying to influence employees' choice of representatives, and refusing to engage in collective bargaining in good faith. Once freed of governmental restraints, under voluntarism, unions could rely solely upon their own economic power and organizing efforts. But under legalism, the state tipped the balance in favour of unions by policing employer behaviour. Legalist regimes do not always operate to favour labour interests, however; changes in labour laws and regulations may favour employer interests. Thus, we should not conflate legalism (or voluntarism or statism) with a robust, growing union movement. Like voluntarism and statism, legalism is a set of institutional relationships, not an indication of which side is winning the industrial relations struggle.

Statism introduces the most extensive level of state involvement in industrial relations, a further movement away from the industrial arena and towards state administrative and judicial venues, particularly regarding dispute settlement (Woods 1973, 346). It shares with legalism significant elements of compulsion that are absent in voluntarist systems. The distinguishing feature of statist regimes is where the compulsion is directed. Legalist regimes provide a regulatory framework that leads up to collective bargaining but does not supplant it. The distinguishing feature of statist regimes is that the state seeks to shape the substantive content of the settlements between labour and capital. Under compulsory conciliation, state mediators can compel the parties to unresolved disputes to go through a process of investigation and conciliation in which the state tries to get the parties to agree to a particular set of terms. Its stronger variants supplant collective bargaining with administrative or judicial determination of wages and working conditions. Under compulsory arbitration and "wages boards," special, permanent courts or boards investigate disputes and make awards that are binding upon the parties.[8] Under the most robust statist regimes, either the state or one of the parties to the dispute can initiate arbitration proceedings and the awards are binding upon both parties. Since only one party is needed to initiate arbitration, the party that is in the weaker bargaining position has an incentive to initiate the proceedings, moving the site of conflict from the industrial realm to the state, from which they may get an award that is more favourable than if they relied on their own bargaining power. The result is that arbitration courts and "wages boards" often supplant much of collective bargaining as the central institution for dispute settlement. Statist regimes usually include other requirements as well. To participate in the system, unions typically must register with the state and are subject to regulation by it. Before conciliation and arbitration, employers and unions are often required to attempt collective bargaining. Strikes and lockouts typically are prohibited or severely restrained during the process of conciliation and arbitration.

While statist regimes typically include the same legally enforceable rights and responsibilities for labour and employers that one finds under legalist regimes, it is possible for the state to impose compulsory arbitration without guaranteeing effective labour rights. Under these circumstances, employers may still refuse to recognize unions and engage in collective bargaining or may bargain only with "company unions" that are not independent of the employer, for example.

Keep in mind that these are ideal types and no political economy in the real world includes all of the characteristics described above or all in the same way. Within each category cases can vary substantially on key dimensions. One legalist regime might include specific regulations that favour organized labour, while others may benefit it less so and be more permissive towards employer practices that work to the detriment of unions. Similarly, while all statist regimes involve direct involvement by the state in industrial relations and an element of coercion, some statist regimes have a much deeper involvement in industrial relations than others. One state may mandate compulsory arbitration of disputes while another may mandate only their investigation and mediation. And as discussed, some repressive regimes act more harshly towards independent labour organizations than do others. Furthermore, no real-world case is exclusively of one type. We may find, for example, that independent trade unions are suppressed in the vast majority of industries, but not all; or we may find a nation that operates under voluntarist principles for most of its industries and during "normal" times but adopts legalist or statist principles for a few industries or during crisis periods.

Comparison with Other Typologies. It is useful to compare and contrast this typology of industrial relations regimes with those that Colin Crouch has developed. Focusing mainly on European nations, Crouch (1979, 179–96) distinguished nations along two dimensions, whether they were "liberal" or "corporatist" and whether they had "weak" or "strong" trade unions. Liberal systems with strong unions he labelled "free collective bargaining" and those with weak unions as "neo-*laissez-faire*." Crouch's other two types were "bargained corporatism" (strong unions) and "corporatism" (weak unions). Crouch (1993) later distinguished among systems characterized by "contestation," "pluralist bargaining," and "neo-corporatism."

Much like the "varieties of capitalism" literature, Crouch's focus on differentiating among mainly European systems led him to lump together all of the Anglophone nations under the "liberal" rubric. About the only distinctions that we can make among Anglophone nations using Crouch's typologies are between those that experienced labour repression at some point in their history and those that moved on to a non-repressive regime. His "neo-*laissez faire*" and "contestation" types resemble labour repression, with weak labour unions and high levels of mistrust and conflict between capital and labour. His "free collective bargaining" and "pluralist bargaining" categories resemble voluntarism. But that is where the parallels end. Except perhaps during wartime, the Anglophone nations were inhospitable to corporatism. Bargained (or neo-) corporatism emerged mainly in Northern Europe. Corporatism was either not attempted in the Anglophone world or it was short-lived, such as in Britain in the 1960s and Australia in the 1980s. It was developed during an era that was far removed from the one in which the industrial relations regimes of the Anglophone world emerged – one in which the state used fiscal, monetary, and "incomes policies" to regulate the macro-economy and during the unravelling of the post–Second World War class consensus that arose out of the slower growth, international competition, and high inflation of the 1970s.[9]

Crouch developed not only a typology, but a typological theory (1993, 31–47). He argued that different industrial relations systems arose out of two variable conditions: the "power of organized labour" (i.e., its ability to "secure concessions from capital") and of capital and labour's "level of organizational articulation" (i.e., their capacity to act strategically and where leaders at the top can commit those whom they represent to negotiated agreements that imposed "discipline" upon those who were represented). Neo-corporatist systems arose where organized labour was sufficiently powerful to extract concessions from employers and where labour and capital were highly organized; pluralistic bargaining and contestation appeared where labour and capital had low levels of organizational articulation (these systems were unstable if labour was powerful; they were stable if labour were weak).

Crouch's typology differs from the one presented here not only because he observed a partially different set of cases, but more importantly because he focused on different dimensions of industrial relations systems. The main distinction between Crouch's typology and the one offered in this book is that he emphasizes differences in the power and capacities of organized labour and capital, while this one stresses the different levels of state intervention and roles for the state in industrial relations. Statist regimes feature high levels of intervention that place the state at the centre of resolving disputes. Voluntarist regimes rely least upon the state, with the state encouraging self-regulation and using non-coercive methods of dispute settlement. Legalist regimes intervene at a level between these two and limit their coercion to setting down each party's legal rights and obligations and policing their pre-collective bargaining behaviour.

Crouch's typology and the one presented in this book are not mutually exclusive, however. We can apply our distinction among voluntarist, legalist, and statist regime types as appropriately to corporatist systems as we can to the liberal Anglophone nations. For example, the corporatist regime that emerged in Sweden has the two essential characteristics of voluntarism – a minimal direct role for the state in industrial relations and widespread employer acceptance of trade unions, which serve as the basis for "self-regulation" (Kjellberg 2009). The main differences between the Anglophone and Swedish cases are the high level of cooperation between labour and management in the conduct of industrial relations compared to the much more competitive and conflictual relationship between Anglophone employers and unions. The other is that industrial relations decisions are much more highly centralized in Sweden than in Anglophone countries, which facilitates the cooperative nature of Swedish industrial relations and exacerbates the competitive nature of the Anglophone. Thus, we might label the Swedish system as *cooperative voluntarism* and Anglophone variety as *competitive voluntarism*.

In contrast to Sweden, another major corporatist case, Germany, has important elements of legalism. According to Silva (2013, 4), "a detailed examination of German labor law ... makes plain the indispensable role of the state in buttressing the postwar German industrial relations regime. Laws, regulations, agencies, and courts unobtrusively sustain a framework highly supportive of 'autonomous' collective bargaining.... German-style regulation relies on maintaining background 'framework condition' (*Rahmenbedingungen*) conducive to the state's objectives rather than remedial intervention." We might label the German system as *cooperative legalism* and the Anglophone nations that adopted legalism as *competitive legalism*.[10]

Some Historical Background

We now return to our focus on the Anglophone nations and a summary of key historical moments in the development of their industrial relations regimes. Industrialization in all of the Anglophone nations began with a period of labour repression, but the length of that period and when and how it ended varied from case to case. The appendix presents the principal legislation (and in one case, government order) that marked the transition from repressive to one of the non-repressive regimes. The period from 1870 to 1920 was critical. During these years, nations either established industrial relations systems that lasted for most of the twentieth century (Australia, Britain, and New Zealand), or they fell short. Starting long before the major innovations that established the industrial relations regimes in each nation, Britain and its colonies jettisoned earlier laws and judicial rulings that rendered unions criminal conspiracies. The process began with the British Parliament's repeal of the Combination Acts in 1824, which protected unions from prosecution for criminal conspiracy. After employers found other laws to continue the prosecutions, Parliament passed the Trade Union Act of 1871, which also barred charging unions with "restraint of trade." This law's protections too were often negated by other laws that made it illegal to coerce employers by various means, which courts sympathetic to employers interpreted broadly in their favour (Clegg, Fox, and Thompson 1964, 44–5). Passage of the Conspiracy and Protection of Property Act of 1875 and the Trade Union Amendment Act of 1876 secured protection against these prosecutions once and for all. Australia, New Zealand, and Canada followed Britain's lead in the 1870s by sweeping away laws that prohibited unionization under criminal conspiracy statutes. Repealing laws that prohibited unions was not necessary in the United States because the mere existence of unions was never illegal in the first place (Forbath 1989, 1149).

Although unions may have been formally legalized in these nations by the 1870s, employers and the state used various means to continue to restrain workers from engaging in collective action and refused to recognize and bargain with them. Resistance to unions varied across the nations, but in all five, workers' civil rights were often violated. Employers refused to recognize unions as legitimate representatives of their workers, harassed and threatened workers who organized or joined unions, used the courts to impede unions by assessing fines and damages or issuing injunctions against them, and by enlisting the police and military to engage in violence.

New Zealand was the first nation to establish a non-repressive regime with the adoption of the Industrial Conciliation and Arbitration Act of 1894. All but one of the Australian states adopted compulsory arbitration or wages boards in the 1890s, leading up to the national government's adoption of the Conciliation and Arbitration Act of 1904, which required de facto union recognition (through a union registration requirement) and set up conciliation boards and arbitration courts, authorizing the latter to enforce their awards. Great Britain came next with the passage of the Trade Disputes Act of 1906, which restored British unions' complete legal immunity from prosecution for civil damages and expanded the unions' freedom to picket and engage in other actions targeted at employers. The turn of the century reform outcomes led to states of equilibrium in the industrial relations regimes of Australia, New Zealand, and Britain for decades afterwards. Subsequent changes in the role of the state in industrial relations took place *within* the contours of the regimes established in the aftermath of the critical juncture or as ancillary to them.

The passage of the National Labor Relations Act of 1935 (Wagner Act) marks the US adoption of the legalist regime, which established the rights of independent labour organizations to organize and bargain collectively with employers and a regulatory agency to decide which actions constituted "unfair labour practices" and issue cease and desist orders that have the force of law.

Canada, like the United States, was a laggard among this group of nations in establishing labour rights and setting up its industrial relations system. It introduced compulsory investigation and conciliation for public utilities in 1907 under the Industrial Disputes Investigation Act (IDIA), which established tripartite boards for investigating disputes. Strikes and lockouts were prohibited during this "cooling-off" period. After the investigative boards published their findings so that public opinion could weigh in, both parties were required to undergo the conciliation process in the hope that it would help bring about a resolution of the dispute. But it took until the Second World War for Canada to complete its hybrid regime. The government issued Order-in-Council PC 1003 in 1944, which mandated rights to union recognition and collective bargaining like those embodied in the American Wagner Act. The reforms were permanently enshrined in 1948 with the passage of the Industrial Relations and Disputes Investigation Act (IRDIA). The IRDIA did not replace the mandatory investigation and conciliation procedures of the IDIA but merged them with the Wagner Act principles.

We now have a clear picture of the similarities and differences among the Anglophone nations in their industrial relations regimes and the timing of policy changes that established the new regimes. The remainder of the book illuminates *why* and *how* these nations developed strikingly different answers to the labour question.

Sources, Scope, and Plan of the Book

This book draws extensively upon the work of historians and other observers who have focused on the establishment of industrial relations regimes in each country. I supplemented these sources where necessary with contemporaneous newspaper accounts, parliamentary debates, and personal memoirs. Most existing historical works focus on one, or much less frequently, two countries. While they have uncovered important information and offer key insights into why these nations made particular choices, they have three drawbacks for our purposes. First, they do not seek to build empirical generalizations across nations and over time. Instead, they mainly focus on the unique circumstances in a given nation that led to a particular outcome. And taken as a group, the country studies do not use a consistent set of concepts and criteria that is useful for analysing patterns across cases. Second, the single country studies are limited because we cannot understand why these nations adopted specific kinds of regimes unless we know the range of alternatives. Studies that focus on a single case may not know about what the alternative outcomes were and what conditions and forces led to the adoption of those alternatives. Comparing cases brings to our attention variables and relationships whose importance would be difficult for us to discern clearly without comparison. Finally, only through comparative analysis can we uncover whether nations pursued different causal paths to the same regime outcome – that is, "equifinality."

A few caveats are in order about the scope and purposes of this study. First, some readers may wonder how well the analysis offered in this book would hold up across cases with more diverse political, legal, and economic systems. While I make no effort to advance a "general theory of industrial relations regimes," there is no reason *a priori* to think that my analysis is time or space bound. We could study other cases of industrialization in which unions, employers, and states struggled to shape and define the state's role. We would then look at the same set of variables and relationships that we use for the Anglophone nations. While it would make little sense to apply the analysis to non-democratic, non-capitalist, or pre-industrial societies, the "scope conditions" of the study are broad enough to permit the analysis of non-Anglophone nations. It will be up to future research to determine if this study's approach, framework, and findings are relevant for understanding industrial relations in other nations or groups of nations.

We also ought to keep in mind that including cases with more diverse political conditions, legal traditions and economic systems would come at some analytical cost. We would face a more daunting task of drawing conclusive inferences. We would have to disentangle an even larger number of possible influences on the outcomes. This is why "most similar systems" designs, like this one, are highly advantageous in small-N macro-historical research. Even though the analysis is restricted to the Anglophone world, we have considerable variation on the dependent variable (industrial relations regimes), which is the main puzzle I seek to address.

Second, the focus of this book is the genesis of the new regimes, not how they were maintained over decades or what forces brought some of them to an end. While the analysis identifies the central importance of critical junctures in the causal process, it does not seek to uncover the "mechanisms of reproduction" that kept the regimes in place or explain why some of them were eventually replaced. Just because we are not analysing the legacies of the critical junctures that we identify does not mean that we have created uncertainty about whether we have identified them correctly as such. The literature on critical junctures suggests that there are two alternative ways to identify critical junctures. One way is to focus on changes that have lasting effects ("legacies") and trace them back to the historical moments in which they originated. The second way is to focus on the historical moments themselves and identify the crises that trigger them and the conditions of "heightened contingency" that arise out of the crises (i.e., the conditions that permitted change to occur and that shaped the specific responses to the crises by loosening constraints on action). Because I seek to understand the origins of these industrial relations regimes, my focus is mainly on the second way, and I use Soifer's (2012) conceptualization of "permissive" and "productive" conditions. At the same time, we know that each of these regimes lasted for many decades, we know when and if they came to an end, and we can trace their legacies back to the critical junctures if we choose to do so.

Which brings us to a final caveat – once established, these regimes were not static and fixed. They sometimes experienced important changes during their existence. Their survival sometimes hinged upon adjusting to new political realities and changes in the economic environment. For example, the Taft-Hartley Act enacted in the 1940s, and some court decisions that preceded it, imposed a series of restrictions on labour unions, just as the Wagner Act had done with employers. However, Taft-Hartley did not change the basic institutional relationships of the regime (nor did it return the United States to company unions, injunctions, and similar repressive tools.) Taft-Hartley rebalanced power between labour and management *within the legalist paradigm* and put the brakes on a greater expansion of union presence in the American economy (Lichtensein 1998). Historians have debated whether Taft-Hartley was a predictable result of decisions that the designers and implementers of the Wagner Act made in the 1930s, or whether it reflected the political resurgence of business and its conservative allies in Congress after the Second World War (Tomlins 1985; Lipsitz 1994, 170). However, few have viewed it as marking the end of the legalist regime and the beginning of something fundamentally different from it.

In other cases, changes threatening the continuation of a regime took place, but they were temporary, and the regime regained its equilibrium. This happened in the 1920s and 1980s, for example, in Britain, when very disruptive strikes led Conservative governments to respond, for example, by declaring secondary strikes aimed at the government and mass picketing unlawful. The next Labour government eventually repealed those changes. Finally, we must be cautious about painting with a broad brush when we talk about entire "nations" following particular regimes. Clearly, some firms, industries, and many workers were in sectors or occupations that were left out of these regimes or were subject to different institutional rules. All of these are topics that researchers should study, and many already have done, but they are beyond the scope of this work.

Chapter 2 focuses on why the Anglophone nations diverged. It starts with an overview of the key actors that shaped the state's response to the labour question: reformers, trade unions, employers, public officials, and political parties. It examines their roles and how different national contexts influenced their potential for shaping industrial relations. Next, I present my main argument, which identifies the importance of contingency and choice in leading to the different industrial relations regime outcomes. Specifically, I argue that employers' acceptance or rejection of trade unions and whether the unions faced a threat to their existence were the two most critical variables leading to voluntarism, statism, or legalism. These variables are the starting points for elaborating longer and more complex causal stories involving their impacts on the preferences and calculations of other key actors, especially trade unions, reformers, and political parties that are elaborated upon in the concluding chapter of the book. Finally, I evaluate several potential rival explanations for the divergence in industrial relations regimes, pointing out their deficiencies.

Chapter 3 focuses on the second question that motivates the study: how did the different regimes emerge? How did each national outcome reflect a distinct combination of processes of historical change? To begin to answer these questions, I use a conceptual framework that combines identifying "critical junctures" and "critical antecedents" for each case. I argue that the emergence of each type of industrial relations regime was the product of both critical junctures and critical antecedents, but that the role and relative causal importance of critical junctures vis-a-vis critical antecedents varied across cases, giving rise to three distinct patterns of institutional change: "breakdown and replacement," "punctuated gradualism," and "breakdown and culmination."

Chapters 4 through 9 present the case studies of the five Anglophone nations, in chronological order from those regimes established the earliest to the latest. Chapter 4 examines the conditions that gave rise to the statist regimes that Australia and New Zealand adopted in the late nineteenth and very early twentieth centuries. Chapter 5 explores the conditions that led Britain to follow the voluntarist path, which was consolidated in the early years of the twentieth century. The presentation of the North American cases takes two chapters for each nation because these nations took the longest and most complicated routes before settling upon a politically viable and enduring industrial relations regime. Chapter 6 examines the forces that made it impossible for the United States to adopt either statism or voluntarism. Chapter 7 covers how Americans finally settled upon legalism during the 1930s. Chapters 8 and 9 examine how Canada ended up with a hybrid system that combined a mild form of statism, which it adopted early in the twentieth century, with American-style legalism, to which it turned starting with the Second World War. The concluding chapter 10 revisits the major questions motivating the study, pulling together the main findings from the case chapters and discussing the analytical arguments from chapters 2 and 3 with greater depth and nuance.

2 Why the Anglophone Nations Diverged

We saw in the last chapter that despite their many similarities, the Anglophone nations adopted a range of answers to the labour question in the realm of industrial relations. The Australasian nations settled on bold statist responses, while Britain developed a vastly different approach – voluntarism. And legalism emerged in North America. This chapter previews my explanation for the outcomes in the five nations. Each nation adopted an industrial relations regime that arose out of a conjunction of historical contingencies and choices; that is, specific combinations and sequences of events as well as decisions and responses to those decisions by key actors involved in the institution-building process.

Before presenting my explanation for why the Anglophone nations diverged, I introduce the major actors who shaped the industrial relations regimes in each nation. The last part of the chapter explores several alternative explanations for the divergent outcomes. I conclude that these rival do not provide plausible accounts for the outcomes, or in some cases, they identify relevant factors but overlook the most important relationships and conditions.

The Key Actors

The approach taken in this book views institutional change as emerging from political outcomes that reflect the purposive actions of individuals and collectivities at decisive historical moments. Although structural factors may play an important role as well, the kinds of institutions that societies develop do not arise inevitably and automatically from impersonal forces like the structure of the economy or the culture. Nor are specific institutional changes understood as simply the result of whether one class or the other gains control over the state. Rather they are contingent on the choices made by concrete actors who possess a degree of agency. Structural characteristics of the economy and polity are only two possible influences on these decisions and choices, along with individual-level beliefs, the goals of the groups and organizations to which individual actors belonged, and each actor's assessment of how other actors would behave.

Five key actors helped to develop the industrial relations regimes in the Anglophone nations – employers, trade unions, political parties and public officials, and in most cases, reformers. These were the most active participants who attempted to shape the state's role by designing alternatives, implementing them, or thwarting their consideration and implementation. Importantly, the preferences of these actors often varied over time and cross-nationally.

For the sake of brevity, I have simplified the discussions of each actor in the process and in so doing I have portrayed them more monolithically than is warranted. "Trade unions" and "employers," for example, include individual unions and firms, but they also include labour movements, occupational groups, industries, and peak associations. Second, individuals could occupy two or more categories at once. For example, some reformers may have held positions in the state as party or legislative leaders or bureaucrats, or they may have been trade union intellectuals.

Reformers

Whether they described themselves as "state socialists," "radical liberals," or "progressives," depending upon the country, reformers were part of a transnational movement of middle-class intellectuals and activists that stretched from Australasia to North America to Europe (Rodgers 1998). Most of the reformers were sympathetic to labour unions' rights and improving working conditions, although to varying degrees. Union leaders and reformers usually came from different class and educational backgrounds and looked differently upon state intervention in industrial relations. Many reformers prioritized the maintenance of industrial peace over labour rights and saw the state as having a legitimate role in protecting the public interest by avoiding strikes, lockouts, and boycotts, which often put them at odds with both the labour movement and employers. Unions, especially strong ones, were usually sceptical towards state intervention.

The main, but by no means only, contribution of reformers to the formation of new industrial relations regimes was in developing and disseminating policy ideas and prescriptions and developing arguments in support of them. Although labour movement leaders and intellectuals contributed significantly to fashioning answers to the labour question in the United States and Britain, in the other nations they had much less impact. It fell to progressive (or "radical") liberal reformers to decide on the over-arching policy prescription, translate it into a concrete legislative proposal and publicize it, and build a sufficiently large coalition to get it adopted. In Australia and New Zealand the leading roles were played by radical liberal reformers-turned-politicians like Charles Cameron Kingston and William Pember Reeves. In Canada, it was William Mackenzie King early on and J.L. Cohen later. In the United States, Robert Wagner played a similar role to Reeves and Kingston, in addition to his aide Leon Keyserling and the many labour relations experts who translated the lessons from the ill-fated National Industrial Recovery Act (NIRA) into a set of principles and practices that would find their way into the National Labor Relations Act (NLRA) of 1935.

Besides developing over-arching policy ideas and concrete proposals, reformers also contributed by controlling how the issue was framed. In most countries reformers framed the issue in terms of a "public interest" in preventing or mitigating the "wasteful," "uncivilized," and "dangerous" methods of dispute settlement to which labour and capital too often resorted, but which could be avoidable under new policies and institutional arrangements. In the United States, Wagner framed the issue in terms of the adverse impacts of industrial unrest on economic recovery and the beneficial impacts for recovery of increasing labor's bargaining power (U.S. Congress 1935, 2371-2).

Reformers' policy preferences as well as their political influence was contingent on a variety of conditions – the scope, severity, and type of crisis that triggered the critical juncture; their understanding of the problem of industrial unrest and economic distress (based upon studying prior experience in their own and other nations); their links to the labour movements and their ability to broaden coalitions for reform by framing the debate and packaging an array of reforms; their access to key institutions within the state; and whether conditions in other nations facilitated or hindered the diffusion of their ideas.

Trade Unions

Ideally, labour unions preferred less state intervention in industrial relations. This was certainly true during times of labour peace and among stronger unions, which were confident in their ability to defend their interests vis-à-vis employers. Stronger unions usually preferred a voluntarist regime, in which employers would voluntarily recognize unions as the legitimate and sole representatives of workers and enter into good faith collective bargaining – without risking a loss of autonomy and organizational purpose that could come from state intervention. Unions wanted to have as much latitude as possible to represent their members unencumbered by legal and regulatory requirements and responsibilities that might constrain the organizations' growth and freedom of action or even favour employers' interests. Not only could the state reduce unions' autonomy, but under certain policies, they could shape the very outcomes that the unions were trying to influence – wages and working conditions – thus undermining the rationale for the unions' existence.

However, industrial relations were embedded in class relations that, under capitalism, were inherently antagonistic. A host of contextual conditions could lead organized labour to accept state involvement. On the one hand, labour movements that had negative experiences with the state, particularly courts, were especially wary of state regulation of industrial relations. Weaker unions and union movements that were in a weakened industrial condition might view the state as a potential ally, or at least an honest broker that could strengthen the unions' bargaining position vis-à-vis employers. Unions that faced more anti-union hostility from employers might also seek a greater role for the state, particularly during crisis periods when organized labour's survival might be at stake. State intervention that promised legal protections for labour and that imposed obligations or restrictions upon employers could induce labour to support state intervention, trading off the risks of state regulation for the benefits of protection from recalcitrant employers.

Apart from their policy preferences concerning state intervention, unions also had varying capacities to influence policymakers, depending upon union density rates, their degree of internal organizational and political unity, their levels of political experience and the strength of their ties to political parties, and whether the institutional structure of the state insulated key policymakers (e.g., judges) from democratic pressures.

Organized labour's mobilization in the industrial and political spheres played a central role in bringing the outcomes covered in this book to fruition. Labour's industrial militancy set off confrontations with employers that put the labour question on the state's agenda, creating pressures for the state to act, mobilizing support for parties and candidates sympathetic to labour interests, and creating political space that allowed reformers to advance new policy ideas.

Labour clearly and solidly backed the new industrial relations regimes established in the United States, Canada, and Britain. In Australia and New Zealand, labour's enthusiasm for compulsory arbitration varied between stronger and weaker unions and across the different provinces and national government. Not only was labour's support necessary at these critical moments for the adoption of a new regime type (or a continuation of an existing one), but also to varying degrees labour initiated and disseminated the ideas that formed the basis for the new regimes. The contributions of the labour movement to the content of the policies were most pronounced in Britain, the United States, and Canada. In Britain, Parliament enacted the labour movement's preference for blanket civil immunity. In the United States, the United Mine Workers played a critical role in getting the Roosevelt administration to incorporate the basic principles in what would become the Wagner Act into its immediate legislative forerunner, the NIRA. In Canada, labour lawyers affiliated with the main labour federation served as agents in the diffusion of Wagner Act principles and their refashioning for the Canadian context.

Employers

Employers shared with trade unions a preference, other things being equal, of having less state intervention in industrial relations. Just as the prospect of state intervention risked trade union autonomy and organizational interests, state intervention could interfere with employers' freedom to control employment contracts and exercise their property rights. Once workers engaged in collective action, however, employers might prefer a stronger state role. Employers had three basic choices on the question of state intervention. They could eschew state involvement by building relations and accommodations with unions outside the purview of the state. They could seek advantages over unions by calling upon courts, police, and other arms of the state to repress unions by making it harder for them to organize or constricting their activities. Thirdly, they could seek a class compromise that gave the state substantial police powers over both themselves and the unions. Employers never voluntarily opted for the third scenario; they signed on to regulation only when it was politically forced upon them (although they sometimes supported it *after* the regulatory regimes were in place). Thus, they were left with either using the state to repress unions or seeking accommodation with unions largely out of the state's purview on a voluntary basis. Employers in most places embraced repressive methods of dealing with trade unions for a long period of time and only accepted state regulation when forced to do so. At the same time, there was significant variation in employer acceptance of unions, from the most accommodating (the British) to the most hostile (the American). These employer attitudes towards unions, as well as their willingness to use the state as an instrument of repression, had profound impacts on trade unions' willingness or reluctance to go along with state intervention.

Public Officials and Political Parties

For most of the nineteenth century or even later in some countries, public officials generally preferred to stay out of industrial relations disputes; or, if they intervened, they weighed in on the side of employers, often with repressive actions and policies that included police violence, criminal and civil penalties, and injunctions. The preferences of state actors – whether they be individual officials or collectivities of them, such as legislative majorities or bureaucratic agencies – were often subject to change, however. As the voting franchise expanded, though in some nations earlier and more rapidly than in others, the working class engaged in the electoral process. Expansion of the franchise and other political reforms opened the door for legislative factions and governments sympathetic to organized labour's interests to come to power. But expansion of the franchise did not necessarily or automatically translate into political influence. Workers and unions had to use the franchise effectively, and to do that they had to be convinced that political mobilization was necessary and would be effective. That, in turn, depended upon how workers and unions related to the party system – whether they had forged strong ties to parties, how dependent parties were on their support, whether the labour movement sought to form an independent labour party, and other aspects of the union/worker–party relationship.

Parties not only responded to organized labour's political mobilization, but they were the mechanisms through which influential reformers gained access to key posts within the state from which they could publicize, build support for, and gain approval for their reforms. The most active and influential state actors usually occupied strategic posts within the state from which they were able to frame the issue, publicize their preferred policy solutions, and build support for their adoption. They included William Pember Reeves (New Zealand), Charles Cameron Kingston (Australia), Robert Wagner (the United States), and William Lyon Mackenzie King and J.S. Cohen (Canada) – all of whom held important legislative or executive posts. Although some scholars have pointed to the importance of the Democratic Party in securing the Wagner Act (Finegold and Skocpol 1995), others have disputed its importance (Plotke 1990) because many Democratic officeholders were not progressives and did not support unions. But the parties in the other nations operated within parliamentary systems in which greater party cohesion and discipline existed.[1] The parties that acted as midwives to the new regimes included, in Britain, the Liberal Party and an inchoate Labour Party that emerged as a new party in response to the judicial attack on the unions. In the Australia states and Commonwealth, it was mainly Liberal parties, sometimes allied with a Labour Party. In New Zealand and the first Canadian critical juncture, it was Liberal parties. In the second Canadian critical juncture it was an insurgent Social Democratic Party that induced the Liberals to act. In the United States workers became a key constituency of the Democratic Party under the New Deal in the 1930s when the party attracted increasing numbers of workers in northern cities in part by pursing policies for labour's benefit (Finegold and Skocpol 1995, 44–50, 72–3).

What we need to explain is *why* these actors favoured certain institutional arrangements over others and what historical forces and conditions impinged upon their decisions. I argue that the industrial relations regime that each nation adopted arose out of a conjunction of historical contingencies and choices. They are the result of a specific sequence and combination of factors that emerged in some cases over many years and in others at specific historical moments. Structural conditions were by no means irrelevant to these outcomes, but they did not lead inevitably to particular answers to the labour question.

Figure 2.1. Employer Acceptance, Trade Union Existence & Industrial Relations Regime Outcomes

		Did Industrial Unrest Threaten Trade Unions' Existence?	
		Yes	No
Did Employers Accept Trade Unions as Partners in Resolving Disputes?	Yes		Voluntarism (Great Britain)
	No	Statism (Australia & New Zealand)	Legalism (U.S. & Canada)

Why the Anglophone Nations Diverged: A Preview of the Analysis

The explanation that I offer for why the Anglophone nations adopted different industrial relations regimes stresses the strategic decisions of the key actors that I discussed in the previous section. Those decisions could affect the preferences, decisions, and relevance of the other actors in the process, which could then alter the industrial and political context. Enduring structural conditions related to the polity undoubtedly had some impact, but they were not as important for the immediate outcome or long-term developments as these more strategic and contingent factors. The explanation for the divergent outcomes begins with two factors that proved to be decisive: *employers' level of acceptance of trade unions* and *whether industrial conflict posed an existential threat to the trade unions or the community, or both*. Figure 2.1 summarizes the five nations' experiences on these two dimensions, which yield three distinct outcomes.

Voluntarism emerged as a viable answer to the labour question where most employers accepted or accommodated labour unions and collective bargaining. Employer acceptance of unions was constitutive of voluntarism; the latter could not exist in its absence. Also, employer acceptance obviously made it much less likely that unions would experience a defeat that would threaten their existence (which explains the empty cell in the upper-left quadrant of Figure 2.1). These conditions thus made it possible to avoid stronger forms of state intervention (statism and legalism). Neither labour unions nor public officials found it necessary to turn to compulsory state measures in industrial relations, and as a result little need existed for reformers to develop new institutional arrangements and persuade the unions and public officials of their necessity.

In the other four Anglophone nations, voluntarism was not a viable option because most employers refused to accept unions and collective bargaining in the absence of state compulsion. This situation induced the labour movement, often reluctantly and after a long period of resistance to the idea, to accept strong state involvement in industrial relations. *Statism* emerged in Australasia when employers vanquished the labour movement in a series of conflicts that posed a severe threat to the economies of Australia and New Zealand. In the aftermath, new liberal-labour electoral coalitions emerged who were allied with "state socialist" reformers that developed new institutions for rebalancing the power between labour and business and maintaining industrial peace. Labour accepted a loss in its autonomy for the state's protection. *Legalism* emerged where employers neither accepted unions nor vanquished them, as in the United States and Canada, but continued to suppress them for long periods of time. Voluntarism was not a viable answer to the labour question in these nations, but neither was statism because industrial unrest did not threaten the unions' existence or endanger the economy. Most trade unions and public officials viewed statism as undesirable or unnecessary. Eventually, organized labour and its allies gained sufficient political leverage to compel the state to force employers to recognize unions and accept collective bargaining under legalist principles and institutional arrangements. Parties, public officials, and reformers played key roles in developing legalist principles and institutions and turning them into reality.

This typological theory has several strengths. First, because it specifies necessary conditions for the outcomes, it correctly predicts all the cases. Second, since it relies on only two variables it provides a parsimonious explanation for why each nation ended up with a particular regime *and* why they did not adopt one of the alternatives instead. Third, the employer accommodation/hostility and existential threat variables provide a foundation for a more complete and complex explanation because they influenced the calculations and behaviour of other critical actors in the process. Employers' stances towards unions had considerable impact on trade unions' preferences for specific industrial relations regimes and what trade-offs the unions were willing to accept in terms of organizational autonomy and state protection. Whether employers viewed unions as legitimate partners in industrial relations also had a large impact on whether trade unions could develop their organizational capacity and in turn, their political resources and ability to mobilize when their interests were at stake. Finally, it impacted levels of industrial strife, which affected the state's propensity to take a more (or less) active role in industrial relations, whether reformers became influential players in the process, and the kinds of institutional reforms they promoted. Likewise, whether industrial strife posed an existential threat to unions and communities motivated reformers to develop new institutional arrangements to deal with industrial conflict and determined their degree of influence over the unions and public officials. It also affected the unions' decisions to develop ties with political parties and engage in political action, and their preferences for and against specific industrial relations regimes.

To understand fully why nations ended up with either "voluntarist," "legalist," or "statist" answers to the labour question, we must also explore why they did not adopt one of the other two alternative regimes. Thus, part of the reason for why some nations came up with a particular answer to the labour question is that alternative answers proved elusive at decisive historical moments. As we will see, failures to develop viable answers to the labour question at earlier points in time shaped the kinds of answers that nations chose later. *When* nations developed viable answers to the labour question often shaped *what* those answers would be. I will elaborate upon all these points in the case chapters and conclusion.

Alternative Explanations

Next, I present several alternative explanations to the one that I have offered for why the Anglophone nations diverged. The explanations mostly focus on the enduring, structural features of each nation's economy and polity. These features had been in place before or at the time the industrial relations regimes were established. A few others focus on more transient and changeable political power relationships.

Economic Structure and Development

Without doubt, the economies of the Anglophone nations had impacts on the emergence of their industrial relations regimes. As we will see in the chapters that follow, economic *climate* – fluctuations in the macro-economy and international competition – often created economic stress and dislocation and contributed to conflict between employers and workers that sometimes developed into crises that triggered critical junctures in each country. These crises gave rise to the permissive conditions that loosened political constraints, which was vital to establishing or consolidating new regimes. We will also see that the *timing* of industrialization had a large impact, particularly on Britain, which for a long time gave it a great advantage in the global economy. This made it easier for many British employers to accommodate the emergence and growth of labour organizations.

But did the different *structural* characteristics of the Anglophone economies give rise to their different regimes? Here we refer to the types of industries, sectors of the economy, and modes of production that dominated at the time each nation experienced a regime change or consolidation. The economies of Australia and New Zealand centred around agricultural and extractive industries, like wool production (pastoralism) and coal mining. Britain had an economy based upon highly developed and specialized manufacturing industries of which many were family owned and run. When the United States and Canada adopted legalism, their manufacturing industries were dominated by large-scale, corporate enterprises that relied increasingly upon Fordist production methods.

It is easy enough to see that these nations had very different economic structures, but it is another thing to draw causal connections between *specific* economic structures and *specific* industrial relations regimes. One must show why each nation's adoption of a particular regime was necessary or more likely because of the intrinsic nature of its economic structure. Australia and New Zealand's reliance upon export markets to sell extractive resources and agricultural products created the need for strong state intervention in the economy. In addition to launching public enterprises and infrastructure building programs in 1860s and 1870s, the state regulated the labour market to address labour shortages (Quinlan 1989, 27; see also Sinclair 1970). "From the very earliest times many of the matters that most immediately concerned workers were significantly affected by government policy including immigration, convict competition and, of course, coercive labour laws" (Quinlan 1989, 43). Australian labour, "even prior to the 'great strikes' of the 1890s had displayed a strong interest in state intervention as a means of securing its object" (Quinlan 1989, 43). The adoption of compulsory arbitration in the 1890s, according to this view, was merely a continuation of a trend established early on. Some historical facts about Australia and New Zealand simply do not fit the theory. What followed the early settlement of New Zealand was Wakefieldism, which was based upon the idea of recreating English conditions for development in New Zealand by maximizing as much as possible individual economic freedom (Sutch 1966; Sinclair 1970, 58–61; 91–100). More importantly, if compulsory arbitration were ordained from the start, then why did it take until several decades after economic development and trade union growth were well underway before its adoption? The imperatives arising out of economic structure might have pushed in the direction of strong state intervention in labour relations, but that could have taken many forms, including vigorous state repression of unions or the legalist systems that emerged in North America. The statist regime that emerged in Australasia included labour rights and protections, which would not necessarily be predicted simply by knowing about the economic structure.

Functionalist explanations may be less helpful for explaining the *origins* of institutions than their persistence (Hall and Taylor 1996, 952). Certain kinds of economic structures do not necessarily lead to the adoption of particular industrial relations systems. Through much of the nineteenth century Canada had a "staples economy" based upon exports of timber, fur, wheat, and fish that was very similar to those in Australasia (Innis 1954, 1956; Watkins 1967). The United States, Argentina, and South Africa were also "settler economies" that endured shortages of investment capital and labour at one point, yet none of them adopted Australasian-style compulsory arbitration and wages boards (Macintyre and Mitchell 1989, 10).

To attribute the regime outcomes mainly to structural economic forces is a form of crude economic determinism that takes politics out of the equation. At best, the explanation implies that employers and/or workers in the dominant industries simply agreed upon a regime that they thought would best serve their interests. Rather than providing an adequate explanation, it raises a host of questions. How did differences in the structure of the economy shape employer–union relationships, political organization, and policy preferences? How did these actors' interests get defined and negotiated? How do we know that broader community interests were not represented? In short, by what mechanisms did the dominant industries get their way in a conflict-ridden, politicized policymaking process?

Finally, this explanation overlooks the problematic and contingent nature of searching for and developing institutional solutions to industrial conflict. It tells us nothing about who was responsible for developing the new institutions, why they preferred those institutions to the alternatives available, and how they translated their ideas into concrete, practical institutional innovations that could garner sufficient political support.

If economic structure played a causal role, it was almost certainly indirect, by influencing one or more intervening variables that had a more direct impact on the outcome. For example, perhaps the economic structure of a country produced more or less severe or widespread industrial unrest that posed greater risk to the social order. The latter, in turn, induced policymakers to turn to more interventionist measures, like compulsory arbitration. Part of the argument in the remainder of the book is that the scope and severity of crises played an important causal role. The industrial unrest (and economic downturn) in Australasia that set off the critical juncture was much more devastating for the society than the one that occurred in Britain, for example. However, it is not clear why different economic structures *per se* would lead to more severe or less severe levels of unrest.

Another possibility is that economic structure could have influenced employers' preferences and behaviour, which could have led to different regimes. As I have argued, employers' attitudes and actions towards unions were critical in shaping the behaviour of the unions and the state, the unions' political capacity, and their regime preferences. Where employers were more accommodating towards unions, less appetite existed for strong state intervention. Economic structure appears to have shaped employers' levels of tolerance for unions in some industries (Haydu 1988; Jacoby 1991). Some scholars have pointed to industrial structure to explain why British employers, for example, were much more accommodating towards unions than their American counterparts. Mass production technologies (Taylorism, Fordism, etc.) had limited applicability for industries like shipbuilding, a mainstay of the British economy, which meant that they could accommodate unions' desires to maintain established craft methods and found alternative ways to increase efficiency. In many other industries employers in both nations sought to take advantage of the new production technologies. Here again, economic structure may have played a role in the differences among employers' attitudes across nations. American industries were more concentrated, and the firms were more specialized, which meant that employers had less need to rely upon unions to moderate wage competition across firms and regions of the country. British industries were fragmented into more specialized, family-run firms.

It is not clear, however, that the source of the difference in attitudes of employers in the two nations was due to economic structure or other factors. American unions were in a weaker position than their British counterparts to resist the new technologies, and American employers were farther along in adopting the new technologies and relied less on skilled workers. Second, the British state was much less willing to help employers resist unions than American courts and police, which were often willing accomplices of anti-union employers (Jacoby 1991; Lorwin 1933).

Another possibility is that economic structure influenced the type of unions that dominated the labour movement, which in turn, may have influenced the unions' preferences for industrial relations regimes. British manufacturing gave rise to several well-organized craft unions, which continued to dominate the British labour movement during the critical juncture of the late nineteenth and early twentieth centuries. Compared to industrial unions, many craft unions were strong, easier to organize, and had some control over labour supply. This gave them a great advantage in dealing with employers, and it reduced the need to rely upon the state to protect their right to strike. Their relative position in the movement strengthened when employers crushed the nascent industrial ("new") unions and craft unions survived the employers' attacks. In the United States, by the 1930s, industrial unions had become increasingly important and were rivals to the established craft unions in the American Federation of Labor (AFL). The United Mine Workers were particularly important in pushing the New Deal to legalist principles in its program (NIRA) for economic recovery from the Great Depression. The Canadian labour movement was more fragmented between craft unions in the east and more militant industrial unions in the west, but by the 1940s Canadian industrial unions had emerged as important. Furthermore, as I will discuss later, the Canadian economy was heavily integrated into the US economy, and many Canadian unions were affiliated with those to the south. Australasian unions in the key industries that were involved in the industrial relations crisis of the 1890s – the shearers, miners, and seamen – were closer to industrial unions than they were to craft unions. Labour shortages in the colonies also afforded workers leverage to organize and resist regulations that favoured employers and encouraged emigration.

The problem with this explanation is that unions in the four non-British cases did not embrace state intervention until the critical junctures of the 1890s (in Australasia) and the 1930s and '40s (in North America). They were not present earlier. Australasian unions showed no signs of favouring compulsory arbitration before the crisis. American unions did not embrace legalism until the 1930s (the Mine Workers did so earlier, but that was because the economic crisis hit that industry earlier). The expected benefits from compulsory arbitration and legalism for workers were much more uncertain and entailed risks because it threatened their autonomy vis-à-vis the state and their bargaining power vis-à-vis employers.

Even if economic structure influenced trade union preferences, it assumes that those preferences alone are what mattered for the choice of regime. The Labour Party in Australia did not hold the effective balance of power in most of the legislatures that adopted compulsory arbitration and wages boards. In New Zealand and the Australian Commonwealth trade unions were usually part of broader governing coalitions. This was the case in Australia, New Zealand, and the United States, in particular, where liberal progressives and other groups were part of the coalition. This explanation also overlooks the fact that progressive and radical liberal reformers were mostly responsible for developing and pushing legalism and statism. Except in the case of progressive Jett Lauck of the United Mine Workers in the United States, labour movement organizations were not central to the development of these novel forms of state intervention. Although they ended up supporting the Wagner Act, most of the American labour movement pushed the New Deal to adopt the "Black bill" rather than what became the National Industrial Recovery Act.

In short, it appears that to whatever extent economic structure had an impact on the outcomes among the five nations, its influence was mediated by, and acted in conjunction with, other factors, that its causal effects are often difficult to disentangle from those of other factors, and that it probably mattered more in some cases than in others.

THE LOGIC OF INDUSTRIALISM

finally, during the post–Second World War era a literature in comparative industrial relations emerged that argued that industrial relations was "common to all nations" and sought to discover a "logic of industrialism" (Kerr et al. 1955, 1960; Dunlop 1958). While these works share this book's view of industrial relations as a web of institutions, they have little usefulness for understanding cross-national differences in the role of the state. They adopted a highly abstract analytical framework – the "systems model" – that deliberately downplayed national differences in search of what was universal. They were less interested in contrasting the role of the state than in describing industrial relations systems as a whole. Their focus was on a convergence in industrial relations systems after the Second World War in which, they argued, the pitched battles of the earlier twentieth century between anti-labour employers and often radical labour movements had dissipated into institutionalized dispute resolution characterized by relative labour peace and consensus (undoubtedly facilitated by post-war economic expansion). In other words, their focus was on what happened *after* the industrial relations regimes were established, not on their origins. To the extent that these works focus on origins, they seek to differentiate among the kinds of elites who ushered in industrialism in different parts of the globe. This bird's-eye view obscures as much as it illuminates because it lumps together countries in very broad categories that fail to take into account the sometimes-dramatic differences among them in their industrial relations systems.

Class Origins and Dominant Ideology

Louis Hartz (1964) and scholars who followed in his footsteps argued that each European colony had distinct origins that influenced their politics long after their founding. The generations that founded these "new societies" determined their ideological orientation and political culture. Hartz argued that the founding generations came from particular strata of European society and carried with them the grievances and political ideas of the time that they left Europe. Upon settling in their new country, these European "fragments" took on new life and were unchallenged because of the absence of competing ideologies. Flourishing in a kind of splendid isolation, the dominant ideology constituted itself as a national identity rather than a mere ideology and perceived alternative ideologies as alien.

Hartz identified three ideologies: feudal (or tory), liberal (or bourgeois), and radical. The American colonial and Revolutionary generations were influenced by the Protestant reformation and Enlightenment. American politics is rooted in Lockean *liberal* ideology with its celebration of individual freedom and responsibility, which legitimated a bourgeois-dominated society and a suspicion of collectivism and state intervention.

The free and convict settlers of Australia brought with them the *radical* ethos of Britain in the early to mid-nineteenth century. Fragments of the British working class left Europe in the first six decades of the nineteenth century and "lodged" in Australia (Rosecrance 1964, 275–313; see also Sutch 1966, 2). These were the casualties of the Industrial Revolution and the Reform Act of 1932, the growing class of wage earners who were left behind as the middle class acquired both economic and political power. The same economic grievances and democratic impulses that inspired Chartists, trade unions, and other radical-inspired movements that were ignored in Britain emerged and demanded greater equality and an end to class privilege. Since "the laboring and lower-middle classes" settled Australia and New Zealand, they "could be expected to react instinctively against any whiff of the mother-country's social stratification" (Lipson 1948, 488).

Canada presents a more complex case. While all proponents of fragment theory agree that French Canada had feudal origins, Hartz (1964, 34) subsumed English Canada under a pan-American liberalism, although he conceded that it had a "tory touch." McRae (1964, 266) likewise argued that Canada was "[b]orn of American liberalism and in many essential respects closely similar to contemporary American society." Horowitz (1966), in contrast, contended that because English Canada remained loyal to the British Crown during the American Revolution and attracted American loyalists, toryism has had a significant presence in English Canada. Important consequences have flowed from that fact, such as Canadians' greater comfort with the state playing a larger role in the economy.

Fragment theory faces a series of challenges as a valid explanation for the divergent industrial relations regimes that emerged in the Anglophone world. First, the theory fails to provide clear-cut predictions that are useful for understanding which countries gravitated to which kind of regime or the facts disconfirm the predictions. Fragment theory is perhaps least helpful for understanding the US case in this regard. There was no single "liberal vision" of how labour relations should be conducted, but several competing ones. One was that employers should be permitted to use the courts, common law, and the police powers of the state to repress unions in the name of "freedom of contract" and to defend against "conspiracies in restraint of trade." Another vision, which the American Federation of Labor championed for many decades, was that the state should remain "neutral" in class relations and allow unions to organize and engage in strikes and boycotts unrestrained by the law. The legalist regime that the United States finally adopted may be viewed either as illiberal because it mandated extensive state regulation of employer and trade union conduct, or a third liberal vision because it left intact essential liberal elements like property rights and private settlement of employment contracts. The root of the problem is that ideologies are broad systems of beliefs and values that are sufficiently malleable to accommodate a variety of specific public policies, legal doctrines, and institutional arrangements. Indeed, if we consider that the industrial relations regimes that *all* the Anglophone nations adopted were in some sense "liberal" because they left intact private property rights and a labour market that still relied heavily upon market incentives, then fragment theory cannot explain the *divergent* outcomes.

Turning to Canada, if we follow Hartz and McRae and consider English Canada to be liberal, then as in the US case, we must be very flexible with what counts as "liberal" so that we include, for example, Canada's adoption (and later expansion) of state-mandated investigation and conciliation of industrial disputes. We are left with asking how and why Canadians translated liberalism into that specific policy. The tory interpretation of Canada is also problematic. First, if the tory tradition had a large role in shaping Canada's industrial relations regime, then we would expect that the Conservative Party would have had a large role in that endeavour since, according to Horowitz (1966, 156–9), the Conservatives have been the most receptive to tory ideas. However, it was Liberal governments, not Conservative, that fashioned and established both the statist and legalist elements of the hybrid Canadian industrial relations regime. Finally, Hartzian logic links toryism with socialism. Countries that had a tory tradition were more likely to develop strong socialist movements because both toryism and socialism have in common a collectivist ethos that rejects liberal individualism. There was no socialist connection with Canada's adoption of compulsory investigation and conciliation. However, we shall see that a Canadian socialist party (the CCF) played a pivotal role in the 1940s in bringing about the adoption of Canada's version of the Wagner Act. Yet, it would be difficult to see how the CCF had much to do with Canadian toryism since toryism was centred in Eastern Canada ("Upper" and "Lower" Canada) and the CCF grew out of the "agrarian ferment" and farmer–labour alliance in Western Canada (McHenry 1950).

Australia is another example of ideology as a poor predictor of the kind of industrial regime that nations ended up adopting. There is nothing in the egalitarian, democratic ethos of radicalism that would predict that Australians would prefer compulsory arbitration over voluntarism or legalism. Radicalism's egalitarian impulses did not offer a clear set of policy prescriptions related to industrial relations the way that it did perhaps with other issues – including the expansion of the franchise, social insurance programs, the eight-hour day, and anti-sweating regulations. While labour movements and the workers that they represent may have supported greater state intervention in social welfare policies – for example, health, retirement, and unemployment insurance – state intervention in industrial relations presented them with a much more complicated situation. *Some* forms of state intervention could help *some* segments of the labour movement, but many trade union leaders and rank-in-file worried that state intervention would reduce their organizational relevance, their autonomy, and their ability to represent and fight for their constituents' interests. Radicalism espoused beliefs and values that supported workers' rights and interests against aristocratic and capitalist privileges and interests, but it influenced both Australian and British labour movements and reformers in very different ways. Australian and British unions and reformers came to very different conclusions as to which kind of regime would best further the interests of the working class.

Another problem with fragment theory as an explanation for divergent industrial relations regimes is the *fixity* of a nation's founding ideology as a causal mechanism, which makes it a poor candidate for explaining the dramatic *change* in industrial relations regimes over time. It cannot account for when nations get off one path and embark on a new one. Fragment theory dismisses as causally unimportant changes that occurred in these nations after the founding era and assumes that ideology, as opposed to many other forces and conditions, drives political outcomes. As such, it is overly simplistic and excessively deterministic. The establishment and failure to establish specific regimes was the product of much more complex causal processes played out over time. We will see the policy preferences of both labour movements and the state varied within each group and changed over time in Australia, the United States, and Canada, sometimes in favour and sometimes against state intervention, and those changes were critical to understanding the outcomes that occurred. If the ideological origins of the nations were such consistently powerful influences, we would not expect to see the changes that we see in the policy preferences of the key actors. Fragment theory fails to recognize that outcomes were *contingent*; that they depended upon the existence of other conditions. Those other conditions were the product of learning and experimentation that nations undertake when they experience major crises. Rather than ideology, we will see that industrial relations regimes were much more driven by a search for practical, effective solutions to the challenges presented by the need to balance competing class interests, avoid repression of working-class organizations, while at the same time minimizing industrial unrest and the disruptions to the economy and public order that could result from it.

A final problem with this approach for our purposes is that it does not have clear relevance for the British case. Hartz and others developed the theory to advance our understanding of politics in European "settler" nations. As the "mother country" of the other nations in our study, Britain obviously experienced tory, radical, and liberal influences. It is not clear that British voluntarism arose out of the influence of any single tradition, and one could make a case that all three had some influence. From the liberal tradition, voluntarism borrowed the minimal and indirect role of law and the state in society. From the tory tradition, voluntarism recognized the collective interests of workers and capitalists alike. And from the radical reform tradition, voluntarism recognized that both classes should operate on a level playing field and that labour unions should be free to act as vehicles for the expression of working-class interests in a democratic society. Since our focus is on explaining why these nations chose the particular industrial regimes that they did, and not one of the alternatives, the theory is of limited relevance for understanding Britain.

While far from satisfactory as a fully developed explanation for the divergent Anglophone outcomes, fragment theory does have explanatory relevance. We can incorporate elements of it carefully as antecedent conditions that contributed to the outcomes. For example, radicalism's strong presence in Britain and Australasia benefited labour in those nations, while its absence in Canada and the United States disadvantaged labour for the reason that Hartz and others have given – the founding generations of Canadians and Americans pre-dated the emergence of radicalism in Britain and thus were untouched by it. The presence (or absence) of radicalism mattered indirectly and did not lead by itself to the adoption of a particular regime type (as is clear in the contrast between the British and Australasian regimes). English radicals provided workers with philosophical arguments and other forms of encouragement to organize trade unions and helped cement the emerging union movements to the Liberal parties in both nations, which were crucial to getting electoral and Parliamentary support for reform.

Political Coalitions

Another approach that might explain why the Anglophone nations developed such different industrial relations regimes points to the importance of the political coalitions that controlled the state at the time of the adoption of their regimes or that put effective pressure on the state from the outside even though they did not hold formal authority at the time.

The Social Democratic Model. One such approach is the "social democratic model" (Korpi 1983; Pontusson 2013; Esping-Andersen 1985; Stephens 1980; Castles 1978). Most of these works try to shed light on why some nations developed more extensive and generous welfare states than others, although Korpi (1983, 159–83) uses the model to explain levels of industrial conflict as well. According to the model, labour union strength and solidarity provided a capacity to elect social democratic governments, which, in turn, legislated welfare state expansion. Social democratic parties stayed in power because (1) workers rewarded them for delivering social protections and redistributive measures, and (2) they built effective political coalitions with other political interests (in the case of Sweden, for example, farmers and, later, white-collar workers and export-oriented firms).

One might argue that the social democratic model is not relevant to explaining differences among the Anglophone nations because none of them followed the model that Korpi laid out. Nevertheless, the variables and hypotheses of that model (especially that variations in trade union organizational strength and alliances with political parties purporting to represent working-class interests) are plausibly relevant to understanding variation among the Anglophone nations.

How well, then, does the social democratic model provide an explanation for the various industrial relations regime outcomes? First, the relevance of the social democratic model is limited to political systems in which workers had already acquired the right to vote in elections as well as the right to unionize. While universal white male suffrage existed when all of these regimes were constituted (except for Britain), unions still faced daunting challenges to organize and operate. Indeed, the struggle at the centre of the establishment of industrial relations regimes was one of the legitimacy of unions, their rights, and employers' rights and obligations to deal with them. Unions as political organizations buttressing social democratic parties could not fully play the role assigned to them in the social democratic model until they secured their rights and were free to organize and operate in a way that grew their memberships substantially. Social democracy made its greatest advances in securing control of governments and legislating welfare state reforms only in the 1930s and after the Second World War.

Second, we need to distinguish between the impacts of labour movements versus "labour" or "social democratic" parties in bringing about industrial relations regimes. Although labour movements were critical actors in support of the regimes, in the vast majority of cases they worked with, through, or pressured liberal parties. Labour/social democratic parties were either just emerging (as in Britain), had yet to emerge (as in New Zealand), were established but not in power (as in Australia), or never emerged (as in the United States). In short, in almost every case, the regimes were established under the auspices of a dominant liberal party, not a social democratic one. The consolidations and expansions of the welfare state that took place under social democratic/labour governments, generally came later, in some cases much later, than the establishment of the industrial relations regimes.

Even if we think of the social democratic model more loosely as labour movements translating their organizational strength into political power, simply knowing labour's level of organizational capacity and political strength does not tell us much about why these nations adopted the regimes that they did instead of one of the alternatives. The positions that labour movements took on welfare state expansion was almost uniformly in favour of greater state involvement. Labour movements' positions on state involvement in industrial relations were far more complex and changeable, however. Trade unions viewed state involvement in labour relations as a much more fraught issue than welfare state provision. Other things equal, trade union movements preferred that the state would stay out of industrial relations, exactly the opposite of their position on welfare state provision. Complicating matters, the prospect of state intervention divided strong and weak unions, and unions versus parliamentary labour parties because it threatened unions' organizational autonomy and mission. We need to be able to take into account why labour movements held the preferences that they did in favour of or against various levels and forms of state intervention. Simply knowing how politically powerful they were is not sufficient.

Finally, the social democratic model exclusively or mainly considers the political strength of the unions and their ties to social democratic parties; it fails to take into account what was happening between unions and employers in the industrial realm, which was critical in shaping the labour movement's acceptance (or not) of strong state intervention in industrial relations. The model also views the state as a passive actor in the process of policy formation. Social democratic parties capture the state to promote the interests of workers. In so doing, it may give too much causal weight to union-inspired social democratic parties as agents for change and too little to other actors, like reformers within or close to the state.

APD Explanations for the Wagner Act. A large literature on American political development (APD) seeks to explain the creation and adoption of the Wagner Act (National Labor Relations Act of 1935, NLRA).[2] Although these works do not have a cross-national focus, the various explanations offered may have important relevance by shedding light on which actors were key in bringing about institutional change and why they were so important. Here we will review explanations that identify several concrete political actors: working-class movements (Goldfield 1989, 1990: Piven and Cloward 1977), state officials and party coalitions (Finegold and Skocpol 1995), and trade unions and progressive reformers (Plotke 1990).[3] The APD approach also draws our attention to the potential importance of "critical junctures" in regime change and consolidation. Although APD studies of the Wagner Act do not explicitly adopt a critical juncture framework, they focus on the 1930s, which constituted such a moment for labour relations in the United States.

The "working-class mobilization" explanation argues that the state introduced labour reforms because it had little choice but to respond to pressures for change from below. It identifies the working class broadly, rather than the labour movement, as the key actor in bringing about industrial relations reforms. Reforms like the Wagner Act came about, according to this view, only when the unemployed and workers generally took their struggle out of the industrial relations arena and brought it into the political arena. Furthermore, these working-class movements often bypassed electoral and other conventional forms of participation in favour of protests and other disruptive activities. The impact of strikes and unions' other actions towards business and the state were limited. The United States went through bitter strikes prior to the 1930s, but none of them led to major legislation (Goldfield 1990, 1305). The broad set of working-class organizations and movements that mobilized in the 1930s – including not only the labour movement (particularly the emerging industrial unions), but also organizations of the unemployed, farmers, African Americans, Huey Long's "Share the Wealth" campaign, and others – induced the state to respond with labour reform legislation (Piven and Cloward 1977, 41–96; Goldfield 1989, 1270–2, 1990, 1305–6). Often led by communists and other radicals, these forces operated outside elections and other regular political processes by engaging in confrontation and disruptive tactics, which "creat[ed] an atmosphere of social protest and radicalism" (Goldfield 1989, 1270–1).

I did not find much cross-national support for this explanation. I found that the trade union movement was usually the key working-class actor pressing for legislation to protect it from anti-union employers (and sometimes the courts), rather than movements consisting of the unemployed and workers generally. In some cases, such as Britain and Canada, the major reforms took place during periods of relatively low unemployment. Even where the rise of "new unions" of unskilled and semi-skilled workers played a role in bringing about industrial relations crises, they engaged primarily in industrial disruption, not political protest, and used trade unions as their vehicle. They were almost always defeated, leaving it to the established craft and industrial unions to lead the ensuing struggles for reform. Second, while the working-class mobilization thesis correctly points out that major breakthroughs in the conduct of industrial relations were ultimately resolved in the political arena, in almost every case the crisis that triggered the critical juncture either began or eventually spread to the industrial relations arena. British trade unions established a voluntarist regime partly through winning or surviving major industrial relations battles in the late nineteenth century. American unions' engagement in strike activity persuaded the unions to turn away from voluntarism, contributed to their electoral mobilization in favour of pro-labour candidates in the 1934 election, and put pressure on the New Deal state to respond favourably or else risk economic recovery. Third, the historical accounts of the political activity that induced the key legislative changes emphasizes electoral mobilization and sometimes realignment, the building of party coalitions and pressuring key elected officials or factions, not frightened governments responding reluctantly to disruptive mass-based protest movements.

The case that comes closest to resembling the working-class mobilization explanation is Canada's adoption of Wagner Act principles in the 1940s. In that case the unions engaged in widespread industrial unrest against the state and employers during the Second World War, demanding the adoption of principles mirroring what the United States adopted a decade earlier. The state gave in reluctantly only when it came under irresistible political pressure from a broad-based urban-rural socialist movement. But that is where the resemblance ends. What induced the state's response was not protest or other disruptive unconventional activity by the unemployed (the war produced full employment), but conventional party politics when the Canadian CCF's electoral appeal grew to such an extent that it became the dominant party in certain provinces and threatened to oust the Liberal Party at the national level.

Finally, even if we interpret the historical record so that it supports the general proposition that working-class pressure (in some form) induced the state to adopt institutional and public policy reforms that it would not have adopted in the absence of such pressure, the working-class mobilization explanation cannot adequately account for the *content and design* of those reforms. There can be no doubt that the substance of those reforms clearly sprang from the minds of experts who were either intellectuals within the established trade unions, or more often, middle-class progressive or radical reformers who held key positions within the state or who had direct access to sympathetic public officials.

What about the other APD explanations? The "state + party" explanation for New Deal labour legislation includes two principal components. First, workers became a key constituency of the new governing Democratic Party. The Democrats attracted the support of increasing numbers of workers, mainly located in northern cities, in a series of elections during the 1930s (Finegold and Skocpol 1995, 44–50, 72–3). Some workers were Democrats loyal to the urban machines, others were northern Blacks who had been voting for the Republican Party or who were immigrants and young people who had not yet formed firm partisan attachments. Workers rewarded the Democrats for policies they instituted for labour's benefit, cementing workers' loyalty to the party. At the same time, "state autonomy and capacity" limited the influence of electoral coalitions on policy. Organizations within the state were "sources of policy initiatives that compete[d] with – and were formulated independently from – the proposals of groups within the governing party" (Finegold and Skocpol 1995, 50–1).[4]

The union + reformer explanation argues that an alliance of trade unions and progressive reformers brought about the Wagner Act in the United States. According to Plotke (1990, 105), "the Wagner Act was passed by Progressive liberals inside and outside the government, in alliance with a mass labor movement." This explanation contends that "labor's mobilization was crucial" in bringing about the NLRA, but it shares with the "state + party" explanation a rejection of the notion that trade unions and other working-class organizations could bring about reform *on their own*. The unions needed the help of progressive reformers who were a major political force in Congress in the 1930s and "developed, proposed and fought" for the Wagner Act (1990, 117, 119). Unlike the state + party explanation, it places less emphasis on the importance of the Democratic Party as a vehicle for reform and on the reformers as state actors.[5]

My findings for the Anglophone nations as a group are largely consistent with the APD studies of the origins of the Wagner Act that identify trade unions, progressive reformers, and political parties as the chief actors who were responsible for the establishment of industrial relations regimes. David Plotke argues that "a mass labor movement" allied with "Progressive liberals" "developed, proposed and fought" for the Wagner Act (1990, 105, 117, 119). Australia, New Zealand, the United States, and Canada are clearly consistent with Plotke's thesis. The British case is more complicated. There, the trade unions were the dominant political actor – basically dictating the terms of the Trade Disputes Act of 1906; even in Britain, the unions could not have prevailed without the support of radicals in the Liberal Party.

Nevertheless, all the APD accounts fall short. First, they largely overlook the role of *employers*. This omission is understandable given that American employers were opposed to the Wagner Act but were too politically weak to prevent its adoption (similar employer opposition to virtually any form of state intervention that infringed upon their prerogatives in labour relations marked the other nations as well). Nevertheless, employers' behaviour made some outcomes more likely than others. Employers' relationships with unions had a major impact on the policy preferences and actions of trade unions, reformers, and state actors during the critical juncture. APD studies of the Wagner Act often overlook the way in which antecedent conditions, in this case the role of employers in the decades prior to the crisis, shaped the outcomes of the 1930s. And despite their often adversarial relationship in the workplace, unions and employers often shared a common scepticism towards a greater state role in regulating industrial relations.

Second, focusing on the roles of the various actors during critical junctures, as most APD accounts do, truncates the analysis by overlooking the important role of "critical antecedents" in the causal process that led to the divergent outcomes. We cannot understand the Wagner Act or any of the key policy decisions in the other Anglophone nations by only looking at the actors and forces that impinged upon the critical junctures in which those decisions were made. We can only unearth the reasons for why the United States and other nations did not adopt one of the alternative regime types by considering conditions that led up to the critical junctures and that were often in place many decades beforehand. Likewise, we can only elucidate the role of employers when we consider their behaviour and relationships with labour and the state that were rooted in longer historical processes. More recent APD accounts of why the United States adopted the Wagner Act have begun to take a longer historical perspective (e.g., O'Brien 1998) rather than explaining its adoption by focusing exclusively on the critical juncture of the 1930s.

Governing Institutions

Institutions are the formal and informal rules or norms that structure collective human behaviour and are separate from individuals' own attributes. Those that deal with governance articulate and aggregate political interests, manage conflict, and make authoritative decisions concerning the allocation of rights and resources. Each Anglophone nation adopted its industrial relations regime in the context of established governing institutions. Did differences among these nations' political and governmental institutions lead them to adopt different industrial relations regimes?

Some institutional differences among these nations constitute important components of the explanation that I put forward earlier in this chapter and more fully in the individual case and concluding chapters. Employer acceptance or rejection of unions had a great impact on whether the labour movement had the organizational strength and trust in political action to develop strong ties between trade unions and political parties, which in turn, were critical for the unions to exert influence over the role the state had in industrial relations. Second, institutions provided reformers with key strategic positions within or close to the state that they could use to formulate, disseminate, and build support for their preferred reforms of industrial relations.

Political scientists who study the domestic politics and institution-building of industrialized nations usually have in mind at least four major types of governing arrangements that vary across nations: the existence of separation of powers or parliamentary government; unitary versus federal system (whether the national government has sole authority to tax, spend, and make laws or if it shares them with subnational governments); whether state bureaucracies have organizational capacities that are appropriate for carrying out particular tasks; and finally, the powers and independence of the courts and the type of legal system in place. We cannot do justice here to comparing all five nations across all these dimensions, but we can ask ourselves whether any critical differences among them on key aspects of each of these dimensions could explain the variation in industrial relations regimes.

It would be difficult to come up with a clear and compelling explanation for the divergence in industrial relations systems based upon any of these four characteristics. For example, only the United States had a separation of powers system. The four nations with parliamentary systems developed widely varying industrial relations regimes; and both the United States and Canada developed legalism despite one having separated powers and the other having a parliamentary form of government. This is not to say that the separation of powers had no impact. It posed significant impediments to government action and often led to pyric legislative victories for the American Federation of Labor, which, in turn, soured labour on the efficacy of politics and governmental solutions to labour's problems. It also made it easy for organized labour to defeat compulsory arbitration proposals at the state level. The centralization of governmental authority in the other Anglophone nations not only made it easier for the state to act, but it left no doubt in the minds of trade unions, parties, and reformers that political mobilization could be a viable route to meaningful reform. The structure of political institutions may have played a role in the process that led the United States to legalism, but the centralization of governmental authority in a majority party in parliament in the other Anglophone nations was a consistent feature that does not help us understand the widely different outcomes among Britain, Canada, and the Australasian countries.

Turning to the federalist versus unitary government comparison, Britain and New Zealand had unitary systems yet developed vastly different industrial relations regimes; of the three nations with federalist systems, the United States and Canada developed legalism and Australia developed statism. Did federalism lead to legalism? It would be difficult to see how that is the case, particularly given that all the major legislative, administrative, and judicial actions in furtherance of legalism in the United States and Canada came from the national governments and not at the subnational levels. One could make a case that Australian federalism helped to diffuse compulsory arbitration and wages boards, but not that American or Canadian federalism helped to do the same for legalism. Arguably in Canada, under the British North America Act and court interpretations of its provisions, the powers of the national and subnational governments were more clearly distinct and separate than in the United States, with labour and civil rights issues falling under provincial control. This barrier to the Canadian federal government's intervention was probably less formidable than it appeared once the political will for national legislative action developed during and after the Second World War. But it was a convenient excuse for Liberal and Conservative governments to use to refrain from pushing labour legislation. It would be most accurate to say that Canadian federalism was an important obstacle to bold state intervention in labour relations, but in a general sense. It would have posed as much a constraint on statism as it did legalism.

Is it possible that differences in bureaucratic organization or capacity help account for the outcomes? In the Australasian cases, government bureaucrats played little role in developing statism, which was drafted by individual reformers who had top positions in newly elected governing coalitions. They played a supporting role in developing British voluntarism by getting behind efforts to encourage voluntarism and providing mediation services when the system broke down. The most far-reaching impact of the bureaucracy was in North America, particularly the United States. The National War Labor Board during the First World War adopted legalist principles, setting an important precedent that would be picked up by reformers and Congress later. Most importantly, the National Labor Board under the NIRA of 1933 played a crucial role in developing case law and learning how legalist principles should be enforced, all of which informed the drafting of the Wagner Act. In Canada during the Second World War, the National War Labor Board, with the guidance of J.L. Cohen and Eugene Forsey, played a very similar role. Nevertheless, it is important to point out that if bureaucratic capacity played an important role in bringing about legalism, the opposite is also true. Making legalism into a viable and enforceable institutional innovation required and induced the development of the requisite bureaucratic capacity.

Perhaps the strongest institutional explanation for the outcomes across the five nations is related to the judiciary and legal systems. American courts were a potent and enduring foe of the labour movement for decades due to their independent and co-equal status in the separation-of-powers and checks-and-balances system of government. This instilled decades of distrust towards the state on the part of the unions. In the other Anglophone countries, parliamentary supremacy meant that it was possible for trade unions to remove the courts as allies of anti-union employers, as they did in Britain. British courts, although frequently hostile to unions, also did not use the labour injunction extensively as their American counterparts did. In Australasia, the absence of a common law tradition to regulate labour relations and of the power of judicial review meant that the courts were not an impediment to labour unions, which made unions and reformers more comfortable with reforms that gave state tribunals the authority to resolve labour disputes.

However, we need to be careful in not exaggerating the structural advantages and power of the courts in the United States as an impediment to reform. Even when Congress decisively removed the courts as an obstacle to trade union organization in the United States in 1932 under the Norris–LaGuardia Act, employers continued to put up effective resistance until Congress passed the Wagner Act and the Supreme Court validated it in 1937. The US Supreme Court also invalidated the state of Kansas's compulsory arbitration policy. However, public support for the Kansas experiment waned and employers only supported the parts that disciplined labour. The fact that only one state adopted compulsory arbitration and that Congress defeated it for the railroads in 1920, the only time it was on the agenda, indicates that it did not have much political support in the first place.

Conclusion

We have seen that some of the alternative explanations, like Hartz's fragment theory, simply do not hold up well. Or, like much of the structural economic and political explanations, their emphasis upon structural constraints and continuities in institutional arrangements over time downplays the importance of contingency and choice that I find to be important in explaining institutional innovations at critical historical moments. Others, such as some of the APD explanations and the social democratic model, are not so much wrong as they are incomplete. They give short shrift, for example, to the important role of employers' behaviour and antecedent conditions generally in building their explanations. The deficiencies in these explanations will become clearer as the analysis in this book unfolds.

Although none of these approaches offers satisfactory explanations for the different national outcomes, some of them include important insights that are compatible with the explanation offered in this book, such as the impact of the structure of the British economy and its early industrialization on the attitudes of British employers towards trade unions. Similarly, we cannot deny the importance of the role of the courts in some nations and their lack of importance in others in shaping the attitudes of the unions towards state involvement and in other ways. Thus, we should regard some of the alternative explanations as supplementing the explanation offered in this book.

3 How the Regimes Emerged

We want to know not only why the Anglophone countries adopted different industrial relations regimes, but also *how* they came to adopt them. What historical processes led to these outcomes? I argue that each regime type arose out of a distinct developmental process that combined "critical junctures" and "critical antecedent conditions." The role and relative importance of critical junctures and critical antecedents varied across our cases. In some, critical junctures were of greater causal weight. In others, antecedent conditions were weightier, or the importance was about equal between them. I use this conceptual framework to organize the individual case chapters (4 through 9) and to analyse what the findings tell us generally about how new industrial relations regimes replaced old ones.

In this chapter, we first explore critical junctures and critical antecedent conditions separately as alternative, but not mutually exclusive sources of institutional change. In the final section I explain how each regime type emerged from different causal combinations of critical junctures and critical antecedent conditions. Chapter 10 pulls together the main findings from the case chapters to illustrate these patterns in greater depth.

Two Sources of Institutional Change

All the Anglophone nations established or consolidated new industrial relations regimes during *critical junctures*, which were crisis periods marked by a relaxation in structural conditions that normally limited the possibilities for change. These key historical moments are marked by "heightened contingency" when the range of choices available to decision-makers expands. The choices made during these critical junctures had lasting legacies that would have been improbable in the absence of the critical juncture (Collier and Collier 1991; Capoccia and Kelemen 2007; Capoccia 2015; 2016; Soifer 2012). The severity and scope of the crises that sparked these historical moments, the coalitions brought together, and the reformers who gained access to state power shaped the regimes that emerged.

Critical junctures rarely provide complete explanations for significant political change, however, because nations are not blank slates when they experience them. The transformative potential of critical junctures is not only determined by what happened at these moments, but also by what came before them – *critical antecedent conditions*, which also shaped the outcomes in each nation. Nations arrive at critical junctures from different starting points – with background conditions that may have important causal impacts on outcomes (Slater and Simmons 2010). For each case chapter, I identify the key critical antecedents and trace out their causal significance for the establishment of industrial relations regimes. Some of the critical antecedents were conditions that made it very difficult or impossible for nations to adopt one or more of the regime alternatives, thus helping to explain why certain paths were *not* taken; other conditions favoured the regime that finally emerged during the critical juncture.

Critical Junctures

My definition of a critical juncture generally follows that of other scholars (Collier and Collier 1991; Capoccia 2015). They are historical moments in which crises produce conditions that could lead to outcomes with lasting impacts on national trajectories that would not have occurred in their absence. They are marked by a relaxation in the constraints on action (or "heightened contingency") that normally operate to limit the choices available to decision-makers. The duration of critical junctures varies, but they are much shorter than the legacies to which they give rise.

Discussions of critical junctures often stress the importance of human agency – that is, individuals enjoying much greater freedom of choice during the crisis periods that mark critical junctures than they do in normal times. However, these choices are not unconstrained volitions. The relaxation of the normal constraints does not mean that new constraints cannot take their place during the critical juncture that limit decision-makers' discretion. In addition to having new constraints on choice replacing older ones, conditions that antedate the critical juncture may also constrain choices during a critical juncture, as noted above.

ELEMENTS OF CRITICAL JUNCTURES

critical junctures are marked by three essential features: *crises*, conditions that lead to *heightened contingency*, and decisions with *lasting impacts*. Crises arise out of (and usually exacerbate) a social cleavage (Collier and Collier 1991, 27). A "crisis" refers to a period of acute difficulty, instability, or conflict fraught with uncertainty or danger. In all of our cases, crises produced a set of conditions that led to the establishment of a new industrial relations regime or the consolidation of an emergent one. Crises do not merely "trigger" critical junctures, however.

The literature on critical junctures so far has overlooked crises as important variables in their own right in shaping and limiting outcomes. Crises differ on several dimensions – their *scope, severity, and timing* – that shape the substance and magnitude of changes that arise out of critical junctures. Scope refers to the number of people or sectors of the economy impacted by it. Some industrial relations crises affect a few industries or regions of a country, while others are more widely felt. Some crises are confined to industrial relations disputes between employers and employees; others encompass broader class conflicts or constitute economic upheavals that disrupt the society broadly. The severity of a crisis simply refers to how acutely the effects of the crises are to those who experience it. Finally, timing refers to whether crises occur earlier or later within a longer historical process (e.g., industrialization) and when they occur sequentially in relation to other historical events and developments.

The scope, severity, and timing of the industrial relations crises that triggered the critical junctures were important in shaping the preferences and actions of organized labour and reformers connected to the state. As a result, crises with broader and deeper impacts, which extended beyond the parties to industrial disputes, generally ushered in more far-reaching breaks with the past. And the crises that came later produced different outcomes than those that came earlier.

It is important to not equate critical junctures with crises, however. All critical junctures are triggered by a crisis, but not every crisis produces a critical juncture. Again, critical junctures are marked not only by crises but also by "structural fluidity and heightened contingency" (Cappocia and Keleman 2007, 352). For example, the United States experienced violent labour unrest in the mid-1880s and the 1890s with the Homestead and Pullman strikes. However, no conditions existed that led to a relaxation of constraints on action ("heightened contingency"). Anti-union Republicans and the judiciary remained in control. We can say much the same about the labour unrest that occurred in 1919–20. And the outcomes of all three episodes were crackdowns on labour that perpetuated the repressive regime in place. In Canada, the Great Depression of the 1930s constituted a crisis for organized labour, but the governments in power did not support labour's demands and no alternative coalition was able to oust them from office. Critical junctures also require lasting effects that we can trace back to them. Sometimes crises have led to the relaxation of political constraints, but without lasting effects. For example, the crisis of the First World War required uninterrupted economic mobilization. The Democratic Congress and Wilson administration were relatively supportive of organized labour. The administration instituted labour regulations that mandated labour's right to organize and engage in collective bargaining. However, this episode does not qualify as a critical juncture because the decision did not have lasting effects. A new Republican administration that took power after the war rescinded the labour rights.

Most of the critical junctures that shaped the industrial relations regimes of the Anglophone nations lasted between four and six years. The statist regimes of Australia and New Zealand arose out of crises that occurred in the 1890s, with major strikes that came in the midst of a depression that started earlier. The 1890 Maritime strike began in Australia and spread to New Zealand. This was followed in Australia by the sheep shearers' strike in 1891, the Broken Hill miners' strike in 1892, and a second shearers' strike in 1894. The unions experienced decisive losses. On the heels of these crises, major political changes took place that led to policy innovations that put Australia on the path to statism. By 1894, New Zealand had adopted compulsory arbitration. The critical juncture lasted longer in Australia as each state adopted compulsory arbitration or wage boards, starting with South Australia in 1894. By 1901, all of the Australian states had adopted such a policy (except for Queensland, which took until 1912). The Australian Commonwealth government, which began in 1901, adopted compulsory arbitration in 1904.

The crisis that set off the critical juncture in the United States was the Great Depression of the 1930s. The first piece of major legislation to emerge was the Norris–LaGuardia Act in 1932, before the New Deal, but on the heels of the emergence of realignment that would put the Democratic Party in power through the rest of the decade. The other principal legislative measures that emerged from the critical juncture were Section 7(a) of the National Industrial Recovery Act of 1933, which set off labour militancy and employer resistance that layered an industrial relations crisis on top of the Depression. In 1935, Congress and the Roosevelt administration approved the National Labor Relations Act of 1935, which established a legalist regime once and for all.

Canada experienced two critical junctures, the first at the turn of the twentieth century and the other during the Second World War. The first was marked by acute industrial disputes centred in the Western region of the country that gave rise to the Industrial Disputes Investigation Act of 1907, which mandated compulsory investigation and conciliation of industrial disputes in several critical industries. Canada's second critical juncture ushered in legalism in the mid-1940s. The crisis was the upsurge in union organizing and severe industrial unrest that accompanied the Second World War. The crisis lasted from the late 1930s when industrial unrest broke out until the adoption of PC 1003 in 1944. Unlike the Australasian and American cases, the crisis did not lead to the demise of an existing governing coalition, but it shook the incumbent coalition to its knees and had the same effect of ushering in a change in industrial relations regimes.

In all the cases discussed above, critical junctures clearly put these nations on new paths. However, not all critical junctures usher in change. Some represent missed opportunities for changing paths.[1] What is common to critical junctures is that they have significant *long-term impacts*, not necessarily that they produce change. They need only have the *potential* for putting nations on new paths.

According to Cappocia and Keleman (2007, 352), "contingency implies that wide ranging change is possible and even likely but also that re-equilibration is not excluded." A critical juncture that *could* have led to a new industrial relations regime but did not is just as consequential as one that does. The British case may be considered one such example of a "near miss," in which the critical juncture at the turn of the twentieth century threatened to take Britain off the voluntarist path that it had been on, through decades of gradual change. Britain suffered major industrial unrest starting with the organization of the "new unions" and the Dock Strike in 1889, followed by strikes in coal mining in 1893 and engineering in 1897. Paralleling these events was a judicial assault on unions that began in 1893 with a string of rulings that culminated in the 1901 House of Lords ruling in the *Taff Vale* case. The acute phase of the crisis began with the 1901 ruling, when it became clear to the labour unions that the unions would be in serious financial jeopardy if employers could sue them for damages for actions that were the result of actions.[2] The critical juncture lasted until 1906 with Parliamentary passage of the Labor Disputes Act. Thus, the outcome of the critical juncture not only avoided sending Britain on to a new path of labour repression but consolidated the voluntarist regime and accelerated its pace of development.

Some historical episodes seem to be candidates for "near misses" at first glance, but upon closer inspection turn out not to be. For example, the American labour movement seized upon the election of Democratic majorities in Congress and Democratic President Woodrow Wilson from 1913 to 1915 to push for legal changes that it thought would remove the courts as a major impediment to unions' ability to put pressure on employers in labour disputes, much as British labour had done with the Labour Disputes Act of 1906. Congress and the president responded with the Clayton Act in 1914, the heart of which ostensibly was intended to deny courts the ability to issue labour injunctions, which had become employers' most potent weapon against the unions. Although labour anticipated that the Act would place the United States on the voluntarist path by removing obstacles to its freedom to act, it was not to be the case. The Supreme Court's interpretation of the Clayton Act permitted the courts to continue issuing labour injunctions. Upon closer examination, however, this episode was not a "near miss." Even if the Court had interpreted the Clayton Act in the way that labour had anticipated it would, or if the Act had been written in a way that would have kept the Court from interpreting it in favour of employers, this alone would not have put the United States on a voluntarist path since employers could have simply continued to refuse to recognize the unions.[3] This scenario re-occurred after Congress passed the Norris–LaGuardia Act of 1932, which finally outlawed the labour injunction, but most employers continued to refuse to deal with unions anyway.[4]

Hence, identifying "near misses" is not always easy since it is often unclear as to whether the conditions that could have led to "wide ranging change" were "possible and even likely." Even after careful analysis, it is possible to disagree about assigning probabilities to a change that did not occur. Not only do we have to estimate the likelihood of a change occurring that did not occur, but we have to assign probabilities to that outcome surviving some length of time into the future that we could consider it placing a nation on a "new path."

Not all historical moments marked by crises, heightened contingency, and lasting changes necessarily qualify as critical junctures. For our purposes, historical moments that bring about lasting change only qualify as critical junctures if all of the essential elements of a new regime are in place at the time of adoption. We need to distinguish between outcomes that fully established a new regime from those where the transformation was incomplete, although perhaps constituted one important step towards such an outcome. For example, the Railway Labor Act of 1926 arose out of a crisis in which changes in the political environment made it possible to consider a range of choices for dealing with railroad labour disputes that had hitherto not existed. The Railway Labor Act also had lasting impacts, including those for the eventual adoption of the Wagner Act because it was the first instance in which the United States adopted the key principles of a legalist regime (outside of temporary wartime regulations). However, the historical moment that produced the Railway Labor Act does not constitute a critical juncture. This is not because it applied to only one sector of the economy, but because the Act did not contain all of the essential elements of a legalist regime that would eventually emerge with the formulation and adoption of the Wagner Act. The missing element from the Railway Act was the enforcement mechanisms that were indispensable for the existence of a viable legalist regime since employers would have continued to resist organized labour in their absence. In contrast, the Canadian IDIA, although it covered a limited number of industries at its adoption, contained all of the elements of a regime that mandated compulsory investigation and conciliation in labour disputes. Several decades after its adoption, the IDIA was "scaled up" to cover the entire Canadian economy, but when it emerged early in the twentieth century it was fully formed.

PERMISSIVE AND PRODUCTIVE CONDITIONS

Soifer (2012) refines the critical juncture concept by distinguishing between the "permissive" and "productive" conditions that constitute them. His distinction allows us to identify the contributions that different kinds of conditions make to the outcome rather than treating them as analytically undifferentiated. Permissive conditions expand the range of plausible choices available to key decision-makers because they relax, destabilize, or overturn the structures and forces that normally constrain choice. Permissive conditions provide a window of opportunity that makes choice and change possible, but they do not shape the *kind* of outcome that emerges from the critical juncture. Productive conditions help to shape the range of choices available, including those that are most preferred by key actors in the process, and ultimately, the outcome of the critical juncture. Both permissive and productive conditions are necessary for a critical juncture to exist.

In the chapters that follow, I identify a set of permissive and productive conditions for each critical juncture out of which new regimes arose or were consolidated. The *permissive conditions* arose out of acute episodes of industrial unrest, economic distress, or some combination of the two. Because their effects were felt beyond the employers and unions directly affected, the conflict expanded beyond the industrial relations arena. These crises were usually instigated by employers and/or trade unions or were exacerbated by their responses to developments in the labour market or economy more broadly. In some cases, employers enlisted the state to strengthen their attack on, or suppression of, the trade unions. In each case, the crisis itself or its resolution put employers and their political allies on the defensive. The *productive conditions* virtually always included the political mobilization of organized labour and its liberal or progressive allies and their capture of the state along with the growing influence of labour and/or progressive reformers who produced or borrowed ideas and concrete proposals for establishing a new regime or consolidating one that was emerging. Employers and their allies within the state, usually reluctantly, acquiesced in these reforms, but sometimes proactively joined the effort to bring them about.

Critical Antecedents

Critical junctures rarely account for institutional change on their own. Conditions that antedate critical junctures may also contribute to the outcomes we observe. As Slater and Simmons (2010) put it, "the cases in any historical comparison might have been very different *places* before a critical juncture sent them on very different *paths*." No nation is a blank slate at the time that a critical juncture occurs. We are interested only in antecedent conditions that Slater and Simmons (2010, 889) describe as "critical" – that is, those having a causal impact. They act in combination "with causal forces during a critical juncture" to "produce long-term divergence in outcomes." Hence, we are not interested in antecedent conditions that were irrelevant to, or inconsistent with, the outcomes in each nation or conditions that were similar across nations (and therefore cannot account for divergent outcomes), or others that represent rival hypotheses. We identify antecedent conditions that are critical in the same way that we do with other causal factors. We need to ascertain whether the antecedent condition was either necessary for the outcome to occur or whether it made the outcome more likely or made an alternative outcome less likely.

Not all antecedent conditions emerge from the same kind of historical process. Some are the result of a single, seminal event or decision that produces a condition that remains fixed and permanent parts of the institutional landscape, such as whether a nation adopts a unitary or a federal system of government or whether the courts have the power of "judicial review." Some antecedent conditions thus emerge out of earlier critical junctures that produce transformative, sharp breaks with the past. Other antecedent conditions are the result of several incremental changes over time, such as the gradual expansion of the voting franchise in some countries or the decrease in union density rates over several decades. It is this latter type of gradual change, which is not sharp and discontinuous, but nevertheless transformative over time, for which Streek and Thelen (2005) have identified several distinct patterns.

Critical antecedents may have a variety of causal impacts. *Crisis inducers* hasten crises that may eventually set off critical junctures. For example, changes in the structure of the economy several years in the making may lead to an upsurge in efforts to unionize previously non-union sectors of the economy that, in turn, sets off a crisis of industrial unrest. Other conditions may act as *facilitators* for bringing about new or consolidating existing industrial relations regimes. For example, the development over the course of decades of strong ties between trade unions and particular political parties facilitates labour's mobilization and influence over the government during the crisis period. A third type of critical antecedent is a *prototype*. These are precursors or rudimentary forms of the kind of industrial regime that will emerge from the critical juncture as fully developed and strengthened. For example, the rapid spread of collective bargaining as a response to an acute crisis of industrial unrest may be preceded by the development in a few industries of informal consultations and negotiations between employers and workers' representatives. Finally, some antecedent conditions serve to foreclose future options. *Foreclosed options* are lost opportunities for certain institutional changes. Once an option is rejected or missed, they may no longer be viable alternatives to be considered during a future critical juncture. Nations that have rejected or been precluded from adopting existing industrial relations regimes may have no recourse but to invent a new alternative during a crisis.

The chapters that follow elucidate the antecedent conditions that appear to have had some causal impact on the outcomes. As we will see, four antecedent conditions were particularly important: whether *employers were relatively hostile or accepting of trade unions*; the extent to which *courts actively repressed unions and whether their power could be checked*; *pre-crisis policy choices that shaped and constrained reformers' influence during the critical juncture*; and whether *trade unions had forged close ties to political parties before the critical juncture*. Not all these conditions may have had the same level of causal impact in every case, but all were important.

As I argued in chapter 2 (and do so in more detail in chapter 10), if forced to choose the most important of these conditions, *employers' orientation towards unions* played a more central and impactful role. Levels of employer hostility (or accommodation) varied both during critical junctures as well as in the years or decades leading up to them. The single most important actor in organized labour's environment was employers, both individual firms and sectors, as well as the "business community" and capitalist class broadly. Labour organizations could only achieve their most preferred, default position in favour of voluntarism if employers went along with it. Voluntarism was, by definition, the absence of state compulsion. Where employers did not embrace voluntarism, which was most places, the labour movement had to accept some sort of state intervention, which was a second-best alternative to voluntarism. Further, if employers were relatively accommodating towards unions, it gave the latter an opportunity to develop the organizational capacity, which they could translate into political capacity during crisis periods.

The courts were often sites of employer hostility towards unions, and they developed a number of legal doctrines and devices to repress unions. Nevertheless, the power and involvement of courts varied across nations. In some places they were heavily and continuously involved in regulating labour relations; in others they were only intermittently so. In some their authority was checked by other state actors; in others, the courts were independent and equal to other governing institutions.

Previous policy choices had a profound impact on future choices. The rejection or failure of policies could foreclose the possibility of their future consideration. The successful implementation of other policies could indicate their practical and political viability.

Whether the unions had forged close ties with political parties also had important consequences. If strong ties already existed before the onset of crisis periods, particularly during times of industrial unrest and attacks on unions, unions could defend their interests much more effectively than if they did not. In addition, the lack of strong ties made it easier for reformers to shape trade union preferences and policy responses during critical junctures.

Not all these antecedent conditions were causally relevant for understanding all of the cases, but that does not make them any less important for understanding those cases for which they are relevant. For example, geographic proximity was important for the diffusion of institutional innovations for Australia, New Zealand, and Canada. Nations facing similar challenges may learn from their neighbours which institutional innovations to adopt and which to avoid. Geographic proximity may facilitate the diffusion process because it may create competition between the neighbouring states or may foster close economic ties and dependencies as well as professional connections between employers, trade union officials, and policymakers.

Explaining How The Industrial Relations Regimes Came to Fruition: Combining Critical Junctures and Critical Antecedents

So far, we have discussed critical junctures and critical antecedents separately. We usually think of critical junctures and critical antecedents as complementary elements in a more comprehensive causal explanation for the outcomes of critical junctures. Their impacts follow a simple additive model of causality. But to understand the kinds of processes of institutional change that are the focus of this book, we ought to examine them as combinations, as causal factors that shape, reinforce, or limit one another's impact. We can gauge which is more important in a particular case and at what point in the regime-building process they are relevant.

The relative contribution of each to institutional outcomes may vary considerably across cases. We will see that antecedent conditions were more important than critical junctures in some cases and contexts; in others, critical junctures were more important. In others, the two were of roughly equal importance. When critical junctures occurred relatively early in the process of industrialization, for example, antecedent conditions may have had less impact (less "critical") or fewer of them may have mattered. When the critical junctures that established or consolidated regimes came later, antecedent conditions may have been more important.

Our analysis of the emergence of new industrial relations regimes among the Anglophone nations reveals three distinct patterns of how regime change came about (see Table 3.1).

- With *breakdown and replacement*, the existing regime rapidly disintegrates and a wholly new regime takes its place.
    "Breakdown and replacement" comes to most people's minds when they think of critical junctures producing institutional change, and it is one of the three patterns of institutional change that Streek and Thelen (2005) identify. The other two patterns do not involve critical junctures.

Table 3.1. Critical Antecedents, Critical Junctures, and Patterns of Institutional Change

Pattern of Change	Causal Importance of Critical Juncture vis-à-vis Critical Antecedents	Regime Type
Breakdown and Replacement	High	Statism
Breakdown and Culmination	Similar	Legalism
Punctuated Gradualism	Low	Voluntarism

However, critical junctures can contribute to institutional changes beyond the familiar breakdown and replacement scenario. What I label "breakdown and culmination" and "punctuated gradualism" are two other patterns:

- With *breakdown and culmination*, again, the existing regime experiences a rapid and widespread disintegration; but the intellectual and institutional underpinnings of the regime that replaces it emerge and begin to take hold well before the old regime's dismantlement. The emergent regime culminates during the critical juncture.
- With punctuated gradualism, a new regime gradually emerges over a long period of time and proves resilient. In a pattern resembling positive feedback, challenges to the regime, such as during a critical juncture, strengthen and accelerate its development and dissemination.

Cases of breakdown and replacement, such as the Australasian nations' adoption of statism, occur when critical junctures have greater causal importance than critical antecedents. Critical junctures determine both the magnitude of change and the development of institutional innovations. Cases of punctuated gradualism, such as Great Britain's adoption of voluntarism, occur when the causal importance of critical antecedents is greater than critical junctures. Antecedent conditions limit the scale of change that is possible and the degree of institutional innovation. Finally, in cases of breakdown and culmination, such as the North American nations, both sources of change are important.

Each of the case chapters illustrate these patterns in greater detail. Chapter 10 brings together the findings from the case chapters to compare and contrast the patterns.

4 The Statist Answer: Australasia

Law is the instrument through which democracy equips a majority to maintain its welfare against the attacks of an anti-social minority.
(Henry Demarest Lloyd, *A Country without Strikes*, 1900, pp. 114–15)

The bold institutional innovations that the Australasians adopted in the area of industrial relations were new not only for them, but for the entire world. New Zealand was the first to establish compulsory conciliation and arbitration in 1894, followed by South Australia in the same year, Western Australia in 1900, New South Wales in 1901 (and 1908), the Commonwealth of Australia in 1904, and Queensland in 1912 (Mitchell and Stern 1989, 104–23). These systems had a basic three-tier structure. Employers and employees would negotiate collective bargaining agreements that the state would register and enforce. If the two parties did not come to agreement, either side could refer the dispute to a conciliation board that would investigate and recommend terms of agreement. Strikes and lockouts were prohibited during this period. If one side or the other did not accept the conciliation board's recommendations, it could bring the dispute to an arbitration court headed by a judge. The court would investigate the dispute and make an award that would be binding upon both sides. To participate in the process, trade unions had to register with the state and were subject to regulation by them (Bray and Walsh 1998, 361–2).

Some Australian states established "wages boards" instead of (or in addition to) compulsory conciliation and arbitration processes. Wages boards were permanent tribunals of employers and employees that determined minimum wages and conditions in each industry, but they were not activated by the need to settle formal disputes; did not require unions or employers organizations to register; and did not ban strikes, lockouts, or other direct action (Macintyre and Mitchell 1989, 6–7). The powers of these boards were the same as the arbitration courts', however, on the key points of obtaining control over dispute settlement and compelling all parties in an industry to comply with court-determined wage levels and working conditions. South Australia adopted wages boards in 1906 and renewed them in 1912, after its 1894 conciliation and arbitration law became a dead letter. Victoria established wages boards in 1896 and renewed them in 1903–5, and Tasmania did the same in 1910. Queensland established wages boards in 1908 but repealed them in 1912 when it adopted conciliation and arbitration (Mitchell and Stern 1989, 104–23; Portus 1958, 104–16).

Australia and New Zealand's adoption of a statist industrial relations regime arose out of the extreme hostility that employers directed at trade unions and the near extinction of the unions in the late nineteenth century. Employers refused to accept unions and a system of industrial self-regulation. Aided by a severe downturn in the economy, employers were able to crush the unions and prevail over them during several severe labour disputes in key industries. The situation led to widespread public fear over the restoration of economic stability and social order in which employers' conduct was perceived as ultimately to blame. It also led to a decline in the political influence of employers and a surge in trade union political activity for the first time in the history of the two nations. The election of new, reformist "lib-lab" governing coalitions afforded an opportunity to progressive reformers who developed and disseminated bold statist solutions to labour unrest, which they viewed as necessary to protect the community from the perils of industrial strife and to rebalance the relationship between capital and labour. Most unions were persuaded to support the new regime, if gradually and reluctantly in many cases. Despite the risks to their autonomy, the new rules would at least guarantee their survival.

The process through which these reforms came about is typical of what we labelled in chapter 3 as a "breakdown and replacement." Australia and New Zealand experienced profound crises in the 1890s that gave rise to a critical juncture. Within about a decade, the permissive and productive conditions in both nations led to the adoption of compulsory arbitration and similar approaches. The crisis grew out of the cleavage between increasingly polarized and organized workers and employers that grew out of industrial capitalism. The Australasian cleavage was distinctive in the acuteness of the crisis that it produced, the crisis's devastating effects, and the political conditions to make a sharp break with the past possible. The political mobilization and acceptance of strong government intervention by the unions, the intellectual breakthroughs in new institutions for the regulation of labour disputes, and the coming to power of a new governing coalition all were the product of the critical juncture.

Of course, neither Australia nor New Zealand was a blank slate when the crisis that set off the critical juncture hit. Pre-existing conditions in Australasia shaped labour's political calculations and policy preferences and facilitated the move to implement bold reforms. Australasian courts lacked the powers to obstruct compulsory arbitration, allowing elected officials and reformers to dominate the institution-building process. The early extension of the voting franchise and the legalization of trade unions that antedated the crisis facilitated and amplified the impact of the electoral coalitions that came to power. Although the critical juncture of the 1890s was necessary and had powerful, immediate impacts on the outcome, the pre-crisis conditions smoothed the way to reform and helped guarantee its long-term viability.

This chapter begins by briefly describing the Australasian context on the eve of the crisis that set off the critical juncture. We then discuss the crisis and the permissive and productive conditions to which it gave rise. Next, we explore the importance of a few critical antecedent conditions and discuss the lasting impacts of both the critical juncture and critical antecedents.

The Critical Juncture of the 1890s

Sweeping reforms of the industrial relations systems of Australasia would have been difficult to imagine in the nineteenth century in the absence of a major crisis. Employers, most politicians, and unions opposed compulsory conciliation and arbitration (Macarthy 1970, 186), but active opposition was unnecessary because the "fairly amicable" relations between employers and employees kept the issue mostly off the agenda before 1890 (Coghlan 1918, 1591). Industrial strife did not present a sufficiently serious threat to public order and economic stability to prompt debate over strong measures. Only proposals that stopped well short of compulsory arbitration – conciliation, and voluntary arbitration – received some hearing (Reeves 1902b, 81–5; Sinclair 1965, 110).

Governments of the day could be relied upon to oppose compulsory arbitration vigorously. Before and after the crisis, employers were solidly opposed to and fought any state involvement in industrial relations that was not clearly in their favour (Patmore 1991, 102–3, 115). They viewed compulsory arbitration as undue interference with their "freedom of contract" and a risk not worth taking given their generally superior resources in industrial relations vis-à-vis labour, particularly since many unions were of recent origin. Employers won most strikes and enjoyed the support of a government that was friendly to property owners in part because systems of "plural voting" remained in place that favoured those with more property (Sinclair 1970, 110–11; Spence 1909, 228). Even for some time after the crisis, they could rely upon the upper houses of colonial parliaments – legislative councils (whose members were appointed by colonial governors or elected in malapportioned districts that favoured rural interests) – to defend their interests (Plowman 1989, 139).

Organized labour generally steered away from political action before the crisis because it sought to develop its industrial strength and distrusted governments that had favoured the propertied classes. For labour, the question of whether to seek state intervention on such issues like the eight-hour day, child labour, and workplace safety was relatively unproblematic compared to industrial relations, where it worried that the state would limit its autonomy and control its organization. As one of Australia's prominent labour leader-politicians at the time put it: "The Trade Unionist did not advocate Compulsory Arbitration without realizing that he, too, was surrendering a very large and important portion of a long-fought-for liberty. The strike had proved to be a powerful weapon, and it was long ere that he was prepared to hand over his destinies to a Supreme Court Judge who, he knew, had come from a different stock, and who had never shown any sympathy with him or his class" (Spence 1909, 312). Strong forms of state intervention would likely reduce unions' autonomy in industrial disputes with employers; on the other hand, they held out the prospect of protection from hostile employers and the avoidance of costly strikes and lockouts. Whether labour would fare better with or without greater state regulation was fraught with uncertainty concerning the unions' future organizational strength and negotiating leverage. As a result of these conflicting considerations, labor's attitude towards compulsory arbitration varied according to the specific context, including whether it was organizationally strong or weak in particular industries and at particular points in time, its level of trust in those who would make arbitration decisions, and specific features of the law that could make compulsory arbitration more or less attractive, such as the permissibility of strikes and whether employers were forced to recognize unions. In the overall Australian context prior to 1890, most unionists were not willing to take the risk of greater state regulation.

Permissive Conditions

Australia and New Zealand experienced very similar and profound crises in the late nineteenth century. The crises were the simultaneous occurrence of a sharp rise in industrial warfare, a deep economic contraction, and, for Australia, a prolonged draught.

INDUSTRIAL UNREST

Unable to raise their wages by controlling labour supply, as craft unions had done, unskilled and semi-skilled workers relied upon organizing drives, collective bargaining, and strikes (Turner 1965, 7–9). The strikes, which met with initial success in the 1880s, continued into the 1890s. They were the largest and most devastating of any in the history of New Zealand and Australia.

Feeling threatened by the upsurge in union strength and pressured by heightened market competition that arose from technological advances, employers built their own organizations and launched counter-attacks to stop the new unionism (as well as to wrest control over production from established craft unions) (Coghlan 1918, 1839–40). The counter-attacks escalated the unrest further. The attacks began in Australia with the shearers' strike, followed by the maritime strike. Ship owners and pastoralists were leading employers of labour in Australasia, and their workers were the most highly organized. The remoteness of the colonies and their heavy reliance upon export markets for primary commodities like wool meant that disruptions in these industries would be felt acutely throughout the region.

The shearers sought to force the pastoralists to employ only union labour, and to that end they enlisted the help of the wharf laborers' union, which refused to handle non-union wool on the docks in Sydney (Coghlan 1918, 1525–6, 1591–3; Patmore 1991, 65; Sutcliffe 1921, 68–71). The Shipowners' Association and Mercantile Marine Officers Association clashed over the officers' attempt to affiliate with other maritime unions in the Melbourne Trades Hall Council (Coghlan 1918, 1593–4). According to one source, the maritime strike "was extensive, had large secondary effects upon industries not directly involved, and affected a buoyant economy" (Bray and Rimmer 1989, 73). These strikes spread throughout most Australian colonies and set the stage for others to follow (Spence 1909, 75–142). The shearers struck again in 1894 and strikes and lockouts roiled other key industries – most notably in the miners' strike at Broken Hill in 1892 where miners were locked out (Sutcliffe 1921, 71–80; Dickey 1966).

The unrest extended to New Zealand. Australia and New Zealand carried on a large volume of trade and labour migration across the Tasman Sea. Unions in both nations had formed Maritime Councils, a conglomeration of several unions, including seamen, wharf labourers, miners, merchant marine officers, and railway servants. New Zealand and Australian unions had close connections because New Zealand unionists sought to be part of Australia's larger and more robust labour organizations. The organization of the employers of maritime labour – the Shipowners' Association – also bridged the two nations. Wharf labourers in Sydney refused to unload cargo belonging to the Union Steam Ship Company, which belonged to the Shipowners' Association. The company then hired non-union labour, knowing that this would set off a strike (Holt 1986, 19–20; Reeves 1902b 87–8). As it had done in Australia, the maritime strike in New Zealand spread to a variety of other unions involving thousands of workers.

Although the strikes began as disputes over wages and conditions, the underlying issue was the fundamental question of employers' acceptance of unions as partners in industrial governance (Portus 1958, 102; Coghlan 1918, 1591). Employers clung to the doctrine of "freedom of contract," which meant that they should be able to hire non-union labour if they saw fit to do so and should control work conditions (Sutcliffe 1921, 67–81). Although "freedom of contract" was very much consistent with laissez-faire capitalism, it also carried over from the pre-industrial era the idea that "masters" should be able to control relationships with their "servants" (Turner 1965, 25). Unionists asserted the principle of "union recognition," which meant the right to organize a union, to strike, to affiliate with other unions, to serve as employers' sole agent in labour disputes, and most importantly, to refuse to work with non-union labour (Gollan 1963, 85; Markey 1989, 156; Macintyre and Mitchell 1989, 15–16; Sutcliffe 1921, 67). Employers were determined to resist, in particular, the demand that they hire only union labour. "In effect, the struggle was as to whether trade unionism was to be made compulsory upon all workmen" (Coghlan 1918, 1591). This was a demand that employers would not countenance, and it led them to attempt to "break the unions" (Gollan 1960, 131).

The employers were well-prepared for the strike, and the bad economic times worked to their advantage, providing a large labour surplus from which they could easily recruit strikebreakers. The employers' victory in the Maritime strike "led many employers to consider the time opportune for further attempts to secure the acceptance by the unions of the principle of freedom of contract. Whatever may have been the initial cause of the Maritime Strike, it certainly resolved itself, so far as the employers were concerned, into a desire to eliminate Trade union intervention in agreements between individual employers and their employees" (Sutcliffe 1921, 74). The employers pressed their advantage to the utmost and refused the pleas of unionists and some politicians to settle their differences peacefully and through compromise (Reeves 1902b, 90; Sutcliffe 1921, 68). In New Zealand and Australia, the public did not immediately sympathize with labour since the maritime unions were among the better paid and resented that they were drawn into an Australian conflict (Sutcliffe 1921, 73). Employers could rely also upon friendly or indifferent, or ineffectual governments. In Australia, "demands for legislation to compel employers to negotiate on wages and to abide by agreements once they had been made were resisted by governments or rejected by property-franchised upper houses" (Turner 1965, 14–15). The government considered the leaders of the Maritime strike "agitators who lead innocent men astray" and refused to either intervene in the strike or provide relief for the unemployed (Sutcliffe 1921, 69). In New Zealand, employers rebuffed the government's efforts to get maritime employees and ship owners to resolve their differences, and similar efforts in Sydney met with the same resistance (Reeves 1902b, 90–1). When a federation of unions pressed the Queensland government to convene a conference between shearers and pastoralists, the government refused and took the pastoralists' side (Reeves 1902b, 92). Governments also called out the police to protect strikebreakers in Queensland and New South Wales (Spence 1909, 90–126; Patmore 1991, 101; Archer 2001; Coghlan 1918, 1841).

ECONOMIC DISTRESS

The strikes came in the midst of a long depression in New Zealand and at the start of a shorter (but no less profound one) in Australia. New Zealand's depression began in 1877, deepened in the 1880s and lasted for eighteen years (Sutch 1966, 60–2). In New Zealand, the decades-long denial of land to the mass of people who wanted to farm exacerbated the problem greatly.

Heavy public and private borrowing to spur development, fuelled by British capital, produced a speculative bubble in land, buildings, and mining (Clark 1981, 63–4). When the bubble burst, a deep downturn ensued that was accompanied by mass unemployment, wage cuts and bank collapses that would rival the Great Depression of the 1930s (Allen 1994, 117; Macintyre and Mitchell 1989, 9). Australia and New Zealand relied heavily upon export markets for their agricultural products, especially wool, and other staples. As the number of sheep rose, pastureland became exhausted. Most importantly, world prices for commodities like wool fell when many countries adopted the gold standard and gold discoveries became depleted. Both countries found themselves in stiff competition to sell their agricultural products with the United States and other nations. With falling prices, the vast amounts of borrowing by private landowners and the government to fund public works could not be repaid (and no protective or preferential British tariff existed at the time) (Sutch 1966, 65). Without social welfare protections, poverty spread. Both nations also had encouraged immigration as part of their development strategy and experienced and end to gold rushes, both of which enlarged the surplus of men in mining and other industries (Coleman 1987, 19–21; Clark 1981, 56). In New Zealand, the immigration reversed itself in 1885 with the depression underway and tens of thousands fled to Australia, until that nation plunged into its own depression in 1891 (Sutch 1966, 64).

A HEIGHTENING OF PUBLIC ANXIETY

The industrial unrest and economic downturn stoked middle-class anxiety that unions could jeopardize foreign investment by shutting down the nations' transportation systems. The maritime strike "paralyzed much of eastern Australia for three months" (Bray and Rimmer 1989, 51; Coghlan 1918, 2100). Where labour was best organized, as in New South Wales and Queensland, the struggle was more bitter and the impacts on the public greater. "[T]he middle class, though winners, were alarmed at the cost of the strife and the temper and number of the unionists" (Reeves 1902b, 98). The employers' uncompromising and harsh approach helped induce public sympathy and calls for reform (Reeves 1902, 90–6). Public sentiment increasingly swung towards labour when employers rebuffed labour's efforts at conciliation: "These encounters profoundly affected the public mind. The sympathy which at first had been widely felt for the attacked masters was now to some extent transferred to the defeated men, who had asked for arbitration and had had their request spurned" (Reeves 1902b, 96). For all Australasians, the crisis dashed the long-held assumption that they had escaped the class warfare of their European forbearers (Patmore 1991, 107; Holt 1986, 21; Reeves 1902b, 96). In New South Wales, the Report of the Royal Commission on Strikes, set up to investigate the causes of the maritime and shearers' strikes, described the unrest as "undeniably the great social problem of the age" and opined that:

> [e]ven those who are least disposed to interfere between the contending forces, and who would prefer to leave the strife to settle itself, admit that the industries

of the colony, and therefore its prosperity, are seriously hampered by the disagreements between employers and employed. Many investors are timid about embarking their savings in any industrial pursuit, which can at any time be brought to a stop by a strike or lock-out; and if this uncertainty could be removed there would in all probability be a great development of industry.... [T]he spirit of enterprise is considerably dampened by the unwillingness of many to set up at their individual risk establishments employing a considerable number of workmen. (1891, 25-6)

In Australia, the depression must have seemed particularly jarring because it came on the heels of a decade of relative affluence. The nation's real per-capita GNP was much higher at the time than that of Canada, the United Kingdom, and the United States (Allen 1994, 117). The depth and length of the depression "seemed to prove that there was little hope for individual improvement within the society," which led to "a popular desire for sweeping change" (Sinclair 1970, 166).

In appearing to threaten social stability and society's liberal underpinnings, the crisis fuelled the arguments of "new" and "radical" liberals that the "needs of the 'community'" were paramount over the economic freedom of private actors and inspired them to push for reforms intended to protect society (quoted in Macintyre 1989, 186; quoted in Holt 1986, 21). Records of Parliamentary debates in both nations noted that major reform would not have been on the agenda in the absence of the major strikes that had occurred in the preceding years (New Zealand Parliamentary Debate 1892, 39, 1893, 158; *South Australian Register* 1890, 6-7). Press accounts give similar credit to the upsurge in industrial conflict for the growing appetite for state intervention: "The apparent disposition in all the colonies to invoke State intervention for the purpose of facilitating the settlement of industrial disputes is a striking sign of the times. It is evidently recognized that under the stress of new conditions the old doctrine of *laissez faire* cannot be allowed such weight as to require Governments to maintain an attitude of absolute inaction, if not of indifference, while society is periodically convulsed by industrial conflicts involving nearly as much bitterness of feeling, and almost as disastrous, as veritable civil wars" (*South Australian Chronicle* 1894a, 5).

EMPLOYERS WEAKENED POLITICALLY

Employers' behaviour during and after the crisis, and the extent of their victory over labour, reduced their political effectiveness in the long run. Their deep hostility, the leverage that they gained from a weak economy, and the help of the police against the strikers, led to the unions' total defeat and near extinction as industrial organizations (Coghlan 1918; Markey 1989, 156; Patmore, 65, 74; Holt 1986, 20-4; Roth 1973, 14-15). Furthermore, employers refused entreaties from unions and politicians to find compromises and peaceful settlements to the disputes, preferring instead to employ strike-breakers and police. Finally, when some governments put in place voluntary systems of conciliation and arbitration, employers refused to cooperate (Plowman 1989, 135). Although the public at first backed the employers, it eventually swung against business (Roth 1973, 14).

The crisis of the 1890s loosened the constraints on change in Australia and New Zealand that had consisted of employer opposition to state intervention, labour's neglect of political affairs in favour of industrial organization, and the state's general orientation towards serving propertied interests. Now, everyone's attention was riveted on the "labour question" as never before and led to a widespread sense of urgency about industrial strife and its pervasive impacts on society. The unrest alarmed the middle class, which feared that it might discourage investment and prolong economic distress; isolated employers' opposition; and led to the near-extinction of the labour movement. In so doing, the crisis opened the possibilities for new political interests to emerge and coalesce and gave the state room to launch bold policies and provided it with a powerful reason for doing so.

Productive Conditions

The crisis made it *possible* for reform to occur, but it did not guarantee that the opportunity would be seized upon or determine what the particular policy response would be. For the permissive conditions to lead to a systemic change in industrial relations, the crisis had to contribute to the rise of a governing coalition that was hospitable to bold change and a process of learning and diffusion that led to specific kinds of reforms.

LABOUR'S ENTRANCE INTO POLITICS AND MOBILIZATION FOR A NEW GOVERNING COALITION

In the wake of the crisis, new interests mobilized, and coalitions emerged that displaced large land-owners and other propertied interests as the dominant forces in Australasian politics (Sinclair 1970, 171; Gollan 1960, 51, 85). Labour had mostly stayed away from politics up until this time, having distrusted a state that was dominated by propertied interests and believing that industrial action was the best way to advance its interests. Most workers were politically "apathetic" (Coghlan 1918, 1591; Spence 1909, 150). Labour's total defeat from the strikes and the response of the governments of the day, which were either impotent or blatantly took the side of the employers, led many of its leaders to conclude that industrial action was insufficient and that they would have to engage in politics on an unprecedented scale (Coghlan 1918, 1841; Sinclair 1965, 114; Reeves 1902a, 75; Spence 1909, 143–8).

In New Zealand and some Australian colonies where Labour parties had not yet emerged, or where workers had not yet developed attachments to them, unions endorsed "lib-lab" candidates who became "labour's representatives" in Parliament. The unions were the strongest supporters of the radical Liberals who came to power in New Zealand in 1891 (Castles, 20; Galenson 1968, 159;

Sutcliffe 1921). The Liberals courted workers and unions in the campaign and the unions endorsed thirty-two Liberal candidates and eight workingmen who ran as Liberals (Woods 1963, 40). The lib-lab alliance was the core of the coalition that passed New Zealand's Conciliation and Arbitration Act of 1894 (Roth 1973, 18–19). The Knights of Labor (KOL), which had sixty district assemblies in New Zealand, started as an American organization, but spread quickly to New Zealand and other countries in the early 1890s just at the time when debate over arbitration got on the agenda (Coleman 1987, 25; Sutch 1966, 68–9, 77). Fourteen members of the Liberal government that swept into power in 1890 were members of the KOL, including Prime Minister Balance and two cabinet ministers.[1] The Liberal government was "anxious to redress the balance [between capital and labour] in favor of the unionists who had contributed so much to its victory, and to provide a framework which would improve the worker's bargaining power" (Roth 1973, 19). According to Reeves (1902a, 76):

> the number of Labour members returned in New Zealand was but five, and they did not attempt to form a separate party. But fully twenty Progressives were generally pledged to the Labour programme, and most of the party owed their election to the Labour vote ... The Labour members did not increase in numbers. Nor did they supply the Progressives with a policy. But the organized support which they and their unions gave the Radical leaders made all the difference. The Progressive leaders already had a policy, and now this was carried through Parliament in a thorough, almost uncompromising fashion.

Passage of compulsory arbitration and other measures cemented the lib-lab alliance further (Holt 1986, 24–5; Sinclair 1965, 116). "In the nineties the Liberal Government was always careful to consult the trade unions concerning labour legislation" (Sutch 1966, 78).

In most Australian colonies and the Commonwealth, labour sought Parliamentary representation through the formation of a new Labour Party. Labour congresses and Parliamentary committees passed resolutions endorsing the idea and organizations like the Labour Electoral League sprang up in the 1880s. The need for a Labour Party was not strongly felt, however, until the crisis hit: "[I]t was not until after the Maritime Strike that there came a full realisation of the advantages that appeared likely to accrue to the unions through their having Labour representatives in the various Parliaments. Up to the end of the eighties the majority of trade unionists were opposed to the [political] course" (Sutcliffe 1921, 101). The post-strike commentaries of many labour activists, such as the New South Wales Labour Defence Committee, also called for political mobilization (see Ebbels 1965, 150–4). The Committee's Report concluded: "This, then, is over and above all others the greatest lesson of the strike.... The rule that trade unionism must steer clear of politics was the golden rule when there was so much work to be done within our present industrial environments. But that time ... is drawing to an end, and we can radically improve the lot to the worker [sic] we must secure a substantial representation in Parliament" (quoted in Sutcliffe 1921, 82). In the election of 1891, thirty-five Labour Party MPs were elected (Gollan 1960, 137). The Labour Party put arbitration into the Commonwealth and most colonial party platforms before Parliamentary adoption (Macintyre 1989, 189). Thus, labour became a key supporter of various lib-lab majorities and coalition governments that supported compulsory arbitration in the two countries.

It may have been that New Zealand adopted compulsory arbitration first because labour had not yet emerged as a partisan rival to the liberals. According to Macintyre (1989, 193), the earlier formation of a Labour Party in Australia may have impeded the introduction of compulsory arbitration because it signalled the crystallization of a class cleavage in politics that had not progressed as far in New Zealand. The New Zealand Liberals were more willing to go along with the demands of one of its own constituency groups than if it had formed a rival electoral organization.

Labour was unable to legislate compulsory arbitration on its own in either country. In New Zealand only 2 per cent of New Zealand's Parliamentarians in 1893 were endorsed by trade unions and other labour organizations (Roth 1973, 18; www.parliament.nsw.gov; www.australia.gov.au). New Zealand labour depended upon a Liberal Party majority that came to power with broad cross-class support and where a Labour Party would not emerge until long after compulsory arbitration was adopted. The Liberal Party held 70 per cent of the seats in Parliament and did not face an opposition party. In New Zealand, almost all of the unions that belonged to the Trades Councils were craft unions that "allowed themselves to be dominated by the Liberal party" (Roth 1973, 19).

The Labour Party emerged in Australia before compulsory arbitration was adopted, but it did not enjoy governing majorities in the Commonwealth Parliament until years after the adoption of compulsory arbitration. In the Commonwealth of Australia, neither the Labour Party nor either of the liberal parties had a majority. Labour's support for the Conciliation and Arbitration Bill was indispensable, but not sufficient to gain passage. Liberals in the government prevailed in their sharp disagreement with Labour over including state employees under the Act. The Protectionist-Labour government resigned after Prime Minister Deakin protested that covering state employees under the federal arbitration law would be an unconstitutional extension of the federal government's power. Labour then took over as a minority government, but it too could not pass the arbitration bill and collapsed. A new liberal government took over with Labour in the opposition and the bill finally passed (Macintyre 1989, 192; Clark 1981, 248–56; Norris 1975, 177–9).

Labour did not hold the effective balance of power in most of the provincial governments that passed the measure. In Western Australia, Labour "played a marginal role in the initiation and passage of" that colony's Arbitration Act of 1900 and had not won any seats yet in Parliament when compulsory arbitration was passed (Plowman and Calkin 2004, 65; see also Crowley 1954, 15). In Victoria, Labour faced the most adamant employer opposition, centred in the Legislative Council (Reeves 1902, 82–3). While it supported the adoption of wages boards, it preferred arbitration; and the wages board system was weak until liberals strengthened it in 1905 after the lib-lab period of collaboration had ended. In Tasmania, Labour supplied Parliamentary support for the passage of wages boards, but Labour MPs were a small contingent and the government did not introduce the legislation to appease labour. In Queensland, Labour supported the passage of wages boards, but it was in the opposition when the liberals passed the measure (Macintyre 1989, 189–93). (As a rule, Labour preferred conciliation and arbitration over wages boards. Wages boards were composed of employees and employers only and employers were thought to hold greater power because they could terminate employees on the job. Arbitration courts, in contrast, were judges who often cast deciding votes [Spence 1909, 311]).

Labour parties did have decisive influence in the passage of compulsory arbitration in New South Wales and South Australia. The government of New South Wales depended upon its support (Labour held 20 per cent of the seats in the Legislative Assembly), but all three of the major parties supported compulsory arbitration (*Sydney Morning Herald* 1901a, 7). In South Australia, a compulsory arbitration scheme that proved unworkable was passed with the support of Labour in 1894, but it turned out to be a dead letter. A lib-lab coalition passed a system of wages boards in 1907 (Macintyre 1989, 190–3). Thus, in most places, "[N]on-labor governments generally implemented a system of their choice ... and did so when they chose" (Macintyre 1989, 189–93).

In sum, the importance of labour's political support varied across Australasia, from very high in New South Wales, and South Australia, for example, to more modest in the other Australian colonies and the Australian Commonwealth. It had a decisive impact in about half of the cases examined here. The importance of labour in arbitration politics was less as a dominant Parliamentary force than as a crucial constituency whose opposition to compulsory arbitration would have made the idea much less politically and operationally feasible. Policymakers knew that a scheme of compulsory arbitration would be difficult, if not impossible, to implement without labour's cooperation with the system. Widespread union resistance to arbitration awards could render the policy unfeasible.

LABOUR'S GROWING ACQUIESCENCE IN STATE INTERVENTION

Although most unions had stayed away from politics and rejected compulsory arbitration before the crisis (Holt 1986, 16–17; Patmore 1991; Mitchell 1989; *New Zealand Parliamentary Debates* 1893, 162), some unionists had begun to support compulsory measures on the eve of the crisis when it became apparent that employers refused to cooperate in voluntary systems (Reeves 1902, 76). The Knights of Labor, an important political and industrial force in New Zealand at the time, favoured arbitration, as did Andrew J. Millar, the head of the Maritime Council, General Secretary of the Seaman's Union, and founder of the Tailoresses Union (Sutch 1966, 68–9, 78–9). The Australian Intercolonial Trade Union Congress began to include conciliation and arbitration on its agenda in the mid-1880s and the Sixth Congress in 1889 passed a resolution calling "for the establishment of Boards of Conciliation and Arbitration for the settlement of all disputes between capital and labour, and so prevent strikes and lock-outs" (quoted in Sutcliffe 1921, 49, 121).[2]

Labour's defeat in the great strikes of the 1890s turned many more unionists into cautious supporters of strong state intervention. The strikes, depression, and drought had been an unparalleled disaster: "There had been setbacks before but they had been short-lived. Now, for the best part of a decade, the labour market was over-supplied; working-class living standards and organizations suffered accordingly" (Turner 1965, 14). In New Zealand, "the remnants of the trade union movement" provided "widespread, though not universal, support" for compulsory arbitration (Holt 1976, 107, 1986, 24). The Trades and Labour Councils scrutinized the bill put forward in Parliament and endorsed it in conferences in 1891 and 1893, as did the Knights of Labor and the working-class members in Parliament (Holt 1976, 107; *New Zealand Parliamentary Debates* 1893, 147). As James Holt put it in the case of New Zealand, "the unions, being industrially weak, lacked the will to oppose [compulsory arbitration], while the employers, being politically weak, lacked the power to prevent it" (Holt 1976, 108–9, 1986, 25). Likewise, most Australian labour unions put aside their distrust of the state in labour relations and acquiesced in compulsory arbitration because it guaranteed their existence, if nothing else (see citations in Patmore 1991, 127; see also Gollan 1960; Macarthy 1967; Rickard 1976). The main labour federation (the Trades and Labour Council) and key unions representing shearers, miners, railway men, and some crafts, supported compulsory arbitration as well.

Labour understood the risk of surrendering so much power to the state, but many in the movement also had concluded that the status quo was no longer sustainable. As W.G. Spence, a leading trade union and Labour Party leader put it in debate over the New South Wales arbitration bill (quoted in Ebbels 1965, 231; emphasis added):

> My opinion is that we shall not be likely to get strikes after this act is passed. I am hopeful of its working successfully, but we realize that there might be, with a great boom of prosperity, which those who favour [Australian] federation have been telling us about, a possibility of the working-classes being in a stronger position

without the bill than with it.... If they go into court the probability is that the decisions will be more in favour of the employers than of the workmen, but we are willing to take that risk. *The trades-unions of Australia are so anxious to avoid these disputes that they will take that risk. They realize more fully to-day than they have before that the present system cannot last; that the present cut-throat policy of competition cannot be a permanent condition of things.* Reform can be brought about by political methods, and, working in that direction, we are willing to sacrifice a good deal in order to avoid serious conflict, in the hope that improved conditions will be brought about by those methods.

Even as late as 1905, unionization rates in New Zealand and Australia were only 8 per cent and 10 per cent, respectively, down from the pre-crisis level of 20 per cent (Stephens 1980, 115; Castles 1985, 21). Labour, in short, was willing to trade off autonomy for institutional security and recognition.

While the crisis led to greater support for compulsory arbitration, support varied across different segments of the labour movement and from one colony to another. Radical unions, wherever they existed were least favourable towards the idea, seeing it as a device for controlling labour and perpetuating capitalism (Clark 1981, 244). The Australian and New South Wales Parliamentary Labour Parties were more strongly in favour of arbitration than many of the unions that supported them (Markey 1989, 169–70). New Zealand Labour backed the idea more quickly and firmly than in Australia because unionism was more recent and less well-developed there. Even in the first decade of the twentieth century, "[i]n a country with no large-scale industry there were few strong unions except on the wharves and in the mines and railways; unions with small or scattered membership found the arbitration system a blessing" (Sinclair 1970, 203). The Labour Party did not put arbitration into its platform until two years before its passage in the Commonwealth in 1904 and four years after it was introduced in Parliament (Markey 1989, 157, 169). Except for Labour MPs, "a larger number of unions [than those that strongly supported arbitration] seem to have merely tolerated arbitration on a conditional basis, often because of political influences from, or loyalties to, the Labor Party." Some historians have greeted Markey's claim that "as many unions opposed compulsory state arbitration as actively supported it" (Markey 1989, 174) with scepticism (Patmore 1991, 102; Brereton 1989, 294–5), though most agree that labour's support was clearest in New South Wales and in the Commonwealth federation.

New South Wales is a good example of how labour's embrace of compulsory arbitration was the result of gradual acceptance through learning. Opinion shifted in favour of "unilateral compulsory referral and enforceable awards between 1895 and 1900" (Patmore 1991, 108). Of the twenty-six workers who appeared before the New South Wales Commission in 1891 and who were asked their opinion on compulsory arbitration, about half favoured the idea, almost one-third opposed it, and the rest were unclear about it (*Royal Commission on Strikes* 1891). Patmore (1991, 107) estimates that while a majority of the union representatives that appeared before the Commission favoured state intervention, only a third of them supported compulsory arbitration. The New South Wales Labor Party, founded in 1893, did not add compulsory arbitration to its platform until 1895 (Norris 1975, 187).

Despite the greater severity of the crisis in that colony than in any other, compulsory arbitration did not appear on the Party platform during the 1894 and 1898 elections, and only did so in the 1901 campaign on the eve of passage of the Arbitration Act (Spence 1909, 150–7). Even as late as 1901, when the first Commonwealth Labour Conference met, its platform did not immediately include compulsory arbitration (Norris 1975, 174–5). The prime minister of New South Wales, upon introducing the 1901 arbitration bill, noted that, "A few years ago the bill would not have met with any support from any labour section" (*Sydney Morning Herald* 1901c, 8). That colony had passed voluntary conciliation and arbitration acts in 1892 and 1894, but employers refused to participate in them. Those who favoured voluntary schemes had argued that the publicity surrounding the investigation undertaken during the conciliation process would bring to bear the force of public opinion on the disputants to follow the recommendations of the conciliation authorities, but this did not happen (Portus 1958, 108; Sutcliffe 1921, 122–3).

Setting aside the complexities and changeability of labour's position on stronger state measures, the best evidence available suggests that, by the time the arbitration acts were passed, most of the labour movements in New Zealand and Australia had come to support them, even if reluctantly in some cases. Thus, the crisis influenced organized labour's preferences directly by changing its calculus of in favour of reform. For all the risks to its autonomy, compulsory arbitration held out the promise of organizational survival and the avoidance of devastating strikes and lockouts. The crisis altered labour's preferences also indirectly by setting off a learning process through which labour concluded that voluntary measures were insufficient to secure its place in industrial governance.

LIBERAL-LED, CROSS-CLASS COALITIONS

The governing coalitions that legislated compulsory arbitration were unusually broad. In addition to middle-class radicals, the New Zealand liberals appealed to "manufacturers wanting tariff protection and abolition of the property tax, the landless and the small farmers wanting land;" other powerful groups were brewers, bankers and merchants with money and influence, the aged and unemployed, and wage-earners with votes and potential industrial might. "With the exception of the big-landowners, these groups all found representation and expression in the Liberal Party" (Sutch 1966, 77; Coleman 1987; Castles 1985, 25). The conflict that erupted in the 1890s was not just between capital and labour but also between the large and small landowners and those who sought to own land (Lipson 1948, 57). The central issue in New Zealand's 1891 election was not arbitration, but land reform. New Zealand's geography, gold rushes and the government's immigration policy led to ever larger numbers of landless citizens (Sutch 1966, 33), which allowed the Liberal Party to forge a strong urban–rural alliance composed of workers and the "land-hungry." The Liberals passed land reform after the election, which boosted their vote totals in rural areas in the 1893 election, allowing them to pursue labour and industrial relations reforms. At the same time, reformers in New Zealand crafted the Arbitration Act to minimize Liberal opposition by excluding farmers from the Act to maintain the support of the "country liberals," given their important role in the Liberal Party at the time (Holt 1976, 107–8). The Liberals thus built a durable coalition of urban and rural interests that benefited the prospects for their passage of arbitration and other labour legislation (Lipson 1948, 203–8; Sinclair 1965, 117).

In the Australian Commonwealth, compulsory arbitration would not have been approved without the New Protectionist policy forged by Labour and liberal reformers in the Protectionist Party (see Macintyre 1989, 180). The coalition brought together labour seeking arbitration and social reforms and manufacturers seeking trade protection. Labour thus capitalized on a split among employers over the tariff issue by marrying industrial relations reform to tariffs. The Employers Federations opposed arbitration, but Chambers of Manufacturers was willing to go along with it in exchange for labour's support for the tariff (Plowman 1989, 146; Macarthy 1970). Australia's first Commonwealth election of a national Parliament in 1901 produced a split among three main parties – the liberal Protectionists, the Free Trade Liberals, and Labour – with none having a majority. The Protectionists formed a coalition government with Labour, using the promise of compulsory arbitration in exchange for labour's support for protectionism. A similar coalition of Labour and the Protectionist Party existed in New South Wales.

THE ROLE OF RADICAL LIBERALS IN POLICY INNOVATION, LEARNING, AND DIFFUSION

Large-scale change would not have occurred in Australasia if progressive liberal reformers had not been in a position to initiate it, develop it as a concrete alternative, and push to get it approved. Reform politics took place before class cleavages had fully crystalized and when working-class parties were only starting to emerge. Yet, even before the crisis, Liberal parties saw labour's demands as increasingly salient and justified given the imbalance in industrial power in favour of larger and larger corporate enterprises and the devastating impacts of boom-and-bust cycles. Of course, they viewed workers as an increasingly important source of electoral support as well. The imbalance in industrial power in favour of capital, the destabilizing impacts of industrial capitalism, along with workers' potential electoral dominance in an increasingly industrialized and democratized polity, created inducements for liberal parties to embrace working-class interests (Clark 1981, 76–8).

Known variously as "radicals," "progressives," and "new liberals," the reformers were deeply committed to gaining the passage of compulsory arbitration by harnessing working-class votes and union support. Progressivism was a transnational reform movement that swept across the Anglo-American world. Its major concern was with the impact of industrialization and class conflict on the working class and social stability. Progressive liberals refashioned the role of the state in an effort to promote class harmony and preserve liberty. Industrial relations reforms were part of a broader effort to refashion the role of the state to meet the challenges of industrial capitalism and urbanization.

Once the scope of conflict moved beyond the industrial arena in which employers and employees had been in control, labour and capital's ability to dominate the discourse of reform diminished. Liberal reformers and politicians dominated the framing of the issue and they emphasized "equity, harmony and public benefit" as much as the interests and demands of either capital or labour (Macintyre and Mitchell 1989, 12). According to Macintyre (1989, 182, 186): "insofar as sections of the labour movement took up arbitration, they did so within a political paradigm that the liberals had established ... [and] liberalism remained a hegemonic ideology." A belief in the possibility of class harmony dominated liberals' thinking during this period of lib-lab cooperation, which lasted until the outbreak of heightened class conflict during the First World War (see Brugger and Jaensch 1985, 20).

The leading reformers were senior members of the Liberal-led governments, including Australians Charles Cameron Kingston (the founder of Australia's system of compulsory conciliation and arbitration), Henry Higgins (who became president of the Arbitration Court), Bernhard Ringrose Wise (the attorney general of New South Wales), and New Zealander William Pember Reeves, a radical in the Liberal Party who served first as education minister and then as the first minister of labour (Patmore 1991, 102, 109). They came from educated, middle- and upper-middle-class backgrounds and took great advantage of their high positions to develop expertise and build support for their initiatives. Kingston and Reeves, in particular, developed compulsory arbitration, advocated its adoption, and built political and legislative support for it (Holt 1986, 17, 24; Patmore 1991, 114–15). Kingston provided significant intellectual and political leadership, introducing a bill of its kind for the first time as a member of the South Australia legislature in 1890, despite determined employer opposition and before labour had come around to embracing it (Glass 1997, 63–4, 101–3). Kingston studied various approaches to ameliorating industrial conflict that a variety of countries had tried and benefited from reports of Royal Commissions established to investigate potential solutions to industrial unrest. His bill passed the South Australia legislature after being substantially weakened by the upper house (Legislative Council) in 1894. Kingston introduced the first Commonwealth arbitration measure as a member of the first Commonwealth cabinet but resigned in 1903 before its passage because he lost in an effort to apply the law to British and foreign seamen (Playford 2013; Norris 1975, 187).

Reeves emerged as labour's champion in the New Zealand Parliament and as the principal author of that nation's legislation (Holt 1986, 17; Roth 1973, 19). By 1891, Reeves had introduced a variety of labour reforms, but he had become "saturate" in the subject of industrial relations, and compulsory arbitration was his "pet measure" (Sinclair 1965, 151). Passage of the Arbitration Act in 1894 undoubtedly owes much to Reeves's single-minded dedication to the cause. Historians and Reeves's biographer credit him as "the chief advocate and driving force" behind compulsory arbitration in New Zealand (Holt 1986, 17; Roth 1973, 19; Holt 1976, 100–1) and argue that, "but for Reeve's [sic] persistence, it is improbable that it would have been introduced" (Sinclair 1965, 151, 185, 205).[3]

For the reformers, the central goal was preventing and minimizing industrial strife in order to protect the community, not taking sides in the capital–labour conflict. As one proponent put it, "it [is] the duty of the State to step in and interfere when the body politics [sic] is in danger from a great industrial strike or lock-out!" (New Zealand Parliamentary Debates 1892, 41). Likewise, upon introducing the Commonwealth arbitration bill, Prime Minister Deakin pointed out that its aim was to "establish industrial peace" (Clark 1981, 245). Similarly, the New South Wales Royal Commission on Strikes, which endorsed some compulsory features of arbitration, concluded that "[i]ndustrial quarrels cannot continue without risk of their growing to dangerous dimensions, and the state has a right in the public interest to call upon all who are protected by the law to conform to any provision the law may establish for setting quarrels dangerous to the public peace" (quoted in Plowman and Calkin 2004, 56). The legislative architects and supporters described strikes and lockouts as "barbarous," "uncivilized," "frightful," and "wasteful" methods of dispute settlement, which caused incalculable "disaster, injury and possibly ruin to capitalists and employees" (*South Australian Register* 1890, 6–7; New Zealand Parliamentary Debates 1892, 34–5, 43). They likened industrial strife to civil warfare, an unenlightened and "unscientific" mode of dispute settlement. Furthermore, because the outcomes of strikes and lockouts reflected which side was more powerful rather than which was right on the merits, they produced inequity and injustice. According to Reeves (1902b, 76), "[i]f the endurance of these hardships and miseries always led to justice, the price paid, though heavy, might be submitted to. But all this may be gone through and yet the party in the right may lose."

In arguing for the need of capital and labour to yield to the interests of the community, reformers called attention to the threat to the public that industrial capital and labour presented. Capital had grown so large and powerful that it threatened to destroy equality and liberty (Sinclair 1970, 173–4). Australasian reformers' brand of liberalism had a strong collectivist streak when it came to using the state to ameliorate the negative effects of industrialization. According to Sinclair, "[l]iberals believed that the state was, in fact, the people" (Sinclair 1970, 176). New Zealand's radicals especially were much more collectivist than British liberals (Sinclair 1965, 172–5). They accepted the notion that the government was responsible for maintaining prosperity, a belief that did not become widespread in other nations until later. Like other radical liberals, Reeves became influenced by Fabian socialism by the early 1890s (Sinclair 1965, 100–4, 207–8). Reeves described himself as a "state socialist," although to him, any activity undertaken by the state constituted "socialism" (Sinclair 1965, 102). Liberal leaders in Australasia and many of their followers drew their ideas from radical liberals like John Stuart Mill and American reformers Henry George and Edward Bellamy. They were influenced by English and French socialists, particularly the Fabians, by American Populists and the Knights of Labor (Coghlan 1918, 1835–8; Sinclair 1970, 172–6; Castles 1985, 20). Their blend of radicalism and socialism was pragmatic and experimental rather than revolutionary and theoretical.

Australasian reformers translated progressivism in ways that fit into their particular setting and how specific problems like industrial unrest manifested itself. Although the liberals' rhetoric stressed class harmony and they proposed that state tribunals constitute open, neutral forums for gathering information, publicizing, and weighing it in the public interest, their proposals deliberately sought to *rebalance* the relationship between capital and labour and clearly weighed in on the side of encouraging the formation of unions and making it possible for the state to cast its deciding vote in arbitration proceedings on labour's side.

Encouraging unionization and compelling employer recognition of unions were other goals of reform that would contribute to industrial peace. Although reformers carefully avoided appearing to take sides in the struggle between capital and labour in presenting their proposals (Coleman 1987, 32, 34–5), their plans for union registration and compulsory arbitration would unavoidably foster unionization and compel employers to recognize unions. Indeed, given that the great strikes had grown out of employers' refusal to recognize unions as the exclusive agents for bargaining over wages and working conditions, future conflicts could only be avoided by legally mandating recognition.

Although Reeves contended that his proposal maintained neutrality between capital and labour (Holt 1976, 108), the preambles of his measure and Kingston's expressly stated the promotion of trade unions as one of their principal goals. Reeves's Industrial Conciliation and Arbitration Act stated that its purposes were "to facilitate the settlement of industrial disputes" and "to encourage the formation of industrial unions and associations" (quoted in Sinclair 1965, 206;

Coleman 1987, 227) and the language in Kingston's 1890 "Industrial Unions Bill" (never enacted) was virtually identical (Spence 1909, 306). Opponents and supporters alike pointed out that benefiting unionized workers was an aim of these measures (New Zealand Parliamentary Debates 1892, 39, 42, 51; *South Australian Register* 1890, 7).

Strengthening unions was not an end in itself, however. It had two interrelated practical purposes aimed at reducing industrial strife. First, workers (and employers) had to be organized in order to make agreements between the two possible, whether concluded through voluntary action or compulsory arbitration. As Reeves put it, "[u]nionism renders arbitration and conciliation much easier, and enables Boards to work in a more systematic way than if the disputes were between the masters and unorganized labour" (*New Zealand Parliamentary Debate* 1892, 31). The elements in the proposals to encourage unions included the minimal numbers of workers necessary who sought to organize, a low threshold for meeting the requirement of a registered union, and provisions that placed unions (as well as employers) under the protection and jurisdiction of the law. Second, strengthening unions would help to prevent industrial conflict by deterring employers from exploiting workers to the point that they would provoke conflict. Reducing industrial strife and restoring a more balanced capital–labor relationship justified strong elements of compulsion while retaining some semblance of a voluntary system (though less, it turned out, than they anticipated). According to Holt, "Reeves, like all advocates of compulsory arbitration, stressed the senselessness and barbarity of unrestrained industrial conflict, and argued that compulsory arbitration provided a rational, civilized, solution to the problem. It 'would never put an end to labour troubles but it would ... put a stop to those disruptions of industry by which factories are closed, enterprise checked, work stopped and misery and desolation brought into hundreds and perhaps thousands of homes'" (Holt 1976, 101).

Australasians did not simply adopt compulsory arbitration, they invented it. The severe and widespread effect of the crisis induced reformers to launch intensive and wide-ranging study and experimentation. "Stronger" state intervention could have included conceivably a range of alternatives, from repression (which was an immediate response of the Australian state to the Maritime strike) to voluntary forms of conciliation and arbitration. Between these extremes were other possibilities, including compulsory arbitration, which in turn, could be designed in a variety of ways that involved greater or lesser state coercion and that favoured one or the other side in industrial conflict. Australasian contributions to industrial governance were twofold – making arbitration (and conciliation) *compulsory* and linking it to a mandate that employers *recognize unions* (Macintyre and Mitchell 1989, 10).

Compulsory arbitration was not an immediate, reflexive response of governments to the crisis, but the outcome of a learning and diffusion process that took years. Only Kingston and a few other notable witnesses advocated compulsory arbitration before the New South Wales Royal Commission on Strikes that convened immediately after the maritime strike in 1890. Most of the trade union leaders and politicians who would eventually support the idea learned the negative lesson that voluntary arbitration had failed (because employers or labour would sabotage it) and, for Australians, the positive lesson that compulsory arbitration (adopted first in New Zealand in 1894) seemed to work.

The reformers studied the efforts that other nations made to use arbitration. Kingston and Reeves knew about early experience with conciliation and arbitration in Britain, France, Massachusetts, and Nova Scotia. Reeves was thoroughly educated in the history of efforts at conciliation and arbitration across the globe and spent a number of pages during the second reading of his bill detailing the failures of these attempts (*New Zealand Parliamentary Debates* 1892, 27–30, 33–4). The New South Wales Royal Commission on Strikes carried out a similarly comprehensive study (Report of NSW Commission 1891, 6–8). All of the earlier schemes were voluntary and often applied only to disputes between individual workers and their employers.

More directly relevant were the recent experiments with voluntary arbitration in the colonies of Australasia. Voluntary arbitration was common in a variety of industries with strong unions in Australia in the decade leading up to the crisis. But industrial relations had become so strained during and after the crisis that voluntary schemes proved unworkable (Coghlan 1918, 1467–8). New South Wales in 1892 and the Commonwealth government in 1899 adopted weak legislation that called only for voluntary arbitration (Reeves 1902b, 99). Kingston, as premier of South Australia in 1894, attempted to pass compulsory arbitration with full powers of compulsion, but the measure that passed was weakened considerably to make it palatable to the conservative Legislative Council (Reeves 1902b, 100–1). Employers easily undermined all these efforts. Reformers became convinced that only compulsory measures would suffice (New Zealand Parliamentary Debates 1982, 1983, 153; *South Australian Register* 1894, 4). Patmore 1991, 108–9; Mitchell 1989, 79–88).

Australian reformers also had some reason to believe that compulsory plans held out promise. They pointed to New Zealand, where they argued, that industrial strife had been reduced and had "not driven capital out of the country" in the years following its adoption. The records of debate in Western Australia and New South Wales are replete with discussion of the relevance of the New Zealand experiment (see Plowman and Calkin 2004, 57; Holt 1976, 109; *Sydney Morning Herald* 1900a, 1900b, 1901b, 1901c). In respects, the New South Wales Act became a model for "all of the other state arbitration systems" and the state arbitration systems in effect at the time became important examples for the adoption of the Commonwealth law early in the twentieth century (Portus 1958, 110–13).

Finally, reformers found a way to make reform more economically feasible and palatable to employers by linking compulsory arbitration and wages boards to trade protection. By reducing competition from abroad, businesses could afford to charge higher prices in order to finance the higher wages that arbitration and wages boards promised to labour (Plowman 1989, 146).

Under Reeves's leadership, New Zealand was the first jurisdiction to adopt compulsory arbitration, in 1894, but the bill that he introduced in 1891 reproduced the conceptual framework and much of the content of the bill that Kingston introduced in the South Australian legislature a year before, including bans on strikes and lockouts, provisions for permanent tribunals with the power to compel arbitration and enforce awards and the registration and regulation of trade unions, and the prohibition of strikes and lockouts (Mitchell 1989, 95–6). Some historians reject any idea that Reeves pilfered Kingston's bill and argue that compulsory arbitration was an idea that was "in the air" (Holt 1976, 100) and that some of the provisions in Reeves's proposal were his own (Holt 1986, 26; Sinclair 1965, 152). At the same time, when the New Zealand Act was approved in 1894, Reeves himself publicly recognized Kingston "as the pioneer of the movement for settling industrial disputes by compulsory arbitration" and sent him his "congratulations on this acceptance of the principle" (*South Australian Chronicle*1894b, 8). Whatever the exact provenance of specific provisions of the legislation in the two nations, the innovation clearly was diffused among the Australian colonies and between Australia and New Zealand.

The Removal of Institutional Foes. Reformers faced two important institutional hurdles. First, Legislative Councils, the upper houses of Parliament modelled after the British House of Lords, were intended to filter and revise ill-considered legislation, but they were bastions of propertied interests that opposed social reforms of every stripe (Clark 1981, 125; Spence 1909, 273). Because members of the Councils were chosen in ways that favoured capitalists and large landowners (for example, through appointment, or through elections in which districts were malapportioned or where property requirements were kept in place for electors), they could frustrate the will of the majority despite the existence of universal male suffrage for elections in the lower houses.

Reeves introduced his arbitration bill in 1891, but it did not become law until 1894 because the upper house blocked it (Sinclair 1965, 148; Spence 1909, 307). Australian opponents used Legislative Councils as a favoured tool for obstruction similarly. Kingston's 1890 arbitration bill was delayed, and then weakened, by the Legislative Council (*South Australian Chronicle*1894b, 5). Employers' federations in at least five states were created or reinvigorated in response to the passage of compulsory arbitration laws (Plowman 1989, 137). Employers in Victoria, for example, fought constant battles to try to eliminate wages boards, while preventing the establishment of arbitration, which they wanted less than wages boards (Plowman 1989, 138–9).

Reformers eventually found ways around the Legislative Councils. In New Zealand, members of the Council were appointed by the British governor on the recommendation of the prime minister (Lipson 1948, 57). The Liberals replaced lifetime tenure for members of the Council with a seven-year term and manoeuvred to get additional appointments (Coleman 1987, 26–7). Even so, the holdovers from Conservative governments frustrated the Liberals' reform program until 1893 when the British Colonial Office agreed, over the objection of the governor, to allow the Liberal government to appoint a dozen new councillors (Sinclair 1965, 147–8). After the election, the Liberals appointed moderate trade unionists to the Council and consulted closely with labour members of Parliament and unions before introducing legislation. In New South Wales, the prime minister appealed to the electorate to remove members of the Council who were blocking progressive reforms. The Councils' powers were not substantially diminished until the creation of Australia's federal, Commonwealth government in 1901, which shifted substantial legislative power away from colonial governments. One of the liberal inspirations for a federal, Commonwealth government was to diminish the power of the Legislative Councils in the colonies (Clark 1981, 125–6).

The second hurdle was the Commonwealth Supreme Court and High Court of Australia, which employers petitioned to circumscribe the authority of the Court of Conciliation and Arbitration Act of 1904. Employers met with initial success in their litigation, but this changed when the first Labour Government came to power in 1913. It enlarged the membership of the Supreme Court and filled a vacancy, thus creating a majority on the Court that expanded the authority of the Arbitration Court (Plowman 1989, 147–53). Ultimately, the compulsory arbitration laws put judicial institutions at the very centre of the new industrial relations process. Once the initial attack on the Arbitration Court was overcome, the centrality of the judicial role in industrial relations reduced further the possibility of judges undermining an institution over which they exerted extensive control. Proponents of ambitious schemes for state intervention would have to contend with the courts' powers of statutory interpretation and with another formidable institutional impediment – the upper houses of Parliament (Legislative Council). They did not need, however, to contend with courts armed with judicial review or a common law tradition in labour regulation.

Summary

The adoption of compulsory arbitration and wages boards occurred because Australasia experienced a critical juncture in the 1890s. The crisis loosened constraints that made it possible for large-scale reform to occur and produced several productive conditions that led to the specific reforms. It mobilized labour and other groups to engage fully in the political process, which helped put in power new reform-oriented governments that were committed to using state intervention to reduce industrial strife both to protect the community and achieve greater balance between capital and labour. Although before the crisis radical liberals had seen the need for government intervention to ameliorate the effects of growing class conflict and sought the electoral support of newly enfranchised workers, the crisis gave them an opportunity to seize power and develop and carry out specific reforms. The crisis set off a process of innovation, learning, and diffusion that led to a rejection of voluntary schemes in favour of compulsory ones that mandated union recognition.

Critical Antecedent Conditions

Four antecedent conditions facilitated Australasian reform. The first was the legacy of pre-arbitral regulation of industrial relations that emphasized statutory over common law approaches. The effect was to remove the courts as a serious potential impediment to establishing unions as legal entities that could act on behalf of their members in disputes with employers. The Trade Unions Acts made unions no longer subject to prosecution as criminal conspiracies and made them organizations subject to regulation by the state. The enfranchisement of the working class made it possible for labour to gain political representation in Parliament. Finally, the spread of unionism posed a greater and greater threat to employers who did not wish to recognize them and agree to their demands.

Parliamentary Supremacy and Judicial Non-Interference

Courts in many nations, as we will see later, often tried (and sometimes succeeded) in constraining the state's role in industrial relations, particularly if it interfered with classical liberal views of the way labour markets should function. Courts in many countries were opposed to unions because they viewed them as illegal combinations and disapproved of organizations and actions that interfered with the rights of employers and employees to freely contract with each other. Legal prohibitions and doctrines against conspiracies in restraint of trade had a long history embedded in the common law and changed slowly because of courts' reliance upon precedent. Courts presented an alternative site within the state for deciding policy and competed with legislative bodies for shaping decisions. Unions suspected, or were convinced, that judges and lawyers were sympathetic to business because they came from similar class backgrounds and knew that judges' removal from direct popular control made it more likely that they would be less susceptible to the demands of newly enfranchised working-class voters. Courts shaped labour's attitudes towards political engagement and their expectations about the court's reaction to laws that helped labour.

Courts can influence policy by declaring laws unconstitutional (where they have the power of judicial review), enforcing their own legal doctrines through the development of common law, and interpreting statutes passed by legislative bodies. Courts in Australasia were unable to use the first two powers to block or weaken compulsory arbitration laws. Parliamentary supremacy in Australasia disallowed the courts from invalidating legislative measures and Australia relied upon statutory, not judge-made common law in labour regulation. Statutes were "an almost complete substitute for common law proceedings" well before compulsory arbitration came into effect (Quinlan 1989, 36). Because of a lack of education in colonial Australasia, the law had to be made comprehensible to magistrates, employers, and employees. Employers, in particular, favoured using masters and servants laws rather than common law conspiracy laws (Quinlan 1989, 37). As a result, elected leaders and legislative bodies, not unelected judges, dominated lawmaking in this area from very early.

Prior to the late 1800s, when a rural and mercantile elite dominated the colonies, local magistrates implemented coercive labour legislation. The magistrates were generally hostile to workers, lobbied legislatures for punitive laws, and interpreted them in ways that made them so (Quinlan 1989, 35, citing Merritt 1981). The expansion of the voting franchise to workers, however, gave labour greater influence over Parliament, and magistrates' decisions changed accordingly. Workers learned the important lesson that legislatures could be responsive to their interests and that the judiciary had little ability to thwart legislative measures.

The Enfranchisement of the Working Class

The expansion of mass democracy in Australasia came just before (or in some colonies, simultaneous with) industrialization and the growth of industrial unrest. Industrial relations reform came *after* universal male suffrage was established in all six Australian colonies and both nations. New Zealand historians see the early 1890s as an important dividing point in that nation's political development. The period before 1891 was a "semidemocratic phase" in which democracy was still evolving and politics was dominated by conservative elites whose stronghold was in rural areas (Lipson 1948). Registered voters as a percentage of the population rose from 18 per cent in 1879 to 29 per cent in 1887, and to 45 per cent in 1893 (Lipson 1948, 24, 168–71). New Zealand adopted the Australian ballot in 1869, manhood suffrage in 1879, abolished plural voting in 1889 and 1893, reduced the tenure of members of Legislative Council from life to seven years, and became the first nation to adopt women's suffrage in 1893 (Sinclair 1970, 185). "Henceforth, there was to be no constitutional check on the expression of the popular will and no political institution designed to conserve the economic interest of one social group in the state" (Lipson 1948, 59–60). Without the expansion of the franchise, it is unlikely that a Liberal Party with a far-reaching populist agenda would have been elected or would have been able to carry out its plans (Lipson 1948, 57). The franchise extended to those mainly non-craft unions that suffered the heaviest losses in the strikes and that were most enthusiastic about compulsory arbitration.

The Trade Unions Acts and Spread of Unionism

The legality of trade unions was also established before these nations attempted extensive regulation of industrial relations. New Zealand's Trade Union Act of 1878 and Australia's Trade Unions Act of 1881 were patterned after similar legislation that the British Parliament enacted for British unions in 1871 and 1876. These laws settled the question that unions were not criminal conspiracies, gave unions the same legal standing as corporations in allowing them to sue and be sued, registered them, and regulated in some detail how trade unions conducted their internal affairs. More importantly for the future, they gave unions legal standing by, for example, making them able to sue and be sued and by permitting unions to register with the state. In bringing unions under the law and giving them a legal personality, the law offered a measure of protection to their organizations, but also made them subject to state regulation, and served as a precursor to the kind of recognition, encouragement, and regulation of unions that came later.

Unions grew in number and variety during the late nineteenth century in Australia and New Zealand. A healthy economic climate in the 1870s and 1880s facilitated the unions' spread in Australia (Sutcliffe 1921, 27–31), but the boom was much shorter in New Zealand. By the 1890s several "new unions" had emerged among unskilled and semi-skilled workers in the pastoral, mining, railway, and maritime industries, which organized seamen, dock workers, coal and gold miners, shearers, shed hands, and general labourers. The new unionism produced more inclusive "mass" unions, a fresh cadre of militant leaders, regional organizations called "trades and labour councils" that brought together several industries, and increased union membership and workers' wages (Patmore 1991, 67). The councils were a step on the road towards a trade union "movement" capable of coordinating unifying a number of disparate unions (Gollan 1963, 65–8).

Conclusion

It is unlikely that Australasians would have adopted compulsory arbitration in the absence of the critical juncture; they certainly would not have adopted it when they did and would not have adopted it through the same causal process. Had labour not been severely weakened by a crisis on the scale of the one it experienced in the 1890s, it is hard to see how they would have been induced to support compulsory arbitration, given the downside that stronger unions would have perceived with the measure. As James Holt (1976, 106) put it, "[h]ad New Zealand's trade unions been as strong as Britain's in the 1890s, a dozen William Pember Reeves could not have made a success of compulsory arbitration there." But, of course, the unions were quite weak because of the profound economic and industrial unrest that occurred. Had it not happened, it is also hard to imagine reformers going through the learning process that they did. We can imagine a more drawn out and delayed process in which industrial strife would have built more gradually or would have not been joined with a depression, so that labour would have been stronger and more able to wage its struggle industrially without getting the state involved. What is clear is that, if not for the critical juncture, compulsory arbitration would never have occurred the way that it did because the lib-lab period of cooperation had died out by the First World War. In the absence of such an alliance, one of two routes might have been possible in the future, either non-labour government would have forced compulsory arbitration upon labour (which might have been impractical given the unions' capacity to resist) or a Labour government would have had to impose it once it had gained power. Thus, Labour was at least as dependent upon Liberal reformers and politicians as the reformers were on labour. "Overall ... legislation would not have been enacted *on such a large scale* if it had not been for the active support of both labor and the liberal progressives" (Brereton 1989, 295).

The systems of dispute settlement and wage setting that Australia and New Zealand established between 1894 and 1904 had profound impacts on the conduct of industrial relations in virtually all major industries. Those who created the systems assumed that the Arbitration Courts would weigh in on only a few difficult cases, but they ended up setting wages throughout most of the economy, thus eclipsing much of the role of collective bargaining (Holt 1976, 108; Portus 1958, 114). The systems went well beyond discouraging strikes and lockouts settling industrial disputes, encouraging the formation of trade unions and employer organizations. Arbitration became a major tool of the state to ensure a measure of equality (through "living wage" and similar standards), distribute the national income, control inflation, and indirectly influence the structure of the economy and adjustment to new technologies and changes in international and domestic markets (Bray and Walsh 1998; 362; Macintyre and Mitchell 1989, 1–3). Arbiters' decisions over wages and working conditions applied automatically to unionized and non-unionized workers alike and bound all employers. Wages were adjusted centrally at the same time through "national wage cases" and "general wage orders." The system also influenced bargaining that went on outside the arbitration system because the two parties knew that they could resort to the formal system to resolve disputes.

The impacts on labour unions were no less profound. Unions were not compelled to register under the law, but employers were compelled to recognize them if they did. The laws permitted small groups of workers to register as unions, created closed shops, and protected the registered unions from other unions that sought to displace them. Most observers agree that the system guaranteed "reasonable and uniform pay and conditions," which were enforced by the state (Brosnan, Smith, and Walsh 1990, 28, 31). On the other hand, registered unions were heavily regulated, limiting the size of their memberships and narrowing the scope of their activities (what constituted "industrial matters" about which unions could represent their members). Thus, the impacts of these systems went far beyond their creators' primary original intention of reducing industrial unrest (see Holt 1976, 108).

Once established, the system became entrenched. By permitting workers to organize and register with small memberships, the state encouraged union fragmentation, which in turn, made it harder for employers and unions that did not want arbitration to build strong organizations to fight the system (Bray and Walsh 1998, 363–4).

The number of labour organizations and employers that were satisfied with the system exceeded those that wanted to change it. After resisting the system at the outset, many employers came to appreciate its stabilization of wage growth, control over militant unions, and the maintenance of managerial prerogatives in areas that the system placed off limits to collective bargaining. The "arbitrationist unions" that the system created "owed their very existence" to the law establishing the system (Holt 1976, 107). Most unions accepted the regulations on their organizations and activities in exchange for the state's guarantee of their organizational survival and other benefits. The unions that sought to do away with the system were either socialist in their orientation or powerful in industry.

Compulsory arbitration remained the dominant industrial relations system in New Zealand and Australia until the 1980s and 1990s, when it was dismantled in favour of neoliberalism. The end of compulsory arbitration came more swiftly and thoroughly in New Zealand than in Australia, where it retains importance in adjusting wages for low-income workers (Bray and Walsh 1998).

5 The Voluntarist Answer: Great Britain

> *There is, perhaps, no major country in the world in which the law has played a less significant role in the shaping of [industrial] relations than in Great Britain and in which today the law and the legal profession have less to do with labour relations.*
>
> (Otto Kahn-Freund 1954, 44)

Self-regulation and joint control of industrial relations were the heart of British voluntarism, which evolved from a set of informal arrangements to regularized and robust structures of collective bargaining, including voluntary conciliation and arbitration. Agreements that employers and labour organizations reached were not formal, legally enforceable contracts, but "gentlemen's agreements" (Portus 1958, 80; Clegg 1979, 291). The agreements imposed moral obligations whose recognition by both sides rendered legal compulsion and enforcement unnecessary and unwanted. Durable collective bargaining institutions and agreements rested upon the existence of strong trade unions, employer organizations that could conclude and enforce agreements, and a relationship between the two in which each one accepted the other as a legitimate. The basic acceptance by each side of the other's legitimacy and the development of "orderly collective bargaining" arrangements should not be confused with industrial peace and calm (Church 1990, 26). Under voluntarism, industrial relations were often unconstrained, competitive, and adversarial contests in which a good deal of conflict could be expected and did occur (Portus 1958, 69). Indeed, the development of joint control presupposed the growth of increasingly organized employer and employee organizations with the potential to cause widespread disruption.

Self-regulation meant that all parties rejected state compulsion except as a last resort under extraordinary circumstances (e.g., wartime). The state's own legitimacy rested upon the perception that it remained neutral in conflicts and competition among the parties to industrial disputes. This did not prevent the state, however, from playing an active role in encouraging collective bargaining by providing indirect inducements and mediating peaceful dispute resolution, as long as it refrained from coercing agreements or imposing its own preferences on the parties. The British state had a long history of facilitating voluntarism in a host of ways, from clearing away legal obstacles to organization and action to setting up institutional mechanisms to promote the spread of joint control; from interventions by high level officials where disputes were intractable to resolution through the normal channels and the conflict was sufficiently disruptive. These efforts began with the repeal of the Combination Acts in 1825 and continued well into the twentieth century with various boards and councils designed not so much to resolve individual disputes but to foster a general climate conducive to joint determination of working conditions and voluntary dispute settlement. British voluntarism lasted until the 1980s when it met its demise.

The explanation for the British case is the mirror image, in essential respects, of the one for the Australasian cases. Most British employers, most of the time, accommodated trade unions and accepted, even if reluctantly, their participation in dispute resolution. Partly because of the employers' behaviour, British trade unions never suffered a defeat that placed their survival in imminent jeopardy. As a result, they saw no need for the kind of compulsory regimes found elsewhere in the Anglophone world. Moreover, because of employer accommodation and the unions' own efforts to be perceived as "responsible," the unions enjoyed levels of legitimacy, organizational strength, political party connections and clout unrivalled throughout the industrial world that they could tap into when the need arose. On those occasions when employers grew hostile towards unions, particularly the industrial relations crises at the turn of the century, the latter were able to defend themselves both in the industrial realm, through strikes and other actions, as well as in politics. The relatively accommodationist stance of British employers and their and the unions' embrace of voluntarism led the state to support voluntarism as well. This meant, further, that reformers and advocates of a more interventionist state role in industrial relations found little support.

The process through which voluntarism triumphed in Britain – what I have described as "punctuated gradualism" – began with a gradual growth in trade unions, of employers' acceptance of them, and of rudimentary collective bargaining. Since this process took place over many decades, we cannot pinpoint one legislative act or series of acts that marked the transition to a new industrial relations regime in Britain, in contrast to the establishment of statism in Australasia. The Trade Disputes Act of 1906 certainly was a great leap forward, but it was consistent with the long-term evolution of British industrial relations. Aside from the gradual growth of accommodation towards unions and spread of joint control, another critical antecedent was Parliamentary supremacy over the courts, which made the unions' pursuit of their rights in the political process worthwhile. Thus, conditions that antedated the critical juncture that began in 1889, had a decisive impact. The crisis that set off the critical juncture that led to the Trade Disputes Act took place in both the industrial and political realms. Periodically acute strikes and lockouts occurred throughout the period; the political crisis was marked by a judicial attack on the unions that the 1906 Act reversed. Yet, by the time that some British employers' actions posed a potential threat to the unions' existence, the unions had acquired enough political resources to extract broad legal protections without acquiescing to compulsory requirements that would curtail their autonomy. Rather than overturn the emerging voluntarist regime, the critical juncture turned out to consolidate and extend it. In sum, antecedent conditions made it highly likely that Britain would stay on the voluntarist path, but the response to the critical juncture pushed it further and faster in that direction.

We begin with a discussion of the crisis that gave rise to the critical juncture and the permissive conditions that raised the possibility for Britain to deviate from the voluntarist path that it had embarked upon gradually over the previous decades. We show why the productive conditions that arose during this period were more conducive to keeping Britain on the voluntarist path rather than pushing it on to an alternative. Following that, we explore several conditions that antedated the critical juncture that contributed significantly to the outcome.

The Critical Juncture: Britain Stays On, and Speeds Down, the Voluntarist Path

From the mid-1870s to 1896, Britain experienced a long period of depression and began to lose its status as the world's leading industrial power as it faced increasingly stiff international competition from the United States and Germany (Brown 1983, 43; Garside and Gospel 1982, 105–6). The result was rising militancy among workers and employer resistance to their demands. Semi-skilled and unskilled workers formed "new unions" starting in the 1880s to demand a "fair" and "living" wage, and craft workers entered into intense struggles with employers who sought greater flexibility in the workplace by ridding themselves of "irksome trade union restrictions on output, the supply of labour and methods of work" (Garside and Gospel 1982, 107). The result was a period of unprecedented industrial unrest and renewed judicial challenges to strikes and other union activities that subjected Britain's emergent voluntarism to a stiff test from 1889 to 1914. Many of the labour disputes during this period "threatened the economy, many of them threatened public order, and in some cases, they even appeared to endanger the stability of society," thus creating considerable concern among political elites and the public (Wrigley 1982,

147; Davidson 1978, 571). The attacks and counterattacks created a situation in which the voluntarist path that Britain had started down years before the crisis could have come to an end.

As in Australasia, the question became not whether the state would intervene in the crisis decades around the turn of the twentieth century, but *how* it would intervene (Wrigley 1982, 150). Faced with unprecedented, periodically acute industrial unrest and a wave of renewed judicial attacks on unions, one could have imagined a number of different outcomes that would have taken Britain off the voluntarist path and in a different direction. One possibility was to resort to the compulsory arbitration or compulsory conciliation that was recently adopted in Australia and Canada, respectively. The multiple crises of the period prompted a variety of proposals by major figures in British industrial relations and government to transform Britain's emerging voluntary system into one characterized by greater state intervention. No proposal that included the slightest bit of compulsion was adopted or had a serious chance of gaining adoption in Parliament, however. A second possibility was for employers to reassert complete unilateral regulation of industrial relations, on their own terms, possibly using the state's coercive powers to repress or severely curtail trade unions. Another possibility was to maintain the status quo. Joint control would continue in those industries that had it prior to the crisis period, but the system would not continue to grow and spread. A final scenario was for workers to wrest control of the state and impose some version of socialism. None of these scenarios came to pass.

Why did these crises, singly or in combination, fail to loosen the political constraints that would allow reformers, employers, or policymakers to install alternative approaches to industrial unrest or arrest the development of voluntarism? How, instead, did they help to advance the spread of voluntarism and contribute to its development?

To answer these questions, we explore the major episodes of industrial unrest, which include the New Unionism uprisings of 1889, the engineering lockout of 1897, the coal mining lockout of 1893 and national strike of 1912, and the railway disputes of 1907 and 1911. We also examine the renewed judicial attacks on the unions during the 1890s and early 1900s.

Permissive Conditions of the Critical Juncture

The "New Unionism" and Employers' Counterattack. As in Australasia, the "new unionism" emerged among unskilled and semi-skilled occupations like seamen, dock laborers, and gas workers starting in the 1870s and expanding abruptly in the late 1880s (Pollard 1985; Pelling 1987, 93–9). The new unions were more confrontational than older craft unions because the latter could raise wages by controlling the supply of their labour. They also drew a similarly harsh response from employers in the Antipodes. The match girls' strike in 1888 was followed by the London Dock Strike in 1889, which was ignited by "cost-conscious employers" who sought to cut wages and job opportunities, although the degree of distinctiveness, causes, and lasting impacts of the new unionism have been a subject of considerable debate among historians (see Pollard 1985; Hobsbawm 1985; Price 1985). The new unionism produced a fresh cadre of leaders and increased union membership and workers' wages (Pelling 1987, 89–106; Clegg, Fox, and Thompson 1964, 55–66, 87–101). The strike received much attention in Britain and abroad. Although they had much initial success, the new unions were eventually crushed, much as their brethren on the other side of the globe had been (Fraser 1999, 78–80). Most employers were prepared to work with unions at this time, but the largest employers and those that had recently federated led the counter-attack (Hobsbawm 1985, 19). The unrest among the new unions spread to the old ones as well. The new unions stimulated growth in union membership, militancy, and acceptance of a broader membership base (Pelling 1987, 100–2, 109).

COAL MINING AND COTTON, 1893 AND 1912

One union that had the capacity to threaten major harm to the British economy was the miners. As in Australasia, the defeat of the new unions was followed by spreading unrest in mining and other industries. Industrial unrest in British mining had been highly localized until 1889, when coal miners formed the Miners' Federation, which became the largest mining union and Britain's largest trade union at the time, representing about one-third of the miners in the country and one in seven unionized workers. Its major goals were the eight-hour day and a minimum wage. It organized around miners' opposition to the sliding scale system that dominated the industry, in which miners' wages fluctuated (often dramatically) with the selling price of coal.

The miners in each district had agreed with the others that, if demands for higher wages were met by a lockout in one district, the miners in other districts would hold a work stoppage. In 1893, the owners locked-out the miners after the miners refused to go along with a wage cut. The miners already had suffered a cut of 35 per cent of their wages when coal prices fell, and now the companies were asking them to take an additional cut of 25 per cent (Benson 1982, 201). The dispute was the largest in British history up to that point, several times larger than the Docker's strike had been, and the miners attracted a good deal of public sympathy (Clegg, Fox, and Thompson 1964, 107). The lockout of so many miners in such a critical industry for three months imperiled fuel supplies and threatened to bring industry as a whole to a halt. Prime Minister Gladstone, who strongly believed that the government should stay out of labour disputes, nevertheless took the unprecedented step of dispatching the Secretary of State, Lord Rosebery, to help settle the dispute (Fraser 1999, 82, 97; Church 1990, 27; Benson 1982). The miners and owners by that time had made sufficient progress in negotiations that Rosebery was able to broker an agreement between them (Brown 1983, 43–4; Wigham 1982, 11).

In 1912, another great coal mining strike threatened the entire economy. The union's main goal, again, was to establish minimum wage rates (Benson 1982, 203). In the early 1890s, the cotton mill owners imposed a lockout in 1892 that brought most operations to a halt.

ENGINEERING, 1897

Employers were not content with defeating the new unions or miners, but also wanted to bring the established craft unions under better control. As part of their counter-attack of the 1890s, employers locked out the Amalgamated Society of Engineers (ASE) in 1897 (Clegg, Fox, and Thompson 1964, 161–78; Brown 1983, 45–6). The employers developed what was an unprecedented level of unity in the mid-1890s by forming the Engineering Employers Federation (EEF) in order to address the renewal of craft militancy among engineers who had lost ground to employers in the 1870s and 1880s when they achieved a good deal of success in introducing piecework, overtime, adding apprentices and making great use of unskilled workers. The ASE sought to maintain engineers' restrictions on which workers could perform which tasks and how they would be performed. Employers chafed under the restrictions as encroachments on their managerial prerogatives and complained that British firms were losing business to foreign competitors, particularly German and American, because the unions resisted the introduction of new machines (which could be run by less skilled and lower paid workers). To address the situation, they established the Employers' Federation of Engineering Associations, whose membership rose rapidly from over one hundred to about eight hundred firms (Clegg, Fox, and Thompson 1964, 163; Brown 1983, 45, 109–11).

RAILWAYS, 1907 AND 1911

The railways were a critical industry that had the potential to deal a major blow to the economy and where employers did not accept the unions. A number of characteristics of the railways made them susceptible to industrial unrest and placed them outside the typically accommodative style of British industrial relations. Foremost among these was the railway companies' steadfast hostility towards the trade unions. In many new industries, like railroads, employers did not have long experience in dealing with demands to continue craft control and in working with unions. Because of the unique features of the business – the safety and convenience of the public – railroad companies believed that their customers could be served well only if management exerted strong, quasi-military discipline over their workers. "Outside interference" – whether from trade unions or the state – would undermine these managerial prerogatives. The railways also argued that Parliament's fixing of the shipping rates that they could charge manufacturers in 1894 made it impossible for them to increase wages because they could not pass the higher costs on to the public and manufacturers (Alderman 1971, 138). Thus, the railroads were sites of frequent resistance to trade unionism, which found its expression in court challenges.

The pivotal position that the railways occupied in the nation's industrial development and military security strengthened their argument that they were unique among British industries in the second half of the nineteenth century. Long before industrial relations on the railways posed a major crisis, the British state was heavily involved in policing the industry, starting with the Railway Regulation Act of 1844. To protect the travelling public it set safety standards, and to protect manufacturers and the public from their monopolistic powers it fixed shipping rates (Alderman 1971, 130). Despite the state's major presence in the industry, but consistent with its adherence to voluntarism, it had left labour relations untouched.

The railways' intransigence on the core issue of trade union recognition collided with the growing organizational strength and militancy of the railway unions. Industrial conflict heightened gradually in the 1890s and became acute in the first two decades of the twentieth century when union militancy and membership rose. The largest of the railway unions, the Amalgamated Society of Railway Servants, launched the "All Grades movement" in 1897, which sought improvements in all grades of rail workers, uniform across railroads, and a united and coordinated labour front vis-à-vis management (Alderman 1971, 133–4).

In the wake of passage of the Trade Disputes Act of 1906, the union was freed of concerns over liability and its membership increased enormously (Askwith 1974, 115). Union membership rose by 22 per cent overall and by considerably more in such occupations as mining, engineering, shipbuilding, and others (Clegg, Fox, and Thompson 1964, 467–9). The effort to build a single, unified union of rail employees culminated in 1913 with the formation of the National Union of Railwaymen (NUR).

Within a few years, it was clear that the conciliation and arbitration scheme of 1907 for the railways was breaking down. The government had been unable to get Parliament to deliver on its promise to the railways to enable them to merge into larger companies as a way to economize (Alderman 1971, 144). In 1911, the four railway unions, in an unusual display of unity, struck after the companies circumvented those processes, making clear that they would not accept "anything less than recognition" (Alderman 1971, 147). The strike spread rapidly, growing to 200,000 men out of work, paralysing rail transport and threatening food supplies. With the transport workers threatening to join the strike, which had become an insurrection accompanied by violence and military involvement, the railway men demanded recognition (Wigham 1982, 25–7). The strike jeopardized rail traffic at a critical time for the government, when a dispute flared in Morocco between the British and Germans (the Agadir crisis) (Askwith 1974, 163–6; Bagwell 1985, 197). "The threat of war demanded the movement of troops and coal for the navy" (Alderman 1971, 146).

RENEWED JUDICIAL ATTACKS AND TAFF VALE

We have seen that rising trade union strength and militancy came up against stiffening employer resistance in the 1890s, brought about by heightened foreign competition and new technology. Employers challenged the unions not only in the industrial arena in the 1890s, but also in the courts. Judges renewed their attacks on unions by issuing a series of rulings that culminated in the 1901 *Taff Vale* case, which threatened the existence of trade unions as effective agents for their members.[1] Unable since passage of the Trade Union Act of 1875 to have the unions prosecuted as criminal conspiracies, employers now sought court rulings that would target unions as civil conspiracies (Pelling 1987, 108, 111, 122).

The events that comprised the crisis period that had the greatest potential to crush the unions was not an industrial dispute, but the judicial attacks that culminated in the *Taff Vale* ruling. Those cases, in effect, paralysed the unions from using their most potent weapon against employers. By outlawing most strike activity, they endangered the unions' existence.

In *Temperton v. Russell* (1893), a Court of Appeal found that local builders' unions had maliciously conspired to injure a third party – a contractor who refused to stop doing business with another employer whose men were on strike. The court awarded Temperton damages. In *Trollope v. London Building Trades Federation* (1895), a court found that union officers, again in a conspiracy to injure, could be sued for damages if they published lists of strikebreakers and non-union businesses. In *Lyons v. Wilkins* (1896), the Court of Appeal ruled that unions could not picket their employer's subcontractors, even in a non-threatening and non-violent manner. The employer in the case sued the union and the Court upheld a judge's ruling that unions could picket only to "communicate" but not to "persuade" (as they would do in a strike). In another case involving picketing, *Charnock v. Court*, the judge found workers guilty of "watching and besetting" (harassment) because they tried to persuade, in a peaceful fashion, other men not to serve as strikebreakers. In *Quinn v. Leathem* (1901), a butcher's assistants union had tried to persuade a butcher not to deal with another butcher who employed non-union employees (Clegg, Fox, and Thompson 1964, 308–12). Using the same conspiracy doctrine articulated in *Temperton*, the House of Lords ruled that, in effect, unions could do nothing to enforce a closed shop without being declared a conspiracy to commit harm. The whole purpose of strikes, of course, was for unions to harm or threaten to harm employers as a way to exert pressure upon them (MacDonald 1960, 55).

The major blow to the unions was the House of Lords 1901 ruling in the *Taff Vale* case. Without official union approval, members of the Amalgamated Society of Railway Servants struck against the Taff Vale Railway in Wales demanding higher wages and recognition for their union. Once the strike was underway, the union's leadership gave the strikers their support. At issue in the *Taff Vale* case was whether employers could collect damages for injuries done to them from unions. Until this time, the unions (as opposed to their individual members and officers), were assumed to have immunity from such claims because they were unincorporated bodies. Immunity from civil damages meant that if workers went on strike they could not trigger damage suits that would deplete union funds. The Lords upheld a lower court's injunction against the union and made it possible for the railway to sue the union for damages for conspiring to get workers to break their contracts and engage in picketing and other activities. Eventually, the courts levied a fine of 42,000 pounds on the Amalgamated Society for damages to the railway.

Productive Conditions of the Critical Juncture

LABOR'S POLITICAL MOBILIZATION AND PARLIAMENTARY INFLUENCE

The unions realized that the *Taff Vale* ruling posed a serious threat to their organizational survival. *Taff Vale* and the cases leading up to it in the 1890s reinforced British unions' bias against state action and galvanized them to pressure Parliament to overturn the ruling, unlike their counterparts in Australasia, whose industrial relations were much less shaped by judicial interpretation of common law.

A consensus emerged that new legislation was needed to rectify the situation, but sharp differences arose both within the unions and among political elites broadly about how much immunity from liability for civil damages the state should accord unions. Many unions echoed the Royal Commission on Trade Disputes of 1893, which had assumed that, as unincorporated entities, unions enjoyed legal immunity and were protected under the Trade Union Act of 1871 (MacDonald 1960, 49, 54–5). They expected Parliament to restore what they understood to be the status quo that existed before *Taff Vale*. Many other observers at the time, and historians who came afterwards, saw the issue as much less clear-cut. Whether unions should have immunity from damage suits, and how much immunity they should enjoy, was a legitimate matter for debate and not easily resolved (MacDonald 1960, 53). "[B]ehind this question lay problems of the relationship between trade unions, the state, and society about which opinion was honestly divided" (Clegg, Fox, and Thompson 1964, 316). This group argued that the 1871 Act protected the unions only from criminal liability, that the Act was silent on whether unions were subject to civil actions, and that giving unions complete immunity would be bad public policy (Clegg, Fox, and Thompson 1964, 320–5).

The Conservative government supported *Taff Vale*, but in response to the uncertainty and controversy swirling in the wake of the Lords' decision, it appointed a Royal Commission to study the matter. The Commission's Majority Report came down firmly on the side of those who thought that unions could be held liable for damages, declaring that the judgment in *Taff Vale* "involved no new principle and was not inconsistent with the legislation [Trade Unions Act] of 1871," and saw "no more reason that [trade unions] should be beyond the reach of the law than any other individual, partnership or institution" (quoted in Clegg, Fox, and Thompson 1964, 393; MacDonald 1960, 56; Brown 1983, 36). The Commission recommended limited immunity in which unions would be declared legal associations with a corporate status that would give them immunity from liability only where suits arose out of actions of its members or local officers that it did not authorize and that the unions' benefit funds would be protected against legal action (Pelling 1987, 125). Sydney Webb, a member of the Commission, leader of the Fabians, and an advocate of trade unionism, insisted that *Taff Vale* was correctly decided, that Parliament had never intended to give unions blanket immunity for civil damages, and that it would be irresponsible to give unions a privileged, unique position that no other organization in British society enjoyed (MacDonald 1960, 55–6). Ernest Aves, another well-known social reformer and union sympathizer, opined that unions should be immune from liability only when its governing body had not authorized or been knowledgeable of activities that inflicted damage.

The thinking of lawyers within the Liberal Party, including one of its leading figures, H.H. Asquith, ran along lines similar to the Commission's. They called for legislation that accepted the essence of the *Taff Vale* ruling but would amend the law of agency so that unions would be immune from damage suits if they arose from the actions of union members or others acting on their own without the union's official authorization (Brown 1983, 36; Clegg, Fox, and Thompson 1964, 369; MacDonald 1960, 60). They believed it would be irresponsible to give unions or any similar large organization the unique status of blanket immunity. According to one of them, it would be tantamount to declaring that "the King can do no wrong; neither can a trade union" (quoted in Brown 1983, 37).

Several trade union leaders also saw advantages in treating unions as incorporated entities that could sue and be sued. Liability, for them, held out the possibility of greater control over undisciplined and "irresponsible" local unionists. Trade union leaders like Richard Bell of the railway workers, George Barnes of the engineers and Ben Pickard of the miners had experienced confrontations with more militant unionists, many of them socialists, who demanded a return to the complete immunity that they assumed unions enjoyed before *Taff Vale* (Clegg, Fox, and Thompson 1964, 318–22; MacDonald 1960, 53–4; Bagwell 1985, 194; Hinton 1983, 72).

In 1902–3, the Parliamentary Committee of the TUC worked with the General Federation of Trade Unions and the Labour Representation Committee (LRC) to come up with a bill that would be acceptable to the Liberal Party lawyers and the Conservative government, neither of which would support granting the unions total immunity. (The TUC had organized the LRC in 1899 in response to pressures for the unions to establish representation in Parliament that was independent of the Tories and Liberals.) The Conservative government brought a proposal, the Trade Disputes Bill, minus the immunity provision, to a vote in Parliament, where it failed to pass on a second reading. Instead of quickly passing new legislation, the government appointed a Royal Commission whose membership included no trade union members (prompting the unions to boycott its proceedings and reject its final report). As time wore on without a resolution to the issue, and as the sum of money that that the Railway Servants had to pay turned out to be higher than anticipated, the hard-liners within the unions gained the upper hand in the internal trade union debate (Clegg, Fox, and Thompson 1964, 323–5; MacDonald 1960, 60; Bagwell 1985, 194). As a result, the TUC changed the Parliamentary Committee's proposal to include complete immunity instead of the limited immunity in its original draft, even though many union leaders still preferred the more moderate alternative (Clegg, Fox, and Thompson 1964, 322–3). In 1904 and 1905, with Conservatives still in power, but an election not far away, the Trade Disputes Bill passed on the second reading, but it had been so altered that its sponsors rejected it.

Taff Vale served as a catalyst for unprecedented trade union political mobilization and institution-building, out of which the Labour Party emerged (Pelling 1987, 122–6; Hinton 1983, 73). When the Conservative government failed to move to restore the unions' full immunity, the unions began affiliating with the Labour Representation Committee (LRC), which had languished until now. The unions now saw the LRC and its transformation into an embryonic Labour Party as a tactic to use against the new Liberal government to force it to repeal the effects of *Taff Vale*. The by-elections of 1902 and 1903 convinced the Liberals that they had to accommodate the unions. The Liberals and LRC agreed on thirty constituencies in which the LRC would be free to run candidates against the Conservatives without competing Liberal candidates (Hinton 1983, 73–4).

The legislative breakthrough came on the heels of the Liberal Party's 1906 landslide election victory in Parliament (Pelling 1987, 124–5; Hinton 1983, 73). *Taff Vale* was not a major issue in the election and the Liberal Party's big victory "owed little or nothing to the Taff Vale issue." But the issue had mobilized many unions and it remained high on the list of the unions' priorities (MacDonald 1960, 59). The TUC's Parliamentary Committee asked workers to vote only for candidates who supported their revised bill. The establishment of the Labour Party in this period for tactical reasons should not be misconstrued as marking a decline in union–Liberal cooperation. The Labour Party remained limited for a number of years and dependent upon its alliance with the Liberals (Luebbert 1991, 24; Hinton 1983, 74). The resolution of the *Taff Vale* threat drew the unions and the left-wing of the Liberal Party into closer cooperation (Clegg, Fox, and Thompson 1964, 377). The Parliamentary Committee's election program "reproduced the demands of the Radical wing of the Liberal Party" (Clegg, Fox, and Thompson 1964, 386).[2] The lib-labs were the largest group of candidates in the 1906 election, but the new Labour Party also ran its own candidates. The Liberals cooperated in some areas of the country with the Labour Representation Committee by not running candidates so that the Labour Party candidates could win (Clegg, Fox, and Thompson 1964, 385). The two groups of candidates' policy positions were indistinguishable (MacDonald 1960, 59).

Despite the serious misgivings of some prominent Liberals about granting the unions full immunity, the Liberal Party's vote-getting organization and the soon-to-be prime minister, Campbell-Bannerman, a Radical, had signed on to the TUC's amended Trade Disputes Bill (Clegg, Fox, and Thompson 1964, 386). After the election, the Trade Disputes Bill "occupied the centre of the stage for all trade unionists." Campbell-Bannerman had met with the Parliamentary Committee "and promised an early measure on 'the general lines' of the Committee's own Bill" (Clegg, Fox, and Thompson 1964, 393). The new prime minister was convinced that, short of a simple, categorical and comprehensive statutory grant of immunity for the unions, lawyers and judges would invent new ways to place the union funds once again in jeopardy (MacDonald 1960, 60; Brown 1983, 37). However, the Liberal members of his cabinet still had strong doubts, which were fuelled by the Majority Report of the Royal Commission (Clegg, Fox, and Thompson 1964, 393). Senior Liberal Cabinet ministers, including Asquith, Haldane, Attorney General Sir John Walton, and the solicitor general, Sir William Robson, were convinced that the Royal Commission had the correct approach and that the unions' proposal for immunity would create "class privileges ... for the proletariat and give a sort of benefit of clergy to trade unions" (quoted in Clegg, Fox, and Thompson 1964, 394). Therefore, they introduced the government's proposal, which adopted the more moderate position that unions could be sued for damages only if they explicitly authorized the conduct that caused the damages. In response, members of Parliament representing the unions embarrassed the government by calling attention to the fact that Liberal Party candidates had declared their support for the Parliamentary Committee's bill during the campaign (Pelling 1987, 125), one member even holding one of Walton's election posters that stated his explicit pledge to support the Trade Disputes Bill.

The Parliamentary Committee and MPs who supported its bill then decided to introduce it and appealed to Campbell-Bannerman for support. The prime minister obliged and took the unusual step of overturning the advice of the lawyers in his government. According to Clegg, Fox, and Thompson (1964, 405), "many of [Prime Minister] Campbell-Bannerman's followers shared his sense of accumulated obligation to the working class." In addition to his Radical orientation, Campbell-Bannerman was persuaded by "the argument from simplicity" (Brown 1983, 37–8). The Labor Disputes Bill passed on its second reading by 416 to 66 votes. Even Asquith, despite his earlier opposition, voted for the Act, arguing now that complete immunity would prevent industrial disputes from getting entangled in the courts, "passing from one stage of appeal to another, and involving loss of temper, money and time" (quoted in Brown 1983, 51). Not only the Liberals, but many Conservatives too, voted for the Trade Disputes Act because the Tories could not afford to lose more popularity than they already had in the last election (MacDonald 1960, 60). After that, the bill was referred to a Parliamentary committee, was read a third time, and gained approval from the House of Lords, despite efforts by employers to weaken it there. Led by Shackleton, perhaps the unions' most seasoned and savvy MP, the Trade Disputes Act gained final approval (Campbell, Fox, and Thompson 1964, 393–5).

As enacted, "the Trades Disputes Act of 1906 gave the Trade Unions all they had asked for" (Cole 1965, 189). One section of the law laid down categorically that "an action against a Trade Union ... in respect to any tortious act alleged to have been committed by or on behalf of the Trade Union, shall not be entertained by any court" (quoted in Cole 1965, 190). In other words, trade unions' actions were immune from civil damages whether they were committed by the union as an official body or by members of the union who were not authorized to take such actions.

While the focus of debate over the Trade Disputes Act was on the immunity issue, the new law made other significant changes to increase trade unions' freedom of action, which altogether thoroughly banished judicial threats to British unions once and for all. The Act followed several recommendations called for by the Royal Commission intended to protect unions' strike activity (Clegg, Fox, and Thompson 1964, 393). Recognizing the growing threat of the court decisions to unions, the Commission sought to get unions beyond the reach of the civil conspiracy doctrine and revised the law on picketing. Even with the immunity issue resolved in the unions' favour, the courts could still prevent unions from striking by issuing injunctions on the grounds that they were civil conspiracies in restraint of trade. To address this issue, the Trade Disputes Act legalized strikes (including sympathetic ones) and calls for strikes. Just as the Act of 1875 had made strikes and other actions of "combinations" outside criminal conspiracies, so the 1906 Act placed them outside of civil conspiracies. Similarly, the Act expanded what behaviour unions were permitted to engage in during strikes. Whereas the existing law made it permissible only to obtain and communicate information, the new law made picketing – intended for communication and persuasion (including persuading others to support the strike) – permissible (Brown 1983, 38–9; Cole 1965, 189–90).

The unions were thus given immense freedom of action, which they used to build up their membership remarkably over the next fifteen years (Booth 1995, 12–13). "Pressure group tactics and political maneuvering," writes Wigham (1982, 17), "had given the unions on extraordinary freedom from legal action which was not interrupted for sixty-five years." The period 1906 to 1910 was the high-water mark of cooperation between the trade union movement and the Liberal Party. During this period, "generally speaking, Lloyd George and Churchill took care to placate the unions, because they wanted the support of their M.Ps. in the Commons debates and the continued backing of the trade union vote at future general elections (Pelling 1987, 27). The unions and Liberals also worked together on a variety of social welfare issues on which the unions had sought action.[3]

LABOUR AND CAPITAL OPPOSED COMPULSION

The major alternative to voluntarism was for the state to take action to prevent work stoppages or shorten their duration through compulsory conciliation and arbitration. Disenchantment with voluntarism, and proposals to reform or replace the system, were not uncommon in Britain during this period. They accompanied every outbreak of severe industrial unrest. A variety of social reformers, public officials, and trade union leaders called for compulsory measures. Many of them drew inspiration and lessons from New Zealand and the Australian colonies, which had recently adopted compulsory arbitration and wages boards. Others looked to Canada, which had instituted compulsory investigation and conciliation of labour disputes.

The Fabian Socialists Sydney and Beatrice Webb, whose outlooks were very similar to the "state socialist" reformers of Australia and New Zealand, promoted arbitration as a "civilized" and "rational" alternative to industrial unrest (Clegg, Fox, and Thompson 1964, 265; Webb and Webb 1897, 244). With the Bishop of Hereford, they decried strikes and lockouts as "barbaric" and "uncivilized" methods of dispute resolution. Several witnesses before the Royal Commission on Labour in 1891–3 called for the kind of compulsory arbitration about to be adopted in New Zealand and Australia (Wigham 1982, 7). Sydney Webb argued that the state should take an active role in preventing and containing industrial unrest and challenged the popular notion that strikes and lockouts arose inevitably from the relationship between capital and labour. He insisted that industrial disputes caused unnecessary harm and disruption not only to the combatants, but to the entire community. "I cannot believe," he wrote, "that a civilized community will permanently continue to abandon the adjustment of industrial disputes ... and incidentally the regulation of the conditions of life of the mass of its people ... to what is, in reality, the arbitrament of private war" (quoted in MacDonald 1960, 57). *The Economist* endorsed compulsory arbitration for the railways during the 1907 strike (Wrigley 1982, 143).

Leaders of several major unions, including George Barnes of the engineers, Ben Tillett of the dockers, and Richard Bell of the railways, strongly favoured compulsory arbitration (Bagwell 1985, 194). Like the Webbs, Tillett had visited Australia and New Zealand and was impressed by their innovations. He brought his proposal for compulsory arbitration before the Trades Union Congress on a number of occasions. Alexander Wilkie, the chairman of the TUC's

Parliamentary Committee, also raised the question of whether the provisions of the 1896 Conciliation Act "should not be considerably strengthened" (quoted in Clegg, Fox, and Thompson 1964, 265). Following that, in response to the disputes of 1897 and 1898, the TUC asked the Board of Trade to convene a conference with the TUC and employers to consider a proposal by Lord Ritchie, the president of the Board of Trade, who called for a National Conciliation Board that would "act in the capacity of an appeal court" on issues not settled by local boards (Clegg, Fox, and Thompson 1964; Wigham 1982, 14).

With the employers' counterattack in full swing in the 1890s, some policymakers also called for legislation that would have gone beyond the purely voluntary Conciliation Act that Parliament passed in 1896. Ritchie, as mentioned, favoured such a course, and so did the influential politician Joseph Chamberlain. While in the Liberal Unionist-Conservative coalition government in 1895, Chamberlain observed in Parliament, "if you are prepared to give to a Board of Arbitration power to compel attendance and to enforce its decisions, you are going to take a great step [towards ending industrial disputes]. Doubts have been expressed as to the possibility of conferring such powers. I do not say that it is possible, but I may point out that in New South Wales they have an Act of Parliament containing provisions to enable Boards of Arbitration to enforce their decrees" (Hansard, March 1895, 405–6). If compulsory arbitration were not possible, Chamberlain then called for "a Board of Arbitration, so influential, so authoritative, so dignified, that no body of employers or workmen would dare to refuse to submit their case to it." According to Davidson (1974, viii), "a succession of Private Member's Bills and amendments" in the mid-1890s proposed "compulsory conciliation or arbitration with legal sanctions." When Winston Churchill was appointed president of the Board of Trade in 1908, he directed Llewellyn Smith, social reformer and the Board's Permanent Secretary, to draw up new proposals to authorize the Board to intervene more decisively in labour disputes that threatened the public interest. Smith modelled his proposal on the Lemieux Act, which Canadians had recently adopted to deal with their industrial disputes. That Act created a conciliation court that investigated labour disputes and ordered a cooling-off period during which both sides would be brought together (Davidson 1974, xi; Wrigley 1982, 145–6). Finally, in 1912, in the face of widespread unrest and rank-in-file militancy, Askwith tried to re-introduce the cooling-off period requirement into a report of the Industrial Council (a body that the state created to encourage capital and labour to cooperate in resolving disputes) (Davidson 1974, xi).

All of these efforts and pockets of support for some form of compulsion amounted to nothing. They could not overcome the adamant objections of most British unions and employers. Tillett's proposal rarely mustered more than one-third support of the delegates who voted in the TUC's annual convention. "Their [the unions'] experience of the law courts in the 1890s did not encourage them to believe in the impartiality of the 'judicial mind'" (Pelling 1987, 119). Key state actors heeded (or agreed with) the positions of labour and capital. The Private Members' Bills calling for compulsory arbitration died when the Board of Trade (echoing the Royal Commission) warned the Cabinet "that any attempt to replace the voluntary system of industrial conciliation already existing in many organized trades by legal compulsion would be certain to produce a confrontation between Labour and the State" (Davidson 1974, viii). Joseph Chamberlain (*Hansard* 1895, 406) opined in Parliament that it might be possible to get Parliament to adopt compulsory arbitration, but it would not be accepted by employers and unions: "I am not certain, then, that you might not have Legislation giving this [compulsory] power to Boards of Arbitration in this country, but I am doubtful whether the employers or the working classes are yet prepared for such a stringent arrangement as that." Some MPs argued in favour of compulsory arbitration, but the consensus view was that the practical obstacles were formidable. The parties to major disputes were unlikely to consent to being bound by awards and if they were, local groups of workers or particular firms might disagree with the awards and make enforcement of them difficult. In addition, "amateur arbiters" would not have sufficient knowledge of local conditions and of particular crafts and workplace circumstances to develop informed and defensible awards (*Hansard* 2 May 1895, 369–74).

Smith asked the Positivist reformer Henry Crompton, who had written an influential book on labour relations, to develop a policy on the state's role in industrial relations. As he had done earlier in his book, Crompton argued in the 1890s that voluntary boards of conciliation and arbitration had spread and proven successful because employers and employees had embraced them: "Where so remarkable a success has been achieved by individual energy and local initiative, the legislature should be most cautious how it interferes. Compulsory arbitration would not be the enforcing of obligations and duties, but the compelling men by physical force and threat of punishment to enter into contracts, a proceeding entirely at variance with the spirit of our civilization, and which I can only compare to conscription, the press-gang or slavery" (quoted in Wigham 1982, 8). The Royal Commission, which similarly saw any form of compulsion as impractical and against the grain of British national character, took a very sanguine view of industrial relations in the mid-1890s, "despite the great strikes and lock-outs of the period" (Wigham 1982, 8): "The course of events is tending towards a more settled and pacific period," which portended, "if not a greater identification of interest, at least a clearer perception of the principles which must regulate the division of the proceeds of each industry, consistently with its permanence and prosperity, between those who supply labour and those who supply managing ability and capital.... As the terms of what is virtually a partnership come to be better understood and the arrangements for adjusting them to the variations of trade are made more perfect in one branch of industry after another, a natural end will be found to the conflicts which have been the result, for the most part, of uncertain rights and mutual misunderstandings, and pursuance of separate interests, without sufficient regard to their common interest, by employers and workmen" (quoted in Wigham 1982, 8–9). The Commission was not much bothered either by industrial conflict that took place, seeing the movement towards large-scale, national conflicts, costly as they were, as preferable to the profusion of local skirmishes of earlier years.

These rosy perspectives were put to a sharp test, however, when industrial strife became even more acute after 1906. Nevertheless, resistance to compulsion remained strong. Askwith's 1911 effort failed also, according to Davidson (1974, xi), because "the hostility of Labour intellectuals was matched by government apathy upon the issue." Like their brethren in other countries, British employers were even more uniformly opposed to compulsory arbitration than the unions. Unlike the TUC, which saw some merit in Ritchie's 1898 proposal, the employers' Parliamentary Federation flatly rejected his overtures. Both the unions and employers rejected Churchill's plan as well, even though it only compelled the parties to enter into conciliation proceedings (Davidson 1974, xi; Wrigley 1982, 145–6; Wigham 1982, 14). In 1912, Sydney Buxton, who replaced Churchill as president of the Board of Trade, considered a compulsory ban on strikes during an investigatory period, followed by the possibility of compulsory arbitration, argued before the Cabinet that, despite public support for such a plan, labour would reject it and it would be impossible to enforce: "Men cannot be made to work if they will not work; men cannot be imprisoned (a million miners for instance) for striking" (quoted in Wigham 1982, 31).

Opposition to compulsion came from the stronger unions of craft workers and "operatives" from major industries. Strong unions, like those representing cotton and coal, defeated Tillett's proposal because they were confident that they would fare better in head-to-head struggles with their employers than if they lost control over their destiny to arbitrators. As a leader of the cotton spinners union asserted, "the best arbitrator in a trade dispute was a strong banking account" (quoted in Clegg, Fox, and Thompson 1964, 177, 265). Unions like cotton and coal were also the best organized in Parliament (because of their regional concentration of voters), which gave them more access than most other unions (Clegg, Fox, and Thompson 1964, 271). Weaker unions lacked the strength from within the movement and in Parliament to get compulsory arbitration adopted.

The older craft unions were less enthusiastic about state intervention because they exercised control over the supply of their labour and had developed into "business unions" that jealously guarded their autonomy, privileges, and established relationships with employers. The newer general and industrial unions were the main supporters of compulsory arbitration because their organizations were less well-established and had less control over the labour market. Once the new unions were defeated, the craft unions asserted even greater influence in the movement. Most unions would accept only the most minimal forms of state intervention, such as the state's facilitation of voluntary conciliation and arbitration and provision of basic legal guarantees so that unions could operate unfettered (Pelling 1987, 119, 142–3). Some unionists had reservations about even *voluntary* forms of conflict resolution. After decades of experience with conciliation and arbitration in some industries, the more militant leaders and members of unions were convinced that they would fare worse under conciliation and arbitration, particularly during the expansionary phase of the business cycle. Under the voluntary arbitration schemes in effect in many industries, umpires used market-based criteria – whether employers could bear higher labour costs – rather than the cost of living or "living wage" criteria that many workers preferred (Davidson 1974, ix, 1982, 165).

According to Holt (1976, 106), in his comparison of New Zealand and Britain, "as long as the big guns in the trade union movement were, in the main, opposed to compulsory arbitration, it was difficult to imagine how such a system could be enforced, and no government was willing to try. By the time the issue was raised in Britain, many unions were strong enough to resist the kind of voluntary arbitration agreement that had been so popular in the 1870s and 1880s. Compulsory arbitration was even less attractive to them. Consequently, it never had a chance in Britain."

As important as it was, the trade unions could afford to be opposed to compulsory arbitration, not just because they were relatively strong, but also because the accommodative posture of many British employers towards trade unions contributed to union calculations that they did not need state protection in the form of compulsory measures. If not for the stance of employers, the unions might have been inclined to accept more intervention (Clegg, Fox, and Thompson 1964, 362–3). Furthermore, the kinds of disputes that emerged – mainly over wages, hours, work restrictions, and working conditions – were much more amenable to voluntary forms of dispute settlement (collective bargaining and voluntary conciliation and arbitration) than if employers did not accept unions as legitimate representatives of employees. As a result, compulsory forms of dispute resolution were much less needed in Britain.

Thus, employers' behaviour and choices made it possible to develop a fairly robust, self-regulated, and voluntarist system of collective bargaining and a set of norms that legitimated the system (Charles 1973, 19–33). Had British employers not committed themselves to joint regulation and built their own organizations to pursue that end, and had Britain been more economically vulnerable, "the pressure to imitate the colonial schemes of state intervention might have been far more difficult to resist" (Clegg, Fox, and Thompson 1964, 265). [For original sources related to the British debate over CA, see the Holt 1976 article in the *New Zealand Journal of History*, 100.]

Official bodies like the Royal Commission of 1894 and the Industrial Council of 1913 also rejected compulsory arbitration, because it would destroy the tradition of "mutual consent" of the two parties (MacDonald 1960, 79). The Commission, appointed on the heels of the unrest of 1889–90, concluded that new laws were not the answer to industrial relations, particularly if they involved compulsion, and that disputes should be settled through "voluntary machinery, relying on moral, not legal, sanctions" (quoted in MacDonald 1960, 48).

Before the turn of the century, voluntarism had become not just a policy preference, but a principle on which much of the British state and most employers and unions agreed. Members of both political parties embraced voluntarism and saw strengthening and supporting it as the only legitimate role for the state (Charles 1073, 28–30). According to MacDonald (1960, 168), "since the State began to take trade unions seriously ... its policy has been, from various motives, to have as little to do with them as possible." Prime Minister Gladstone emphasized that despite the suffering caused by the shipping strike in Hull in 1893, "Her Majesty's Government in an official sense...had no right whatever to intervene" (*Hansard* 1893). The Industrial Council came to the same conclusion as the Royal Commission of the 1890s. The Report that it issued twenty years later, in 1913, maintained that, despite the intervening years of acute industrial strife, strong employer and employee organizations engaged in voluntary dispute resolution was still the best approach: "We regard it as axiomatic that nothing should be done which would lead to the abandonment of a method of adjusting the relationships between employers and workpeople which as proved so advantageous throughout most of the trades of the country" (quoted in Wigham 1982, 32).

All of these forces left the advocates of compulsion politically scattered and stymied. No committed advocate emerged who combined the sustained intellectual and political commitment and cabinet-level access to power of a William Pember Reeves or a Charles Cameron Kingston. Churchill, for example, who might have fulfilled that role, quickly dropped his plan for compulsion once it met opposition. Fabian reformers like the Webbs, though very visible and prolific as scholars, did not have close ties to the governments in power and were ineffective in generating support for any of their social reforms (Hobsbawm 1968, 250–65).

TRADE UNIONS SURVIVED, GREW, AND PROMOTED (OR SUBMITTED TO) COLLECTIVE BARGAINING

British unions would have been less opposed to compulsion, or at least less capable of resisting it, if they had suffered devastating losses. Employer and judicial attacks challenged British unions, but they were never decimated by them as Australasian unions were. British unions survived and grew over the long-term without the state having to rescue them. Although the defeat of the new unions of unskilled workers was about as complete in Britain as it was in Australasia, it was not nearly as consequential for the labour movement generally. The established craft unions were not driven out of their industries; nor did many employers withhold recognition from them. Craft unions in Britain were left largely unscathed by the new unionism's defeat and, in fact, were a beneficiary of the defeat by being better able to consolidate their memberships (Berkowitz et al. 2004, 238–9). The strength of the craft and operatives unions was not tied to the new unions as much as to the health of the economy. Economic conditions were not nearly as advantageous for employers as they were in Australia. The new unionism in Britain rode in during a boom time in the late 1880s that lasted until 1892 (Fraser 1999, 82). Even when a depression came in 1895, the downturn was not as acute. British workers did not suffer as much as they did in other countries, because even though wages did not rise, industrial production increased and prices fell, so the standard of living did not decline (Macdonald 1960, 44).

Although its status as the "workshop of the world" was slipping, Britain was still a major centre for the production of cotton textiles, tools and implements, iron and steel, ships, and coal. Throughout the 1890s, shipbuilding, metals, engineering, and textiles were the leading employers in Britain (Clegg, Fox, and Thompson 1964, 97). Despite the unrest of the 1890s, the bulk of the British trade unions at the turn of the century remained committed to working with employers to resolve disputes and saw strikes as wasteful and bad for international competition (MacDonald 1960, 51).

Although much of the attention on the new unions' rise and fall focused on semi-skilled and unskilled occupations, we have seen that established unions of craft workers and operatives also grew more militant and encountered stiff employer resistance to wage demands and work restrictions in the 1890s (Brown 1982, 119). The infamous British employers' counter-attack decimated the new unions, but it did not destroy the established ones. According to Clegg, Fox, and Thompson (1964, 175), "in terms of crippling the unions [the employers' counter-attacks'] accomplishment was negligible." The older unions remained strong and grew despite the losses of the new unions. For example, only a few of the new unions were among the twenty largest unions in the country in 1900. The rest were the separate unions in the mining and textile industries (Pelling 1987, 117).

The outcomes of the major strikes from 1893 to 1914 were mixed for trade unions, but in no instance was a major union destroyed. The mining strike of 1893 posed a serious problem for the British economy and a challenge to the state, but it did not lead to the defeat of the union. The stakes in the conflict were confined to pay and conditions; recognition of the union was not an issue. The union did not get the minimum wage that it had sought, but nor did the mining companies get the wage reduction or a pure sliding scale for wage determination that they sought. Instead, a Wages and Conciliation Board was created that approved and regulated wage increases and a minimum level to base-rate wages (Garside and Gospel 1982, 105; Church 1990, 27). Some historians have seen this as a defeat for the union because the conciliation board appointed to settle the dispute reasserted the sliding scale and the miners failed to establish a real minimum wage. On the other hand, the Miners' Federation avoided the wage reduction that the companies sought to impose and the conciliation board softened the effects of the sliding scale by avoiding the most extreme fluctuations in wage rates and maintaining them well above the "standard" 1888 levels (Benson 1982, 201–2). All in all, "the events of 1893–4 cannot be described as either a victory for either the owners or for the miners" (Church 1990, 28). In the longer term, the miners became one of the most cohesive and powerful British unions to the point where it was "blackleg proof" (Clegg, Fox, and Thompson 1964, 108–11; Church 1990, 28). According to Hinton (1983, 65), the very survival of the [Miners'] Federation in 1893 was itself a significant victory, providing a secure framework for the systematic encroachment of union power at pit and local level during the ensuing years of prosperity and expansion in the industry." And although it took until 1908, the miners did achieve the eight-hour day over the objections of their employers. Looked at in a broader perspective, the 1893 miners' strike shored-up the voluntarist system. The broad unity and aggressiveness of the Miners' Federation helped stimulate employers to build their own organizations and the spread of collective bargaining throughout the coal mining regions (Benson 1982, 198–9).

The resolution of labour disputes in the textile industry in the 1890s also demonstrated the resilience of British unions and helped the spread of collective bargaining. Although the Spinners union lost ground on wages and control over work conditions, there was no question that the union survived intact, partly because of its considerable resources to withstand the lockout (Clegg, Fox, and Thompson 1964, 115–17; Garside and Gospel 1982, 109). The 1893 settlement – known as the Brooklands Agreement – set up a new, elaborate structure of joint boards at local and national levels to resolve disputes, which came to be considered a success in reducing strikes and lockouts (Porter 1967, 53). Although the Agreement may have constrained labour from taking strike action and redounded to the benefit mainly of the employers and senior spinners, it clearly developed and diffused collective bargaining arrangements (Burgess 1975, 286–93). In 1895, a similar agreement – Terms of Settlement – appeared in the footwear industry (Garside and Gospel 1982, 105; Pelling 1987, 119).

The engineering lockout of 1898, while a considerable victory for employers, did not pose a serious threat to the union's status as the representative of the engineers in collective bargaining. Although the engineers lost the strike, they did not lose the union, which after a lull, continued to grow briskly. The engineers demonstrated a great deal of resilience and enjoyed the support of the public (and fifteen Oxford dons). According to Hinton (1983, 68), "the employers, here as in other industries, had failed to smash trade unionism." Employers prevailed in their lockout of engineers in the 1890s, establishing the Terms of Settlement of 1898 (Garside and Gospel 1982, 105), but the importance of their victory is marked both by what it did and did not achieve. Of long-standing significance, the employers won considerable concessions from the engineers in what they sought most – greater managerial control over production. No longer would the craft unions be able to control how many apprentices would be employed, how machines would be manned, and other work arrangements, and they were subject to piecework rates and working more overtime. The unions also accepted new collective bargaining arrangements that weakened local work groups, entrenching a more centralized system of collective bargaining as well as a more centralized disputes procedure at the regional and national levels (Clegg, Fox, and Thompson 1964, 175; Pelling 1987, 119; Zeitlin 1991, 57). The union's leadership was also strengthened because strikes could not be authorized until the union executive conferred with the EEF, which would discourage local resistance (Garside and Gospel 1982, 109; Zeitlin 1991, 57). Moreover, the employers failed to cripple the ASE as an organization representing their members' interests. The ASE's membership had grown from 61,000 in 1889 to 91,500 in 1897 on the eve of the lockout. It dipped temporarily, but recovered to 87,500 by 1900 (Clegg, Fox, and Thompson 1964, 175).

Despite their victory in 1898, the employers' unity was precarious and jeopardized by divisions across firms and regions. Their unity and influence were highly contingent and more limited after 1898. Further, after 1898, employers' unity declined and many of the issues settled in the Terms of Settlement were reopened (Zeitlin 1991). Many of the issues that were settled to its satisfaction were reopened later for reconsideration. Furthermore, the employers were limited by the continued dependence of employers on skilled labour (Zeitlin 1991, 57–75).

The outcomes of the major post-1906 disputes were similarly mixed. The railway unions failed to secure union recognition in the 1907 railways strike, but the companies' acceptance of boards of conciliation and arbitration was a step along a road that finally led, as a result of the 1911 strike, to recognition. The outcome of the 1912 miners' strike was not deemed adequate by a majority of the union members, but it resulted in a law establishing minimum rates. According to Wrigley (1982, 149), this episode "revealed clearly the power of organized labour in putting pressure on a government." Unable to get a compromise accepted by the two parties, Parliament passed the Minimum Wage Act, which created joint boards in each mining region, under an independent chairman, that were responsible for establishing minimum rates (Wrigley 1982, 149). A majority of the miners (who preferred uniform minimums rather than variations across regions) voted to continue to strike, but it failed to meet the requirement of a two-thirds vote for continuing a strike, and so the dispute came to a close. Although they enjoyed only a partial victory, the miners showed that they were capable of sustaining a long strike and effectively pressuring the government to intervene and pass legislation (Church 1990, 29; Brown 1959, 325–8; Pelling 1987, 136). The miners' ability to exert pressure continued during the First World War, although it suffered stinging defeats after the war and its influence waned considerably during the interwar period (see Church 1990, 30–42).

The interlude of industrial peace that lasted from 1899 to 1907 is sometimes explained in terms of the chilling effect that *Taff Vale* had upon the unions. Unions abstained from strikes to avoid having employers sue them for damages. Clegg, Fox, and Thompson (1964, 327–63) produced considerable evidence to show that industrial peace varied widely across industries, that it began before *Taff Vale* and lasted beyond the time that it was in effect, and that high unemployment and "an unwillingness of the employers to counter-attack" (rather than any chilling effect from the court ruling) is what prevented the unions from taking defensive actions.

What is clearer is that unionization rates rose in Britain from the mid-1800s up through the 1920s, particularly from 1890 to 1914, and most dramatically after the passage of the Trade Disputes Act of 1906 (see Cronin 1985). Unionization expanded in waves, most notably in 1871–3, 1889–92, 1911–13, and 1915–20 (Pollard 1985, 33; Booth 1995, 12–13). The pattern ratcheted downwards during trade cycles and major employer victories, but the trough of each downturn was higher than the previous one and the long-term trend was upward.

Trends already underway accelerated during this period. Union membership, employer organization, and collective bargaining grew dramatically between 1896 and 1914. Union membership rose from 1,466,000 in 1896 to 1,868,000 in 1900, to 3,708,000 in 1914 (Rubinstein 1982, 63; Bain and Price 1980, 37; 466; Wigham 1982, 33). The union density rate rose from 10.5 per cent in 1896 to 13 per cent in 1900 and 15 per cent in 1910, 24 per cent in 1915 and 45 per cent by 1920 (Bain and Price 1980, 37; Booth 1995, 13). Almost one-third of the male population was unionized by 1910 (Clegg, Fox, and Thompson 1964, 467). Similar growth occurred with employers' organizations. In 1895, 336 employers' organizations existed. That figure rose to 675 in 1898 and 1,487 in 1914 (Garside and Gospel 1982, 104). Growth in labour and employers' organizations made a concomitant growth in collective bargaining and joint conciliation boards possible (Wigham 1982, 33). According to Clegg, Fox, and Thompson (1964, 471), only cotton weaving had collective bargaining in 1893, but by 1910, among major industries, only railways did not. Engineering, shipbuilding, cotton spinning, building, printing, iron, steel, and footwear had national agreements, and all of the others, like coal, had agreements on district, regional or some other subnational basis. According to Benson (1982, 200), 20 per cent of the labour force was covered by collective bargaining agreements in 1910, but it was much higher in critical industries, like coal, where it was virtually universal.

The unions did not just survive and grow during the crisis period, however. They also helped extend collective bargaining, spearheading efforts in some cases to take negotiations from the district to the national level, particularly after the labour market tightened after 1914. According to Hinton (1983, 65), "the limitations of the [employers'] counter-attack ... resulted not so much in defeat for the unions as in industrial truce and the expansion of collective bargaining." Although many accounts place employers at the centre of efforts to establish national collective bargaining, that depended upon the particular industry and other conditions. Sometimes the unions demanded collective bargaining through strike action or took advantage of crisis situations to manoeuvre employers to accept it or capitalized on the growth of employers' organizations to institute it. Unlike craft unions, which had ways to control wages and work conditions through autonomous regulation, operatives unions in mining and textiles could not and viewed collective bargaining as the next best alternative (Turner 1962, 188, 201–7). The unions often leveraged periods of low unemployment and their potential to disrupt war production during the First World War to gain national wage settlements. Adams (1997, 508) has shown how trade unions "forced the pace of industry-wide bargaining" in "coal mining, rail, shipping and port transport." Employers were "steadfast opponents" of national pay bargaining in these industries." National collective bargaining machinery was, for example, "forced upon the ship owners by a combination of union and state pressure in 1917" (Adams 1997, 510). And although engineering had been the model of employer-driven national bargaining, "unions in the engineering industries managed to secure a national agreement in 1917 and another more satisfactory to them in 1919 which officially recognized not only the shop stewards but also the numerous works committees set up by them" (Fox 1985, 289).

EMPLOYERS' STRATEGIES FAVOURED THE SPREAD OF JOINT CONTROL
Although many employers became more confrontational as they faced increasing competitive pressures and more militant unions in the 1890s, most employers remained accommodative towards unions even during the tumultuous period between 1890 and 1914 (Fraser 1999, 104, 126; Gospel 1987, 163–4; Coates and Topham 1991, 247). Unlike employers in other countries, most British employers continued to recognize unions and did not seek confrontation or address employee grievances with the aim of destroying the unions. Had British employers decided on an antagonistic course towards the unions rather than accommodative one, as their counterparts did in other nations, the preferences of the unions and public officials might have been much more favourable towards greater state intervention.

Instead of using industrial conflict to get rid of or circumvent unions, employers used them to establish collective bargaining arrangements and grievance procedures where they had not existed, or they used such arrangements to negotiate wages and working conditions that were more advantageous to them. In an increasingly competitive economic environment, their aim was to constrain trade unions in order to assert or reassert their managerial prerogatives so that they could gain greater control and bring greater stability to their industries

(Garside and Gospel 1982, 104–5, 109). In three major industries – mining, cotton, and engineering – industrial peace was the result of the establishment of collective bargaining arrangements in the 1890s (Clegg, Fox, and Thompson 1964, 362; Garside and Gospel 1982, 105). Similar arrangements were established in footwear (1895), building (1904) and ship building (1908), and the railways (1911–13) (Garside and Gospel 1982, 105). Employers initiated these arrangements, which grew out of the unrest of the 1890s and early 1900s, but both sides wanted them to work (which they largely did), helped along by the depression. In many of these cases, the unions both lost and won. Employers gained greater authority over wages and production. On the other hand, "[t]he position of union officials as mediators of conflict was enhanced through an elaborate grievance procedure" (Garside and Gospel 1982, 109).

Employers who were staunchly anti-union, notably the railways and Shipping Federation, were exceptional. "Of the employers' suggestions for preventing or settling disputes, which the Board of Trade collected in 1889–90, only 20 percent were hostile to unions or intransigent, and the percentage tended, if anything, to diminish over the next four years" (Hobsbawm 1985, 19).

A little later, during the engineering lockout, some employers embraced tactics for smashing the union. Colonel Dyer, the director of the Employers' Federation of Engineering Associations, for example, was a noted admirer of anti-union American employers, like Andrew Carnegie, who succeeded in doing away with unions in his plants. A large Free Labour Association – whose mission was to supply strikebreakers to employers who sought them –was established in the 1890s and the TUC feared for the worst (Clegg, Fox, and Thompson 1964, 164–72; Pelling 1987, 109–10). Yet, from a broader perspective, Dyer's Employers' Federation was "not representative of the employers, even in the engineering and shipbuilding industries." The employers who uncompromisingly fought the unions' fundamental rights to exist, like Dyer and most of the railroad executives, were a minority of all employers. Both before and after its existence, employer federations arose that recognized the legitimacy of trade unions and sought accommodation between capital and labour (Clegg, Fox, and Thompson 1964, 175–6; see also Fraser 1999, 86).

Most employers did not take advantage of the *Taff Vale* decision to attack unions either (Hinton 1983, 68). According to Clegg, Fox, and Thompson (1964, 362–3, "[h]ad British employers wished to be rid of trade unions, the depression years of 1902–05, with the *Taff Vale* precedent valid in every court, were as favourable an opportunity as ever presented itself." Other historians contend that attacks on the unions would not have succeeded in getting rid of them (and argue that employers gained handsomely from union control over rank-in-file militants). Whatever the case might have been, there were "relatively few instances of organized employers taking advantage of [*Taff Vale*] to attempt to weaken or destroy the unions." Despite *Taff Vale*, "the majority of organized employers preferred to make a serious attempt to work with the unions" (Clegg, Fox, and Thompson 1964, 362–3). Similarly, employers put up very little resistance to the Trade Disputes Act of 1906 when it was under consideration in Parliament. According to Lord Lansdowne, the House of Lords did not try to block the Trade Disputes Act from taking effect because "throughout the discussions on the Bill the employers of labour in Parliament did not, as far as I know, raise a little finger to arrest its progress" (quoted in Brown 1983, 53).

Why did employers continue to accommodate the unions or come to accept accommodation? The competitive pressures and worker militancy that employers experienced beginning in the 1890s might have convinced employers that further accommodation and spread of joint control would be too costly. Indeed, some employers made that calculation. What explains the continued accommodation despite increased worker militancy and competitive pressures from abroad? As we will argue later, a good part of the answer to that question is that many employers already had several years of experience dealing with workers and setting up rudimentary institutions of joint control and had come to accept them. However, employers still faced a choice of how to respond to the unions during the crisis and pre-crisis developments would have a hard time explaining the ultimate triumph of joint control in industries that did not have a history of employer accommodation of unions.

Some employers who had held out against granting recognition, notably the railways, came under intense pressure from the unions and the state to grant it, and a younger, ascendant generation of railway executives adopted a more pragmatic vision of industrial relations. In 1907, a railway strike over recognition that "would have threatened large sectors of the British industry" was averted (Wrigley 1982, 143; Alderman 1971, 139–41; Fraser 1999, 112). The unions had the public's sympathy, the railways were divided over how to deal with the unions, and a younger group of railway executives, who had less interest in traditional anti-union principles than in the practical economics of their industry, had begun to play a larger role in the industry (Alderman 1971, 141, 149). In response to the All Grades movement, for example, the North Eastern Railway agreed to negotiation and arbitration with the unions, even though the other companies maintained their policy of non-recognition. The new generation of executives realized that continued refusal to budge on the recognition issue was counter-productive and they secretly developed the substance of the new settlement, known as the Conciliation Scheme.

Other employers, who had already worked with unions, remained accommodative because they saw advantages in extending and shaping collective bargaining. They responded to the new unionism and to their victory in the *Taff Vale* decision by building their organizational capacity to engage in collective bargaining, particularly centralized dispute resolution at the national level (Garside and Gospel 1982, 108–11). National wage bargaining became a strategy for dealing with competitive pressures by taking the variability in labour costs out of the equation (Adams 1997, 519, 522). As they had done earlier in their showdowns with the miners, spinners, and engineers, employers used *Taff Vale* to organize new employer federations and strengthen existing ones (Clegg, Fox, and Thompson 1964, 363). In the wake of their victories against the engineers' union and the *Taff Vale* ruling, employers seized upon the vulnerability of the unions, but *not* to destroy the labour movement. As British employers intended, *Taff Vale* also induced craft unions to fall more in line with employers' desires that they relinquish their craft controls over production (Clegg, Fox, and Thompson 1964, 328–5). Class analyses of this period argue similarly that employers turned to collective bargaining, conciliation, arbitration, and the like to wrest control over production away from craft workers and that they worked with union leaders and bureaucracies to control and deflect pressure from rank-in-file militants who fought against relinquishing their control (see Hinton 1973; Price 1980; Burgess 1975; Hyman 1979). In short, employers used the opportunity to reduce the craft unions' ability to make workplace decisions unilaterally by developing a stronger system of collective bargaining (Clegg, Fox, and Thompson 1964, 175; Charles 1973, 19–33).

Other historians have argued that businesses had no choice but to maintain accommodation. Efforts by employers to eliminate trade unions, even during a time when they were scoring victories, would have been futile and counter-productive (Saville 1985). "[E]mployers came to realize that the unions in their industries were here to stay" (Pelling 1987, 118). While employers' use of "free labour" (strike-breakers) in the dock strike was effective, it was much less so in industries like mining and textiles that relied upon skilled workers. Their efforts to use them during the 1890s in engineering, shipbuilding, railways, and iron and steel were not very effective (Garside and Gospel 1982, 107). The "blacklegs" could not usually be isolated from the community and the bitterness that they caused prolonged strikes rather than brought them to closure (Pelling 1987, 107).

Employers' authority in the workplace was relatively weak. Unions grew stronger and unionization continued to spread during the crisis period, particularly after 1906. Far from being manipulated by employers as instruments of social control over workers, union leadership structures and collective bargaining emerged and spread because they were effective instruments for craft workers to continue to retain control over their jobs and limit managerial power (see Zeitlin 1987, 171–2; and cites therein). Furthermore, British employers' often did not seek greater control over the work process because they found other ways to compete, or their efforts to wrest control over the craft unions did not succeed because they were highly dependent upon their skilled workers (see Zeitlin 1987, 171–2; and cites therein). According to Garside and Gospel (1982, 108): "Many employers, anxious to retain their authority, but keenly aware that successful adaptation to market pressures against a background of inferior technology and inadequate re-equipment of industry required the skill, effort and co-operation of trade unionists, encouraged further extensions of formal collective bargaining and dispute procedures. Granting concessions by negotiation in return for adjustments in working practices and the guarantee of stability of production clearly had some advantages over risky attempts to weaken the unions and to replace union by non-union labour."

Employers' effectiveness in imposing their authority on craft unions was limited because British manufacturers produced differentiated goods for the domestic and foreign markets which did not lend themselves to mass production, capital-intensive machine production and centralization of managerial control. Further, British industry consisted mostly of a plethora of family-owned enterprises that often specialized in one phase of the production process, which militated against the formation of cartels and monopolies and the development of elaborate systems of managerial control over workers. Businesses tended to stay in "families, partnerships, and private companies" instead of being taken over by banks or shareholders before the 1920s (Church 1990, 17). "The growth of monopoly capitalism in the sense of industrial concentration, the growth of modern mass-production, etc. was abnormally slow [in Britain] compared to Germany and the United States" (Hobsbawm 1968, 317). In ship building, employers "were inevitably committed to labour-intensive, low supervision and to a workforce with high levels of technical skill and task discretion" (Reid 1991, 46). Skilled workers often retained supervisory status over other workers. Finally, the competitive, fragmented, and family-run structure of British manufacturing industries produced "inward looking," competitive firms that made developing a capacity to coordinate and build effective national industrial and political organizations difficult (the Engineering Association of the late 1890s being an exception) (Zeitlin 1987, 174-6; Brown 1959, 265-8). Even in industries where employers demonstrated a remarkable degree of unity and scored major victories, like in engineering in 1898, their unity and success could not always be maintained over the long term (Zeitlin 1991).

Still other scholars argue that British employers' "national character" – specifically, "a dislike of regulation and an avoidance of conflict" – inclined them towards passivity when it came to dealing with unions. British employers were conflict averse, preferring to get along with their workers and not to lord over them, even if it made it more difficult for them to regain their competitive edge globally (Brown 1983, 107-15).

Whatever may explain employers' relatively accommodative posture vis-à-vis organized labour, particularly when compared to their counterparts abroad, it made it more likely that unions, collective bargaining, and other voluntary institutions of joint control would emerge and grow strong. According to Hobsbawm (1985, 18-19), "[t]he lasting success of new unions or of union expansion depended on the readiness of employers to accept them. As it happened, British employers were quite prepared in principle to do so."

A PROACTIVE STATE REDUCED THE NEED FOR STRONGER INTERVENTION DURING AND AFTER THE CRITICAL JUNCTURE

An elite consensus had emerged by the 1890s that, on balance, unions and voluntarism were beneficial. According to the Final Report of the Royal Commission on Labour in 1894, "[p]eacable relations are, upon the whole, the result of strong and firmly-established trade unionism" (quoted in Pelling 1987, 118). The governments in power clearly preferred voluntarism over other alternatives, notwithstanding the Board of Trade's proposals for some form of compulsion. Leading Liberals like Campbell-Bannerman and Asquith "subscribed to a minimalist policy of state intervention industrial relations, determined by the 'impartial' needs of the community rather than any class or interest" (Davidson 1978, 579). Clearly, however, the state was prepared to do more than remain disengaged. Although the state scrupulously sought to appear neutral in conflicts between employers and workers, and the state was constrained by employers and unions insofar as neither would countenance compulsory measures, the state was prepared to promote voluntarism in various ways. We have seen that it took affirmative action in removing the legal barriers and judicial threats to trade union organizations and activities in Parliamentary acts in the 1870s and 1906.

Although the industrial unrest of the 1889–1914 period in Britain was not accompanied by an economic contraction whose severity was on a par with Australasia's (Bray and Rimmer 1989; Clegg, Fox, and Thompson 1964), the industrial unrest of 1893, 1907, and 1911–12 posed serious threats to the economy and the convenience of the public. The state intervened when exigencies arose to buttress the voluntarist system by fashioning and using new, non-compulsory policy tools at its disposal. The state's contribution to keeping Britain on a voluntarist path was important during the crisis years. The state responded to the unrest associated with the new unionism by creating the Royal Commission on Labour (1891-4), adopting the Conciliation Act of 1896, and creating the Labour Department of the Board of Trade. All three affirmed the basic tenets of voluntarism – joint regulation by strong unions and employer associations – and rejected any form of state compulsion. By the time the commission issued its final *Report*, the new unionist uprisings and crushing defeat were becoming a memory that had come and gone with striking rapidity. The much larger strikes in coal mining and cotton had taken their place as the more salient labour disputes. Those disputes were not about the spread of unionism to new occupations and industries and demands for recognition and management's rights but sprang out of depressed economic conditions. These industries had established unions and, to one degree or another, joint regulation, so that compromise was a real possibility. Thus, the focus of the Commission's recommendations was on this more tractable industrial relations problem than the one that prompted its creation (Bray and Rimmer 1989, 64–5). Like the 1867 Commission, the 1893 *Report* gave a ringing endorsement to the "voluntary approach": "When organizations on either side are so strong as fairly to balance each other, the result of the situation is a disposition, already realized in certain cases, to form a mixed board, meeting regularly to discuss and settle questions affecting their relations.... The most successful of these institutions are those which have been formed in the trades where organisations on either side are strongest and most complete.... We hope and believe that the present rapid extension of voluntary boards will continue" (quoted in Clegg, Fox, and Thompson 1964, 485). The *Report* was also clear about the appropriate role for the state, which was to encourage robust voluntary business and labour organizations (Fraser 1999, 97).

Adoption of the Conciliation Act of 1896 was another government response to public concern over industrial unrest. The Act permitted the Board of Trade to inquire into the causes of work stoppages and, with the consent of the union and employer, to appoint a conciliator or arbitrator (Fraser 1999, 97). It provided for no cooling-off period, no compulsion for both sides to meet, and no binding arbitration awards (Davidson 1982, 163). Unlike the many earlier legislative efforts at conciliation and arbitration that were launched in 1824, 1867, and 1872 and that failed to have much impact on industrial relations (Davidson 1974, vii; Bray and Rimmer 1989, 53), the 1896 Act encouraged and supplemented the already extensive network of boards of conciliation set up voluntarily by unions and employers. While the 1896 Act had little impact in the years immediately following its passage, despite the "very slight legislative base" that the Act provided for the Board of Trade to intervene, the Board made tremendous use of its warrant in the years after 1906 when industrial unrest increased sharply. The number and magnitude of the disputes in which the Board intervened rose considerably, as did its success rate. Its arbitration awards were generally followed and the Board had a hand in preventing a large number of strikes through its interventions (Askwith 1974, 78; Davidson 1982, 167–9). Finally, in creating the Labour Department, under the Liberal Mundella in 1893, the state sought to build its informational capacity for dealing with disputes. The effectiveness of collective bargaining and arbitration were hampered by a lack of reliably non-partisan data related to conditions in trade and industries (Wigham 1982, 1–4).

As in other nations, the state's primary interest was in avoiding costly disruptions from industrial unrest. Because the state was interested in industrial stability, it worked with moderate trade union leaders and employers – that is, those who supported the accommodative orientation. It viewed militant union leaders and rank-in-file and anti-union employers as obstacles.

The response to the 1893 miners' strike signalled a sea change in the state's posture towards major industrial disputes. No longer would the state remain on the sidelines or limit itself to legislation that created fruitless conciliation and arbitration schemes. Thus began a series of interventions by high public officials into labour disputes that lasted for decades.

The Board of Trade took the lead in fashioning a policy, particularly before 1911 when the Cabinet paid little attention to industrial relations. The Board argued vigorously against the railways and shippers that refused to recognize their unions and sought to minimize labour's vulnerability to anti-union judicial rulings. In the railway strike of 1907, it fell to the president of the Board of Trade, Lloyd George, with his "captivating eloquence with ruthlessness and cunning," to intervene personally in a series of separate meetings with the companies and unions that led both sides to accept the Scheme (Alderman 1971, 140–1; Bagwell 1985, 196; Pelling 1987, 132). George used carrots and sticks – at one point threatening the executives with compulsory arbitration if they did not accept the conciliation boards, and in the end, promising them favourable consideration of their requests for mergers, route consolidations, and rate schedule revisions. These changes would make more generous wages more affordable. The unions fell short of their goal of gaining recognition in 1907. However, the railways' acceptance of conciliation boards (and arbitration, if the boards failed) meant that they had retreated on one of their cherished principles – not permitting third parties to get involved in their labour disputes (Alderman 1971, 141–2). Although the Board was motivated by a desire to reduce industrial unrest rather than take labour's side in the class struggle or improve the lives of workers, its efforts "helped to erode some of the most dictatorial forms of industrial management surviving at the turn of the century" and bolstered the accommodative position that most employers had taken by that time (Davidson 1978, 576).

Second, government leaders and the Board acted to preempt work stoppages and worked hard to hasten the resolution of many disputes, particularly those in key sectors of the economy. High-ranking officials intervened directly in disputes to pressure the two parties to come to agreement, actions that Australasian governments failed to take when confronted with an industrial relations crisis that was similarly grave. From the very first such dispute – the 1993 miners' strike – when Gladstone dispatched Lord Rosebery, a pattern was set for such emergency interventions. The most important instances of key officials brokering agreements were Lloyd George in the 1907 railway strike, Churchill in the 1908 cotton spinners strike, and George Askwith in the seamen and dockers strike of 1911 (Fraser 1999, 115–16; Wigham 1982, 18–24). George's actions were particularly decisive, as he used a foreign crisis and threatened the railways with compulsion in order to preserve the voluntarist system. Churchill's successor at the Board of Trade, Sidney Buxton, was more reticent about intervening personally in disputes, but the Board continued its success in resolving disputes under Askwith's able leadership (Wrigley 1982, 147). "Askwith and his Board of Trade associates worked tirelessly as conciliators and never lost the belief that the voluntary system could work.... In a whole variety of ways government was keen to create a new consensus which would bring social harmony and revitalize economic efficiency and saw trade union officials as crucial figures in achieving such a consensus" (Fraser 1999, 123–4; Wigham 1982, 19–20). After 1906, these initiatives not only helped the parties reach settlements of the immediate disputes, but put in place machinery – boards of voluntary conciliation and arbitration – to try to prevent and manage future disputes (Davidson 1982, 168). Between Lloyd George's success in the 1907 rail dispute and the end of 1909 sixty-seven new boards were set up.

In the 1911 rail crisis, George and Churchill (now in control at the Board of Trade), used the foreign crisis to pressure both sides to meet (Alderman 1971, 148; Pelling 1987, 134–5). Finally, the railway executives agreed for the first time to sit down with the unions, effectively granting them recognition (Bagwell 1985, 197). George, with members of his government, brokered an agreement to end the strike, which included the appointment of a Royal Commission (Askwith 1974, 161–7). The government pressured both sides to accept the findings of the impending Commission and threatened to impose the Commission's recommendations through legislation if they did not (Askwith 1974, 166; Charles 1973, 41). In the face of public opinion that did not support them, the railway companies remained deeply split on the issue of union recognition and continued to insist on a relaxation of shipping rates to have the revenue to pay higher wages (Alderman 1971, 146–9).

By the end of 1911, the railway executives again agreed to meet with the unions to negotiate an agreement based upon the Royal Commission Report, which recommended that the railways give partial recognition to the unions. The Report stated ambiguously that the railways should negotiate with the unions over "conditions of service" and "rates of wages and hours of labour," but that "matters of management or discipline" should be excluded (Stephenson 1911). The two sides were again brought together by the government (this time under the leadership of George Askwith, the Board of Trade's Permanent Secretary) and a settlement was concluded along the lines of the Commission Report to continue the Conciliation Scheme. While the railway companies never expressly granted recognition to the union, the practical effect of the companies' agreement to meet with the union officials constituted recognition. According to Askwith (1974, 169), "no railway company subsequently raised the point of non-recognition as an answer to claims of grievances." Finally, in 1913, Parliament kept the government's promise to allow shipping rates to rise, which encouraged the companies to negotiate further with the unions. With the railways' financial situation eased, their final rationale for refusing recognition vanished and the more moderate railway executives gained greater influence in the industry (Alderman 1971, 149–51). Thus, collective bargaining had come to the last remaining major industry that had held out against it.

Starting with the strike wave in 1911, the state established a series of councils and conferences whose principal task was not to settle particular disputes but to promote "cooperation and consultation" more broadly between labour and capital. They included the Industrial Council (1911–13), the Whitley Committee, Report and Scheme (1916–39), the National Industrial Conference (1919–21), and the Conference on Industrial Reorganization and Industrial Relations (1928–9). According to one perspective, the primary purpose of these efforts was to formulate and inculcate procedural and substantive norms that would guide collective bargaining (Charles 1973, 28–33).[4] According to another perspective, these efforts were naïve because they failed to compel labour and capital to behave any differently and they assumed a large identity of interest between the two parties that was incompatible with the intrinsically opposing interests between them under industrial capitalism (Fox 1985, 294–7). While these initiatives mostly failed to reduce industrial unrest and eventually were ignored or abandoned, they fulfilled the symbolic function of reassuring the public and mass media that the state was making some effort to deal with disruptive industrial relations disputes (Wigham 1982, 31).

Although the British state was limited to purely voluntarist policy tools, it used them frequently and skillfully, which helped to maintain the viability of the system through the crucible of the immediate pre- and post-First World War period. The emergency dispute resolution efforts that key officials undertook and the machinery set up under the Conciliation Act of 1896 most likely reduced the likelihood of adopting more interventionist policies by helping to prevent disputes or bringing them to a resolution. Furthermore, some unions found the Conciliation Act constraining, which may have hardened their already negative feelings towards stronger state intervention.

The state's role in industrial relations also underwent unprecedented and permanent changes in this period. Until this time, the state was either complicit with employers in repressing unions or it confined pro-union actions to the removal of legal barriers to their organization. Now the state intervened for the first time to try to prevent and settle disputes. The state also encouraged union membership by designating unions as agents for carrying out labour exchanges, unemployment insurance and other social reforms (Booth 1995, 19). Finally, unionization spread to occupations where it had not existed earlier, or at least reached a critical mass that was not extinguished simply through downturns in the trade cycle.

Finally, while the British system rested on "the primacy of voluntary action" in which "all statutory methods of fixing wages and other conditions of employment were considered as a second best," two exceptions existed (Kahn-Freund). First, during the First and Second World Wars, the state banned strikes and lockouts and imposed compulsory arbitration. Second, the state established minimum wages in industries where workers were not organized (Clegg 1979, 296). Trade Boards started setting minimum wages in 1909, but the policy was a very limited and cautious one that took many decades to develop a national minimum based upon what it took to live (Blackburn 2007).

Widespread outbreaks of unrest that threatened the economy and national security (during the First World War) often prompted these initiatives.[5] The first of these was the Industrial Council (1911–13). The Council was followed by the Whitley Councils (1916–39) and its successors, such as the National Industrial Conference (1919–21), and Council on Industrial Reorganization and Industrial Relations, 1928–9. According to Charles (1973, 20, 29–33), these institutions were "attempts by the parties to collective bargaining, with or without outside help, to work together in establishing the norms governing their relationship: they therefore assumed that the interests of capital and labour could somehow be reconciled, however fumbling and imprecise their approach to the problem might be."

Critical Antecedents: How Britain Got on the Voluntary Path in the First Place

The crisis of 1889–1913 did not occur in an historical vacuum. Three early developments in British industrial relations during the mid-Victorian era proved critical in putting Britain on the voluntarist path. Nothing assured that it would stay on that path, but these conditions made it much more likely. First, by the middle of the nineteenth century, many employers came to accept, and some even to value, trade unions. Their acceptance opened the way for rudimentary forms of collective bargaining and boards of conciliation and arbitration to develop. Having committed itself to accommodation and having seen the advantages in doing so, employers were less likely to abandon this posture during the crisis period. Second, trade unions often encountered judicial hostility to their organizations and activities, which made them distrustful of state intervention in industrial relations. Third, the unions responded to the judicial assaults with political mobilization, which resulted in legislative measures that addressed their demands.

Employer Acceptance of Trade Unions and the Emergence of Joint Control Institutions.

Efforts to outlaw unions began with the Anti-Combination Acts of the late eighteenth century. These laws probably dampened union organizing efforts, but they appear not to have had a significant effect on trade unions in existence and were "used very rarely to suppress" them (Fraser 1999, 10–11). Opinion is divided about whether employers were hostile to unions before the 1860s. During the 1850s, the Amalgamated Engineers won recognition (Pelling 1987, 43). Some historians assert that "from an early stage it became common for employers to recognize the existence of trade unions and to confer with them to agree on terms and conditions of employment (Portus 1958, 70; see also Brown 1983, 19–26, but others argue that employers only dealt with unions when they felt they had no choice (Hobsbawm 1968, 319). Compared to their counterparts in the United States and other nations, British employers were noted for attempting few attacks on unions in the nineteenth century (Brown 1959, 269).

Most agree that by the 1860s and 1870s many employers saw unions and collective bargaining as acceptable. Fraser (1974, 99) states that "[b]y the 1880s, over a substantial section of British industry a pattern of collective bargaining had emerged" and that unions "had gained recognition from most substantial employers in the staple industries" (Fraser 1999, 69).

Widespread employer and governmental acceptance of unions was indispensable for the establishment of collective bargaining (Brown 1983). Before collective bargaining, or joint regulation, industrial relations operated, in craft-dominated industries at least, on the basis of "autonomous regulation," in which the workmen or their masters (depending upon which was the most powerful), set wage rates and other conditions of employment unilaterally (Price 1980; Fraser 1974, 42; Turner 1962, 204). Under autonomous regulation, workers often formed "work groups" (not unions), which informed employers what they would charge for producing goods and how the goods would be produced (Price 1980). Unions, by contrast, often did not begin as workers' representatives in relations with employers but began instead as "friendly" societies of workmen in the same craft that would provide benefits during hard times.

Rudimentary forms of collective bargaining began with informal talks and impromptu meetings between employers and employees as issues arose. As early as 1860, "the main channel of British industrial relations" was for employers to meet with union representatives to negotiate wages. Employers saw an advantage in doing so because it established a floor for the price of labour and thus avoided cut-throat competition just as when they bought raw materials from the same source as their competitors (Brown 1959, 124). According to some historians at least, the development of a formal, procedural system of collective bargaining that involved the participation of third parties (trade unions and employer associations) in the employer–employee relationship arose in the 1850s and 1860s as an effort on the part of employers to wrest control over production away from craft-dominated industries like building and engineering (Price 1980). However, unions in industries that were not dominated by craft workers who were able to control of their supply of labour, often turned to collective bargaining backed up by strike action. These included operatives unions in industries like coal mining and cotton, and later, the "new unions" of the 1880s. Still others "combined systematic collective bargaining with an exclusive restriction entry" to their occupation, such as the United Society of Boilermakers and Iron Shipbuilders (Turner 1962, 201–7).

Another important innovation in these years was the spread of joint boards of conciliation and arbitration on a local basis in a variety of industries (Price 1980, 116; Bray and Rimmer 1989, 52–3; Fraser 1974, 110–15). "Conciliation and arbitration" were often used interchangeably in those days to mean collective bargaining (Fox 1985, 159). In some industries, like iron-making and hosiery, employers' associations took the lead in establishing collective bargaining (Armstrong 1984, 46). The major breakthrough came in 1860 when A.J. Mundella, a hosiery manufacturer, union supporter, and later, Liberal member of Parliament, established the Nottingham Board of Arbitration (Wigham 1982, 1; Brown 1959, 126–7). The Board brought peace to what had been a dispute-prone industry. Rupert Kettle, an arbitration judge in the building trades, developed a more procedurally elaborate system (Brown 1959, 126). In mining and some other industries, unions initiated the boards (at the district level in the case of mining) (Church 1990, 21–2). Unions and employers realized the advantages of these boards. They gave the unions a route to recognition as agents for their members, raised the status of union officials, and helped to avoid costly strikes; they gave employers a tool to impose discipline and order on the workforce, predictability in labour relations, and the chance to work with union leaders who were often more moderate than their rank-in-file. These advantages loomed increasingly important as employers found themselves between increasing trade union demands and sharper fluctuations in market conditions (Brown 1983, 106). For the long term, the "arbitration craze" of the 1860s softened the attitudes of many employers towards unions (Fraser 1974, 114–15).

Thus, the introduction of joint boards and the movement away from the informal process of autonomous regulation to the formal one of mutual negotiation pushed unions further away from their role as friendly societies into becoming representatives of workmen in a system of jointly regulated industrial relations (Price 1980, 123). Second, the success of these boards in many cases, and by contrast, the failure of many legislative attempts to encourage conciliation and arbitration, suggested that private, voluntary efforts were likely to succeed while government-sponsored ones were not (Fraser 1974, 110; Bray and Rimmer 1989, 51–4).

How do we account for the mid-Victorian acceptance of trade unions by many British employers? First, trade unions campaigned assiduously to make themselves acceptable. They evolved from confrontational to conciliatory bodies (Fraser 1974, 53). This change reflected a conscious strategy on the part of unions to burnish their public image and reduce middle-class concerns about them. Industrialization at first threatened craftsmen's status and economic security and inspired Owenite and Chartist ideas, which fuelled confrontations between unions and employers in the 1830s and 1840s. But in the 1850s, bolstered by rising wages and prosperity, most workers came to terms with laissez-faire and industrialization and credited it with rising living standards (Fraser 1999, 35–6). Conciliation-oriented unionists embarked on a campaign of "image building" tailored to gaining middle-class acceptance (Pelling 1987, 49). They demonstrated their support for widely shared middle-class values like self-improvement, respectability, industriousness, temperance, and moderation (Fox 1985, 135–6). Unions portrayed themselves as agents of social improvement that could "elevate the character" of workers by promoting education, temperance, and other endeavours popular with the middle class. According to Hobsbawm (1968, 319), "the transformation of militant Chartist workers into respectable aristocrats of labour ... took place 'spontaneously,' without any important change in capitalist policy, and with relatively small conscious changes in labour policy."

The "Sheffield outrages" of the 1860s, in which unionists were accused of resorting to violence against non-unionists, posed a new threat to the unions' reputation. At around the same time, court rulings placed unions outside the law. In response, the unions launched a campaign to guarantee unions' standing as legally valid organizations. First, they urged the appointment of a Royal Commission in 1868, before which they testified to their moderation, respectability, and responsible behaviour (Brown 1982, 116; Fraser 1974, 62). Although union supporters were a minority on the Commission, they were represented ably by middle-class reformers and union sympathizers Thomas Hughes (a Christian Socialist) and Frederic Harrison (a Positivist) who shaped its majority and minority reports in ways favourable to the unions. Whatever damage to the trade unions' reputation had been done in Sheffield, the testimony and report of the Commission resulted in "a remarkable change in the public's attitude to trade unionism" in a positive direction (Pelling 1987, 63). In addition to the testimony of the leaders of the large, amalgamated unions, which reassured the Commission that the unions' interests were limited to wages and hours, union supporters like the hosiery manufacturer A.J. Mundella testified to the constructive role of unions.

Much of the credit for the legal emancipation of the unions in the 1870s goes to the Positivists and other middle-class, educated union sympathizers who served as "labour's intellectuals" in the latter half of the nineteenth century. Henry Crompton, in particular, rallied the unions to get Parliament to overturn the adverse court decisions and, later on, to repeal the Criminal Law Amendment Act of 1871 and gain passage of the Trade Union Act of 1875. Crompton, and Harrison from inside the Royal Commission, supplied the rationales and concrete proposals that led to the 1875 Act (Harrison 1965, 282–308). Harrison had considerable impact in shaping both the majority and minority reports, but signed only the latter, which contained recommendations that Parliament eventually adopted, ensuring that unions would be able to recover damages from unscrupulous union officers, but avoided any state supervision and legal incorporation that would make them liable for damages. At the same time, economics treatises appeared that debunked the "wage fund theory" (which said that if one union secured a wage increase it would be offset by a decrease in wages for other workers) (Pelling 1987, 61–3). The Commission's recommendations were used as the basis for the Trade Union Acts of the 1870s, which banned prosecutions of trade unions as criminal conspiracies (Brown 1982, 117; Fox 1985, 150–7). These measures, like others that came later, encouraged union growth and militancy (Wigham 1982, 2–3).

Leading British political economists of the nineteenth century also viewed unions as positive and necessary. John Stuart Mill (1852) argued in his revised *Principles of Political Economy* that unions were an important vehicle for workers to advance their interests within a competitive economy (Fraser 1999, 41; Pelling 1987, 50). Later, Alfred Marshall argued that unions were beneficial because they raised workers' productivity and morale, which redounded to the benefit of employers. Once unions were seen as compatible with and beneficial to a market economy, then voluntarism was the system of industrial relations most compatible with a laissez-faire approach to economic affairs. Prime Minister Gladstone supported the 1871 Trade Union Act, which protected trade union funds and attempted to put them beyond the reach of criminal law, on the grounds that "in all economic matters the law to take no part" in regulating private parties (quoted in Fraser 1999, 47).

Crompton and other intellectuals and reformers of the pre-crisis period, not only saw unions as beneficial, but institutions of dispute resolution as well, as long as they were voluntary in nature. In *Industrial Conciliation* (1876, 40) Crompton had extolled the conciliation boards set up under Mundella and Kettle starting in the 1869s and carried forward their argument that "these boards ought to be voluntary, and not compulsory. They believe that compulsion is fatal to conciliation. He argued further that, on practical grounds, compulsory arbitration would not work because no way existed (in his view) to compel workers to accept arbiters' awards. Moreover, he underscored the philosophical principle that served as the linchpin of voluntarism's rejection of state compulsion in industrial relations of any sort: "Moral means are in fact the true protection against such breach of faith. It is better, therefore, not to depend on legal means, but for both sides to rely solely on moral means and to endeavor to strengthen that in every way. By trusting to legal redress, I cannot but think that an obstacle is put in the way of the development of the mutual trust between employers and employed which is the only real reconciliation" (Crompton 1876, 144).[6]

Second, Britain's early international lead in manufacturing gave rise to comparatively strong craft and operative unions, which employers could accommodate in the context of the nation's economic dominance. Skilled workers were in high demand in Britain, and employers were able to pay higher wages, at least for a time. "Many manufacturers had been sheltered from international competition by the technical lead" that British industry held in the mid-nineteenth century. British firms "compete[d] with one another in the home market, but according to accepted rules of the game." British employers were thus in a position to "take a more accommodating view of trade unions than those whose selling prices were held down by forces beyond their own control" (Brown 1983, 107). According to Burgess (1975, 306): "There were several aspects of Britain's dominant position in the international economy which helped shaped the future structure of industrial relations.... The net result was that labour was able to obtain a greater share of increasing wealth, at least in the 1870s and 1880s, without seriously threatening the share of profit.... It is difficult to escape from the conclusion that British firms thrived in a relatively 'soft' market environment.... This made for a situation favourable to the resolution of conflict between employers and employed by means of voluntary collective bargaining."

British economic dominance also provided positive feedback that encouraged the unions' conciliatory orientation towards employers. According to Fraser (1974, 69), unions persisted in conciliation "because it was working.... Unions were getting as much, if not more, from negotiation as from confrontation." The booming economic times of the third quarter of the nineteenth century also strengthened unions by putting them in a stronger bargaining position, particularly skilled workers, who were in short supply and were the workers most able to unionize (Fraser 1999, 65). Even when the period of strong growth came to an end with the Depression of the 1880s, unions remained moderate because the poor economy drove out many militant union members and "singled out for survival the well-organized union of higher-grade workmen, led by cautious men of limited aims" (Brown 1983, 105). Britain's early industrial lead also meant that the British labour movement would be dominated early on by strong, exclusive craft and operative unions. Members of the craft and operators unions identified with their craft rather than with their industry or economic class (Brown 1959, 118–19, 121). British unions eschewed socialism and developed a "labourist" style of politics that looked to Parliament for legal protections. The movement realized, early on, that "they had much to lose in revolutionary upheaval and much to gain from a cooperative legislature" (Coates 1975, 7; Cowley 1967).

Third, while unions were still relatively new and weak, employers and other elites believed that they were not powerful enough to inflict market harm. Employers were willing to negotiate with them as long as their dealings were confined to demands over wages and hours. Employers realized that they could bargain over wages and hours for labour, much as they did for any commodity needed in their business, without giving up their managerial authority. "The employers granted the trade unions recognition on the tacit condition that it be only for a restricted agenda" (Brown 1983, 107). Collective bargaining throughout most of the nineteenth century was conducted in a manner that was least problematic for employers. Negotiations with craft and operator unions took place on a district level, instead of at the plant level. This had two advantages. One, negotiations left untouched specific plant-level workplace issues where employers continued to maintain control. Thus, negotiations did not encroach on "the immediate relations of management and within the firm" where "most employers remained authoritarian, within the limits set by custom and practice." Two, since all employers were required to pay the same negotiated wage rate, they did not have to worry about being undercut by competing firms (Brown 1959, 123–5).

Fourth, employers came to appreciate the advantages of working with unions, or, viewed working with them as preferable to more uncertain and disorganized labour relations (Brown 1959, 270). "Of forty-seven trade societies and branches who submitted answers to the Royal Commission on Trade Unions in 1868, thirty-one claimed to have some measure of recognition from their employers" (Fraser 1974, 100). Once employers accepted unions and allowed them to organize, they recognized their value. "[O]ver a wide range of industries employers had come to accept unions as natural and inevitable" and "not a few employers saw strong unions as positively desirable" (Brown 1983, 107). "Before the 1890s, employers in general came to recognize" that collective bargaining, conciliation, and arbitration arrangements "could effectively diffuse the 'tyranny' of the unions if it operated to establish or reimpose managerial authority." Of course, it was the existence of unions themselves that permitted employers to engage in these forms of dispute resolution, which compared to the lack of institutionalization of conflict resolution that existed earlier, "seemed to promise industrial peace, regularity of production and flexible costs of production" (Garside and Gospel 1982, 104–5). "We have come to the conclusion," wrote Crompton in 1876 (95), "that permanent boards, either of arbitration or conciliation, are not possible unless the [workers] are united together in some form of permanently established organization, without which there is no guarantee that the men will abide by the decisions of the board." Many employers realized that a moderate, conciliatory union movement that accepted the capitalist system's basic structure could be advantageous to them. Skilled workers, who were most likely to be union members, served as trainers and supervisors of less-skilled workers. Many union leaders were moderating influences, helping to control more militantly minded rank-in-file (Fraser 1974, 64–5, 1999, 55, 62, e86). They were usually more pragmatic and conciliatory and more supportive of boards of conciliation and arbitration than rank-in-file members, partly because union executives saw strikes as putting their large reserves at risk, and in some cases, sought middle-class electoral support in a future run for Parliament. Mundella and Kettle recognized the value of trade unions when they were setting up boards of conciliation: "They [trade union leaders] have been the greatest barriers we have had between the ignorant workmen and ourselves" (Mundella quoted in Crompton 1876, 42).

Fifth, as unions became more widespread and stronger, "the desire for industrial peace often forced recognition of unions on even the most recalcitrant of employers" (Fraser 1974, 100). British employers had limited collective capacity to fight unions once they had become entrenched in an industry. Employers' associations were weak because they were fragmented at the local level and found it difficult to perceive common interests (Brown 1959, 269–72).

Judicial Hostility to Trade Unions and Unions' Distrust of State Intervention

Because the unions' rejection of proposals that involved state compulsion proved so critical during the critical juncture, we need to be clear about why they took that position. (British employers' opposition to compulsion was typical of employers in all industrial nations, but union opposition varied across nations and over time). While many employers gravitated towards accommodating the unions, the courts posed a frequent threat to them. Wherever the common law played a central role in the conduct of industrial relations, it posed a challenge to trade unions. The emphasis on the protection of individual rights in the common law raised a legal presumption against combinations, which inevitably compromised the freedom of individual employers and employees alike (Brown 1983, 27; Fox 1985, 160–1). In contrast to Australasia, common law doctrines played a central role in the development of industrial relations in Great Britain from the start and had a profound impact on the unions' views of the state.

The repeal of the Combination Acts in 1825 protected trade unions from being charged as criminal conspiracies as long as they focused on negotiating wages and hours and refrained from violence, obstruction, threats, intimidation, and similar actions. The legal status of unions remained uncertain, however, because when negotiations broke down they often resorted to actions that courts could construe as threatening and coercive. Under the Master and Servant Laws and a string of court decisions, unions remained highly vulnerable to attack. "[T]he failure of the Combination Laws Repeal Amendment Act of 1825 to offer precise definitions of terms such as 'threat,' 'molestation,' 'intimidation,' and 'obstruction' had left the unions very much at the mercy of judicial whim" (Brown 1982, 116). In *R. v. Duffield* and *R. v. Rowlands* in 1851, for example, the courts said that while unions were legal organizations, most of the activities in which they engaged were not. In *Hornby v. Close* in 1867, the Queen's Bench upheld a lower court ruling that trade unions were "in restraint of trade." The decision impelled the unions to petition Parliament to address the adverse rulings.

From early on, organized labour acquired a deep mistrust of legal authorities, whom they believed held class prejudices against them and were incapable of knowing enough about the particular industries and work situations to make qualified judgments. Decades before *Taff Vale*, judges "reflecting ... the social prejudices of their time, and in particular the bias towards individualism," had ruled that unions were illegal combinations. While unionism spread and unions found ways around the courts (partly by petitioning Parliament for legal reform), they would not accept relinquishing their autonomy involuntarily to arbitration boards given the legacy of judicial hostility towards them (MacDonald 1960, 23–4). The unions' adamant opposition persisted even when labour suffered industrial defeats in the 1890s (MacDonald 1960, 46).

Labor's Political Engagement, Parliamentary Responsiveness, and Supremacy

British unions' hostility towards the state, especially the judiciary, did not mean that they rejected politics and abstained from political engagement. Nor did it mean that elected officials were politically unresponsive to their grievances. From early in the nineteenth century onwards, British unions showed that they were capable of mobilizing and worked with radical liberal allies to defend themselves. Both major British parties came to support social reform as the nineteenth century wore on, helped along by the gradual liberalization of the franchise, the growth of misgivings about laissez-faire among left-wing liberals, and rising public support that came in response to widely publicized investigations of social conditions (MacDonald 57–8). By the 1870s, the Liberal Party had emerged as labour's champion in Parliament, especially among its Radical wing, which had much ideological sympathy for its aims (MacDonald 1960, 43). The Trades Unions Congress (TUC), formed in 1868, established a Parliamentary Committee, which served as a pressure group within the Liberal Party and the first lib-lab MPs – working-class MPs affiliated with the Liberal Party – were elected (Pelling 1987, 64–7, 79). The memberships of important "moderate and reformist" unions, such as the miners, developed close ties with the Liberals, strengthened by miners' identification with religious non-conformity (Church 1990, 23). The close ties between the "labor aristocracy" and radical wing of the Liberal Party had "deep historical roots" in shared religious outlooks, temperance, and political radicalism and was a major reason why Socialist doctrines, which came later, had a difficult time gaining converts among British workers (Fox 1985, 137–8). The Labour Party that emerged in 1906 displaced the lib-labs, but the new party also inherited the "non-revolutionary tradition of working-class politics ... which focused on parliament for the redress of social and economic grievances" (Shepherd 1991, 189).

Unions began agitating for the repeal of the Combination Acts soon after they were adopted, and upon their repeal in 1825 workers were once again permitted to organize to negotiate wages and hours (Fraser 1999, 13). Middle-class allies, including the followers of Robert Owen, the Christian Socialists, the Positivists, and the Radicals, were crucial for trade unions to gain access to the state (Fox 1985, 155). These movements of the early nineteenth century, which stood at the intersection of religion, philosophy, and politics, recruited many of their members from the trade unions, many of whose members were Methodists or belonged to other sects (French 1962, 18). In a pattern that would repeat itself throughout the nineteenth century, Radical reformers and unionists like Francis Place of the

Breechmakers Benefit Society, Benthamite economist J.R. McCulloch, and likeminded officials at the Board of Trade, the Home Office, and in Parliament, gained passage of the Combination Laws of 1824–5, which repealed all of the anticombination laws "to form the nucleus of the trade union movement as we know it today" (Pelling 1987, 20–3). In Parliament, the "friends of labour" group was led by Thomas Hughes and A.J. Mundella from 1869 to 1874, the critical period in which unions gained their legal legitimacy, who worked closely with trade union leaders like Robert Applegarth and George Howell in the Parliamentary Committee of the TUC (Spain 1991, 110–11). Middle-class, radical reformers were vital allies because Parliament extended the voting franchise very slowly. The reforms of 1867 and 1885 resulted in only 28 per cent of all adults eligible to vote. Until 1918 only 44 per cent of males (and no women) could vote (Fox 1985, 137). But the radicals did not just supply votes, they also supplied concrete proposals that came to fruition in abolishing the Criminal Law Amendment Act of 1871 and designing the 1875 Trade Union Act, and more broadly, intellectual arguments that justified unions' autonomy from the state and a limited role for the state in industrial relations that lasted until after the turn of the twentieth century. In response to the unions' opposition to *Hornby v. Close* and similar decisions, and with the key assistance of Hughes and Harrison in formulating the unions' demands and translating them into concrete proposals, Parliament passed the Trade Union Act of 1871, which explicitly stated that unions could not be prosecuted as criminal conspiracies in restraint of trade (Fox 1985, 152–5). However, Parliament also passed the Criminal Law Amendment Act, which prohibited unions from engaging in numerous activities, including "persistently following" and "watching and besetting" if done by one or more individuals. Employers brought suits under this statute and judges resumed issuing anti-union rulings, this time finding that unions were not conspiracies in restraint of trade but conspiracies to coerce and intimidate (Brown 1982, 118; Spain 1991, 112–13). Trade unionists mobilized at the 1875 election and put pressure on Parliament for electoral reform (Pelling 1987, 56–7). The government responded by appointing another Royal Commission, which employers dominated, and the unions boycotted. The unions launched a four-year campaign to get the law repealed (Fox 1985, 153–4). Union membership was growing, and the franchise had expanded in 1867. Disenchanted with Gladstone's government that had enacted the Criminal Law Amendment Act, the unions threw their support in the 1874 election behind candidates who favoured legal reform. The Conservatives won the election and Disraeli, ignoring the pro-employer recommendations of the Commission and eager to attract working-class support for the Tories, pushed through the Conspiracy and Protection of Property Act of 1875, which also had considerable Liberal support and the Liberals were responsible for working with trade union leaders in drafting major portions of it (Spain 1991; see also Fox 1985, 156; Brown 1982, 117–19; Clegg, Fox, and Thompson 1964, 44–5). The 1875 Act secured, once and for all, immunity from prosecution for the unions under criminal law and elevated employers and employees to a formally equal status by repealing the Master and Servants Laws (Price 1980, 129). The courts receded into the background again until the 1890s, but the British had established an important pattern of judicial hostility followed by labour mobilization and Parliamentary responsiveness.

The electoral cooperation and legislative lobbying that the unions engaged in with Parliament during the crisis may not have been effective if not for the British system of parliamentary supremacy, which made it possible for Parliament's legislative authority to trump the courts' ruling. The unions' definitive victories over the courts removed an impediment to union growth and confidence, which made the adoption of compulsory measures less likely and allowed union membership to grow dramatically and the system of self-regulation to continue to develop. British unions could reject stronger state intervention because, through their Radical Liberal allies and emerging Labour representatives, they had effective access to Parliament. Parliament was not only highly responsive to labour's mobilization on industrial relations policy issues, but it was in an institutionally privileged position vis-à-vis the courts, which allowed the unions to leverage it to neutralize the greatest threat to their existence and autonomy.

In sum, before the crisis period of 1889–1914, much of the foundation of the voluntary system was in place. The existence and legitimacy of trade unions was no longer an issue for the majority of employers. Trade unions had become more established in Britain than they had anywhere else on the globe in the nineteenth century. Union moderation and British industrial dominance led to employer acceptance. Employers' experience with unions, in turn, led them to discover their usefulness. Collective bargaining and voluntary forms of conciliation and arbitration gradually emerged as unions and employers realized the advantages in resolving disputes through increasingly regularized and formalized mechanisms for carrying out joint regulation of industrial relations. If needed, each party could resort to strikes and other activities to put pressure on the other. At the same time, judicial hostility induced a deep scepticism among the unions towards state invention in industrial relations. Labour also learned that it could exert effective pressure upon Parliament for protection, by mobilizing and appealing to their supporters for redress when employers or the courts threatened their activities.

Conclusion

Before the critical juncture that began in the late nineteenth century, Britain was already on a path that would lead to a voluntarist industrial relations regime. Not only had unions emerged and were no longer considered criminal conspiracies, but many employers had already accepted unions and at least rudimentary forms of collective bargaining had taken hold in many industries. As Charles

(1973, 27) puts it, voluntarism develops "where there is no ideological objection on the part of unions to employers and vice versa. The two sides must accept each other as legitimate representatives of legitimate interests." In exchange for employers' recognition of their legitimacy, the unions did not challenge private ownership of the means of production and embraced collective bargaining and other forms of joint control and dispute resolution.

Furthermore, British unions had a history of political mobilization and workers had developed strong ties to the established parties, which became more consequential after the Reform Act of 1867 expanded the franchise. They had also learned that their political participation could be effective, even in the face of judicial hostility, because they could rely upon Parliamentary supremacy. None of these conditions guaranteed the survival of voluntarism in the face of heightened conflict between workers and employers, but they made it less likely that Britain would switch to an alternative path. These antecedent conditions contributed to the survival of voluntarism in two ways. It made it more likely that, once the crisis came, employers would refrain from attempting to eliminate the unions, but seek more advantageous terms on wages and working conditions and attempt to strengthen collective bargaining and other modes of peaceful dispute resolution. Returning to a form of unilateral, employer control of industrial relations was not a plausible alternative to voluntarism given the strides that both labour and business had made towards joint regulation. Returning to unilateral regulation under employers would have set off labour unrest and necessitated a level of repression that the political parties would not have tolerated. Thus, the state's only realistic choices were to do nothing or to buttress and help extend voluntarism. As industrial unrest worsened after 1889, it redoubled its efforts in that direction. Second, labour's involvement in politics before the crisis occurred meant that labour unions were in a better position to survive the crisis and defend themselves against employers who continued to resist voluntarism. The unions generally held their ground, and many had expanded their memberships considerably by the First World War.

While it may not be so surprising, then, that voluntarism survived the crises that beset British industrial relations in the 1889–1914 period, what is remarkable is that many of the responses to the crisis helped to consolidate the emergent voluntarist regime and accelerate its development. The antecedent conditions do not explain what transformed the emergent system into a fully consolidated one and accelerated its spread, or how Britain stayed on the path for decades to come, despite frequent upheaval in industrial relations in the crisis years. Rather than push Britain off its course, or maintain the status quo, the crises diffused and consolidated the voluntarist system that had begun to emerge in the preceding decades. First, during the crisis period significant institutional innovations occurred. Employers in particular industries organized on a national basis and established the first peak association (The Employers' Parliamentary Council). These organizations, in turn, enabled collective bargaining to move from districts and regions to the national level. Major disputes emerged over whether employers or workers would control the work process (Booth 1995, 18).

Although the critical juncture offered a genuine opportunity to turn in a different direction – more repression, or more state regulation of industrial relations, or some combination of voluntarism in some industries and repression or regulation in others – the nature of the crisis and the conditions that emerged immediately from it help to explain why none of these alternatives occurred. As bad as the industrial unrest became during this period, it did not have the devastating impacts on British society and the economy as those experienced in Australia and New Zealand. The industrial unrest was not accompanied by as deep an economic downturn and public fears that the collapse would continue and that investment would not return. Conditions never got bad enough for reformers pushing a statist answer to the labour question to gain traction within the state, which remained as wedded to voluntarism as most employers and labour unions did. Most critically for the prospects of a statist solution, and most in contrast with the experience in Australia and New Zealand, the crisis never created an existential threat for the unions. Without at least reluctant support from the unions, compulsory measures would not move forward. Not only did most unions, including the strongest, not believe that state compulsion was unnecessary, but their experience with the judiciary before and during the crisis reinforced their prejudices against compulsory measures.

A second possibility was for the employers to crush the unions and impose an employer-based system of unilateral regulation. A minority of employers tried to do just that, both through industrial actions and judicial attacks on the unions. Anti-union employers' most lethal weapon against the unions was a judiciary and common law that were hostile to most trade union activities designed to put pressure on employers. Had the courts' rulings prevailed and not been reversed by Parliament, employers could have been emboldened to ignore or crush unions; over time, the voluntary system may have become eroded. Employers who sought to crush unions got little help from the state, which viewed the refusal of some employers to recognize unions as provocative actions that would only spawn more unrest. Here, the unions' victory was complete and decisive. Armed with the powerful tool of Parliamentary supremacy, the unions banished the judicial threat. The Trade Disputes Act, enacted on terms virtually dictated by the unions and despite opposition and reservations from many Liberal cabinet members, was the result of the support that workers had given to the Liberal Party, their skill at manoeuvring the Liberals into a position where the Party had to retreat, and Prime Minister Campbell-Bannerman's Radical leanings. But it also stemmed from a feeling in Parliament that MPs shared with the unions that the courts constituted a real threat to the future of unionism that had to be addressed. Not only did the legacy of judicial hostility fuel a mistrust of state interference among the unions in industrial relations, it also induced Parliament to respond to the courts in a manner that pushed policy further in the voluntarist direction than it might have gone otherwise. The rulings impelled the unions to pressure Parliament for a policy on immunity that was extreme in its complete absence of legal liability. Although many reformers, politicians, and legal experts had misgivings about blanket immunity, they supported it over a more limited one ultimately because they argued that anything less would fail to provide unions with "freedom from the embranglements of litigation and the unforeseeable developments of case law" (Asquith quoted in Brown 1983, 51).

The state also passed legislation throughout the nineteenth century to encourage conciliation and arbitration. Most of these laws were unused or failed to resolve conflict until after 1906, when industrial unrest skyrocketed, and the Board of Trade made external use of the Conciliation Act of 1896 to create numerous boards of conciliation and arbitration. Finally, the state created new corporatist institutions whose aim went beyond settling specific disputes in particular industries or localities. These entities brought capital and labour together on a regular basis to engage in "consultation and cooperation."

Ultimately, all three actors – employers, unions, and the state – saw advantages in its expansion. For the state, the voluntary system offered a way to resolve or at least manage industrial disputes with minimal state intervention. For employers, it brought predictability to labour relations, constrained worker militancy, and offered the possibility of reducing unilaterally imposed and maintained work restrictions. For the unions, particularly union leaders and bureaucrats, it provided an organizational purpose and status and jointly shared authority to make decisions. Whether rank-in-file union members, much less those who were not in craft unions or who were non-unionized, benefited from this system or would have fared better under an alternative remains a debate among labour historians.

6   Elusive Answers: The United States before the 1930s

Under a law based upon compulsory arbitration ... we would be compelled to work or to suffer the state penalty, which [is] not one scintilla distinction, not one jot removed from slavery.

(Samuel Gompers 1920, 261)

Employers in no other country, with the possible exception of those in the metal and machine trades of France have so persistently, so vigorously, at such costs, and with such conviction of serving a cause opposed and fought trade unions as the American employing class.

(Lewis Lorwin 1933, 35)

The US response to the labour question remained mainly one of repression for an unusually long period of time. Adoption of the Wagner Act in the 1930s occurred only after decades of stalemate and drift over a viable, long-term policy. Alone among English-speaking nations, the United States failed to adopt any form of statism or voluntarism. All that existed was a patchwork of state laws that had limited success in providing peaceful means of dispute resolution well into the twentieth century. American unions existed in a state of "semi-outlawry" for an unusually long period of time, despite never being illegal organizations per se and enjoying growth in membership, especially in the first two decades of the twentieth century (Forbath 1991, 60). Except for the railroads, proposals for compulsory arbitration and conciliation rarely reached the agenda, were usually defeated, or lasted only a few years. The quest for a voluntarist system also came up short. Capital and labour reached no accommodation backed by the state in most industries.

Highlighting the reasons for Americans' failure to adopt the two major alternatives existing at the time is important because adoption of legalism would have been unnecessary had the United States adopted one of them. Thus, Americans' turn to legalism in the 1930s owed as much to what failed to happen in the prior decades as it did to the immediate circumstances of the 1930s.

The first part of this chapter addresses why the United States failed to adopt any form of compulsion, like those that Australasia and Canada adopted. American employers were at least as hostile to trade unions as their counterparts in Australasia, but the American labour movement did not suffer the kind of threat to its very existence that led Australian and New Zealand unions to accept compulsory arbitration and wages boards. With few exceptions, American unions could thus persist for decades in their demands for a voluntarist system and remain adamantly opposed to compulsory arbitration or even more mild forms of statism. Opposition to compulsion was one of the few things on which labour and employers agreed. The US economy did not suffer the kind of acute economic crisis that Australia and New Zealand experienced until the 1930s, and when it did, employers were not able to vanquish the labour movement. By that time, compulsory arbitration was not a viable option since the US Supreme Court had invalidated Kansas's compulsory arbitration law in 1923.

The second part of the chapter addresses why the United States did not embrace the voluntarist regime that Great Britain adopted, or something similar. Conditions in the United States were no more hospitable to voluntarism than they were to statism. Voluntarism was only possible where the business community accepted unions as partners in the conduct of industrial relations and where businesses felt that the benefits of joint control of industrial relations outweighed the costs. Although some employers early in the twentieth century were willing to work with the unions, it was short-lived. American business continued to refuse to recognize unions for decades and enlisted the help of the state to make sure that the unions were kept mostly at bay. Organized labour was too weak politically to overcome the influence of business in the state (particularly the judiciary) and never developed a viable labour party or ties to the Democratic Party that were as strong as British unions did to the Liberal Party. Yet, even when these obstacles were swept away in the 1930s, employer resistance to voluntarism remained a decisive impediment.

The Rejection of Statism

Unlike the other major English-speaking "settler" nations, compulsory forms of industrial relations policy failed to take root in the United States prior to the 1930s. Reformers at both the state and federal levels made several proposals for compulsory investigation, conciliation, and arbitration between the 1870s and 1920s, particularly when unions grew in strength and labour disputes periodically became violent (Abrams and Nolan 1983, 378; Fisher 1922). One state, Kansas, experimented with compulsory arbitration in the 1920s, but that ended after a few years. No fewer than twenty-five states adopted statutes providing for boards of arbitration between 1878 and 1900. Only a handful of these boards accomplished much.[1] Most laws that called for investigation, conciliation, or arbitration made them voluntary, which resulted in the laws having modest impacts. The federal government adopted several measures that provided for voluntary arbitration on the railroads starting with the Arbitration Act of 1888 and followed by the Erdman Act of 1898, the Newlands Act of 1913, and the Railway Labor Act of 1926 (Abrams and Nolan 1983, 380; Ellingwood 1928; Fisher 1922). Only the Transportation Act of 1920 approximated compulsory arbitration, but it was repealed and replaced in 1926 after it was widely viewed as a failure.

What accounts for the broad rejection of compulsory measures for the resolution of industrial conflict in the United States? Part of the answer lies in the fact that the conditions that were hospitable to the adoption of compulsory measures in Australasia did not exist in the United States, except for employers who were hostile to unions. As noted, industrial strife in the United States never got to a point where organized labour was in danger of being destroyed. Key state actors at the national level, who were members of pro-labour governing coalitions, never initiated and committed themselves to pushing for compulsion. Organized labour never embraced or acquiesced in such a policy. And even if they had, the Supreme Court was almost certain to strike it down.

We begin by addressing how conditions in the United States deviated from those in Australasia and then turn to the possibilities for reform under anti-labour auspices.

The Lack of an Existential Crisis and Americans' Reliance upon Repression

The scope and severity of economic and industrial relations crises reduced enthusiasm for compulsion among US workers, reformers, and policymakers. In Australia and New Zealand, the state had much greater leverage to introduce compulsory measures because the crises loosened the constraints that employers and labour normally imposed. Organized labour was nearly obliterated, and the level of public alarm about the economy was widespread. The crises lowered the ability and inclination of employers and unions to block compulsion, tipped the balance among unions in favour of it, and induced bold actions from reformist policymakers.

Few serious proposals for compulsion were entertained in the United States in part because the crises were different from, and less severe than, those in Australasia. Except for the Pullman strike of 1894, none of the other eruptions of major industrial unrest took place simultaneously with a severe economic downturn. A comparison of the economic contractions that took place in the 1890s in the United States and Australasia reveals that the one in Australasia was much more severe. In Australia, the best estimates are that GDP fell by between 17 and 18 per cent between 1892 and 1893 (Maddison 2006; Fisher and Kent 1999). For the United States the highest estimate is 10 per cent for 1892–3 and 1893–4 (Kuznets 1961; Kendrick 1961) and more recent estimates are much lower (5.2 per cent for Balke and Gordon 1989). Economists debate whether the contraction in the 1890s in the United States was a depression or a severe recession; they are agreed that what occurred in Australia and New Zealand was a depression. That the American labour market was much larger and more geographically decentralized than those in Australasia and Canada also helped diffuse and absorb economic disruptions. Without the catalyst of a crisis that spilled outside to the boundaries of labour-management relations in particular industries, and threatened widespread economic hardship and public disorder, progressive reformers in the United States had less urgency to push for reforms that included compulsion, could make a less compelling case for them, and had less of a chance winning over labour and business.

American labour never faced a crisis in these years that weakened it to a point where its very survival was at stake. The United States surely had its share of industrial unrest before the 1930s. Major strikes occurred including the Homestead and Pullman strikes in 1892 and 1894, the rail strike of 1912, and most acutely after the First World War (1918–19). By the early 1900s, labour unions that were strong enough to organize and compel employers to engage in collective bargaining were free do to so by American courts. The courts' use of the injunction mainly thwarted secondary boycotts and sympathy strikes that the unions used to organize non-union plants that undercut those firms that were organized in individual industries (Gregory 1958, 174).

The depression that began in 1893, coming in the first decade of its existence, was an important challenge to the American Federation of Labor (AFL). Businesses that avoided bankruptcy turned to cutting jobs and wages. Union membership declined, but the AFL survived (Greene 1998, 37). The AFL's survival of the crisis of the 1890s depression is like the experience of British labour during the late nineteenth century. The newer industrial unions suffered the most and the labour movement became more craft-dominant and exclusive coming out of the downturn (Greene 1998, 38). But no industrial relations crisis ensued that brought the economy to the brink. Major strikes like Pullman and Homestead did not become so disruptive that the public was severely inconvenienced.

REPRESSION KEPT CRISES IN CHECK

The industrial relations crises were held in check by the courts, police, and military, which crushed and demoralized the strikers. And the AFL demurred from expanding the conflict in ways that could have led to a more general breakdown in order (Forbath 1991, 74–7). Repression helped to limit the severity and scope of industrial relations crises, which in turn, reduced public pressure on the state to introduce compulsory arbitration. In effect, the state relied upon repression – injunctions, fines, arrests, and violence – as an alternative to boards and courts that would adjudicate labour disputes. The use of repression also enabled employers to disregard the rights of labour organizations and their demands for recognition, which were prerequisites for the establishment of Australasian-style compulsory arbitration. Some have argued that American employers were philosophically more hostile to unions than those in other nations, while others have argued that employers were emboldened to take a harder line because they knew that they could rely upon state repression (Voss 1993; Friedman 1998; Archer 2001). Whichever may be the case, repression almost certainly helps explain why industrial relations crises in the United States were relatively contained. Repression not only helped to shorten the duration of industrial relations crises. As a result, employers were spared blame for a crisis that created much public anxiety and pain (as happened in Australasia).

American Labour's Strong Aversion to Compulsion

American labour organizations and employers were hardly unique in their reluctance to go along with compulsory state policies in the arena of industrial relations. Since both employers and labour organizations distrusted handing control over industrial relations to a third party with police powers, opposition to compulsory measures was the default condition in all nations, not just the United States. Employers saw it as their prerogative to set wage rates and working conditions and were often under competitive pressures to maintain that control. Labour unions usually viewed a large role for the state in industrial relations as potential interference in their basic mission to fight for higher pay and better working conditions. Compulsory arbitration impinged not only on labour's ability to promote workers' interests, but also to function and thrive as an autonomous organization. They saw compulsory arbitration as undercutting collective bargaining and their role in it. Labour unions, thus, had a strong incentive to mobilize and punish politicians who did not support an industrial relations regime that enabled them to maintain strong, autonomous organizations. Buttressing these rational incentives to protect their organizational self-interest, the AFL developed an ideology in which economic power, not political power, was the appropriate route to follow to pursue workers' interests and that "the trade union was glorified as the soundest basis of all workers' progress" (Lorwin 1933, 46).

American labour's embrace of voluntarism and opposition to compulsion were the opposite sides of the same coin. As we have seen, voluntarism was a policy of self-help with minimal state involvement in the relationship between employers and employee organizations. In its purest form, voluntarism held that unions were private and voluntary institutions that sought nothing from the state and sought absolute freedom from state regulation. This view also emphasized "pure and simple" material gains for labour, particularly better wages, hours and working conditions, as opposed to "ultimate aims" of challenging the system of capitalism and realizing socialism (Robertson 2000, 66).

Given the pivotal role of labour's support in Australasia for compulsory arbitration, we need to explain labour's implacable opposition to *any* compulsory measures and why it persisted for such a long period of time. Although our focus in this section focuses mostly on the American labour movement's rejection of compulsory arbitration, it is important to recognize that labour objected to measures that fell short of arbitration, including compulsory investigation and conciliation, and it "rejected the proposal for compelling corporations by law to deal with unions" (Lorwin 1933, 46). Labour would not abandon its opposition to the last form of compulsion until the New Deal. The vast majority of the American labour movement rejected state regulation of industrial relations in favour of voluntarism throughout the pre–New Deal era (Fisher 1922, 7), several decades after unions in Australia and New Zealand signed on to extensive state supervision and Canadian unions went along with compulsory investigation and conciliation.

American labour's opposition to compulsion was neither ordained at the outset of the labour movement nor held universally within the movement, however. Early on, support for compulsory arbitration existed within the movement. The forerunner organization of the AFL (the Federation of Organized Trades and Labor Unions) advocated it (Witte 1952, 10). The Knights of Labor – the AFL's main rival early in the movement – listed arbitration as a goal in its constitution and many of its local chapters lobbied Congress for such a law, although whether they meant the "compulsory" variety remains unclear (Abrams and Nolan 1983, 378; Fisher 1922, 11). Many individual officers and members of labour unions supported compulsory arbitration in the 1880s and some states established boards "as part of the union agenda" (Robertson 2000, 74–5). Railway unions also supported compulsory arbitration early in their history. Labour organizations were also often at the forefront in pushing for voluntary arbitration laws in the states in the 1870s and 1880s. As in other countries, the weakest unions were those most inclined to support arbitration (Abrams and Nolan 1983, 378). Opposition to arbitration came from employers who refused to participate, not wanting to relinquish control over wage determination to a third party (Witte 1952, 10).

Despite this modest, but genuine, support for compulsory arbitration early on, what made American labour become an enduring foe of any form of compulsion? One was the AFL's takeover of the labour movement under Samuel Gompers and its experience with the state-sponsored social reform and voluntary arbitration. Another was conservative elites' eventual embrace of compulsory arbitration.

THE TRIUMPH OF SAMUEL GOMPERS AND THE AFL

The growing ascendance of the AFL and Samuel Gompers, and the decline of the Knights of Labor after 1886, consolidated and strengthened labour's opposition to compulsory arbitration. The reasons for the rise and fall of the Knights has been a subject of considerable academic discussion, but labour's position might have been more open to compulsory measures if Gompers had not occupied such a pivotal position within the AFL for such an extended period. Gompers led the AFL from its creation in 1886 to his death in 1924, except for one year (1894–5). In 1894, John McBride, president of the United Mine Workers, defeated Gompers. Notably, McBride supported compulsory arbitration (Gompers 1925, 156). Gompers returned to power the following year, by winning a narrow majority of eighteen out of hundreds of votes cast. McBride was an abrasive personality and not a stranger to controversy, among them his public endorsement of compulsory arbitration despite the AFL's 1893 convention (Taft 1957, 126–7).

The labour movement's positions on public policy, particularly before the First World War were largely decided by the AFL and the national and international craft unions with which it affiliated. The unions enjoyed considerable autonomy in running their local affairs, but the AFL played the leading role on matters of political involvement, interest representation before government, and defining the movement as representing exclusive, craft-dominated, and conservative business unionism. Gompers was a formidable force who, with his top lieutenants and the presidents of the major craft unions, steered the organization for most of its first four decades. He controlled a staff and budget, maintained a network of loyal allies throughout the movement, and presided over annual conventions. With the national and international unions, he worked to head off or weaken rival labour organizations like the Knights of Labor, industrial unions, local federations, and central labour unions (Greene 1998, 42–7). Before the 1890s, the central labour unions had been important political arms of organized labour. Their decline coincided with the AFL's emphasis on economic rather than political action in the last three decades of the nineteenth century.

Gompers rejected even the most limited forms of compulsion, such as Canada's mandatory investigation and conciliation of disputes (Craven 1980, 5). He opposed compulsory investigation, when it was proposed in Congress, on the grounds that it could lead to compulsory arbitration (Fisher 1922, 40). When unions lobbied for voluntary arbitration in the 1880s, Gompers accepted it only if labour's bargaining power matched that of employers and if employers were unable to hire cheap labour (Abrams and Nolan 1983, 378). The Erdman Act, which called for voluntary arbitration of railroad disputes, passed when Gompers reluctantly withdrew his opposition to it, in deference to the railroad brotherhoods' demand for it. But Gompers worked to contain its spread beyond the railroads (Fisher 1922, 24–5; Robertson 2000, 75). It took until Gompers's death and the cataclysm of the Great Depression of the 1930s to reduce employers' influence and convince labour to abandon voluntarism.

LABOUR'S EXPERIENCE WITH STATE ACTION

Students of this period in American labour history have offered various explanations for why Gompers and the AFL were so wedded to voluntarism. These works have not specifically addressed labour's rejection of compulsory measures in industrial relations, but since voluntarism and compulsion were antithetical to one another, their explanations for labour's adherence to voluntarism should be helpful for understanding labour's rejection of compulsion. The most widely embraced explanation for labour's turn to voluntarism emphasizes the opposition of the courts to labour's interests (Hattam 1993; Forbath 1991). In the latter part of the nineteenth century, labour often turned to the state for protective legislation when economic pressure did not work (Robertson 2000, 41). Labour was sometimes successful at the state level in getting regulations passed regarding hours of work, workplace conditions in factories and mines, immigrant labour, and similar issues, only to have courts invalidate the new laws.

Through their power of judicial review, courts overturned eight-hour day legislation, bans on tenement sweat labour, and similar paternalistic legislation on the grounds that adult workers should be free to contract with employers (Forbath 1991, 37–57). Courts also used labour injunctions as a principal weapon against unions that attempted to pressure employers through boycotts, sympathy strikes, and control and recognition strikes, and they often called out police and troops to enforce their orders (Forbath 1991, 65–7). Courts also invoked the Sherman Act, which Congress intended to curb business monopolies, to attack unions as "combinations" in restraint of trade (Forbath 1991, 71). The state's resort to police and the military to quell unrest made labour organizations further distrustful of state intervention, particularly any kind of compulsory measures, and thus more adamant opponents of such measures.

Other scholars have argued that labour's turn to voluntarism cannot be attributed only to the hostility of the courts and the use of police, but to its frustration with the elected branches of government as well. Two legislative chambers and the governor of the state had to approve legislation. If labour's opponents did not block legislation at some point in the process, they often weakened it in the process of garnering sufficient support for passage (Robertson 2000, 53). Robertson's (2000, 45 and 51) study of eight-hour day and child labour legislation suggests that the legislature and bureaucracy had more to do with labour's disappointing experiences rather than the courts.

Gompers blamed legislators as well as judges for rejecting labour's claims on the grounds of unconstitutionality. Gompers's early experience as a labour activist with attempting to get factory reforms in the cigar-making industry through the New York state legislature led him to conclude that political action was ineffective compared to industrial action, a point of difference between him and Ferdinand Lasalle and other socialists. He and his associates had worked assiduously to get the state legislature to pass a law regulating manufacturing in tenements only to see the law overturned by the state's highest court. Gompers's disenchantment with the legislative route for regulating hours, factory conditions, and similar reforms, and his embrace of achieving labour's goals through economic power is something that stayed with him for the rest of his life (Reed 1930, 47–9). Labour would succeed in achieving its goals, according to Gompers, only after it turned to strikes and other forms of agitation (Gompers 1925, 58–62).

The state's impact went beyond hamstringing unions and blocking labour legislation. Its actions also shaped the AFL's ideology, agenda, and membership composition. Labour abandoned the republican idea that workers were citizens rather than sellers of labour and adopted the courts' freedom of contract rhetoric that treated labour as a commodity (Forbath 1991, 128–39). Because legislation was difficult to enact and enforce, the labour movement focused on those parts of the workforce that were the easiest to organize and that had the highest chance of success – the labour aristocracy of craft unions (Robertson 2000, 72). The courts helped to narrow the reform agenda of the AFL so that it was not inclined to push for social welfare policies and it affirmed labour's belief that positive state intervention would be either futile or used against the labour movement.

Eventually, Gompers and the AFL would be forced to re-engage in politics in order to secure labour's ability to challenge employers in the industrial arena, but political action in favour of positive state intervention became circumscribed towards a narrow set of objectives, that would avoid having the state compete with the unions for workers' loyalties and "threatened to make union activities like collective bargaining seem less vital" (Greenstone 1977, 26–7). Legislative lobbying was to be employed to address the needs of particularly vulnerable groups in the labour market who were difficult to organize, such as women and children, and, the reform of labour laws so that employers and courts would no longer hinder organizing drives, strikes and picketing and other activities that unions undertook to force employers to bargain (Robertson 2000, 71; Greene 1998, 256). When Gompers and the AFL entered the political fray after 1900, it was to insure a reliable voluntarist system.

Gompers's view of the state as an unreliable ally of labour was not just a pragmatic strategic response to an often hostile or indifferent state but reflected his and the AFL's ideological commitment to voluntarism: "I saw in the proposal to establish arbitration carrying any degree of compulsion a blow at the fundamentals of voluntary institutions, which to my thinking are the heart of freedom" (1925, 158). He viewed politics as unnatural and believed that the state had no legitimate interest in industrial relations. Gompers believed that the growth of large organizations in industrial society was a natural and scientifically based evolution of society, but that politics was outside this process. According to Gompers (1925, 134–5):

> Several times the plain question has been put to me by members of the Senate Judiciary Committee: "Mr. Gompers, what can we do to allay the causes of strikes that bring discomfort and financial suffering to all alike?" I have had to answer,

"Nothing."... Foremost in my mind is to tell the politicians to keep their hands off and thus to preserve institutions and opportunity for individual and group initiative and leave the way open to deal with problems as the experience and facts of industry shall indicate. I have, with equal emphasis, opposed submitting determination of industrial policies to courts. But it is difficult for lawyers to understand that the most important human justice comes through other agencies than the political.

Reformers abroad often invoked the public interest as a rationale for compulsory arbitration, but Gompers believed that "[t]he public has no rights which are superior to the toilers' rights to live and to their right to defend themselves against oppression" (quoted in Reed 1930, 121). According to Salvatore (1984, xxii), Gompers believed that: "Employers and workers through their unions were the only legitimate actors ... and the inevitable struggle between them would be fought directly in the economic arena without regard for political concerns. As Gompers explained to a Senate committee in 1883, the U.S. Constitution 'does not give our National Government the right to adopt a law which would be applicable to private employments.'" The AFL's ideological commitment to voluntarism survived Gompers's death in 1923. As late as the early years of the Great Depression, the AFL's support of voluntarism led it to oppose unemployment insurance despite a very high jobless rate (Greenstone 1977, 26).

LABOUR'S CHECKERED EXPERIENCE WITH VOLUNTARY ARBITRATION
By the early part of the twentieth century, schemes for voluntary arbitration had spread to some industries. Had labour viewed its experience with voluntary arbitration as successful, that might have softened the AFL's position on compulsory arbitration. But experience with voluntary arbitration was often disappointing either because the procedures were unused, or because employers refused to follow the arbiter's decisions, or because labour perceived the decisions rendered as unfair. The railroads were the major industry in which voluntary arbitration had been the most promoted by the government. Unlike many American unions, the railroad brotherhoods were adverse to strikes in the late nineteenth century and were very open to government-sponsored voluntary arbitration as late as the turn of the century when Congress passed the Erdman Act. The unions in this period were still weak vis-à-vis the railroads and therefore were not averse to government involvement. Employers took the opposite stance towards the Erdman Act. For a long while, the Act was unused because employers refused to accept offers by the Interstate Commerce Commission (ICC) and Commissioner of Labor to arbitrate (Lecht 1955, 18–19). The Act began to be used after 1906, and in 1912 the unions and carriers agreed to arbitration of a major dispute involving the eastern engineers that would set a pattern for the entire industry. When the unions did not receive what they thought was a favourable award, they soured on arbitration. Employers, who

had shied away from using the procedure previously, now grew fond of it. Not only did employers win numerous awards under the Erdman Act, some calling for wage cuts, but they dominated the implementation process. A poll of railroad managers indicated that a majority favoured having the government set wages (Lecht 1955, 21–4). The brotherhoods complied with anti-union awards, but the employers refused to follow awards that went against them (Zakson 1989, 329–35). These experiences seemed to validate the scepticism that Gompers and the AFL greeted schemes for voluntary arbitration, and they further hardened their opposition to compulsory measures.

LABOUR'S OPPOSITION STIFFENED FURTHER WHEN CONSERVATIVES TURNED TO COMPULSORY ARBITRATION

As union membership grew in the early part of the twentieth century, some business interests and their conservative allies in government began to view compulsory arbitration as a tool to limit labour's disruptive potential. This, in turn, increased the opposition of labour and progressives to arbitration. Particularly after the First World War, conservative forces began to take a serious interest in compulsory arbitration in crucial industries like coal and railroads. Although unions had been enthusiastic about voluntary (and in some cases compulsory) arbitration before the 1890s, unions lost faith in voluntary arbitration and grew suspicious of it (Witte 1952, 12). Thus, what began as a union initiative in many places eventually attracted the support of employers in the wake of the Pullman strike in 1894–5 to prevent strikes. "The Pullman strike prompted seven states to enact [voluntary] arbitration laws in 1894–95. In these states, notably Illinois, support for this legislation came from conservatives reacting against the disorder resulting from the strikes" (Robertson 2000, 75). By the 1890s, labour had turned against arbitration, fighting against proposals that the US Strike Commission and members of Congress proposed in the wake of the Pullman strike (see Fisher 1922, 22; US Strike Commission 1895, XLVII, LII–LIV; Abrams and Nolan 378; Fisher 1922, 21). Thus began a pattern that would continue – occasional interest among conservatives for compulsory arbitration.

LABOUR'S VETO POWER WITHIN A FRAGMENTED STATE STRUCTURE

Until the 1930s, in the face of an often hostile state and employers, labour could do little in a positive way to shape industrial relations policy to its liking. But it used the influence and leverage at its disposal to veto proposals to strengthen state regulation of industrial relations. Labour's opposition to arbitration was often effective. The fragmented structure of the American state afforded labour opportunities to block efforts to enact compulsory measures. Gompers worked to defeat compulsory measures whenever they appeared on the agenda between the late 1800s through the First World War (see Fisher 1922). "I regard no public service of mine of greater importance," he stated, "than my efforts extending over forty years to prevent the enactment of legislation of this character" (Gompers 1925, 149). According to Robertson, "when conservative legislators introduced compulsory arbitration bills, Gompers and other leaders often successfully maneuvered to ensure that the bills died in committee" (Robertson 2000, 53–4; see also Yellowitz 1965, 142). The same outcome ensued at the federal level when Congress debated compulsory investigation and conciliation measures (Fisher 1922, 41–2). Although organized labour had less influence in Washington once the Democrats were out of power after the First World War, they were part of a coalition that defeated efforts to include compulsory arbitration in the Transportation Act of 1920, which governed industrial relations in the railroad industry (discussed in more detail below).

A Lack of Progressive Commitment to Compulsory Measures and Strong Ties to Labour

In Australia and New Zealand, compulsory arbitration sprang from the minds of public officials who were deeply committed to the policies and who occupied key positions in the state from which to launch the reforms. The governing coalitions that adopted the measures were either dominated by labour or led by pro-labour liberal parties. The labour movements were important for agreeing to go along with them, but the measures constituted one element in a broad "state socialist" set of experiments and compact between labour and the state.

In contrast, until the 1930s, American labour's ties to the Democratic Party and to progressivism were complicated and often tenuous (Yellowitz 1965, 44–70, 128–44). The unions began forging stronger ties to the Democrats during the Wilson Administration, but labour remained officially non-partisan. American labour's strongest allies in government were progressives, particularly those in the Democratic Party, but progressivism was a broad, diverse reform movement, as many commentators have noted. It spanned both political parties and championed a variety of causes. Many progressives were sympathetic to the working class and committed to social reform, but they viewed organized labour as a private interest group whose demands for "class legislation" were often inconsistent with the "public's interests" (O'Brien 1998, 27–30). Labour and progressives did not share similar class backgrounds, and they often held different beliefs about the appropriate role of government in society (Yellowitz 1965, 143). Progressives were disproportionately educated, middle-class citizens who worked through organizations that mostly wealthy patrons supported (Yellowitz 1965, 40–87). Labour's distrust of the state partly rested upon fears that it would be risky to place the fate of working-class interests in the hands of middle-class individuals. Many American progressives also saw a much more legitimate role for the state in industrial relations than organized labour. They thought that strikes and other tactics were "barbaric" and destructive for all parties involved. Even those progressives that supported labour's rejection of compulsory arbitration believed that the state had an obligation to protect the public's interests, particularly when labour disputes created major disruptions. For example, according to Rep. Townsend (R-MI), the sponsor of one of several measures to establish compulsory investigation of labour disputes, "whatever maybe the effect upon the employers and employees, it is our duty to legislate for the people. Special interests, however powerful, must, if needs be, give way to the public good. Neither capital nor labor would be safe under a Government controlled by any other principle.… We simply ask by this bill for a fair, just, and impartial publicity of the causes which bring disaster to the people whom we serve" (quoted in Fisher 1922, 41).

Many American progressives put forward measures like those in Australasia. Proposals for compulsory and voluntary arbitration were so popular in the late nineteenth and early twentieth centuries among American economists, civil servants, and other reformers that it was dubbed the "middle class panacea" (quoted in Abrams and Nolan 1983, 378–9). American progressive reformers inside and outside of government made "numerous proposals for compulsory arbitration laws … following the bitter and sometimes bloody labor disputes of the 1870s and 1880s" (Abrams and Nolan 1983, 378). In New York State, these efforts gained strength in 1901–4, but ultimately failed when labour and many businesses opposed them (Yellowitz 1965, 142). In the first decade of the twentieth century, members of Congress introduced several bills for compulsory investigation of industrial disputes (though not arbitration) in industries involving interstate commerce. Reflecting progressives' faith in the influence of public opinion, and in the state's capacity to act as a neutral third party in industrial disputes, sponsors of these bills believed that the public awareness of the findings from such investigations would bring about public pressure to moderate the demands of each side and hasten an agreement (Fisher 1922, 39–40). Only one of these bills made it out of committee with a favourable recommendation.

Over time, progressives became less and less interested in compulsory arbitration. No progressive champion of compulsory arbitration with ties to labour ever emerged at the national level, and supporters of such measures were never more than a minority in the US Congress. Progressives' waning interest in compulsion may have been due to labour's adamant opposition to it and its ability to use the fragmented state structure in America to defeat compulsory proposals, or it may have been due to the growing interest in compulsion that anti-labour conservatives exhibited, particularly by the 1920s, when progressives became as opposed to compulsion as labour was.

An Alternative Path for Compulsion? Conservative Elites in Search of Order

Although the Australasian route to compulsory arbitration was unattainable in the United States, another plausible pathway existed. Like many public policies, compulsory arbitration did not necessarily favour one side or the other in industrial relations. Compulsory measures were not intrinsically progressive and pro-labour. Indeed, many Australasian labour organizations had misgivings about supporting compulsory arbitration, supported it only because employers and economic conditions threatened their survival, and because their closest political allies in government sponsored the legislation. Compulsory arbitration could also be attractive to governments that were not supporters of (or supported by) labour organizations but that were under pressure to maintain industrial peace. Although compulsory arbitration in Australasia was part of a compact between the state and labour, in which labour gained security and recognition in return for its willingness to cede much of its autonomy in labour negotiations, it was possible to adopt the measure without such an arrangement. As some American employers and their allies in government figured out, compulsory arbitration could be fashioned in a way that constrained labour without guaranteeing workers' rights to join unions and freely choose their representatives (Lecht 1955, 39).

The American state's most serious flirtations with compulsory measures came under the auspices of conservative responses to unrest from within the Republican Party in the 1920s. The immediate post–First World War period was one of intense conflict between capital and labour. In 1919, with the cost of living rising and the constraints of wartime lifted, unions became aggressive; most employers, meanwhile, remained implacable foes of unions and readied themselves for battle. Particularly in critical industries where unions were strong, such as railroads and coal mining, businesses and conservatives began to reconsider their opposition to arbitration schemes. As unions grew in strength, outbreaks of industrial unrest became more frequent, with serious impacts on those industries. In addition, many businesses were now under the regulation of the Interstate Commerce Act, making it more difficult for them to engage in the kind of anti-competitive behaviours in which they could easily pass along higher labour costs to consumers. By the first decade of the twentieth century, many railroad managers, such as F. A. Delano, president of the Wabash Railroad, came out in favour of compulsory arbitration (Fisher 1922, 44; Typographical Journal 1911, 520). The 1902 Industrial Commission recommended strengthening the Erdman Act "by imposing penalties on the party which refused to accept arbitration ... and prohibiting strikes and lockouts before a case was submitted to arbitration" (Lecht 1955, 24). In 1905, President Theodore Roosevelt and the Republican Party endorsed compulsory investigation of industrial disputes, similar to the policy recently adopted in Canada, and several bills were debated in Congress in the years leading up to the First World War containing such provisions, particularly for the settlement of railway conflicts (Fisher 1922, 41–2; Lecht 1955, 24). The railroad unions and the AFL strongly objected to those bills, and they never reached the floor for a vote. But that was not to be the end of Republican efforts to legislate compulsory measures.

FEDERAL RAILROAD LABOUR POLICY

The disruptive potential of often violent railway strikes that began in the 1870s and 1880s led to a succession of federal laws to cope with them. Although Congress endeavoured to foster voluntary dispute resolution throughout the history of the railroad industry, compulsory arbitration was seriously considered on multiple occasions, especially during the 1920s (Zakson 1989). The first piece of railroad labour legislation, the Arbitration Act of 1888, set up a system of voluntary arbitration after Congress rejected an alternative bill that contained compulsory arbitration (Lecht 1955, 15). Some members called for more interventionist measures, but the opponents of compulsory arbitration argued that trying to enforce arbitration awards over the objections of thousands of railroad employees who might refuse to work would be impractical and would amount to involuntary servitude (Zakson 1989, 324). The rarely used Arbitration Act of 1888 was followed by the Erdman Act in 1898, and following that, the Newlands Act of 1913. All relied upon voluntary measures.

The Erdman Act was inspired by Richard Olney, the attorney general during the Pullman strike of 1894, and the US Strike Commission appointed by President Cleveland in the wake of the strike. Olney orchestrated the hardline federal response to the strike and conceived of using the Sherman Act to justify getting the courts to issue an injunction against the American Railway Union, the first use of what would become the most potent weapon in the hands of anti-union employers (Eggert 1967, 152–85). After the strike, Olney evolved in his thinking about the best policy to handle strikes. He still believed that sympathy strikes should not be permitted, but he also concluded that compulsory arbitration was needed to avoid the damage that strikes wrought to both employers and employees (Eggert 1967, 203, 210). Like Olney, the Strike Commission, recommended arbitration as an alternative to the "barbarism" of the "wars" between capital and labour and called for compulsory enforcement of arbitration awards (Magnusson and Gadsby 1920, 40). Two of the commissioners worked with the House Labor Committee to draft a bill to replace the 1888 Arbitration Act that was like Olney's proposal. A federal strike commission would have the power to investigate disputes and publicize them. Following that, as with the Act of 1888, either one of the parties to a labour dispute could submit their complaints to arbitrators. Unlike the 1888 Act, the arbitrators' decisions would be binding upon them as long as both sides agreed to abide by the decisions at the time, they submitted the dispute to arbitration. However, the compulsory features of Olney's proposal were weakened when the final legislation excluded Olney's recommendation that, in the case of serious strikes, if "parties refused to arbitrate or abide by the award of an arbitration commission," the government would issue an injunction to seek to restrain employees from striking or it would take over the railroads. The railroad unions and operators objected to this provision, although both ended up supporting the bill

(Eggert 1967, 216–17). (Labour supported the bill enthusiastically because Section 10 prohibited yellow dog contracts and threatening employees who joined labour organizations, which the Supreme Court would later nullify [Lecht 1955, 18].) Erdman, the bill's floor manager, argued that voluntary arbitration was better than compulsory arbitration because both labour and management were opposed to compulsory measures (Eggert 1967, 222).

The closest the federal government came to adopting compulsory arbitration came in the debate over post–First World War railroad labour policy. At the war's end, the question arose as to how to settle labour disputes in the railroads and similar industries once they were turned back to private owners. The conservative and progressive wings of the Republican Party reunited in 1918 and re-gained control of Congress, vowing to return the railroads to private owners and to clamp down on the unions, which had done well during the war. With wartime machinery for avoiding industrial unrest disbanded, labour militancy increased. In many instances, labour leaders were unable to control rank-in-file sympathy strikes. The Republicans returned to power by exploiting public fears over the unrest and promising a "return to normalcy." They blamed the unrest on the Wilson administration's wartime policy of granting unions the right to organize and bargain collectively, in addition to the other concessions, in exchange for a no-strike pledge (O'Brien 1998, 74–5).

How to restore industrial peace in the railroads became the focus of debate over the Transportation Act of 1920 (the "Esch-Cummins Act"), and specifically the powers of a new Railroad Labor Board (RLB) created under it. Compulsory arbitration had widespread public support and split the business community, with the railroads in favour of it (Witte 1952, 35). Once again, labour rejected compulsory arbitration and the weakening of the legal status that it enjoyed during the war, which included the right to join unions and a prohibition against carriers that interfered with employees' selection of their representatives (Fisher 1922, 79; Lecht 1955, 39). Within Congress, the "old guard" Republicans pushed for it; Democrats and progressive Republicans opposed it. The bill that passed the Senate, sponsored by Senator Albert B. Cummins (R-IA), included compulsory arbitration and a strike prohibition; the one in the House did not. When the bill introduced by Rep. John J. Esch (R-WI), the chair of the House Energy and Commerce Committee, came to the floor, a group of conservative Republican members offered an amendment to include compulsory arbitration. The amendment was defeated by a coalition of Democrats and progressive Republicans, 203–189. Esch opposed the amendment, arguing that, while compulsory arbitration was good in theory, it was unworkable because it would be too difficult to enforce awards if thousands of employees refused to work under them (O'Brien 1998, 79, 234 note 150). This was a frequent criticism of compulsory arbitration and had appeared in debates over earlier proposals (Eggert 1967, 221). The anti-strike language was also deleted. When the bill went to a conference committee, "[f]or three weeks, House and Senate conferees fought about whether this machinery [the Labor Board] would provide compulsory or voluntary arbitration" (O'Brien 1998, 88). In the end, the Senate conceded to the House and the committee excluded compulsory arbitration from the final legislation.

Although the Transportation Act of 1920 did not contain compulsory arbitration, it strayed a good distance from the earlier statutes' total reliance upon voluntary methods of dispute resolution. The federal government became heavily involved in determining wages and other conditions of employment on the railroads (Lecht 1955, 46). One of the parties to a dispute could petition for an "adjustment board" or, where the RLB thought that a dispute was "likely to substantially interrupt commerce," could establish a board in order "to decide all disputes involving grievances, rules or working conditions." The RLB also had the authority to hear and decide all disputes concerning wages and issues the adjustment boards left unresolved (Guaranty Trust Company of New York 1920, 25–6; Zakson 1989, 355). However, the Board could not compel compliance with its decisions. It could rely only upon the pressure of public opinion, which the Supreme Court eventually affirmed in a case brought against it (Lecht 1955, 45). The Transportation Act thus included a mix of compulsory and voluntary elements, stopping just short of compulsory arbitration.

It did not take long before the unions and railroad companies objected to the RLB's decisions. The breaking point came over the Board's handling of the Shopmen's strike of 1922. These workers were not members of the four established railroad brotherhoods, and the rail operators insisted on an open-shop strategy and cut their wages. After the walkout of hundreds of thousands of workers, the Board encouraged the rail operators to hire replacement workers and declared that the strikers had given up their arbitration rights. The Board's decision ended any faith that the railway unions had in the RLB and fuelled further unrest. The RLB's efforts to resolve the dispute through negotiation failed and the unions boycotted the RLB (Lecht 1955, 43). Following that, Supreme Court decisions found that the Board had overstepped its authority. Its *Pennsylvania Railroad* decision in 1923 undercut the RLB's powers and encouraged the brotherhoods to ignore the Board's decisions (Zakson 1989, 358; Lecht 1955, 44–5). In the end, the RLB's authority was not commensurate with its efforts to resolve railroad disputes by setting wages (Lecht 1955, 46).

The RLB's failure to end the 1922 strike, the widespread perception that its actions made reaching a settlement more difficult, and the court's weakening of its authority, renewed debate in Congress about whether the Board's powers should be strengthened. In response, anti-labour, "old guard" Republicans in Congress once again pushed for compulsory arbitration, this time with the backing of President Harding, who sought to expand the Interstate Commerce Commission's jurisdiction to include the arbitration of industrial disputes. Harding had appointed Ben W. Hooper, a strong advocate of the Kansas Industrial Court, to head the RLB. But the turmoil that that the Board caused under Hooper in the 1922 shopmen's strike made it more difficult to argue for further strengthening the state's coercive powers in handling industrial disputes. The split between the anti-labour "old guard" and progressives within the Republican Party over compulsory arbitration persisted. Harding's death in 1923 denied the supporters of compulsory arbitration a key ally, effectively ending the federal government's consideration of compulsory arbitration. Harding's successor, Calvin Coolidge, shared neither the old guard's support for compulsory arbitration nor its desire to discipline labour (O'Brien 1998, 96–113; 122–3).

THE KANSAS EXPERIMENT

The singular instance in which American policymakers adopted compulsory arbitration took place in Kansas in the early 1920s. The Kansas experiment was short-lived and failed to spread to other jurisdictions. Nevertheless, how this anomaly came to fruition sheds further light on the overall American failure to adopt compulsion. Some of the circumstances that gave rise to Kansas's adoption of a compulsory measure were similar to the adoptions in Australasia and Canada. An industrial relations crisis that severely affected the public order and convenience set off a search for a bold policy innovation. After the First World War, a nationwide miners' strike ensued after mine owners rejected the miners' demand for a substantial wage increase. Kansas, in particular, was hard hit. The strikers shut down the mines in the state, and the nationwide strike prevented the importation of coal from elsewhere. The state experienced hardship and widespread anxiety – "people were suffering, schools and churches closed, public utility services curtailed and thousands in industrial establishments unemployed because coal was lacking" (Gagliardo 1941, 25). The governor's attempt to negotiate with the union, which was led by an uncompromising local president, proved fruitless. Railway unions, which refused to haul non-union coal, ignored a court injunction and orders to return to work. The state recruited volunteers to mine coal, but this proved difficult because of their lack of experience.

Also, like Australasia and Canada, the Kansas experiment was the brainchild of a progressive reformer-policy entrepreneur, William Huggins. The Pullman strike of 1894, in which many men lost their jobs and were blacklisted because of their involvement, had a major impact on Huggins. Like his counterparts in Australasia, Huggins believed that the state could play a constructive role in controlling industrial conflict in an age when large concentrations of capital and labour unions, acting irresponsibly, could do grave harm to the public. He believed that a "legal substitute for the strike" could be devised that protected the public and workers from costly strikes and still ensured that workers were treated justly. Like other reformers, Huggins saw a legitimate place for unions in industrial relations in protecting workers and advancing their interests, but he criticized "radical" union members whom he considered bad citizens (Gagliardo 1941, 28, 41). Huggins cited a Supreme Court case in 1916, *Wilson v. New*, that made it possible for Congress to intervene to avert strike-induced emergencies, as legal authorization for laws intended to protect the public. The Industrial Court would have jurisdiction over essential industries like food products, fuel, utilities, and transportation. Similar to the Australasian statutes, the law incorporated and recognized unions, gave workers the right to join them, and gave unions the right to represent their members and bargain collectively. Unincorporated unions were given the same rights. The Court had great powers to modify any agreement between the parties if it found it unreasonable. Strikes, boycotts, and the like were outlawed, although workers were free to quit employment. Unlike the Australasian laws, citizens who were not parties to labour-management disputes could initiate proceedings and the Court had perhaps somewhat more expansive powers over industry (Gagliardo 1941, 248).

What distinguishes the Kansas experiment from those in Australasia was the lack of support from labour for the policy. Even though American unions enjoyed much of the same level of security in law as those in Australasia, it remained outside of the governing coalition in Kansas. This made it possible for organized labour to remain unanimously and adamantly opposed to the Industrial Court (Gagliardo 1941, 242). The unions viewed the Court as an effort to destroy them and impose "involuntary servitude."[2] Employers supported the restrictions on labour, but opposed any that were placed upon themselves (39–40). During the years in which the Court existed, both the unions and employers chafed under its authority to control wages and working conditions (Gagliardo 1941, 203–15). Within Kansas, the Republican Party took pride in passage of the law, which had considerable public approval for a while; the Democrats exploited labour's opposition and the problems that the Court eventually encountered (Gagliardo 1941, 238–40).

In the end, compulsory arbitration did not survive judicial scrutiny either. The Kansas Supreme Court upheld the law, but the US Supreme Court in 1923 invalidated most of its important provisions and left it a dead letter in *Chas. Wolff Packing Company v. Court of Industrial Relations of the State of Kansas* (Gagliardo 1941, 180–93, 227; O'Brien 1998, 113). The Court's ruling made it certain that other states would not follow Kansas's lead and indicated that a federal law would have been struck down as well. The Court signalled that point in the *Pennsylvania Railroad case*, when it ruled that the RLB should not have compulsory powers if Congress thought about giving it to them (O'Brien 1998, 113).

The judicial impediment to compulsory arbitration was undeniably significant in understanding why the United States never had such a policy. However, any explanation for the failure of such a policy needs to begin with the role of the American labour movement, progressives, and conservative policymakers at the state and federal levels. The adoption of the Kansas Industrial Court and the serious consideration given to compulsory arbitration in Congress in deliberation over railroad legislation in the early 1920s shows that compulsory measures could reach the agenda and even be adopted, despite labour's opposition. In Kansas, an acute crisis, a committed policy entrepreneur, and a Republican Party that was open to the idea, and importantly, not dependent upon labour's electoral support, made the innovation possible. A very similar set of conditions existed in Congress, except for the lack of Republican unity.

A policy of compulsory arbitration without labour had a greater chance of adoption than one that included labour, but not a greater chance of survival. In the wake of the defeats for compulsory arbitration in the Kansas experiment and the Transportation Act of 1920, neither national party supported compulsory arbitration in their 1920 platforms, even for public utilities; the Republican platform rejected it in 1924 and the Democratic platform made no mention of it (Gagliardo 1941, 204–6, 227).

Voluntarism Eludes American Labour

We have seen that Gompers and the mainstream of the American labour movement were staunch advocates of voluntarism. Labour sought to pressure and bargain with employers free of state regulation. Yet, no real-world industrial relations system could be totally self-regulating. Unions might avoid incorporation, registration, and compulsory mediation, conciliation, and arbitration, but at minimum, they needed the state to legalize their organizations and nonviolent activities and protect them from employers who refused to recognize their legitimacy and used the courts to hobble them. British labour had achieved these basic protections by the first decade of the twentieth century.

Americans adopted the legislative framework for a voluntarist regime by finally outlawing the labour injunction and other roadblocks with the passage of the Norris–LaGuardia Act in 1932, but it was quickly superseded by New Deal labour legislation in 1933 and 1935. Why did Americans fall short of establishing a voluntarist industrial relations regime? Based upon our analysis of the British case, the United States lacked two key conditions that made voluntarism possible in Britain. First, by the turn of the century, many American employers had become adamant foes of unions, while most British employers, having established an accommodative relationship with organized labour decades ago, remained resigned to working with the established unions. In both nations, judges mainly supported the employers, but in the United States, parliamentary supremacy did not exist. But even after the judicial impediments were swept away, American employers continued to resist unions and any industrial relations policies that sought to assist them. Second, American unions lacked for many years the kind of strong attachments to political parties that helped British labour translate political mobilization into statutory changes that effectively banished employer and judicial threats to unions. Even though labour eventually forged stronger ties to the Democratic Party, it eschewed the option of forming a labour party. Of these two conditions, as we shall see, employer hostility proved to be the most consequential and enduring obstacle to voluntarism.[3]

Hostile Employers

American employers, by and large, were adamantly opposed to unions and were much less inclined to make their peace with them than their British counterparts. Arthur Shadwell, a British observer who conducted a first-hand, detailed study of industrialization and social conditions in Britain, Germany, and the United States in the first decade of the twentieth century, wrote (1913, 552):

> Nothing has struck me more in the course of this investigation than the remarkable difference of attitude towards trade unions displayed, in private, by employers in this country [Britain] and in the others. I have not heard a single word in favour of trade unions from any employer in Germany or America.... [T]he prevailing feeling is strongly hostile; employers hate and dread the unions. In England I have met with no such feeling at all. I have heard the unions unfavorably criticized and sometimes condemned, but without bitterness; I have far more often heard from employers and managers fair and even friendly expressions of opinion.

Writing in the 1930s, the historian Lewis Lorwin (1933, 35) echoed this judgment when he concluded that "in no other country" had employers "so persistently, so vigorously, at such costs, and with such conviction of serving a cause opposed and fought trade unions as the American employing class." More recent scholarship has come to the same conclusion. In his study of the American steel industry's destruction of unions in the late 1800s (lasting until the 1930s) and the survival of British unions, Holt (1977, 30, 34) found that "the most striking difference between the two situations concerns the behavior of employers," which is that "British employers were more willing to tolerate the existence of unions in their mills than their American counterparts" and "offered little resistance to union growth while [Americans] generally fought back vigorously." Similarly, Brown (1983, 112) writes that British employers were "passive in their relations with the unions, less aggressive individually than American employers [and] less willing to combine for defense and attack than employers in both continents."

American employers had a long list of tactics with which to fight unions. There were, of course, the liberal ideological arguments that individual businesses and business groups deployed before courts and legislative bodies. The National Association of Manufacturers, for example, fought the union shop by arguing that the individual worker's right to contract without a union was infringed upon. Business appropriated the labour movement's own devotion to voluntarism against it. They invoked the core principle of voluntarism – freedom from coercion – to argue that they should be free to make contracts with individual employers and not be forced to accept unions (Salvatore 1984). These arguments were often supplemented with an array of practices meant to coerce and intimidate. According to Morris (2005, 21), "companies inundated their employees with anti-union propaganda and threats, frequently enforced yellow dog contracts, employed labor spies, organized company unions, discharged union adherents, exchanged blacklists of union militants, obtained labor injunctions to suppress union activity."

American employers were not only less tolerant of unions than their counterparts in Britain, but their confrontations with them were more violent, which may be a manifestation of the depth of resolve to resist unions (Jacoby 1991, 183; for comparisons between the United States and other nations (see also Jamieson 1973, 3; Clegg 1976). American employers "resorted to the use of goon squads and armed force" (Morris 2005, 21). According to Dulles (1966, 247), "strong-arm guards were often employed to beat up the trouble-makers while incipient strikes were crushed by bringing in strikebreakers under protection of local authorities."

Rarely did British industrial disputes involve violent confrontations between workers and the police, whereas major strikes in America often turned bloody, as in the cases of Homestead, Haymarket, Pullman, and the steel strike of 1919. According to Jacoby (1991, 191), "British employers received far less government support whenever they sought to use the state's repressive apparatus in disputes with organized labor," which he and others have traced to the political influence of the landed aristocracy's lack of sympathy for employers' interests and their desire to avoid social conflict. Instead, "at a relatively early date the British state began to apply pressure on its employers to eschew violence and to recognize unions and bargain with them, long before the emergence of [the] Labour [Party]," such as through the reports of royal commissions and the government's efforts to mediate industrial disputes. Fox (1985, 78) identified the British state's reluctance to get involved in and prosecute parties to labour disputes as far back as the early nineteenth century. Bringing to bear the coercive powers of the state on labour relations contradicted the voluntarist ethos of a neutral state that did not compel either side to take action.

American employers were not only resistant to unions, several studies suggest that their resistance shaped the American labour movement in ways that weakened it and made it more conservative. In comparing American and French unions' propensity to strike, Friedman (1998) notes that American unionists learned to be cautious and restrained because of the dominant hostility that they faced from employers and the state. Voss (1993) attributes the demise of the Knights of Labor, in part, to the activities of employers' associations. In the short run, the defeat of the Knights provided an opportunity for the AFL to fill the vacuum. In the longer term, the lessons learned from the Knights' demise inculcated a cautiousness and sectarianism to American labour. Had the Knights survived, the American labour movement would have been more inclusive, egalitarian, radical, and more inclined towards mass political mobilization than the AFL turned out to be.

Why were American employers so much more resistant to unions than their counterparts in Britain (and other industrial nations)? British and American managers operated in very different social, economic, and political contexts that shaped their values and calculations in ways that induced varying levels of acceptance of unions.

SOCIAL AND ECONOMIC DIFFERENCES

Scholars have developed several explanations for why most American firms resorted to union-busting and the open shop while most of the British accepted unions and engaged in collective bargaining and trade agreements. Some have argued that the very different social status and position in the class structure of businessmen in Britain and the United States shaped their political influence and orientation towards labour. Entrepreneurship was not considered as socially prestigious in Britain as in the United States, and British businessmen had to contend with a landed aristocracy that still had considerable social standing and political influence in the nineteenth century. To be accepted by the aristocracy, British businessmen were expected to demonstrate some measure of *noblesse oblige*, avoid conflict, and not appear rapacious. According to Jacoby (1991, 191), "compared to American management in its reaction to the Wagner Act, British employers were more receptive to their government's message because of the respect accorded to a monarchical state and because, from the very beginning, necessity had forced them to get along with other powerful groups ... whose interests were different from their own." Without a landed aristocracy and monarchy, American business, by contrast, had no powerful interests with which to contend (Jacoby 1991, 189–90; Lipset 1962). They were much freer to run their businesses in a way that treated workers as they would any other commodity, even if it created considerable conflict. They constructed their identities around their success as businessmen and "success" meant the growth and profitability of their enterprises, which they believed was the source of American prosperity (Ernst 1991, 135).

Others contend that British business lacked the superior financial and organizational resources that American employers possessed to fight unionism. Many American industries were far more concentrated than those in Britain. The Carnegie Company in 1892 and U.S. Steel in 1902 squeezed the steelworkers' union into submission by maintaining full production and profits in some plants while others were shut down because of strikes (Holt 1977, 29). American companies also had more money to spend on "employee welfare and personnel management" that discouraged non-union employees from joining unions (Jacoby 1991, 190). Small to mid-size firms did not have the immense resources of the giant corporations, so they engaged in cooperative employers' associations, which emerged between 1895 and 1920 with the main purpose of busting unions by supplying strikebreakers and other assistance. They often accomplished their goal (Harris 1991). According to Bonnett (1922, 24), from the turn of the century up to the outbreak of the First World War, "there was a distinct evolution in belligerency [towards unions] among old [business] associations and in numerous newly formed ones." British employers' associations, in contrast, were comparatively weak due to "the large number of relatively small and independent companies and the divisions of interest between [sic] them" (Reid 1991, 36–40). American companies also had their own armed guards and police, or rented them, an option not available in Europe, where the state had a monopoly on arms and the use of force (Jacoby 1991, 183).

Industrial structure and the timing and pace of the introduction of new technology and of unionization also varied across nations and industries, which meant that British employers faced different economic incentives than their American counterparts. Although many American and British industries faced sharp competition in the late nineteenth century, they responded to different incentives. In some British industries, such as ship building, employers "lacked a strong desire to move away from established craft methods" (Reid 1991, 48). They found ways to increase efficiency that did not involve challenging craft production, and in fact, preferred craft controls over the new technologies and management practices. Mass production technologies in ship building had limited applicability. Craft production could more efficiently accommodate fluctuations in demand for products, the customer-specific nature of the products, the need for highly skilled workers and labour-intensive production (Reid 1991).

But in many other industries, employers in both nations sought to take advantage of new technologies and management practices that would cut costs and raise productivity. Craft workers stood in the way because they insisted on controlling production. American firms dealt with the situation by resisting unions, while the British worked with them, as best exemplified by the survival of the Terms of Agreement into which British machinists and engineering firms entered and the demise of the Murray Hill agreement in the United States (Haydu 1988, 29–33; see also Derber 1983; Robertson 2000, 98–9). According to Haydu (1988, 34), "American managers had less to gain from trade agreements, and less to lose from abandoning them, than their British counterparts." First, American firms were further along in adopting new technologies and management tools, which meant that they relied less on skilled union workers and found craft restrictions more onerous. Second, American unions were weaker than British unions, making it easier to fight them. Employers who wished to collaborate with unions were likely to make their unions stronger, putting them at a disadvantage with competitors who still enjoyed weak or non-existent unions. Third, because American industries were more concentrated and firms more specialized, employers found less of a need to use unions to moderate competition across firms and parts of the country. American collective bargaining took place at the firm level, which made it enticing for individual firms to gain a competitive edge by keeping unions out. The structure of British industry – small, more specialized, family-owned firms – induced multi-employer bargaining because such firms could not tolerate cost differentials. The British organized unions and collective bargaining on a district level, which brought together multiple employers (Jacoby 1991, 190). Wage rates tended to be uniform and stable since individual firms could not undercut each other.

Haydu argues that "these differences" between Britain and the United States "were long standing" and grew out of the timing of economic development in the two nations. Recall that British employers enjoyed the advantage of early industrialization, allowing them to dominate world markets and making it easier for them to accept having to deal with unions. "Export demand could be met through an expansion of employment within the technical status quo, avoiding confrontations over established work practices" (Haydu 1988, 35). Although British firms came under sharp competition by the late nineteenth century, unions had by that time taken firm hold for forty years in Britain and most employers pragmatically accepted the fact that they were there to stay. By contrast, "no legacy of collective bargaining existed to sustain the Murry Hill Agreement in the face of widespread disputes over wages in 1901," except in Chicago, where collective bargaining survived because conditions were close to those experienced in Britain – strong unions and a history of collective bargaining (Haydu 1988, 36). Economic growth in the United States came later and more rapidly in the nineteenth century, led by the development of new product markets and labour scarcity. Rather than expand traditional manufacturing practices, American employers sought out new labour-saving production technologies and practices. Strong unions emerged at a time when skilled craftsmen were already under pressure and in this context they "seemed to endanger both employers' right to manage and the success of their businesses."[4]

Haydu's analysis also casts doubt upon broad-brush explanations based upon "national character" – such as the celebration of individualism in the United States and paternalism in Britain. How employers should treat unions was a matter of debate around the turn of the century, with elite economic organizations like the National Civic Federation promoting trade agreements and other forms of employer–union cooperation. Employers and unions, such as the International Association of Machinists and the National Metal Trades Association had set in place a foundation for a more cooperative industrial relations system. Employers' associations did not reflexively fight unions, and some sought to work with them on trade agreements until after 1901 when they turned against them (Bonnett 1922, 24). Furthermore, Haydu (1988, 36–9) shows that where industrial conditions in the United States were like those that dominated in Britain, the open shop was more likely to be rejected (e.g., the railroads, printing, the building trades, and coal mining); conversely, where conditions in Britain resembled those in the United States, employers were less likely to accept unions (bicycles and automobiles).

POLITICAL DIFFERENCES

American business usually could rely, as we have seen, upon powerful state actors to protect it from unions. Employers had no reason to recognize and bargain with unions knowing that they could call upon the courts, military, and police to restrain them. Employers might have been forced to accept the union shop and collective bargaining had they not found a powerful ally in these institutions. Much more than in Europe, American governments used police, militias, and occasionally federal troops to come to the aid of employers, usually to put down violent confrontations between union men and strikebreakers (Jacoby 1991, 183; Lorwin 1933, 355).

Much of the literature on why voluntarism was so difficult to establish in the United States identifies the courts, along with the police and military, as major impediments (Forbath 1991; Hattam 1993; Archer 2001). Courts used common law doctrines, like "freedom of contract"; the injunction; and statutes like the Sherman Act to bring a wide range of union activities under the "unlawful" rubric of equity law (Forbath 1991; Hattam 1993). In *Buck's Stove and Range Co. v. AFL*, *Loewe v. Lawlor*, and other cases, they turned the Sherman Act's anti-trust provisions against unions (Greene 1998, 153–5). Courts ruled that not only could the unions be ordered to cease and desist from strikes, boycotts, and the like, but they could be sued for damages. State and federal injunctions numbered in the thousands in the last decade of the nineteenth and first decades of the twentieth centuries. The courts reasoned that strikes, boycotts, and other tactics to bring pressure on employers infringed upon their property rights. Several American legal experts eventually assailed the abuse of the injunction, most famously Frankfurter (1930).

Temporary injunctions could immediately delay strikes and other union actions. By the time a trial was held to see if the action was lawful, the strikers were long ago forced to disband and employers had time to hire strikebreakers and make other adjustments. Judges, without the use of juries, often issued sweeping injunctions restraining everyone "whomsoever" got involved in a labour action, often in the absence of consideration of the context in which the action was taken and without a legal theory or proof that the specific action was unlawful and used technical legal language that laypersons could not understand (Robertson 2000, 183–5; Gregory 1958, 97–104). The state also deployed the police and military, and employers used private security forces, to intimidate, arrest, and violently repress strikers.

The courts continued to issue injunctions even after organized labour secured the Clayton Act in 1914. Although the Act appeared to deny the courts the authority to issue injunctive relief in most labour disputes, it also included a clause that stated injunctions were permissible "to prevent irreparable injury to property, or to a property right, of the party making the application" (quoted in Forbath 1991, 157; see also Greene 1998, 248). In *Hitchman Coal and Coke Co. v. Mitchell* (1917) the US Supreme Court ruled that the United Mine Workers union infringed upon the coal company's property right in its workforce when it tried to unionize miners. The employment contract between the company and its individual workers, which included a yellow dog contract that forbade workers from joining unions, was sacrosanct. In *Deering v. Duplex Printing Company* (1921) the Court sided with employers' interpretation of the Clayton Act, which was that courts could enjoin labour unions from engaging in secondary boycotts. What Gompers had declared "labor's Magna Carta," was, according to the Supreme Court, simply a codification of the common law that already existed regarding labour injunctions (Lovell 2003, 101).

Thus, American courts gave American employers critical institutional leverage and emboldened them to continue to resist unions. The courts' rulings in favour of employers' property rights and "freedom of contract" claims must have bolstered their resistance to labour organizations.

While British courts were also hostile to unions for a time, culminating in *Taff Vale* and similar cases involving civil liability, American courts were much more threatening to labour unions for a prolonged period of time for two reasons. First, the injunction was aimed at virtually all economic actions in which unions engaged. Federal courts and most state courts considered a very broad scope of activities enjoinable, including most strikes, picket lines, and boycotts (Gregory 1958 103–4). In contrast, British courts applied injunctions against labour unions sparingly. Keeping with tradition, they issued injunctions only if labour unions' actions threatened irreparable damage to tangible property (e.g., broken windows, damaged equipment). American courts, on the other hand, construed any economic pressure brought by unions as harming or threatening to harm "property" that included intangible losses in production and customers that were not necessarily irreparable (Gregory 1958, 97–8). Second, American courts had an institutional advantage that British courts did not, which augmented their influence. The British system of parliamentary supremacy gave the legislature the last word on the law of the land. Once Parliament weighed in with the Trade Disputes Act of 1906, the courts retreated from playing a large role in industrial relations. American courts, on the other hand, were an independent, co-equal branch of government with the power of judicial review, which helped sustain their attacks on unions (Hattam 1993).

We should not exaggerate the importance of the courts and the absence of Parliamentary supremacy, however, in trying to explain the failure to establish a voluntarist industrial relations system in the United States. The courts were not omnipotent, and they eventually curtailed their anti-union actions. Employers, though, continued to thwart labour's efforts to establish a voluntarist system even *after*

Congress curbed the courts' ability to restrain unions under the Noris–LaGuardia Act of 1932. Ultimately, then, it was employers who remained the implacable foes of labour. It is chiefly because employer recalcitrance in recognizing unions persisted after 1932, that a voluntarist system would never become a viable option in the United States and make a greater role for the state inevitable in industrial relations. We shall return to this point in the conclusion to this chapter and in chapter 7.

Labour's Legislative Weakness and Union–Party Ties

While employer and judicial hostility towards labour proved to be potent obstacles to achieving the kind of voluntarist system to which the AFL aspired, labour's lack of political capacity and effective strategy to overcome the opposition was also part of the story. British labour, after all, had to win a decisive legislative victory to guarantee voluntarism's survival in the face of employer and judicial assaults at the turn of the century. The United States would finally adopt legislation removing the courts as a threat to labour unions in 1932, twenty-five years after it came to Britain, but not primarily because of labour's political influence.

THE FAILURE OF LABOUR'S ANTI-INJUNCTION LEGISLATIVE EFFORTS
American labour was not so weak that it could not get labour law reform on legislative agendas at the federal and state levels. But until 1914, it faced serious obstacles in getting proposals enacted into law. Although House Speaker Joseph Cannon and members of the Labor Committee were sympathetic, Congressional Republicans blocked labour legislation in Congress until 1910. After that, anti-injunction bills either died in the Senate, which was not popularly elected until 1913, or President Taft (the "injunction judge") vetoed measures that reached his desk.

The AFL's seemingly golden opportunity came during the Wilson administration with legislation that culminated in the passage of the Clayton Act. The AFL launched its campaign to end the courts' use of injunctions against unions by supporting bills introduced by Rep. Pearre (R-MD) whose language was unambiguous.[5] Instead of passing the Pearre bill, Congress drafted the Clayton Act, which Gompers hailed as "labor's Magna Carta," but as we have seen, turned out to be a hollow victory because judges continued to issue injunctions against unions in the years that followed passage of the Act (Lovell 2003; Eskridge 1994, chapter 3).

A debate exists over whether American jurists interpreted the Clayton Act contrary to clear Congressional intent, or whether Congress wrote the law in ways that enabled the courts to continue using the labour injunction (Gregory 1958, 167–73; Lovell 2003, 101–54). The most recent scholarship argues that organized labour was aware that the courts could use the ambiguous language in the Clayton Act to rule against the unions, but that they lacked sufficient political power to force Congress to pass, and the Wilson administration to accept, stronger legislation that labour preferred (Lovell 2003, 154–7). Section

20 of the Clayton Act was not as clear about restricting labour injunction as the earlier Pearre bills had been and left interpretation in the hands of the courts. According to Lovell (2003, 154), "Instead of using the new law to establish a clear congressional position on the injunction and antitrust issues, legislators deliberately created conditions that allowed judges to continue to make crucial policy decisions. Because the confusing language in the labor provisions could support multiple interpretations, the justices who settled interpretive questions faced a choice between plausible alternatives rather than a choice between following or rejecting the clearly expressed will of Congress." Lovell's (2003, 155) explanation for this outcome rests on the conclusion that labour was insufficiently influential in Congress: "there were no labor organizations in a position to force legislators to pass anything but a very compromised bill in 1914." Labour was unable to get its allies, including President Wilson, to go along with key amendments that would have crafted the statute more to its liking. Nor was it able to defeat the amendments of its proponents to add qualifications and ambiguous language that afforded the courts opportunities to interpret the statute against labour's interests. Thus, the same provisions in the Clayton Act that the labour movement criticized earlier, it ended up supporting because "labor leaders were well aware that they did not have the political power to produce the kind of legislation that they thought would best control the courts" (Lovell 2003, 46–7).

Why did labour lack the necessary political influence to force the enactment of stronger legislation? As we have seen, British labour also faced hostile courts and employers at a decisive point in the development of its industrial relations system. Of course, Parliamentary supremacy was an important institutional advantage for British labour, but it would have been useless if the movement had been unable to bring effective political pressure to bear upon Parliament and win a sweeping victory that cemented the voluntarist system for decades to come. Thus, we need to look more closely at the reasons for American labour's inability to secure more effective legislation.

One place to look is how the two nations compared in their rates of labour union density. Labour's political strength rests typically on the size and strength of trade unions. Highly unionized workforces provide critical resources for labour's electoral and legislative mobilization. In the years in which the British Trade Disputes Act and American Clayton Act were adopted, 1906 and 1914, respectively, the differences in labour density between the two nations was modest, around 12–13 per cent in Britain and 9.7–11.5 per cent in the United States (Bain and Price 1980, 37, 88; Booth 1995, 13; Friedman 1999, 77). It seems unlikely that union density would account for the divergent legislative fortunes of labour in Britain and the United States, given the low absolute levels of unionization in both nations and modest difference between them. Even if British unions had higher density rates, they had to *translate* that advantage into effective political influence.

Of greater significance than union density was the relationship between the unions and the established political parties in the two nations. Labour movements in the Anglophone world at the time had three broad choices for how they would position themselves vis-à-vis the party system. They could maintain non-partisanship by eschewing alliances with specific parties and "rewarding friends and punishing enemies" of both parties instead. Two, they could develop close relationships with one of the major, established "bourgeois" parties. Or three, they could cultivate independent labour representation that would eventually culminate in the formation of a working-class party that would compete with the established parties.

The strategies that the mainstream British and American labour movements pursued were strikingly different. British labour in the years leading up to the passage of the Trade Disputes Act of 1906 pursued options two and three. It worked very closely with the Liberal Party and had begun the process of establishing the Labour Party. The American movement got off to a halting start in developing its ties to the Democratic Party and the ties that it developed prior to the New Deal were more tenuous. It also decisively rejected the formation of a working-class party. We address the links between the unions and the established, "bourgeois" parties first and follow up with a discussion of the working-class party option.

TRADE UNION – "BOURGEOIS" PARTY TIES IN BRITAIN AND THE UNITED STATES

Decades before passage of the Trade Disputes Act, British unions established close ties with the Liberal Party's radical wing, which was highly supportive of their aims in Parliament. Working-class members of Parliament, most of them trade union and labour leaders, began running as Liberals in 1874, long before the adoption of the Trade Disputes Act of 1906. These "lib-labs" were bound to the party by their long-lasting attachment to radicalism (Biagini and Reid 1991). The Trades Union Congress (TUC) became a key pressure group within the Liberal Party, and several unions identified with the party on a number of socio-political dimensions. Before the 1906 election, the Parliamentary Representation Committee of the TUC and the Liberals reached an agreement where they would not run candidates to compete with one another in a number of constituencies. It was these strong links that the unions had forged with the Liberals that allowed them to bring substantial pressure on Parliament. The Liberals increased their seat total from 183 to 397. The radicals, led by Prime Minister Campbell-Bannerman, dominated the Liberal government (Greene 1998, 100). Thus, the Liberal Party that swept to power in a landslide in 1906 was the unions' primary instrument for enacting the Trade Disputes Act (despite the misgivings of some of their key Liberal allies that they were being granted excessive immunity).

American labour was far behind the British in forging ties with one of the established parties. The AFL decided in the 1890s to eschew not just parties but political action altogether in favour of confronting employers in the industrial sphere. By the turn of the twentieth century it was clear that its approach would not work and it would have no choice but to turn to politics to remove court-imposed barriers to collective action. The failure of efforts at business–labour collusion, rising employer insistence on the open shop, and increased judicial protection of employers' interests spurred labour's political action. "The union shop strategy [of the AFL] made it imperative that government fully protect unions' ability to strike, boycott and picket employers" (Robertson 2000, 73). Gompers and the AFL clung to their anti-statist beliefs, but they realized that they could only attain their goal of a voluntarist industrial relations system if they mobilized politically.

Now that the AFL embraced political action, it had to decide *how* it would engage innational politics. The AFL rejected party politics and moved instead to develop into a non-partisan lobbying organization at the federal level. By 1896, the AFL was lobbying on a host of issues including an eight-hour day, immigration, the injunction, and arbitration. The lobbying campaign encountered two obstacles that rendered it ineffective. First, Republicans showed no interest in giving labour a hearing and the Democrats were out of power until 1913 (Salvatore 1984, xxxv). Second, employers counter-mobilized. To prevent the AFL from securing legislation that would enable it to exert economic pressure on employers to secure the union shop, the National Association of Manufacturers (NAM) emerged as a key business group opposed to unions and launched an aggressive grassroots campaign focused on Congress.[6] Opposition to labour became an objective that cut across an otherwise diverse set of business interests, but businesses that were the most attracted to the open shop drive were headed by "wealthy businessmen one significant step below the trusts" in more competitive sectors of the economy (Greene 1998, 92).

Labour realized by 1906 that lobbying was fruitless, and it needed to mobilize in the electoral process to make its influence felt. Its anti-party commitment meant a rejection of any formal alliance with the Democrats or Republicans as well as an independent labour or other third party representing workers (Greene 107–11). Instead, labour would follow a policy of "rewarding friends and punishing enemies," regardless of party affiliation. Like labour, business was officially non-partisan, but because it worked most closely with Republicans, the AFL started aligning itself with the Democrats between 1908 and 1910, initially in the race for president, and then for Congress (Greene 1998, 104, 159–62). Most trade unionists who ran for office did so as Democrats, and the AFL supported mostly Democratic candidates (Greene 1998, 138). Although still officially non-partisan, from 1906 until 1922, the AFL informally backed Democratic candidates in most races for Congress and the presidency, though unfortunately Democrats controlled Congress and the presidency in only six of those years (Greenstone 1977, 31). In the decades preceding the New Deal, the unions were not fully integrated into the Democrats' campaign operations and did not enjoy the close ties that their counterparts did in Britain with the Liberals. The AFL's attachment to the Democrats waned in the 1920s when the Party nominated candidates who were less committed to labour's interests.

BRITISH UNIONS EMBRACE AND AMERICAN UNIONS REJECT A WORKING-CLASS PARTY

While their alliance with and pressure on the Liberal Party was the primary means by which the British unions succeeded in getting the Trades Unions Act accomplished, part of that pressure included the continued development of the Labour Party. The *Taff Vale* decision had been the catalyst that accelerated the unions affiliation with the Labour Representation Committee and the unions' push to formally establish the Labour Party in 1900. The alliance between the Liberals and the Labour Representation Committee was based upon a 1903 agreement in which Liberals and Labour agreed not to compete head-to-head in about fifty constituencies where Labour was stronger. The agreement worked to the advantage of both the unions and the Liberals in 1906, but the pressure of independent labour representation was a serious long-term threat to the electoral base of the Liberals. While the Liberals' gains in the House of Commons dwarfed Labour's in the 1906 election, the threat of independent labour representation was clearly an effective political tool for the unions.

Likewise, while the American labour movement's comparatively weaker ties to the Democratic Party prior to the New Deal was the primary reason for labour's political weakness in Washington, the AFL's rejection of forming a working-class party was also relevant. Just because the British Labour Party was not the main mechanism for translating union political strength into favourable legislation does not mean that an American working-class party might not have been of great help to American labour's efforts to do the same.

The mainstream of the American labour movement considered whether it should form a party expressly devoted to representing working-class interests most critically during the industrial unrest and economic turmoil of the 1890s. While industrial unions were more supportive of a working-class party than the craft-dominated AFL, the AFL held a dominant position in the movement as a whole. The Morgan program was brought before the AFL's 1893 convention along with a proposal from the Knights of Labor to endorse People's Party candidates. An English expatriate socialist who settled in Chicago pushed the idea and patterned his plan after the British movement's activities in independent labour politics. It consisted of ten policy planks ranging from the AFL's long-standing demands for the eight-hour day to public ownership of the means of production. At the same time, workers were increasingly attracted to populism and a new People's Party was gaining adherents. Through a series of parliamentary manoeuvres at the 1894 convention, Gompers prevailed in blocking the AFL from endorsing a labour party. Virtually all the AFL-affiliated unions voted in favour of the Morgan program, and hundreds of union members ran as People's Party candidates.

Attendees at the 1894 AFL convention approved all the Morgan program's individual components except for collective ownership of industry, but then voted the entire program down by a vote of 1,173 to 735. It also rejected a resolution praising British labour for pursuing independent labour representation. Gompers assembled a broad coalition of unionists who were willing to get the Federation involved in politics without involving it in political parties. His coalition united the unions that wanted either no involvement in politics or only non-partisan involvement, which left the socialists and populists in the minority.

At the same convention, the supporters of the Morgan program elected John McBride as president of the AFL and sent Gompers into exile for one year. McBride was more favourable towards independent labour politics than Gompers, but he ran into illness and corruption charges during his presidency, giving Gompers the opportunity to return as AFL president. Gompers won back the presidency by a narrow vote of 1,041–1,023 and reconsolidated his control over the organization. The Morgan program was once again voted down and the convention adopted an explicit declaration that "party politics shall have no place in the conventions of the AFL" (Greene 1998, 63-4). The AFL debated whether to form a labour party next at its 1901 convention in Scranton but rejected it again in favour of "pure and simple" union politics. Gompers defeated socialist and non-socialist supporters of a third party in 1902 and 1903 as well (Greene 1998, 77-8).

The consequence of the AFL's rejection of independent labour politics and its anti-partyism limited labour's strategy for attaining anti-injunction legislation became apparent twenty years later, when the time was most auspicious for gaining adoption of anti-injunction legislation once and for all. Although it clung to an official position of non-partisanship that "rewarded friends and punished enemies," it supported Wilson and other Democrats in the election of 1912 on the promise that they would pass injunction relief. Having settled on a political strategy that favoured "pure and simple" unionism and the rejection of a labour party, Gompers was under pressure from within the labour movement to show that his approach could produce results. This pressure grew, and along with it calls for an independent labour party, when efforts to get Congress to pass an anti-injunction bill went nowhere in the first year of the Wilson administration. Gompers warned Wilson and the Democrats in 1913 (as he had done a few years earlier) that continued lack of responsiveness to labour's legislative demands could result in the AFL's endorsement of an independent labour party over his opposition (Foner 1980, 98). Neither Wilson and the Democrats nor Gompers wished to see an independent labour party emerge, but that did not mean that Wilson would capitulate to labour's specific preferences on how the anti-injunction bill would be written. According to Lovell, Wilson knew that Gompers needed a concrete legislative achievement more than he needed an ideal bill since "the danger for Gompers was that holding out for the strongest possible law would leave him with nothing to show for his endorsement of

Wilson, and thus little basis for resisting calls to form an independent labor party in time for the 1916 presidential election" (Lovell 2003, 159).

Whether the AFL could have gained stronger legislation if it had not compromised and supported the Clayton Act is doubtful. British unions were in a much stronger position vis-à-vis the Liberal Party in 1906 than the AFL was with the Democrats in 1914. Fifty-four trade unionists were elected to Parliament in 1906 compared to only seventeen trade unionists (which was a record number) elected to Congress in 1912 (Foner 1980, 118). And British labour enjoyed a Liberal prime minister (Campbell-Bannerman) who was a much stronger and more consistent supporter of trade union demands than President Wilson (see chapter 4 and Foner 1980, 131).

REASONS FOR THE REJECTION OF A WORKING-CLASS PARTY
The reasons for the absence of a working-class party in the United States have been the subject of scholarly examination for at least a century and are at the centre of many debates over "American exceptionalism." Attempting to resolve that debate here would go beyond the purpose and space limitations of this volume. Robin Archer (2007) conducted the most recent exhaustive examination of this question in his comparative study of the United States with Australia. After rejecting a long list of reasons frequently given for this phenomenon, Archer concluded that two "proximate factors" along with more deeply entrenched conditions seem to explain it. One is the weakness of "new unions" of unskilled and semi-skilled workers that emerged in industries across the Anglophone world. The new unionists had stronger class identities than craft workers and were the most enthusiastic proponents of the formation of a labour party. American new unionists experienced higher and more severe levels of repression than their Australian counterparts, which weakened them and left the more cautious and less inclusive craft unions in a dominant position especially within the AFL.

The other proximate cause was the fear throughout the AFL leadership that pursuit of a working-class party would further weaken the labour movement by fostering dissention within its ranks. The potential for dissention and fragmentation arose, first, out of the "intense Democratic and Republican loyalties of American workers" (Archer 2007, 239). American workers had already developed strong ties to the existing parties given the early extension of voting rights to all white males early in the nineteenth century. These attachments cut across regions, communities, and ethnic groups. Gompers feared that endorsing candidates of a particular party, or organizing a labour party, would create disunity and friction within the movement. Local unions also saw advantages in not having the AFL affiliate with a particular political party because it made it much easier for them to support whatever party they wished in their areas (Greene 1998, 70). The divisions that emerged in the labour movement when labour engaged in nationwide voter mobilization efforts for the first time in 1908, confirmed

Gompers's view about the difficulties and risks entailed in trying to persuade American workers to support one particular party. Labour parties emerged in some big cities where considerable union support existed for creating "independent political action [i.e., a labour party], but Gompers and the AFL leadership opposed them" (Greene 1998, 218–19). The AFL developed a close relationship with the Democratic Party nationally in 1908 to advance its two most important issues – anti-injunction legislation and amending the Sherman Act (Greene 1998, 162–3). Analysing a series of state and local races in the 1908 election, Greene (202) revealed "the difficulties involved in attempting to tie organized labor to one party across the United States." A prosperous economy gave the Republicans and NAM an electoral advantage. They framed the campaign for workers in terms of Gompers trying to "dictate" to workers whom to vote for and painting organized labour as a "special interest" (Greene 1998, 162–76). Democrats and labour focused on the issue of labour's legal rights, but that issue proved insufficiently inspiring for many workers. In the end, a great many workers remained loyal to the socialists or the Republicans, and did not heed Gompers's advice to vote Democratic, or they supported the Democrats' presidential candidate, William Jennings Bryan, for national office, but fell back on their traditional partisan loyalties by voting against Democratic candidates in state and local races (Greene 1998, 211–13). The election ended badly for labour and the Democrats with the reelection of President Taft (the "injunction judge") and several of labour's Congressional enemies, including Speaker Cannon (Greene 1998, 217). Labour turned to more elite-oriented politics after 1908 and never again engaged in mass mobilization during the remainder of Gompers's lifetime (Greene 1998, 225).

AFL leaders also perceived that "religious conflicts" and "socialist sectarianism" also threatened the unions' existence. A labour party that was forced to take sides in disputes between Catholics and Protestants would pit workers' loyalties to their deeply held religious beliefs against their class interests. Religion played a less important and divisive role in Australia (Archer 2007, 239–40). While both the US and Australian trade union movements were divided along various reformist and socialist factions, the more doctrinaire European socialist camps had a much stronger presence in the United States and were thus a more divisive force. Gompers associated the formation of a labour party with the AFL's socialist adversaries. Gompers's embrace of "pure and simple" unionism was inconsistent with the socialists' more radical policy proposals and their goal of capturing state power through the election of socialist majorities. Ironically, the socialists aided Gompers's efforts to block the formation of a labour party because they saw labour parties as a moderate alternative (in both goals and tactics) to their own Socialist Party. Gompers teamed up with left-wing socialists to defeat the formation of a strong American labour party (Greene 1998, 220–1).

Third, Gompers feared that the creation of a labour party would compete with the unions for workers' loyalties and that they would be an autonomous actor that might threaten the primacy and autonomy of unions in the labour movement (Greenstone 1977, 29). The AFL saw weakening workers' partisan attachments as necessary for strengthening their attachments to unions and to strengthen the AFL's control over workers' loyalties (Greene 1998, 69). Gompers seized upon the remarks of British unionists visiting the United States at the time, who urged American workers to turn away from the "plutocratic" Democratic and Republican parties just as British workers had turned away from the Liberal and Conservative parties in Britain (though he ignored their suggestion that they follow the lead of their British brethren and form a labour party) (Greene 1998, 67, 70). Gompers clung to the belief that trade unions were "natural" organizations that worked best for workers when they operated on their own (Greene 1998, 60). He shared the view of many of the progressive reformers at the time that party bosses and machines were corrupt. He likened party domination to "slavery" for workers because the parties kept workers "chained" and only unions could free them from the parties so that they could pursue their interests (Greene 1998, 66–7). Greene (1998, 67–8) argues that anti-partyism was congruent with the strong republican streak in American political culture and was an important value for nineteenth-century American workers. The factionalism of parties was viewed as incompatible with civic virtue and concern with the welfare of the nation as a whole.

Conclusion

The adoption of legalism in the United States is partly accounted for by Americans' rejection of the two main alternatives – statism and voluntarism. Statism involved a measure not only of compulsion, but of direct involvement by the state in setting wages and other work conditions. This was particularly the case in the strongest version of statism – compulsory arbitration. Except for employer hostility towards unions, none of the other conditions that led to the adoption of compulsory arbitration in Australia and New Zealand were present in the United States. The conditions in Australasia were very special. The nature of the crisis there that drove both the state and organized labour towards compulsory arbitration was acute industrial unrest combined with a very severe depression. The unions were decimated in the process, and fear that the economy would not rebound permeated these nations. American labour's negative experience with the courts and politics generally and Gompers's devotion to voluntarism through his long and powerful tenure as head of the AFL eclipsed the enthusiasm for compulsory arbitration from some quarters of the American labour movement. Only a crisis on the scale experienced in Australasia would have shaken labour's opposition to compulsion and might have pressured American progressives in government to turn to compulsory arbitration. Industrial unrest in the United States was partly kept in check through repression, which was in some sense a substitute for compulsory arbitration. In the United States, a comparable crisis did not occur until the New Deal period when compulsory arbitration was already off the table and elements of the legalist approach had emerged. Until the New Deal, progressives in the Democratic Party and organized labour had a more tenuous relationship than they did in Australia and New Zealand. Progressives were unable to control the national government, and even under the Democrats and President Wilson, progressives made few efforts to convince labour that compulsory arbitration could work in its interests.

At the turn of the century, the main alternative to statism in the United States was voluntarism. The mainstream of the American labour movement tried to follow the British example by establishing voluntarism, and it worked to pressure employers and eventually policymakers to achieve that goal. Compared to their British brethren, most American employers were much more hostile towards unions and worked assiduously to thwart their efforts to build their organizations, gain recognition, and represent their members. In this, they had a powerful ally in the judiciary and could often enlist the coercive powers of the police and military. While British courts were often similarly anti-labour, they were not willing to use the labour injunction on a frequent basis, as American courts were. And British employers did not have the police or military to rely upon. Finally, not only did Congress not enjoy supremacy over the courts, as the British Parliament did, but American labour was in a politically disadvantageous position to exert pressure through the party system. Even after the American labour movement abandoned non-partisanship and lobbying, and began to ally itself closely with the Democrats, it simply did not have sufficient leverage over the party to push through legislation to remove the courts as an obstacle, a task that it made all the more difficult by rejecting the formation of a labour party or any other mechanism for independent labour representation that might have put pressure on the Democrats to be more supportive. There were opportunities to establish closer ties between the unions and the established parties or to launch a working-class party. But these opportunities were either lost due to chance (John McBride's shortened tenure as AFL president) or were rejected because they went against the grain of the interests and calculations of Gompers and the movement that he led.

The anti-union activities of American courts and the political weakness of American labour were mainly important components of the causal story for why voluntarism did not emerge mainly insofar as they prolonged the period in which it would become clear that labour's quest for a voluntarist industrial relations regime was a fool's errand that could not be accomplished through legislative means. Of all the reasons for why a voluntarist regime eluded labour and the United States, employer hostility stands out as the most formidable and persistent obstacle. Eventually, Congress removed the injunction as an anti-union weapon when it enacted the Norris–LaGuardia Act in 1932, though notably less because of labour's political clout than for other reasons. Labour also overcame Gomperism when it constituted itself as a key part of the New Deal Democratic coalition. But even that could not bring about a durable voluntarist regime, as we will see in the next chapter when the Roosevelt administration tried to implement the National Industrial Recovery Act's labour code according to voluntarist principles. From the perspective of the 1930s and the decades to follow, American labour's quest for a voluntarist regime had indeed turned out to be quixotic. It missed the fundamental reality that voluntarism could not be achieved through the removal of legal obstacles, since the role of policy was very limited and subordinate to the basic relationship between business and labour organizations, and specifically whether the two accepted each other as legitimate partners in industrial relations.

Voluntarism in Britain rested only partly on Parliament's willingness to tame the courts and enact legislation, giving labour wide latitude to pursue its interests in its confrontations with employers. The establishment of these broad legal parameters was only part of what was necessary for voluntarism. The other part was a willingness of employers to permit labour to freely organize, to establish collective bargaining institutions, and follow through by bargaining in good faith. As the name implies, "voluntarism" rested on the voluntary acceptance of unions and collective bargaining. That, in turn, rested on the belief that both sides were legitimate partners or at least that acceptance of the other side and a willingness to work together was more expedient than refusing to do so. Ultimately, then, it was employers who remained the implacable foes of labour. It is chiefly because employer recalcitrance in recognizing unions persisted after 1932, that a voluntarist system would never become a viable option in the Unitd States, making a greater role for the state necessary in industrial relations. But the many anti-union employers in the United States regarded decisions related to working conditions as exclusively under their control and part of their managerial privileges. The continued resistance of business led inevitably to the need to construct an elaborate, ongoing regulatory apparatus to police industrial relations.

7 The Legalist Answer: The United States

The breakdown of voluntarism was a function of adversity, the unions coming to the government when hard times set in.

(Irving Bernstein 1950, 23)

The national labor relations bill which I now propose is novel neither in philosophy nor in content. It creates no new substantive rights. It merely provides that employees, if they desire to do so, shall be free to organize for their mutual protection or benefit.... [T]his principle has been embodied in a long train of other enactments of Congress.

(Sen. Robert F. Wagner, *Congressional Record*, 74th Congress, 1st Session, Volume 9, 21 February 1935)

Americans fashioned a unique answer to the labour question that we call *legalism*. In no other country did legal concepts and arguments figure so prominently in how reformers and advocates of every stripe defined industrial relations issues and the solutions that they devised. Nowhere else was labour policy so entangled in judicial decision-making. Legalism culminated in the National Labor Relations Act (NLRA) of 1935, or "Wagner Act," which put in place labour rights and employer responsibilities and an independent regulatory agency with the capacity to promulgate and enforce regulations policing the conduct of industrial relations.

Legalism involved far more state involvement in industrial relations than the voluntarist answer and far less than the statist answer. At some risk of oversimplification, legalism constituted a "third way" between statism and voluntarism, both of which Americans rejected. It did more than guarantee unions freedom to organize and the remove judicial impediments that employers could use to thwart trade unions, as voluntarism did. Under the legalist regime, the state mandated that employers recognize unions, refrain from discrimination or threats against organizers and members, and bargain in good faith. It empowered a regulatory body to make rules and rulings on myriad issues pertaining to the conduct of representation elections, "unfair labour practices," the size of bargaining units, and to issue cease and desist orders. However, unlike statism, it did not arbitrate disputes or in other ways seek to directly influence the outcomes of collective bargaining.

The explanation for the adoption of legalism in the United States parallels some of the same conditions that led Australia and New Zealand to adopt statism: employers refused to recognize unions and bargain with them in good faith and sought ways to undermine strikes and other union tactics; the state was compelled to regulate employers' behaviour and unions would have to work within a regulatory framework to secure their rights; these rights were won when employers' political power ebbed and the labour movement's political mobilization helped a liberal-labour governing coalition take power (which also parallels the British case); finally, progressive reformers devised and implemented a far-reaching set of principles and processes that constituted a new industrial relations regime.

That is where similarities with the other nations ends, however. Because American employers never destroyed the American labour movement, unions and most public officials could avoid imposing a statist answer to the labour question and by the time the unions and their allies had the political and constitutional leverage to create a new regime, statist solutions were no longer viable, if they ever were. As a result, American progressives and their labour union allies turned to legalism, which created a legal framework for the recognition and certification of trade unions and mandated collective bargaining but did not outlaw strikes and lockouts or prescribe the terms on which disputes would be settled.

The process that led to legalism – "breakdown and culmination" – was one in which both the critical juncture set off by the Great Depression of the 1930s as well as antecedent conditions played critical roles. In the absence of the critical juncture, either pro-business Republicans would have continued to control the federal government, or a Democratic majority would have been highly constrained and less responsive to the demands of labour and progressives. When the crisis of the Great Depression brought the Democratic Party to power in the 1930s, employers' influence was diminished and labour's rose. Since organized labour was a key component of New Deal coalition, the Roosevelt administration's recovery program mandated labour rights. Implementation of the program exacerbated industrial strife and fuelled a decisive showdown between labour and employers. Organized labour prevailed when progressives, led by Senator Wagner, strengthened their numbers in Congress in the 1934 election and passed the National Labor Relations Act (Wagner Act), whose constitutionality the US Supreme Court upheld. Certain antecedent conditions were also critical to the adoption of legalism. While the Wagner Act applied legalist principles of industrial relations through virtually the entire economy and the implementation of labour rights in Section 7(a) of the recovery program created vital enforcement mechanisms, legalism as an overarching policy prescription had developed over several decades prior to the crisis in the work of progressive jurists on new legal doctrines that conceived of unions as agents for workers and "responsible unionism," regulatory actions of the First World War Labor Board, and the Railway Act of 1926. For all its innovation, the Wagner Act represented continuity with the pervasive legalism of what had come before it. In the second quote at the beginning of this chapter, no less authority on the importance of these critical antecedents than Senator Wagner commented on the contributions of these earlier efforts to enshrine labour rights in American law. Finally, as recounted in the last chapter, the failure of efforts to institute compulsory arbitration in the 1920s cleared the way for legalism by removing that option from consideration in the 1930s.

The Critical Juncture: Voluntarism Fails and a Legalist Answer Emerges

Permissive Conditions of the Critical Juncture

ECONOMIC DEVASTATION AND SOCIAL DESPAIR

The Depression began in 1929 with the stock market crash and lasted for a decade. The crisis grew deeper as time wore on, so that on the eve of the new Roosevelt administration in 1933 it had taken a devastating toll. The litany of casualties is well known: unprecedented levels of unemployment, wage and profit declines, bankruptcies, stock losses, bank closures, and various manifestations of social and psychological suffering (Kennedy 1999, 162–7). The nation's gross national product had fallen to half of its 1929 level, and business investment represented only a fraction of what it was a few years earlier. Production of materials like lumber and steel plummeted, creating ripple effects throughout the economy for the production of finished consumer goods like automobiles. As a result, one in every four workers was unemployed, about 17 million male and female wage earners, in every conceivable occupation. Three-quarters of the value of stocks had vanished, wiping out the holdings not only of many wealthy Americans, but also of middle-class retirement accounts and the savings of college endowments, community banks, and other organizations. Bank failures numbered over 5,000, hundreds of thousands of individuals and families lost their homes and businesses due to foreclosures and bankruptcies. Municipalities ran out of money as tax revenue dried up and demands for relief shot up. Combined with a long drought, farm income fell precipitously, and many farm families were driven off the land. As David Kennedy (1999, 172) summed up the situation, "[t]he Depression was a wholesale social catastrophe that fell indiscriminately on vast sectors of American society."

REDUCED POLITICAL INFLUENCE OF EMPLOYERS AND REPUBLICANS

The crisis loosened the constraints on industrial relations that anti-union forces in American politics had imposed for half a century. It reduced the political power and legitimacy of the business community. Business retained considerable economic power, to be sure, but it was politically weakened. The Republican Party's "old guard" was decimated as well, as progressive factions of both parties made gains in 1930 and the GOP's electoral fortunes continued to decline in succeeding elections.

THE CRISIS WITHIN A CRISIS: THE NIRA RAISES LABOUR'S EXPECTATIONS AND INDUSTRIAL UNREST

We shall discuss the NIRA in detail under the productive conditions of the critical juncture, but the promulgation and implementation of Section 7(a) of the NIRA created such a high level of industrial unrest and conflict within the Roosevelt administration and between various agencies and employers and labour unions that it was seen as endangering economic recovery. The situation was untenable, had all the appearances of heightening class warfare, and gave further warrant for those who sought a sharp break with the politics and policies of the past.

Productive Conditions of the Critical Juncture

LABOUR'S POLITICAL MOBILIZATION AND THE NEW DEAL REALIGNMENT

While the elections of the early 1930s were permissive conditions because they greatly weakened the political power of business and their allies in government, they were also productive because they did not bring to power just *any* new government. They brought the Democratic Party to power, with its history of support for labour (no matter how tepid it had been in the 1920s). More importantly, the 1930, 1932, and 1934 elections bolstered the influence of the progressive wing of the party. Even before Roosevelt came to power, Democrats wrested control of the House in the 1930 midterm elections. The composition of Democratic Congressional delegation also changed, with declines in the share of Southerners and increases in the ranks of northern urban liberals and Midwestern progressives (O'Brien 1998, 164–5).

The Democratic electoral gains in 1930 made it possible to enact the Norris–LaGuardia Act in 1932, which the previous Republican-dominated Congress had blocked (Forbath 1991, 163; O'Brien 1998, 158–9). Stimulated by the Depression and the presidential election of 1932, labour's participation in electoral politics rose and it helped elect Roosevelt and the Democrats, paving the way for the enactment of the NIRA; its support for the Democrats rose further in the 1934 and 1936 elections as millions of workers in Northern industrial cities flocked to the party (Bernstein 1950, 43; Sundquist 1983, 214–18). The party benefited greatly from reapportionment after the 1930 census, which increased the number of urban House districts (Finegold and Skocpol 1995, 136). Besides the unions, a broader set of working-class organizations and movements mobilized, including the unemployed, farmers, and others (Piven and Cloward 1977, 41–96). These groups created an "atmosphere of social protest and radicalism" by operating outside conventional channels of political participation and engaging in confrontation and disruptive tactics (Goldfield 1989, 1270–1).

The Democrats' huge victory in the 1934 midterm election, combined with the failure of the NIRA's Section 7(a), opened the door for the enactment of the Wagner Act (Gross 1974, 139). Given the typical pattern of the party in control of the White House losing seats in Congress during mid-term elections, the Democrats' gains of nine seats in the House and ten in the Senate was (and continues to be) a historical record (Brookings Institution 2016). Organized labour augmented its support for the Democrats, which made it a potent force in Congress and led directly to the passage of the Wagner Act (Bernstein 1950, 88; Gross 1974, 142–3). Despite solid and adamant business opposition, organized labour now had an overwhelming advantage. Even legislators who otherwise would not have voted for the Wagner Act did so, in part, to avoid opposition from the AFL at the polls and in part because they assumed that it would be declared unconstitutional.

THE LABOUR MOVEMENT ABANDONS VOLUNTARISM

The AFL's abandonment of voluntarism is linked with the dire circumstances of the Great Depression. Not surprisingly, the unions' concern with the high jobless rate led them to abandon voluntarism most clearly in their endorsement of government provision of relief for the unemployed and unemployment insurance, a sharp break from Gompers's opposition to these ideas and his insistence on self-help (Bernstein 1950, 23–5). The AFL did not abandon voluntarism until the spring of 1933, just as the Roosevelt administration took office and began formulating its economic recovery program.[1]

PROGRESSIVE REFORMERS DEVELOP AND CONGRESS ADOPTS THE NORRIS–LAGUARDIA ACT

The crisis induced Congressional progressives to adopt three principal pieces of legislation in the area of industrial relations. The last was the Wagner Act, but the first – the Norris–LaGuardia Act of 1932 – mixed elements of voluntarism and legalism. On the one hand, it clearly aspired to establish a voluntarist labour regime; indeed, it "usher[ed] in a period of almost complete freedom for union expansion through economic self-help" (Gregory 1958, 223). By ending (in most cases) the labour injunction and the yellow dog contract, Norris–LaGuardia embodied the core idea of voluntarism, which was that of "insuring free enterprise for all" (Gregory 1958, 225). It declared labour's right to organize and bring as much economic pressure to bear upon employers as they could muster, without any aid or hindrance from the government.

It might be more apt to label US labour policy *quasi*-voluntarist for two reasons. First, under it American unions never attained the legal immunity that the British enjoyed. Norris–LaGuardia did not set out to distinguish between legal and illegal union conduct, but merely to deny the federal courts' equity powers in the use of the injunction. Even if labour union conduct was no longer enjoinable, it still might be illegal; under the anti-trust laws, for example, if strikes and boycotts were found to be conspiracies in the restraint of interstate commerce. Money damages and criminal prosecutions were still a possibility (Gregory 1958, 253–76). Writing just after Congress adopted Norris–LaGuardia, Lorwin (1933, 400) observed:

> the right of trade unions to use the methods they have developed to obtain and enforce collective contracts remains uncertain. The legality of a strike is still contingent on its purpose, which may be declared unlawful according to the judgment of the courts. Sympathetic strikes, picketing, and boycotting have been severely restricted by court decisions, and may still be enjoined. The opportunity of the courts to interpret "threats and intimidation" in relation to the conduct of strikers so as to obstruct the success of a strike remains unrestricted. Damage suits and criminal prosecutions against strikers and active unionists remain a possibility.

The supporters of the Wagner Act would have to keep this in mind when they drafted the legislation.

The text of the Norris–LaGuardia Act also included important language on the rights of labour that anticipated the legalist regime that was to come soon and that New Deal labour statutes would essentially reiterate:

> Whereas under prevailing economic conditions, developed with the aid of governmental authority for owners of property to organize in the corporate and other forms of ownership association, the individual unorganized worker is commonly helpless to exercise actual liberty of contract and to protect his freedom of labor, and hereby obtain acceptable terms and conditions of employment, wherefore, though he should be free to decline to associate with his fellows, *it is necessary that he have full freedom of association, self-organization and designation of representatives of his own choosing, to negotiate the terms and conditions of his employment, and that he shall be free from the interference, restraint, or coercion of employers of labor, or their agents, in the designation of such representatives* or in self-organization or in other concerted activities for the purpose of collective bargaining or other mutual aid or protection. (quoted in Morris 2005, 18; emphasis added)

Thus, the transition to legalism, which would eventually culminate in the Wagner Act, had already begun, even before the Roosevelt administration's response to the Great Depression.

WAGNER AND OTHER PROGRESSIVES CHAMPION SECTION 7(A) OF THE NATIONAL INDUSTRIAL RECOVERY ACT (NIRA)

After Roosevelt's election, reformers and experts of various stripes offered a number of diagnoses for the Great Depression – overproduction (caused by cutthroat competition that depressed wages), misguided pro-cyclical actions by the government and lack of spending by the private sector, and under consumption (technology displaced workers, so that insufficient demand existed for what the economy produced) (Bernstein (1970, 18–27). Each diagnosis had a corresponding policy recommendation: allow businesses to fix prices and agree to limit output, expand public works, and cut workers' hours without cutting their incomes. Although the United Mine Workers called for a law that mandated collective bargaining rights, the AFL and most of the labour movement adhered to the third diagnosis and backed a bill that Senator Hugo Black introduced, which called for spreading employment by shortening work hours. Wagner and other members of Roosevelt's "brains trust" rejected the Black bill as unconstitutional (Gross 1974, 11).

At Roosevelt's request, Wagner assembled a group of reformers who came up with the National Industrial Recovery Act (NIRA). Wagner was the link between the Roosevelt administration, reformers, and the labour movement. The NIRA embraced the idea of overproduction and at its heart was government encouragement of collusion among firms in the same industry and a suspension of the anti-trust laws. Each industry developed and followed codes of conduct in order to fix output and prices (Gross 1974, 10; Bernstein 1950, 32, 131). From the drafting of the labour provisions of the NIRA to the passage of the Wagner Act two years later, Senator Wagner stands out as the pivotal figure without any doubt. Along the way, President Roosevelt and many members of his administration either were opposed to Wagner's support for labour's legislative interests or they remained on the sidelines and gave only tacit support. As Bernstein (1950, 128) put it, "the result [NLRA] was primarily the work of the Senator whose name it bore. He mobilized the draftsmen, devised the political strategy, and carried the brunt of the fight with the public, Congress and the White House."

Roosevelt did not view labour rights as integral to economic recovery, but Wagner added Section 7(a) to the NIRA, which echoed the language in Norris–LaGuardia, guaranteeing workers the right to organize, choose their own representatives, and bargain collectively with employers.[2] The key individuals who were responsible for the inclusion of the labour provisions (Section 7(a)) in the NIRA were Jett Lauck, the United Mine Workers economist; Wagner; Wagner's former law partner and legislative aide Samuel Rifkind; and Donald Richberg, a labour lawyer. All of them had extensive experience as progressive reformers earlier in the twentieth century. According to Bernstein (1950, 37), "the impetus for including it in the Act came from the union movement, spearheaded by the Mine Workers." And it was Lauck who was chiefly responsible for convincing UMW president John L. Lewis to abandon voluntarism and pressure Franklin Roosevelt as a presidential candidate for federal assistance in mandating collective bargaining in the coal industry (Bernstein 1950, 24).

Given the importance of labour to the New Deal coalition and the unfairness of having the NIRA facilitate business collusion while denying labour the same opportunity, they decided to add Section 7(a) (Bernstein 1970, 28; Bernstein 1950, 29–33, 37). According to one contemporaneous source, "all labor, and especially organized labor, would have been put into an ugly, resentful mood, if not given equivalent rights and opportunities" (Lyon et al. 1935, 417). AFL leaders and the UMW considered Section 7(a) a major breakthrough, and the *New York Times* opined that it signaled labour's rise to power (Bernstein 1950, 38). Once the NIRA was in effect, labour unions took their struggles for recognition out of the exclusively industrial sphere, where they were usually at a disadvantage vis-à-vis anti-union employers, and into the new administrative venue that the NLB provided, which included quasi-judicial hearings and deliberative sessions directed at cases brought before them.

The NIRA's design included important elements of voluntarism both conceptually and, as we will see later, in practice. The NIRA's labour policy was voluntary in the sense that it did not *require* that workers join labour unions or engage in collective bargaining, did not establish unions as the exclusive agents for collective bargaining, and left the door open for workers to join company unions. Organizationally, the National Labor Board (NLB), which the NIRA established for resolving labour disputes, was dominated by representatives of labour and business, with three members from each and Senator Wagner acting as its chairman. Because industrial unrest posed a threat to economic recovery, the NLB's main task was to resolve disputes as quickly as possible (Gross 1974, 20). The NRA conceived of the NLB's role as a mediator of disputes, again, in line with the NRA's neutral and voluntary ethos (Lyon et al. 1935, 461–6).

The NIRA's voluntaristic aspirations notwithstanding, key provisions of the NIRA drifted some distance away from voluntarism. Labour organizations, in particular, viewed the statute's declaration of workers' rights and employers' obligations, not as the government remaining neutral in industrial relations, but as coming to their aid. The statute admonished employers that employees were to be "free from the interference, restraint or coercion of employers" in organizing themselves, in choosing their representatives, and in "other concerted activities for the purpose of collective bargaining or other mutual aid or protection," and listed other restraints on employers. Second, at least theoretically, no longer would the collective bargaining agreements be only between private parties, but their terms would be binding legal commitments that could be enforced against employers who were not signatories to the agreements but that were in the same industry. Most importantly, the NIRA made clear that the coercive powers of the state could be used to achieve its goals by declaring that Congress sought "to induce and maintain united action of labor and management *under adequate governmental sanctions and supervision*" (quoted in Lyon et al. 1935, 415; emphasis added).

THE NIRA'S IMPACTS: UNION MILITANCY, EMPLOYER RESISTANCE, AND THE END OF VOLUNTARISM

Labour union militancy and political mobilization did not result mainly from the dire economic conditions of the Depression. More important were the New Deal and pre–New Deal policies of the early 1930s. The sharp rise in labour militancy that helped induce Congress to enact the Wagner Act did not occur until after Congress adopted Norris–LaGuardia and Section 7(a) of the NIRA. The first made labour organizing easier by removing the injunction and yellow dog contracts from employers' anti-union arsenal. The second encouraged unions to organize and demand that employers recognize labour organizations and engage in collective bargaining. For labor, passage of the NIRA signalled that the government considered unions and collective bargaining in the national interest, emboldening the unions to undertake organizing drives and strikes (Gross 1974, 14; Millis and Brown 1950, 22; Piven and Cloward 1977, 113–14; 121–51). The resulting upsurge in labour organization and militancy rivalled earlier episodes, like 1886 and 1894 (Bernstein 1970, 37, 40–53, 217–317). According to a study by the Brookings Institution at the time:

> [b]efore the Industrial Recovery Act was many days old, it became evident that Section 7(a) was operating as a potent factor in stimulating trade union growth and expansion. An organizing fever spread through the ranks of American labor recalling in scope and intensity the greatest labor organizing periods of the past.... The fear of employers which had long kept workers from joining trade unions was for the time being overcome. Paid trade union organizers, as well as voluntary self-appointed ones, not only emphasized the new freedom to organize, but asserted that the NIRA required the organization of both employers and workers to carry on collective negotiations. (Lyon et al. 1935, 489)

And according to Morris (2005, 25): "the trade union movement undertook a massive organizational campaign that exceeded any such activity since World War I, and ... immediately after passage of the Act, a wave of strikes swept over the country."

Passage of these laws also influenced employer behaviour, which further fed into the growing labour militancy. Most employers, who had opposed the labour provisions of NIRA, actively resisted the law's implementation (Bernstein 1970, 30, 32). The anti-union resistance constituted "an organized campaign of non-compliance in which entire industries acted in concert, supported by their trade associations and by the leading employer organizations" (Lyon et al. 1935, 483). As labour militancy and the employers' counter-offensive escalated, the number of industrial disputes in the United States doubled in 1933–4 from what they had been the year before. The number of workers involved in disputes, the number of working days lost to them, and the number of workers involved as a percent of union membership, all rose sharply (Ross and Hartman 1960, 194–205; Gross 1974, 15).

Employers resisted union recognition and collective bargaining in many of the largest and most critical industries, such as steel, automobiles, and rubber; in other cases, organizing drives petered out or achieved only partial success (Bernstein 1970, 93–115). ("Recognition" meant that a union was vested with exclusive authority to negotiate collective agreements on behalf of a relevant group of workers.) No longer able to avail themselves of yellow dog contracts and injunctions, employers turned to an alternative anti-union weapon – the company union – which they had originated during an earlier period of labour militancy, 1919–22 (Lyon et al. 1935, 523; Gross 1974, 22–4). "During 1933–34 company unions, in the form of 'employee representation plans,' experienced a growth even more remarkable than that of the trade unions" (Lyon et al. 1934, 523). Until passage of the Wagner Act, Conference Board survey data revealed that employers were making widespread use of company unions (see Morris 2005, 29). Employee representation plans enabled employers to exert greater control over workers by excluding "outsiders" (i.e., established, independent unions) and thus undermined the principle of workers being able to choose their own representatives (Bernstein 1970, 38–40). Thus Section 7(a), whose purpose was partly to help independent labour organizations grow by putting an end to company unions, stimulated the growth of the latter and, in turn, fuelled further labour unrest (Lyon et al. 1935, 526).

When we say that Section 7(a) had an impact on labour union and employer behaviour, we do not just mean the text of the statute and how it was interpreted. The lack of effective enforcement of NLB and NLRB decisions also had important effects. Inadequate enforcement shaped the perception among labour unions that the government was not interested in, or capable of, enforcing the law in a way that would benefit them and it emboldened employers to keep up their resistance to those decisions (Gross 1974, 129).

The Roosevelt administration was unprepared for the rise in union organizing efforts and the industrial unrest that ensued upon the adoption of Section 7(a). The upsurge in labour militancy and employer resistance led it to worry that they would forestall economic recovery (Bernstein 1970, 173; Lyon et al. 1935, 471). With Section 7(a) subject to conflicting interpretations and the National Labor Board given inadequate enforcement powers in the law, the National Recovery Administration dealt with the pressures and counter-pressures often by interpreting Section 7(a) in ways that bolstered the position of business in disputes that arose between labour and business (Gross 1974, 12–15), which fuelled further labour militancy and employer recalcitrance (Gross 1974, 62). Organized labour lost faith in the government's willingness to enforce Section 7(a) when President Roosevelt and the NRA intervened in the automobile strike and made a settlement that undercut the NLB's position.

We have seen that the NIRA included elements of both voluntarism and legalism. In practice, Section 7(a) operated, at least initially, in a voluntaristic fashion (Morris 2005, 25). The leaders of the NRA, General Hugh S. Johnson, and General Counsel Donald R. Richberg, adopted a decidedly voluntarist view of the NIRA statute. The government was to maintain a posture of "perfect neutrality" and detachment from the struggles between business and labour. The law, in their view, sought neither to promote nor to hinder labour organization or show a preference for one type of labour organization over another. Individual workers who chose to join labour organizations were to be protected from employers who would coerce or discriminate against them, but issues of recognition and representation were left up to individual workers and negotiations between them and employers. Senator Wagner also began his chairmanship of the NLB with strong voluntarist aspirations, commenting that the purpose of the NLB's labour and business representatives was to replace "war" between labour and management with "agreements through mediation" and conciliation (Morris 2005, 26). Writing shortly after the NLB's creation, Wagner noted: "The very brief experience of the National Labor Board has already demonstrated that practically all of the recent industrial conflicts can be amicably settled when the parties have been brought together to discuss their differences in an atmosphere of calmness and disinterestedness and with a clearer knowledge of their respective rights and duties. Cooperation based on mutual trust and understanding must be the keynote henceforward" (quoted in Gross 1974, 16).

For a few months, this approach worked (Gross 1974, 20–2, 31). According to Wagner, the NLB's main assets were the elite reputations of its members and the public's support for its work. Beyond that, the Board relied upon voluntary cooperation between the disputants.

If anyone had any doubts about the viability of voluntarism under the NIRA, experience with the law dispelled it. Over time, the NLB achieved fewer and fewer settlements through voluntary agreements (Gross 1974, 45). Within months after its creation, it moved away from trying to mediate disputes to handing down rulings on how labour representation and collective bargaining should operate. The root of the problem was that "almost all employers vigorously resisted union recognition unless it was forced upon them by strikes or boycotts. Not surprisingly, most of the strikes then occurring were for recognition" (Morris 2005, 26). In the context of heightened labour militancy and an employer rejection recognition of independent unions as exclusive bargaining agents, it quickly became clear that the NLB would have to act as a quasijudicial body rather than a mediator of disputes that would rest on voluntary cooperation. (Lyon et al. 1935, 490–1; Gross 1974, 46).

Neither organized labour nor independent observers viewed the NRA leadership as acting in a neutral fashion, despite its pretenses to such an image. As the labour scholar Lewis Lorwin concluded at the time, "the NRA ... threw its weight against labor in the balance of bargaining power between capital and labor" (Lyon et al. 1935, 465). Except in the few cases where unions were already strong and collective bargaining established, employers unilaterally wrote the labour standards contained in the codes, and the NRA did not insist that employers involve labour representatives (Lyon et al. 1935, 427, 442–3). Employers, similarly, dominated the enforcement of the codes' labour provisions and denied labour representation on the bodies that enforced them (again, except where the unions were well-entrenched) (Lyon et al. 1935, 458–9).

The NRA was "neutral" only in the passive sense of going along with whichever party applied the most pressure, which meant employers in most cases (Lyon et al. 1935, 443, 461). The NRA's hands-off policy in the resolution of industrial relations disputes was effectively anti-union. It permitted employers to set up company unions (as long as employees were not forced to join them). It did not require employers to extend exclusive recognition to labour organizations that represented majorities of employers (giving organizations that represented minorities of workers the same claims on legitimacy). And it allowed individual workers to make individual contracts with employers.

Conversely, employers increasingly saw the NLB as biased in favour of labour unions. These conflicts over the meaning and intent of Section 7(a) played out in a long series of cases in which the NLB tried to overcome employers' resistance to union recognition, collective bargaining, and their insistence on company unions (Lyon et al. 1935, 467, 490). Anti-union employers refused to permit the NLB and the NLRB from conducting elections for employee representatives, accept the principle of majority rule, bargain in good faith, and reinstate workers who had been dismissed for their union activities (Lyon 1935, 483). Convinced that the NLB was biased in the unions' favour (Gross 1974, 43), employers insisted that NLB/NLRB decisions were at odds with established legal interpretations of the rights and obligations of employers and employees and that the NLB would force unionization upon all businesses. Employers continued their resistance to administrative efforts to strengthen labour, often exploiting divisions between the National Recovery Administration and the NLB (Bernstein 1950, 100–2).

IMPLEMENTATION OF SECTION 7(A): POLICY LEARNING AND THE
CONSTRUCTION OF A LEGALIST REGIME

If the abandonment of voluntarism happened quickly under the NLB, the development of a viable legalist alternative did not. It took two years to resolve the difficulties related to the implementation of Section 7(a) with the eventual adoption of the Wagner Act. The source of the problems that the NRA and NLB encountered was the ambiguous language of Section 7(a), which permitted alternative interpretations on such contentious issues as company unions, exclusive representation, and the government's role in actively promoting independent trade unions (Gross 1974, 11). The law left unclear the procedures and principles that should guide the selection of employees' representatives and what actions by employers were prohibited in specific contexts. Its wording "was susceptible to interpretations that would sanction company unions, proportional rather than exclusive representation, and individual rather than collective bargaining ... [and] would also permit an employer to avoid bargaining with a labor union which represented his employees" (Gross 1974, 11). Section 7(a) also failed to provide the NLB with clear enforcement powers and procedures to follow in order to effectuate its orders. Employers were thus able to flout the law's intent that they recognize workers' duly elected representatives and engage in collective bargaining (Bernstein 1970, 192, 331). The same was true of its successor agency, the "old" National Labor Relations Board (NLRB) (Gross 1974, 128–9). As a result, Section 7(a) created more industrial unrest than it resolved.

The conflicting interpretations of Section 7(a) cut along several lines – between labour and business, between organized labour and the NRA, between the NRA leadership and the NLB, and finally, between Senator Wagner and President Roosevelt. The NRA and employers were often at odds with the NLB and organized labour over whether "the right of employees to organize and bargain collectively through representatives of their own choosing" implied representational "pluralism," where a body of employees could be represented by several unions consisting of minorities or whether a single union representing a majority of employees would have exclusive representation (Morris 2005, 35).

The test for the NLB came when it had to deal with disputes involving large, powerful industries like automobiles and steel. Mediation and voluntary cooperation in these cases simply failed. The decisive showdowns were the Budd Manufacturing and Weirton Steel Co. cases, which "conclusively demonstrated the weakness in the Board's total dependence upon the voluntary cooperation of employers and unions" (Gross 1974, 41). The NLB was powerless to enforce its decisions (Gross 1974, 60–1; Bernstein 1970, 172). The NLB depended upon the NRA's Compliance Division and the Department of Justice to enforce its rulings. These bodies had to accept NLB and NLRB decisions as final, but they were not obliged to act on them. Neither of the boards established good working relationships with either of the enforcement agencies. The Compliance Division was hesitant to penalize employers by taking away their "Blue Eagle" designation, which would disqualify firms from government contracts and invite popular boycotts. The Justice Department often disagreed with the boards' determination that employers' behaviour constituted clear-cut violations. When it did agree to prosecute, the process was long and cumbersome, with employers delaying final decisions in the federal courts for months (Lyon 1935, 484–7). And when the NLB had to defend its decisions in court, it found itself understaffed to handle the litigation (Gross 1974, 48). The agency finally collapsed when Roosevelt resolved the automobile case in a way that contravened the NLB's principles (Gross 1974, 61).

The NLB's successor, the (old) National Labor Relations Board (NLRB), suffered a virtually identical fate. The NLRB had only the power to investigate disputes and left enforcement power with the Compliance Division and Justice Department. The Houde Engineering Company, an auto parts supplier, refused to comply with the board's decision that it the company must grant the duly elected union (United Auto Workers), which won a majority vote, exclusive representation and bargain with the union in good faith. A concerted effort by several other employers to block or delay other NLRB decisions ensued (Gross 1974, 92–8). Then, in the case of the San Francisco *Call-Bulletin*, a local newspaper, the publishing industry refused to consent to the NLRB's jurisdiction on the grounds that publishing was a special industry protected from government regulation by the First Amendment. After a protracted stalemate, Roosevelt and the NRA took the side of the newspaper publishers by taking away the NLRB's jurisdiction over the industry (Gross 1974, 109–22). As with the NLB, the Justice Department failed to enforce most of the board's decisions (Gross 1974, 129).

The reformers and experts charged with implementing and evaluating Section 7(a) eventually overcame the problems that the law presented through a two-year learning process that culminated in the drafting and implementation of the Wagner Act. The Wagner Act would have been necessary even if the Supreme Court had not struck down the NIRA in May of 1935, because of the upheaval in labour relations that the weaknesses in Section 7(a) had produced. Indeed, the Court's decision to invalidate the NIRA came just days before the scheduled vote in Congress on the Wagner Act.

Wagner's proposed solution to these problems – the Labor Disputes Act of 1934 – failed to gain Congressional passage because of employer resistance. Employers rallied strongly against its provisions that outlawed company unions and allowed independent unions to secure closed-shop agreements (Morris 2005, 46). Roosevelt too came out against Wagner's bill because of his concern with keeping business on board with the NIRA in order to aid economic recovery (Lyon 1935, 487). Rather than support Wagner's bill, the president issued Public Resolution Number 44, which simply authorized him to establish boards to resolve industrial disputes. The NIRA collapsed as a viable labour policy before the Supreme Court declared it unconstitutional in May 1935. Thus, while Congress adopted Section 7(a) in fairness to labour and as a political concession to it (having rejected the Black bill), the Wagner Act grew out of a deep concern within the government that the industrial disputes that arose during the implementation of Section 7(a) became an obstacle to economic recovery. Industrial conflict was now perceived as integral to the crisis and a roadblock to its resolution (Bernstein 1970, 173).

Although Wagner's Labor Disputes Act failed in 1934, its solutions to many of the problems with Section 7(a) eventually reappeared in the National Labor Relations Act of 1935. It did so by linking "the right to organize for collective bargaining to six employer 'unfair labor practices' and to a national labor board empowered to conduct representative elections and to prevent these unfair labor practices by using cease and desist orders" (Gross 1974, 65). The Act forced employers to recognize labour organizations that were of the workers' own choosing, outlawed company unions, and compelled employers to bargain in good faith.

The experience of Wagner and others involved with implementing the NIRA aided efforts to refine the principles and develop the working rules of a legalist industrial relations regime and design a regulatory agency that would be able to enforce them effectively (Gross 1974, 3, 91, 132; Gross 1981, 1–2; Bernstein 1950, 18). Some of the labour boards set up under the NIRA, such as the one for petroleum, served as sites of administrative learning where experts, like Professor William M. Leiserson, "tested basic concepts and procedures" related to collective bargaining and developed "a 'common law' of Section 7(a), out of which evolved a set of guidelines for how employers and employee organizations would go about selecting workers' representatives, how labor organizations would be certified as exclusive bargaining agents, and how bargaining would be conducted" (Bernstein 1970, 112–14).

Basing their decisions on the cases that came before it, the NLB engaged in ten months of "intense testing and experimentation" (Gross 1974, 71). The most common labour dispute that came before the NLB was employers' refusal to recognize unions in the context of competing company unions. The NLB chose to institute secret ballot elections in order to overcome this obstacle in its implementation of 7(a). Workers must be empowered freely to choose their representatives, it decided, through secret ballots in which the majority would rule in deciding whether they would be represented by an internal or external union, or whether they would forego representation and collective bargaining. Through the *Denver Tramway* decision, the *Houde Engineering Company* case, and others like them, the NLB (and its successor the "old" NLRB) established fundamental principles like majority rule elections and exclusive representation (Morris 2005, 36, 48–50). Once an election was held, employers had to recognize the labour organization chosen by the majority as exclusively authorized to bargain over the terms of agreements and had to bargain with them in good faith and work to maintain such agreements (Lyon et al. 1935, 470–4; Gross 1974, 91; Morris 2005, 30–1). The NLB's successor agency, the NLRB, both affirmed and carried forward with the development of labour law principles, particularly by ruling that the purposes of Section 7(a) could be achieved only by accepting non-interference by employers in elections, majority rule, rights of exclusive representation, and by severely constraining employers' use of company unions (Gross 1974, 91). Thus, even before Congress enacted the Wagner Act, the labour boards created under the NIRA developed a body of case law that effectively "enacted" the Wagner Act (Gross 1974, 123; Tomlins

1985, 134–5). The NLRB also learned that in applying majority rule in representation elections, first it had to carefully ascertain the appropriate scope of the bargaining unit – the group of workers that should be represented by a single labour organization (Gross 1974, 98).

While the old NLB had three representatives each from labour and employers, with Senator Wagner as chair, the NLRB did away with partisan representation and was composed of three impartial experts. NLB staff members Leiserson and Handler argued that the mediators should not represent either labour or employers because of the pressure on them to remain as advocates for their own side (Gross 1974, 27, 55). The NLRB thus strengthened the position of autonomous state actors and diminished those of societal interests. As time went on, the labour boards deemphasized mediation and informal processes and increasingly turned to adjudication and formal rules and procedures (Gross 1974, 82). The NLRB also rejected the role of mediator and adjudicator of disputes and instead sat as judges exclusively and left mediation up to regional boards (Gross 1974, 71).

Out of the ashes of the NIRA, finally, arose the National Labor Relations Act of 1935, which cemented the legalist regime that still exists today, by codifying the rights and responsibilities of employers and labour organizations and strengthening the state's capacity for adjudicating claims of "unfair labour practices" and issuing and enforcing decisions of the National Labor Relations Board. The "new" NLRB was constituted as an independent agency with decisive decision-making and enforcement powers (Tomlins 1985, 133).

Wagner began drafting the Wagner Act (S. 1958), a revised version of the earlier Labor Disputes bill in 1934, which incorporated the NLB and NLRB precedents, including the majority rule established part of the statute. The NLRB's legal staff worked closely with Leon Keyserling, whom Wagner instructed to draft the legislation (Gross 1974, 131). Keyserling included almost all the "necessary features" that the NLRB suggested the legislation should contain. S.1958 constituted a new NLRB as an independent agency, composed of three independent members (devoid of representatives of labour or business), with the task of enforcing rights rather than mediating disputes. It included the same guarantee of rights contained in Section 7(a), made employer coercion and restraint of employees in their exercise of their rights an "unfair labour practice," and mandated that employers bargain in good faith. The new NLRB was given wide latitude to determine the appropriate size of the bargaining unit and to issue cease and desist orders if it found employers engaging in unfair labour practices. The Justice Department lost control over the enforcement of NLRB decisions, which was now placed in the hands of federal circuit courts.

The failure of Section 7(a) strengthened the validity of the broad public interest rationales that Wagner put forward for the National Labor Relations Act (NLRA). Giving labour a greater voice in industrial life was consistent, Wagner and other progressives pointed out, with widely cherished values like "democracy" (see Gross 1974, 64; Bernstein 1950, 90, 100, 115). Second, the weaknesses of Section 7(a) and the labour boards had aggravated industrial unrest rather than lessened it, which in turn, disrupted economic recovery (Bernstein 1970, 324). The problems encountered with Section 7(a) affirmed Wagner's argument that guaranteeing labour's rights to organize and bargain collectively with employers was needed to redress the imbalance in bargaining power between employees and employers. The individual worker lacked any significant bargaining power vis-à-vis the large modern corporation. Allowing corporations to continue to resist independent unions by installing company unions curtailed employees' rights of free association and weakened labour's bargaining power. The resulting lower wages and purchasing power was cited as a major cause of the Depression and impeded the recovery (Bernstein 1970, 192–3, 325, 331–4; Finegold and Skocpol 1995, 137).

THE SUPREME COURT STRIKES DOWN THE NIRA AND WAGNER BUILDS CONSTITUTIONAL DEFENSES

Wagner and his assistants were very concerned that the NLRA would suffer the same fate as other New Deal legislation, so they drafted the NLRA with particular concern for the constitutional objections that its opponents would probably make in court challenges. In the midst of the floor debate over the Wagner Act, the Supreme Court declared the NIRA unconstitutional in the *Schecter Poultry Corporation* decision (Bernstein 1950, 116; Gross 1974, 145). In the wake of the Supreme Court's *Schecter* decision, the Wagner Act's opening declaration was revised to emphasize the impact of industrial unrest on interstate commerce, in the hope of avoiding the same fate that befell the NIRA when it came before the Court (Gross 1974, 132–9, 144). The other major concern about the Wagner Act's constitutional vulnerability was that the Supreme Court might consider its regulation of the employer–employee relationship a violation of due process because it made unlawful several "unfair labour practices" and gave powers to an administrative body to adjudicate whether they had been violated without the procedural guarantees afforded in a court of law (Bernstein 1950, 104, 107). Even after passage of the Wagner Act, the NLRB worked for several years on a legal strategy that would maximize its chance for surviving the Court's test for constitutionality, which it did in the 1937 *Jones and Laughlin* case (Gross 1974, 223–30).

Although Roosevelt had assured Wagner that he would not block the legislation he had offered no active support for the bill. On the heels of *Schecter*, Roosevelt spoke affirmatively about the need for its adoption in private, but his support remained lukewarm in public. In spite of Roosevelt's lack of presidential lobbying for the bill, the Wagner Act passed both chambers of Congress with overwhelming margins, however (Gross 1974, 141, 145–7).

THE "SWITCH IN TIME THAT SAVED NINE"

A final productive condition was changes on the Supreme Court in the 1930s, not for the adoption of the new labour policy, but to guarantee its survival. The long history of the judiciary coming to the aid of employers led Senator Wagner (D-NY) and other progressives to worry that the Court would strike down the NLRA. The National Association of Manufacturers and other opponents of the Act argued that Congress had no authority to regulate interstate commerce and that the powers given to the NLRB violated due process (Bernstein 1970, 336). When it became clear that the public supported the New Deal, and FDR threatened to pack the Court, a former member of the anti–New Deal bloc on the Court voted to uphold the constitutionality of the Wagner Act in *Jones and Laughlin* (Bernstein 1970, 635–46). The legalist industrial relations regime was now permanently in place.

Critical Antecedent Conditions

As important as the critical juncture of the 1930s was, we cannot ignore a set of antecedent conditions that contributed to the formation of the legalist regime that emerged. Here we look at two sets of critical antecedents, the rejection of alternatives that would have precluded the adoption of legalism and pre-Depression events and conditions that positively contributed to the outcome of the critical juncture.

The Rejection of Compulsory Measures and the Failure of Voluntarism Prior to the Great Depression

The importance of these negative outcomes, these paths not taken, cannot be overstated (see chapter 5). The failure to adopt compulsory arbitration or voluntarism prior to the New Deal laid a foundation for the development of legalism by making such an outcome more likely. Americans would not have adopted a legalist industrial relations regime in the 1930s if they had adopted one of the alternatives to it in the decades preceding the Great Depression. If compulsory arbitration or voluntarism had taken root in the United States, it seems very unlikely that the Depression would have led the United States to switch on to the legalist path, and in that case, as bad as the crisis was, it would not have constituted a critical juncture for the conduct of industrial relations. Britain, Canada, and Australia and New Zealand all experienced the same depression but maintained the industrial relations regimes that they had established decades earlier.

The rejection of compulsory arbitration and conciliation made legalism possible not only because it left the need for the creation of an alternative, when combined with the passage of the Norris–LaGuardia Act, it left the unions largely unconstrained in the field of industrial relations. Like British unions and unlike Australian unions, American unions were unincorporated bodies and acted as agents for their members rather than as principals. Once the New Deal encouraged independent labour organizations and collective bargaining, as it did through the NIRA, the unions were in a much better position to bring pressure to bear upon employers and the state, through strikes and other actions, than if they had been hemmed in by compulsory processes that would have required no-strike and "cooling-off" periods.

While it is true that the state and the AFL did not abandon their efforts to establish a voluntarist regime until during the critical juncture, the failure of voluntarism played out over several decades and the root causes were long-standing. Employer hostility towards unions was the most enduring and decisive reason for the failure of voluntarism to take root in the United States. Although the final nail in voluntarism's coffin came with the implementation of the NIRA, the employer recalcitrance that helped lead to the failure of Section 7(a) was only the latest chapter in a long history of such resistance that grew out of employers' privileged socio-economic position and their experience with success in pursuing an anti-union strategy.

Employers' deep historical antipathy towards trade unions also made the Norris–LaGuardia Act and Wagner Act more likely because it fuelled labour organizing drives, strikes, and militancy in general. The industrial unrest, in turn, had the potential for halting economic recovery. It also helped mobilize labour and New Deal supporters in the 1934 elections, which strengthened progressive forces in Congress, allowing them to push through the Wagner Act.

The Pre-crisis Foundations of Legalism

PARTISAN REALIGNMENT

Affirmative developments also played an important role in setting up a permissive environment during the 1930s. Even before the crisis of the Depression, an electoral realignment was underway that favoured the Democratic Party. By the late 1920s, progressives in both parties were gaining traction with the electorate, and the number of pro-business "old guard" Republicans was beginning to decline. Tens of millions of new voters came into the electorate in the 1920s, including many newly enfranchised immigrants, many of them Catholics, and women. Black Americans began shifting towards the Democrats, as did the majority of Americans, especially the working class, who now lived in cities (Lubell 1965, 48–68). Many of these new voters aligned with the Democrats under Al Smith, the first Catholic presidential candidate, in the 1928 election.

DECLINING SUPPORT FOR LABOUR INJUNCTIONS

Although Congress did not pass the Norris–LaGuardia Act until the crisis, the movement that would lead to its passage started earlier in response to the abuses.

Support for ending the labour injunction broadened and intensified prior to the crisis. American courts, as we have seen, made increasing use of the labour injunction in ways that many observers who were not affiliated with the labour movement saw increasingly as abusive and arbitrary. In the 1920s, the courts and business community overreached in their use of the labour injunction and yellow dog contracts. The number of injunctions soared to over 2,100, covering 25 per cent of all strikes, figures considerably higher than in previous years. United in its opposition, the labour movement engaged in unprecedented acts of civil disobedience. As the resistance mounted, lawyers and reformers grew worried that "government by injunction" was fostering disrespect towards the law and distrust of the judiciary and exacerbating industrial unrest. Progressives, led by Senator George Norris, enlisted Felix Frankfurter and other legal reformers to write legislation outlawing the injunction in most labour disputes and blocked a federal appeals court appointment supported by "old guard" Republicans (Forbath 1991, 158–62; Lovell 2003, 211–16).

All of these developments, culminating in the Norris–LaGuardia Act, encouraged American unions to grow more militant. Norris–LaGuardia had lifted the largest impediment to strike activity, the injunction. As a result, what started out as an economic crisis evolved into one that included significant levels of industrial unrest, which led, in turn to major labour law reforms in the 1930s.

THE PRE–NEW DEAL LEGAL THINKING AND POLICY BREAKTHROUGHS

The Wagner Act's approach to industrial relations – providing a legal framework and developing a detailed body of case law for the enforcement of labour rights – was partly rooted in earlier efforts to craft an industrial relations policy. Starting in the early part of the twentieth century, progressive jurists began developing a common law reform that would change labour unions' legal standing. Unions were unincorporated bodies, and thus had no legal personality. As totally unincorporated bodies, they could not sue or be sued, which was consistent with Gompers's preference that they remain totally voluntary organizations that were able to compete with business without state interference. Rather than have unions incorporate, the reform that the progressives developed was to use the "law of agency" to establish limited liability. Unions would make agreements *for* workers, acting as their agents. Agency would hold unions legally accountable and allow unions to negotiate enforceable collective bargaining agreements. Unions would be legally entitled to both the state's assistance as well as its regulation. "Responsible unionism" would get the AFL around the political and judicial attacks on its claims as a special class deserving of immunity under the law, which was an ongoing concern through the adoption of the Wagner Act and the Supreme Court's validation of it (O'Brien 1998, 6). By the mid-1920s, the doctrine of responsible unionism was fully developed and was enshrined in Republican-crafted railroad labour legislation that guaranteed collectivities of workers (though not unions) freedom of association in representing their interests in disputes with employers (O'Brien 1998, 63–7).

Legalism also had roots in the National War Labor Board (NWLB) of the First World War. In the First World War, the government sought to use labour unions to preserve industrial peace so that industrial unrest would not interfere with preparedness for the war. Although it was not the immediate goal of the policy, unions and workers benefited greatly from the wartime experience (Zakson 1989, 346). Because of the Wilson administration's pro-labour policies during the First World War, by the end of the conflict, all categories of railway labour (not just the brotherhoods) were organized and recognized on virtually all railways, which had not existed previously, in addition to the establishment of specific rules and procedures for collective bargaining and dispute adjudication and enhanced wages and working hours. The unions' role in labour relations approximated that of an equal participant in resolving labour matters on the rails (Zakson 1989, 341–3). President Woodrow Wilson encouraged workers' rights to organize and bargain collectively and gave them a voice on the corporatist NWLB in exchange for a pledge not to strike (see cites in O'Brien 1998, 72; Zakson 1989, 344). The following language from a 1918 NWLB is virtually identical to the language from the Norris–LaGuardia Act of 1932, Section 7(a) of the 1933 NIRA, and the Wagner Act of 1935: "The right of workers to organize in trade unions and to bargain collectively through chosen representatives is recognized and affirmed. This right shall not be denied, abridged, or interfered with by employers in any manner whatsoever" (quoted in Morris 2005, 18).

Also important were statutes that addressed industrial relations in the railways from the 1880s to the 1920s. The state had a strong interest in maintaining industrial peace on the railroads. The railways were vital to regional and national economies in the late nineteenth and early twentieth centuries, and their clear interstate character eliminated a key constitutional stumbling block to Congress's authority to regulate the industry. The distribution of employees and work areas over vast geographic distances made industrial relations more complicated than localized production of traditional industries. Early on, railroad workers in the four "brotherhoods" (engineers, firemen, trainmen, and conductors) organized and eventually won a significant degree of recognition from railroad operators. Over the decades leading up to the 1930s, the federal government sought to promote industrial peace on the railways by guaranteeing protections for the brotherhoods and promoting voluntary dispute resolution in exchange for restraints on unions' ability to disrupt the industry. Negotiated settlements were only feasible where unions were permitted to organize and operate, thus contributing to orderly dispute resolutions by speaking for workers with a single voice. The general thrust of the policy was to foster voluntary cooperation between labour and management, although the degree of interventionism varied from statute to statute (Zakson 1989). Providing state support for labour organizations was incidental to the basic aim of industrial peace. (Note that once the state got involved, it had to traverse a major obstacle in order to gain sufficient political and judicial support: it could not be perceived as "class legislation" – that is, biased in favour of one side or the other. It had to be perceived as in the "public interest" instead.)

The first of the statutes related to railway labor were the Arbitration Act of 1888 and the Erdman Act of 1898, which were similar, although the latter was more interventionist (see Bernstein 1950, 18, 40–1). The Erdman Act was the legislative response to the Pullman strike, a major industrial relations crisis in 1893, which employers and the federal government repressed. It contained several features that would reappear or be elaborated upon in the legislation of the 1930s (Zakson 1989, 326–9). For the first time, Congress placed limits on employers, including prohibiting yellow dog contracts, blacklisting employees who joined unions, and engaging in other forms of discrimination against union members (Stromquist 1987, 262). These provisions won the support of the railroad brotherhoods, although they would be struck down by the courts later (Lecht 1955, 17–18). It also provided for labour organizations to represent employees before arbitrators (the last stage in the Act's voluntary dispute resolution process) and elections by majority vote of representatives in cases where employees were not members of any labour organization. Furthermore, the Act's basic rationale, that it was in the public interest to avoid disruptions to interstate commerce, would reappear in the 1930s as well.[3]

Although intended to make railroad unions more "responsible," the Transportation Act of 1920 also protected railroad workers' right to organize for the purpose of selecting representatives who would appear before the Railroad Labor Board (RLB), which was charged with investigating and rendering (nonbinding) decisions on collective bargaining agreements (O'Brien 1998, 89). When the RLB failed to get the Pennsylvania Railroad to accept its jurisdiction and prevent the 1922 railway shopmen's strike, Congress passed the Railway Labor Act of 1926. The Railway Labor Act was the first federal law that explicitly stipulated that employers had an obligation to bargain with employees' freely chosen representatives (Zakson 1989, 372–3; Zieger 1969, 205).

We should not overstate the importance of the railway legislation, which dealt with a single and somewhat atypical industry. The focus upon that legislation, particularly after the First World War, was in coming up with a workable process for dispute resolution where workers were highly organized and their unions established (Morris 2005, 31). The railways had, if only reluctantly in many cases, come to recognize the unions and engage in collective bargaining. This was not the case with the Wagner Act, which was less about adjudicating disputes over wages and working conditions and more about the basic rights, privileges, and obligations of the two parties. Whereas the railways more or less went along with legally mandated employee rights, the Wagner Act contained enforcement mechanisms to bring recalcitrant employers into line. Second, although the 1926 railway legislation specified a duty on the part of employers to bargain, it did not provide for elections and did not obligate employers to recognize and bargain with representatives of a *majority* of employees and left the door open for representation by company unions, major issues that would have to be resolved in the 1930s (Zakson 1989, 373; Zieger 1969, 205–6; Morris 2005, 21).

Nevertheless, railroad legislation represented important innovation and experimentation with state involvement in labour legislation. First, Congress smoothed the way for collective bargaining to take root as a voluntary means for conflict resolution by eliminating the courts from interfering with labour organization, thus serving as a precursor to the Norris–LaGuardia Act of 1932. Second, Congress stipulated railway labour's rights to organize, which were broadened to all private-sector, nonagricultural workers in the National Industrial Recovery Act of 1933 and the Wagner Act of 1935. Third, Congress promoted collective bargaining as the preferred way to resolve industrial disputes over other alternatives, including state repression, laissez-faire voluntarism, and compulsory arbitration.

KEY UNIONS ABANDONED VOLUNTARISM

Although it took the Great Depression to get the AFL finally to break with voluntarism, key unions had already done so prior to the Depression. We have already discussed the railway unions' embrace of government-enforced labour rights. The United Mine Workers (UMW) and garment workers also abandoned voluntarism. Dire economic circumstances in these industries began before the stock market crash and led to a search for solutions that involved greater state involvement in the economy than had occurred ever before in peacetime. The UMW, led by John L. Lewis, was at first firmly in the voluntarist camp. But he became the first major labour leader to abandon it in the late 1920s. It signed on to Commerce Secretary Herbert Hoover's "new capitalism" that involved industrial self-regulation. Jett Lauck, an economist who was deeply influenced in the progressive experiments during the Wilson administration, influenced the evolution of Lewis's thinking on the economy and labour relations. Lauck, who believed that labour unions were as integral to industrial capitalism as corporations, promoted area-wide collective bargaining agreements between the coal industry and UMW. Self-regulation in mining, however, could not deal with the problem of overproduction and wage and price cutting. New mines continued to be opened up even as new fuels (like natural gas) came on board, reducing prices and wages in the mining industry. Lauck argued in favour of greater federal control over the market and pushed Lewis to abandon voluntarism and replace it with a regulatory system that enabled coal mine operators to end price cutting and gave the unions collective bargaining rights (Johnson 1979, 122). The result was Lewis's endorsement of a Coal Commission in 1928 to regulate wages, prices, and profits and mandate collective bargaining (Fink 1997, 225–6). In 1932, this idea became the basis for the Kelly–Davis bill, which prefigured the Roosevelt administration's National Industrial Recovery Act by allowing coal companies to combine into syndicates to sell coal, essentially engaging in government-approved price-fixing as long as they recognized the UMW and engaged in collective bargaining. Lewis became a successful, ardent advocate of including Section 7(a) during the New Dealers' formulation of the NRA (Johnson 1979, 144). The principles of 7(a) thus closely resembled those in the Watson-Rathbone and Davis-Kelly coal bills (Fink 1997, 226; Lorwin 1933, 496–7; Bernstein 1950, 24). According to Lauck, 7(a) "was taken verbatim from the Davis-Kelly Bill. I know this because Congressman Clyde Kelley and I did this in drafting the Recovery Act" (Johnson 1979, 144).

Conclusion

The long period of state-supported labour repression in the United States came to an end in the 1930s. By that decade, the United States had come some way in deciding what regime would replace repression. Statist solutions that involved compulsory conciliation and arbitration were not on the agenda and had become infeasible. The most favourable conditions for its adoption, in the early 1920s under Republican auspices, came and went without mustering a Congressional majority and then the Supreme Court ruled the Kansas Industrial Court unconstitutional. Three options remained. The first was voluntarism. The Roosevelt administration and Senator Wagner had high hopes for a voluntarist approach to the fulfilment of Section 7(a) of the NIRA, but those hopes were soon dashed. Voluntarism became untenable when the mandates on employers in Section 7(a) encountered intractable employer opposition. A second possibility was a continuation of labour repression, which was not out of the question. The business community adamantly opposed state intervention to enforce labour rights, and the Roosevelt administration, particularly the National Recovery Administration, was attuned to business's demands given the administration's overriding goal of economic recovery. But the industrial unrest the New Deal helped unleash with Section 7(a) was also a threat to the recovery. Thus, Americans had to invent a "middle way" between these two models that would garner enough support and pass judicial muster. The resolution of this dilemma came in the wake of the 1934 elections, which strengthened the hand of Congressional progressives to pass the Wagner Act, the Roosevelt administration's acquiescence in its adoption (and for some legislators, a mistaken assumption that they could support the Wagner Act knowing that the Supreme Court would overturn it.)

Clearly, the United States would not have adopted a legalist regime, at least not in the 1930s, had the conditions constituting a critical juncture not occurred at that time. The findings of this chapter are consistent with some of the explanations for the adoption of the Wagner Act put forward among scholars of American political development. Three actors, in particular, played crucial roles in the Act's adoption – organized labour, the Democratic Party, and progressive reformers. The trade union movement mobilized politically and helped strengthen and broaden the New Deal coalition in the elections of 1930, 1932, and most important of all, 1934. Perhaps as important as its political support was the organizing activity and militancy that the adoption of Section 7(a) induced. Once labour's expectations were dashed when the Roosevelt administration took the side of oppositional employers and the NLB was unable to enforce its decisions, the intensification of the crisis pushed Wagner and other progressive reformers to resolve the issue in labour's favour. As in the past, labour's support for policy change was often important, but it was not able to dictate the substance of the changes.[4]

The incorporation of Section 7(a) in the NIRA, a seminal event in the history of American industrial relations policy, is due to the joint efforts of organized labour and progressive reformers. Although most of the labour movement preferred a different approach to economic recovery (the "Black bill"). The United Mine Workers, in particular, played an important role in pushing for its inclusion in the NIRA due to the work of Jett Lauck in persuading John L. Lewis. Wagner played the pivotal role brokering between the labour movement and the New Deal in getting Section 7(a) incorporated in the NIRA (Bernstein 1970, 130). It was also Wagner, and a handful of others, including Lauck, Leon Keyserling, and those who served with Wagner on the NLB (and later, the old NLRB), who were the architects of the legalist approach to industrial relations under the NIRA and Wagner Act. Aside from drafting the legislation, they took advantage of the experience with the implementation of Section 7(a), producing a body of administrative law that contained important principles and procedures that constituted the new legalist regime and formulated effective enforcement mechanisms that were lacking in the earlier legislation. Finally, the Democratic Party provided the vital institutional and political linkages among labour and other elements in the New Deal electoral coalition, progressive reformers, and key leaders within the state, particularly Senator Wagner.

The critical juncture framework contributes to efforts to reconcile some of the differing explanations in the APD literature. By distinguishing between "permissive" and "productive" conditions, we do not need to choose among the various actors as the decisive one that brought about the outcome. Permissive conditions, such as the shifting electoral prospects of the two political parties opened a window of opportunity for labour and progressive reformers to engage in policy learning and launch specific and significant reforms (productive conditions). The critical juncture approach helps us to understand the outcome as part of a causal process rather than simply a search for one or two "key actors."

The findings in this chapter also correct two other deficiencies in APD accounts of the Wagner Act. First, in focusing on key actors – individuals or organizations in the political and policymaking process – they give insufficient weight to public policy itself as a key causal variable. Existing policies "feedback" into the political arena – mobilizing the union movement in this case – that in turn, set the stage for the enactment of the Wagner Act. Section 7(a) the NIRA contained bold mandates that for the first time applied to all American employers. The rights guaranteed to labour organizations and the obligations placed upon employers, backed by state power, energized the labour movement, and shifted the ground from under employers. It created a crisis within a crisis and contributed significantly, both politically and substantively, to the content and eventual adoption of the Wagner Act. It exemplified how public policies, once implemented, can have profound political effects.

Second, because APD explanations are limited to the critical juncture, they truncate the historical analysis by overlooking the causal impact of several "critical antecedent conditions." First and most obviously, there would have been no legalism and no need for it if the United States had turned to statism or voluntarism in the preceding decades, or if it had laid a foundation for doing so. The legalist path that Americans took cannot be fully understood unless we place it in the broader context of paths that were not taken. Second, and perhaps most importantly, these explanations understate the critical role of employers. They focus on those actors that acted affirmatively to usher in a new regime – worker organizations that mobilized, reformers who developed solutions, political leaders who built support for new proposals. Weakened politically, employers mostly drop out of these analyses. Yet, employers played a pivotal role in shaping the outcome both during and before the New Deal. American employers were comparatively extreme in their hostility towards unions, which was deeply rooted historically in the privileged place of the employer class in society and how the structure of American capitalism during the critical years of industrialization in the late nineteenth and early twentieth centuries. And during the crisis, they fought actively and for a time successfully to create more company unions than did the labour movement form independent ones. Finally, APD accounts sometimes do not do justice to the way in which the New Deal borrowed from and built upon policy breakthroughs and intellectual building blocks like the labour policies of the War Labor Board and the 1926 Railway Labor Act.

8 Limited Statism: Canada's First Answer

All industrial strife is a form of anarchy.... Private rights must cease when they become public wrongs.... It cannot be contended that what is a matter of grave concern to the public is a matter of exclusive concern to private parties. There is no right superior to that of the community as a whole.

(William Lyon Mackenzie King, *Industry and Humanity*, 1918 [1973 reprint, 313–14, 329])

The search for a viable, non-repressive industrial relations regime took an exceptionally long time in Canada. Not until the 1940s, when Canadians experienced their second critical juncture, did they settle on their unique "dual experiment," a hybrid system that grafted the American legalist approach on to a system of compulsory investigation and conciliation (Woods 1973, 347). Because Canada first adopted compulsory investigation and conciliation, it placed less confidence in collective bargaining once it adopted its version of the Wagner Act several decades later. The 1944 legislation did not articulate a principled commitment to collective bargaining as the Wagner Act had done. "Any support for collective bargaining," by the state, "was incidental to the conciliation and investigation of specific disputes" (Woods 1973, 82).

The Canadians distinguished themselves at the turn of the century by turning to a form of industrial relations regulation that pursued a "middle way" between the voluntarism of Britain and the statist approach of Australia and New Zealand for select industries. Canada's statist approach (the Industrial Disputes Investigation Act of 1907, IDIA, or "Lemieux Act") was limited, however, compared to the one in Australasia. The IDIA built upon the Railway Labour Disputes Act (RLDA) of 1903, which made investigation and conciliation of disputes mandatory for the railways. The IDIA went beyond the RDLA by prohibiting strikes and lockouts during a "cooling-off" period. The state did not mandate the terms of settlements, however, as it would under compulsory arbitration and wages boards. Furthermore, these requirements initially applied only to a select group of "public utilities," like transportation and mining; they covered all other industries much later.

Why did Canada turn to statism in the early part of the twentieth century? As in the United States, Canadian employers were largely hostile to organized labour. Therefore, voluntarism was not a viable answer to the labour question. Though Parliament formally established the unions' right to exist as far back as 1872, employers were not compelled to recognize unions, could fire employees who belonged to unions, and could hinder the unions' ability to engage in strikes and other activities through the courts. Employers were also free to call in strikebreakers and ask the government to call out troops to put down strikes. Second, while Canadian trade unions were never on the verge of extinction the way they were in Australia and New Zealand, they were arguably the weakest and most fragmented in the Anglophone world. More importantly for understanding the turn to statism in 1907, industrial strife in parts of Canada became so acute and lasted long enough that it posed an imminent danger to the public, similar in kind to the dire situation that existed in Australasia in the 1890s. Western Canada was a hotbed of labour militancy where protracted strikes broke out in the early years of the twentieth century in the railways and mining. The strikes led to a great public outcry when it endangered fuel supplies in the region.

Canada's statist response was limited because the crisis that impelled policymakers to respond was localized; it did not threaten the existence of the labour movement as a whole or cause the kind of disruption to the national economy that occurred in Australia and New Zealand. As a result, the crisis did not produce the kind of nationwide political upheaval that occurred in Australasia. Little appetite existed for compulsory arbitration or wages boards within the labour movement (which by that time had come mostly under the control of the anti-statist American Federation of Labor), employers, or the state. Given the geographic and economic containment of the crisis, these actors viewed a limited form of statism as appropriate. Labour's disappointment centred on the lack of a guarantee of labour rights in the IDIA, but in the absence of the kind of broad political mobilization of broad labour and a lib-lab coalition that favoured an Australasian-style "state socialist" reform program, such a goal remained elusive.

Adoption of the IDIA comes closest to the breakdown and replacement pattern of institutional change because of the causal importance of the critical juncture of 1900–7. An acute crisis created a critical juncture when the effects of industrial conflict spilled over into the broader community, serving as a catalyst for a significant institutional change. But because the crisis was circumscribed by geography and the industrial sector, it did not lead to the kinds of political and governmental change that might have led to more significant institutional change. Mandatory investigation and conciliation as a set of principles and institutional arrangements emerged directly from the crisis and William Lyon Mackenzie King's extensive experience as a mediator of industrial disputes. A liberal reformer, King served as deputy labour minister, a strategic position within the state that helped him get the reform on the agenda and gain the backing of the unions and the Liberal government in power. Aside from the long-standing hostility of employers towards unions, most antecedent conditions were not critical to the outcome.

This chapter explains the emergence of Canada's limited statism as an its initial answer to the labour question. The remainder of the chapter focuses on what did *not* happen – why Canadians did not follow the Australasian example and adopt a stronger statist response or British voluntarism. Chapter 9, which follows, focuses on Canada's turn to legalism several decades later.

The Critical Juncture of 1900-7

Permissive Conditions

INDUSTRIAL UNREST IN THE CANADIAN WEST

As unions spread gradually in the 1880s and 1890s, so did the frequency of industrial disputes. Labour's organizational strength rose, and as it turned more towards business unionism, it demanded recognition and higher wages from employers. As in the United States and Australasia, employers responded with a "rising determination to crush the unions" (Lipton 1966, 80).[1] Initially, the state responded to these clashes with measures emphasizing voluntary approaches to dispute resolution, culminating in the Conciliation Act of 1900, which established a Department of Labour and authorized the labour minister to intervene in industrial disputes to try to get the parties to come to a settlement. However, the unrest intensified rather than diminished. A series of strikes at the turn of the century posed more significant threats to public order and convenience than the earlier ones. Unrest was greatest in the West, where more militant unions organized, often along industrial lines and often inspired by socialists. These unions affiliated with the American Labor Union and were like the "new unions" that emerged a decade earlier in Britain and Australasia. Like those unions, they had a tense relationship with older craft unions, and many were eventually defeated by employers, often with the help of the police (Bothwell, Drummond, and English 1987, 96). The disputes began with rail strikes from 1901 to 1903 (Cameron and Young 1960, 41). In 1901, 5,000 maintenance-of-way trackmen struck the Canadian Pacific Railway (CPR) for recognition. The action disrupted rail traffic across the nation. In 1902, another protracted strike took place against the Canadian Northern Railway in Manitoba. In 1903, the most controversial and dramatic strike occurred when a new industrial union (the United Brotherhood of Railway Employees, UBRE) organized strikes of clerks and other non-unionized categories of workers.

MORE STRIKES AND PUBLIC OUTCRY

As the organization drive and strikes on the railways gained momentum throughout Western Canada, unrest spread to mining and other industries (Tuck 1983, 63). A few years later, a second industrial relations crisis occurred in the mining industry. A string of bitter strikes in coal mining over union recognition, wages and working conditions threatened public safety (Craven 1980, 264–5; Baker 1983). The nine-month-long strike in 1906 in Lethbridge, Alberta, led to a public outcry when it jeopardized the fuel supplies of residents of Alberta and Saskatchewan as winter approached (Craven 1980, 260; Jamieson 1968, 128, 148–9).

Productive Conditions

A LIBERAL REFORMER WITHIN THE STATE DEVELOPS A SOLUTION TO INDUSTRIAL UNREST

As in Australia, New Zealand, and the United States, most of the impetus for change and the source of policy innovations came from individual reformers within the state. While organized labour weighed in on proposals to deal with industrial unrest, it did not do much to initiate them. The IDIA "was not an offspring of the labor movement but was a government measure designed to protect the public interest through preventing any precipitate dislocation in the operations of industries of a public-utility character, including coal mining, transportation (railroads and street transit), telephone and telegraph" (Logan 1928, 217–18).

Most of the credit for the IDIA goes to the deputy minister of labour, William Lyon Mackenzie King. King was a liberal reformer, policy intellectual, and innovator with an interest in labour reform who attended graduate school at the University of Chicago and Harvard University. He was among a new breed of university-trained experts and progressive reformers who grasped the enormous changes wrought by industrial capitalism and envisioned a legitimate and vital role for the state in protecting the public and preventing or mitigating the system's "abuses," while preserving it. In 1900, he turned down a faculty appointment at Harvard to take a job as editor of the *Labour Gazette*, a new government publication of the Labour Department that was created under the Conciliation Act. King quickly rose in the civil service to become deputy minister of labour and the department's chief conciliator, which put him at the centre of the state's efforts to settle labour disputes. Eventually, he became labour minister and would go on to serve three times as prime minister later in the century.

Most historians consider King to be the sole and undisputed architect of the state's response to the industrial relations crisis.[2] According to Kealey (1995,

Limited Statism: Canada's First Answer   201

432), "by 1907 King's status was such that neither the minister responsible nor any other cabinet minister even saw the draft legislation before it was introduced in Parliament (see also Craven 1980, 289). Perhaps more than Pember Reeves in New Zealand and Charles Kingston in Australia, King dominated policymaking at this critical time. The compulsory features of investigation and conciliation that he devised were truly new for Canada and marked a "middle way" between voluntarism and compulsory arbitration. Understanding his thinking and experience goes a long way in helping us to understand why Canadians came up with a unique approach to the industrial relations crisis. King developed his own social theory over the course of his academic training and professional experience that culminated in his book *Industry and Humanity*. Like most liberal reformers at the time, King rejected the notion of the inevitability and irreconcilability of class interests under capitalism and insisted that labour and employers shared a common interest. For King, the impersonal nature of class relations under industrial capitalism undermined social cohesion that was necessary for workers and employers to recognize and take into account their common and mutually interdependent interests. King also shared with other reformers the assumption that the public had a legitimate interest in peaceful industrial relations that did not necessarily coincide with the interests of labour and employers. According to King, the "Labor Question" was a misnomer because the question did not involve labour alone or labour and business, but also the community. Each had its proper role and responsibilities. Industries operate to the mutual benefit of the private economic interests involved in them only because the community, through the state, makes their activities possible. The community provides, among other things, "law and order and promoting orderly organization and peaceful behavior." The private parties must be held responsible for their actions when those actions harm the community: "in any civilized community private rights should cease when they become public wrongs" (quoted in Craven 1980, 81, 268). King, like other reformers, saw that the public's growing dependence upon modern transportation and communications infrastructure and other utilities, plus the utilities' status as natural monopolies, gave them tremendous market power, and their access to public resources (e.g., streets) provided a compelling case for various forms of government regulation (Webber 1991, 26). Therefore, the community had the right to intervene and require the parties to relinquish exclusive control over their relations when they were unable to resolve serious conflict on their own.[3]

King used the considerable experience that he gained as a mediator not only to burnish his reputation as an effective and honest broker, but also to develop and refine his ideas about the role of the state in resolving industrial disputes. King helped settle numerous labour disputes during the first decade of the twentieth century (Bothwell, Drummond, and English 1987, 94). The Conciliation Act envisioned a more modest role for the state in settling disputes than

King did. Rather than seeing his task under the Act as simply bringing together workers and employers and encouraging them to bargain, King actively suggested points of settlement, which was compatible with his view of his role as an "*interested* third party to the dispute ... [who] represented the interests of the public" (Craven 1980, 232).

Given his experience as a mediator and his study of efforts to reduce industrial unrest in New South Wales, Illinois, New York, British Columbia, and Ontario, King realized that the three least interventionist options – doing nothing; continuing to intervene in strikes on an ad hoc, emergency basis; and strengthening the purely voluntarist approach adopted under the Conciliation Act of 1900 – would not work. Experience with laws in the two Canadian provinces and New South Wales taught him that requiring the consent of both parties to a dispute was ineffective because at least one party would not agree to conciliation (Webber 1991, 35). He concluded that voluntary measures were not sufficient, particularly when severe outbreaks occurred in crucial sectors of the economy that could threaten the public safety and convenience. Even if industrial unrest in Canada had not reached a point where it threatened nationwide social disorder, it was increasingly disruptive, especially in Western Canada. The Conciliation Act of 1900 did not work well to prevent unrest, given that most of the disputes handled between 1900 and 1906 "resulted in strikes before the intervention of the Department of Labour was requested" (Cameron and Young 1960, 41). According to Webber (1991, 32), "despite his successes [at mediation] during these years, King's conciliation suffered from some of the defects of purely voluntary intervention. King could initiate contact with the parties, perhaps beginning conciliation in circumstances where neither party would seek outside assistance, yet both would cooperate. But King could do little in those disputes where the employer resolutely refused any intervention, resisting even the modicum of recognition implied in mediation. Indeed, the government, rather than risk an embarrassing rebuff, adopted the practice of intervening only after both parties had given their consent. This meant that in some of the fiercest disputes the government was powerless to intervene."

King designed the RLDA as "a happy medium between the Conciliation Act, ineffective because it was purely permissive, and compulsory arbitration" (Craven 1980, 278). Its centrepiece was compulsory investigation and conciliation. The RLDA authorized the labour minister to appoint an ad hoc tripartite committee of investigation, mediation, and conciliation if either of the parties to a railways dispute (or an affected municipality) asked for it, or if the minister initiated it. The law compelled the parties to the dispute to enter into conciliation proceedings, but they were not required to enter into collective bargaining. If the conciliation committee could not forge an agreement, the labour minister could refer the dispute to an arbitration board that had the power to investigate the dispute (including subpoena power) and publish its findings. The board's findings would not be binding on the disputants; however, King anticipated that public opinion would be brought to bear upon the parties once the findings of the board were published (Craven 1980, 278).[4]

King next became involved in 1906 in the Lethbridge mining strike in Western Canada, both as the government's conciliator as well as secretary of a Royal Commission established to investigate the strike. Although the state had little experience yet under the RDLA, King's deep involvement with the mining strike led him to capitalize on the dire conditions that the strike produced to push to extend the approach in the RDLA to other industries and "public utilities." Parliament responded with passage of the IDIA in 1907, which covered the railways, mining, transportation, and communications (Cameron and Young 1960, 44). The IDIA added a new feature that was not included in the RDLA – a "cooling off period" during which it prohibited strikes and lockouts during the investigation and conciliation stages.

ORGANIZED LABOUR SUPPORTS THE IDIA

Most of the Canadian labour movement embraced the IDIA, including the Trades and Labour Congress (TLC), Canada's trade union federation, and the Toronto District Labour Council, which actively supported the government's measure. Lib-lab members of Parliament, including Ralph Smith, came to the aid of the government when the opponents attempted to kill it, arguing that the bill was needed to deal with the likelihood of industrial unrest soon (Craven 1980, 282–3). Some lib-labs favoured extending the reach of the bill to all Canadian industries. A delegation from the TLC, which met with the prime minister, labour minister, and other top officials to express their support, argued that labour preferred to resolve disputes through means other than strikes, which it saw as its last resort, that the IDIA process would deprive employers of an excuse for not recognizing unincorporated labour unions, and that "in every great industrial struggle the public have a large interest as well in the result as in the means adopted to reach that result" (quoting lib-lab MP Alphonse Verville, who summarized the TLC executive body's views, in Craven 1980, 285). Attendees at the 1907 TLC convention supported the IDIA by a vote of 81 to 19; moreover, according to Craven (1980, 286), "it appears that the convention wanted the Act to be extended to cover all industrial disputes" (see also Bothwell, Drummond, and English 1987, 98). The TLC's embrace of the IDIA arose out of labour's overall industrial weakness. According to Craven (1980, 286–7), most Canadian labour unions "were still struggling for their lives, and when the IDI Act came along with its promise of forcing a hearing of their grievances and demands, and its apparent *de facto* recognition of their organizations, it seemed likely to circumvent the weary cycle of recognition strikes that had so often been lost."

Only the railway unions opposed the IDIA, because it included the no-strike "cooling off" period and they feared that it would lead to compulsory arbitration. Samuel Gompers of the AFL, which had by this time penetrated the Canadian labour movement, also opposed any compulsory measures (Craven 1980, 5). However, the railway unions were isolated and the AFL's influence was muted.

Critical Antecedent Conditions

Hostile Employers

Our knowledge of Canadian employers' stance towards unions before the crisis is sketchy, but Canadian employers were about as hostile to unions as Americans were. According to Coats (1913, 295), "trade unions till that period had been no factor in the public life of Canada.... In 1870 opinion was less tolerant [of unions] in Canada than in Great Britain. Even by the liberal statesmen and press of the day, labour unions were considered as perversions ... 'whose aims were mischievous where not utopian.'" Employers in Western Canada were particularly "ruthless" (Abella 1975, 5). The 1870s saw a fair level of worker solidarity and mobilization, much of it centred around the "nine-hours movement," was met with employer resistance. When the printers' union launched a strike in furtherance of the nine-hour day, newspaper publisher George Brown took the union to court on conspiracy charges, which took the wind out of the unions' sails (Heron 1989, 15). In the latter part of the nineteenth century, three Canadian provinces experimented with what were at the time novel mechanisms for dispute resolution. Ontario and British Columbia laws encouraged the formation of conciliation boards, but these were little used because both parties had to agree to participate in them. Most employers at the time resisted collective bargaining and thus were unlikely to submit to conciliation (Webber 1991, 19). Unions grew in the last quarter of the nineteenth century in Canada as they did elsewhere, but organized labour remained a tiny proportion of the labour force mainly due to the employers' hostility towards them.

Theoretically, policymakers had several alternatives for addressing, on a permanent basis, an increasingly organized labour movement and the heightened unrest between it and capital: continuing on voluntary dispute resolution by intervening in an ad hoc basis during the most serious strikes and continuing to rely upon the Conciliation Act of 1900; removing the courts as impediments to union organization and activity and broadening the legal sanction for picketing and other types of union activity as the British did; or moving in a direction to guarantee labour rights by mandating that employers recognize unions and engage in collective bargaining (as later would happen in the United States) either as a stand-alone policy or linked with compulsory arbitration (as in Australasia).

Why did Canadians turn to compulsory investigation and conciliation instead of these alternatives? A large part of the reason is that the permissive conditions of the critical juncture discussed above – mainly a crisis that was limited in scope and scale – failed to create enough political upheaval that would loosen political constraints enough to allow for more far-reaching institutional change. Within those constraints the productive conditions – especially King's ideas and arguments and his ability to define his preferred alternative – determined the specific response. But another part of the explanation lies in the fact that neither before nor after the crisis was either compulsory arbitration or voluntarism viable. We turn next to those options.

Why No Compulsory Arbitration in Canada?

We have not fully explained Canada's adoption of a limited statist regime unless we examine why it did not follow the examples of Australia and New Zealand in adopting compulsory arbitration or of Britain in removing legal obstacles to voluntarism during this same period. This section first turns to why Canada did not adopt a more interventionist statism.

A LIMITED CRISIS WITH LIMITED IMPACTS
The timing and limited scope and severity of the Canadian crises decreased the likelihood that the state would launch a bolder and broader approach to managing industrial relations conflict. The crisis of industrial relations in Canada was less severe and prolonged than those in other nations in several ways. First, strikes and lockouts were not as frequent or severe in Canada in the 1890s as they were in Britain and Australasia (Logan 1928, 77–8). The Knights of Labor, which remained a force until the turn of the century, preferred to avoid strike activity, and the Canadian economy was in relatively good condition during that decade, in stark contrast with Australia and New Zealand. Canadian employers did not face competitive pressures as severe as the British did.

While many of the Canadian strikes were bitterly fought, starting in 1899 with the Grand Trunk Railway strike, their impacts were felt less widely and profoundly than those that occurred in New Zealand and Australia. The 1901 CPR trackmen's strike had nationwide impacts, but the 1903 CPR strike and the Lethbridge mining strike were felt acutely, mainly at the provincial and local levels, not across the wide expanse of Canada. Craven (1980, 241) describes the turmoil in mining as a "war at the periphery of Canadian industrialism" (Craven 1980, 241; Tuck 1983, 63 and 65). According to Bothwell, Drummond, and English (1987, 99), "the [mining] industry was not profoundly important" to Canada as a whole. "[C]entral Canada ran on imported coal and processed few of its own minerals." Despite industrial expansion, coal mining accounted for only 1 per cent of the workforce, and mining in general a bit more than that. "[I]t is absolutely certain that the small groups of isolated miners, whether in Sydney, Nova Scotia, or Rossland, British Columbia, could not possibly have changed Canada's socio-economic order. They were too few, too scattered, too weak."

Second, the industrial unrest in Canada was not accompanied or followed by an economic downturn, much less the profound ones that Australia and New Zealand experienced in in the 1890s. Instead, from the mid-1890s to 1910, Canada experienced one of the greatest economic booms in its history. Canada was a "settler" nation with a "staples economy" in the nineteenth century, like New Zealand and Australia – dependent upon exports of agricultural products, timber, and minerals. But Canada "was better able to utilize its resource base to form linkages that increased the growth of final goods sectors than other settler economies" and "was better able to exploit global market conditions in the pre-World War I period in order to support its export-oriented growth strategy" (Zammit 2011, X).

Third, the Canadian trade union movement did not suffer the decisive, devastating defeats that their Australasian counterparts did as part of, or because of, the crisis. The outcomes of major industrial disputes were a mixed bag of victories, partial defeats, and stand-offs. In the seven-month mining strike, the unions had to give up on two fundamental goals – a closed shop and recognition from the mining companies – but they won a wage increase and the recognition of a limited number of rights (Lipton 1966, 107). The CPR trackmen gained recognition in their 1901 strike (Tuck 1983, 65; Webber 1991, 32). The CPR defeated the UBRE industrial union in 1903, but the railway brotherhoods (which represented a series of strong craft unions) opposed the UBRE and came out of the strike unscathed (Tuck 1983, 87–8). In short, Canadian unions were not vanquished industrially, and as a result, were not induced out of desperation to resign themselves to compulsory arbitration.

Fourth, as in Britain, and unlike Australasia, the state moved to contain and shorten the disputes. Creation of the Labour Department and passage of the Conciliation Act of 1900 provided the state with some capacity to intervene to shorten disputes and save the unions from total defeats. The department was conceived originally under Labour Minister Mulock as a "ineffective sop to labour pressure" – a source of patronage jobs for the unions, but under his successor and protégé, King, the department became a highly active intervener in bringing parties into conciliation (Craven 1980, 209–10). King's interventions were particularly helpful in avoiding a total defeat and possible extinction of the United Mine Workers of America in Canada during the Lethbridge strike (Baker 1980, 116). Thus, officials' ad hoc interventions in disputes before and after the Conciliation Act (reminiscent of the intercessions of high-level British officials in their industrial crises) blunted the severity and scope of the industrial relations crises, which also gave labour little reason to change its opposition to stronger state measures and lessened the state's need to resort to them.

THE ABSENCE OF A CHANGE IN THE GOVERNING PARTY OR COALITION

Bold policy innovations in the other nations were not possible without major political transformations that swept through governments. The crises in

Australia, New Zealand, and the United States led to significant shifts in control of government under a new majority party or new coalitions. Even in Britain, where the Liberal government remained in power, the party (and the "lib-lab" faction within it), enlarged its majority in the election before passage of the Labour Disputes Act of 1906. But because the Canadian crisis was less severe and widespread, it did not instigate a significant rise in labour's political mobilization that would help to usher in a new majority party or electoral coalition. The Liberal government that had begun in 1896 under Prime Minister Laurier continued in office.

THE AFL'S TAKEOVER AND LABOUR'S ABANDONMENT OF SUPPORT FOR COMPULSORY ARBITRATION

We have seen that the adoption of compulsory arbitration in Australia and New Zealand took a push from reformers within the state as well as the labour movements' acceptance of the idea. Support for compulsory arbitration existed in both the Canadian labour movement and within the state around the turn of the twentieth century but at different times.

The Toronto Trades and Labour Council in 1883 began calling for boards of arbitration "to which all disputes between workmen and their employers shall be submitted" (quoted in French 1962, 92). Although the Canadian Trades and Labour Congress' support for compulsory arbitration wavered somewhat throughout the 1890s, the TLC came out in favour of compulsory arbitration in 1892, 1894, 1898 (as part of its "Winnipeg Platform of Principles"), and at its 1900 annual convention "definitely declared for the compulsory feature" (Scotton 1956, 11; Logan 1928, 66; Kealey 1995, 422). The TLC supported the Conciliation Act of 1900 but had wanted it to include compulsory arbitration (Craven 1980, 238). Ralph Smith, president of the TLC, was a strong proponent of compulsory arbitration even after he was deposed as the organization's leader in 1902. The railway and mining unions "assumed that arbitration would encourage bargaining because it would limit the employer's power to act unilaterally" (Fudge and Tucker 2001, 41).

Two forces seem to account for labour's early and largely favourable position towards compulsory arbitration. One was the influence of the Knights of Labor, which persisted throughout the 1890s. The Knights listed arbitration as one of the ten points in their Declaration of Principles (Kealey and Palmer 1982, 111; French 1962, 9). The Knights had a presence in upper Canada where they were influential within the Provincial Workmen's Association of Nova Scotia, a miners' union. The miners struck four times during the 1880s, but its leadership opposed strikes as a method of dispute resolution. As a result, the PWA became one of the proponents of the Arbitration Act of 1888, which the Liberal government of Nova Scotia passed with the mine owners in opposition. Nova Scotia's experience with compulsory arbitration was one of a handful of early experiments with the idea that Australasian reformers studied before embarking on their own experiments.

Perhaps a more important reason for labour's support of compulsory arbitration was its industrial weakness (Logan 1928, 77). Even without the kind of deep crisis that Australian and New Zealand workers faced, Canadian unions were weak industrially for reasons discussed later in the chapter. According to Coats writing shortly after this time (1913, 297), "[t]hat labour at [sic] this period was content to leave its claims to compulsory arbitration is a striking commentary on the reasonableness, or perhaps on the weakness, of the early movement. It is a policy which has all but disappeared in the strong unions of to-day."

Finally, as indicated by Ralph Smith and the TLC, Canadian labour had greater faith in the state than their American brethren did (Craven 1980, 144). According to Fudge and Tucker (2001, 34), "[w]orkers in the transportation and resources sectors were much more willing than their craft counterparts to look to the state for assistance. In these strikes, federally appointed conciliation boards, rather than the courts, provided the template of industrial legality." And although the Canadian state resorted to the use of police and militias to repress mass unrest, the federal government left that to the local authorities in order to maintain the perception of the state's neutrality in class relations (Fudge and Tucker 2001, 286).

Despite these conditions that were auspicious for labour's support of compulsory arbitration, the TLC reversed its position on that policy option at its historic 1902 conference in Berlin, Ontario. "[T]he [Trades and Labour] Congress, after further study of the matter, was forced to concur in the opinion of the [railway] brotherhoods. It immediately proceeded, by a vote of 78 to 12, to pass a resolution of disapproval of a bill which, if enacted, 'would rob the railway employees of their constitutional rights, destroy their organizations, and place them absolutely in the hands of railway companies,' and promised its best efforts to secure the defeat of the measure" (Logan 1928, 67).

The reversal was a direct result of the takeover of the TLC by the American Federation of Labor (AFL) and the ascendance of the American-led international unions over purely Canadian national unions (Logan 1928, 129). At the 1902 Berlin, Ontario, convention of the TLC, the AFL, led by President Samuel Gompers, gained significant control over the organization. The AFL unions voted to expel all Canadian unions that were against the AFL. The AFL's penetration of the Canadian movement had begun years earlier. Under John Flett, a Canadian organizer, the AFL organized more than seven hundred locals of craft unions in Canada between 1898 and 1902 (Bothwell, Drummond, and English 1987, 95). The AFL induced the TLC to reverse its previously favourable stand on compulsory arbitration, (Cameron and Young 1960, 41), dealing a fatal blow to the TLC's continued support for compulsory arbitration. As we saw in chapter 5, Gompers was uncompromisingly hostile towards the idea, which he likened to "slavery" (Craven 1980). Smith, deposed as head of the TLC, criticized Gompers for assuming that the same conditions in the United States that made compulsory arbitration unattractive existed in Canada (see Craven 1980, 144). The TLC dropped the word "compulsory" from its declaration of principles and substituted the word "voluntary" instead. According to Logan, "[d]oubtless the change in attitude with regard to compulsory arbitration was influenced by the outspoken denunciation of the principle" by Gompers (Logan 1928, 67). The TLC remained staunchly opposed to compulsory arbitration and registered a "vigorous protest" against the idea when efforts to pass such a law in the Dominion Parliament reappeared in 1910 (Logan 1928, 217).

THE STATE'S INTEREST IN COMPULSORY ARBITRATION EMERGES TOO LATE FOR LABOUR AND IS ABORTED

The TLC's commitment to compulsory arbitration before the crisis and prior to the AFL takeover found little support from the state. The delay in the onset of industrial and economic crises meant that the state had little incentive to push for strong measures to deal with disputes and to address the place of labour unions in the Canadian economy. The 1889 Royal Commission on the Relations of Capital and Labour recommended a network of voluntary boards of conciliation and arbitration, but rejected any compulsory features (Kealey 1995, 421). Commissioners sitting on other official investigations came to the same conclusion. The Dominion Parliament passed the Conciliation Act of 1900, which was essentially like the British Conciliation Act of 1896 – setting up a Department of Labour to collect statistics and with the task of encouraging the spread of voluntary conciliation boards. (see Cameron and Young 1960, 40–1). The Canadian state up until the crisis mainly followed the British predilection that voluntary measures would suffice and were much preferred in order for the state to remain "neutral."

State actors' interest in compulsory measures rose once industrial unrest rose in the first years of the new century. Webber (1991, 17) reports that from 1900 to 1907 "at least ten Members of Parliament – many representing labour constituencies and several identified with the government – declared their support for the judicial settlement of disputes." And during the debated over the IDIA in 1907, the Conservative Opposition leader argued in favour of giving the idea consideration, but it was the 1903 railway strike that prompted the most serious interest in compulsory arbitration. The Royal Commission to Investigate Labour Unrest in British Columbia, established in the wake of the railroad and mining strikes, recommended compulsory arbitration in "special cases," which included public services (Kealey 1995, 430). Following that, the Labour Ministry introduced a bill providing for the compulsory arbitration of labour disputes on railroads. It prohibited strikes and lockouts and empowered the government to levy heavy fines on those who resorted to them. Labor Minister Mulock put forward the measure as a trial balloon with no expectation of its immediate passage (Craven 1980, 273–6). The genesis of the proposal remains unclear. Mulock had travelled to Australasia in 1901, but he did not come back as a supporter of compulsory arbitration (Webber 1991, 32). Outside pressure in favour of the measure came from Ralph Smith (recently deposed head of the TLC), the former British Columbia mines minister, and the president of the Canadian Pacific Railway, Sir Thomas Shaughnessy (who sought a way to outlaw strikes) (Webber 1991, 33).

The government withdrew the trial balloon when it ran into the opposition of the railway unions and the AFL (Webber 1991, 33). The interest of Mulock and other Canadian elites in compulsory arbitration came after the AFL's penetration of the Canadian movement. More importantly, the railways were among the few unions that belonged to "the aristocracy of the North American labour movement." Their opposition to compulsory measures, according to Craven (1981, xxx), arose because the unions "had no worries about union recognition or having to wage lengthy strikes merely to establish bargaining relations. They insisted that they had managed to develop an intricate and institutionalized mechanism for resolving grievances and carrying on collective bargaining, and they were concerned that the compulsory features of the Act would disrupt this.... They were fully fledged business unions and as such were opposed to state intervention in their affairs."

The AFL's opposition to compulsory arbitration was important, but we should not exaggerate its control over the Canadian movement. Even that part of the movement most closely associated with the American movement, the TLC, had different policy preferences from the AFL and enjoyed a degree of autonomy to pursue them. (This is evident in the TLC's later embrace of social legislation and public ownership of industry, which diverged from the AFL's distrust of state action and commitment to voluntarism (Robin 1968, 277–88).

While it is unlikely that the railway brotherhoods would have accepted compulsory arbitration, it is plausible that the unions covered by the IDIA a few years later, would have supported such a measure. Except for the railway unions, the TLC and the other unions covered by the IDIA accepted the provision for a "cooling off" period in the IDIA. It is possible that the TLC would have accepted compulsory arbitration if the government had combined it with legal reforms guaranteeing labour rights and obligations on employers to recognize unions and bargain collectively, particularly since many Canadian employers refused to recognize and bargain with the unions. These conditions helped lead the Australasian nations to adopt compulsory arbitration.

KING'S OPPOSITION TO COMPULSORY ARBITRATION
With compulsory arbitration off the table, it fell to the Deputy Minister of Labour, William Lyon Mackenzie King, to fill the vacuum created when the Labour Department's compulsory arbitration trial balloon burst in 1903. King opposed compulsory arbitration in part because of labour's opposition to the

idea, but King might have overcome labour's opposition to compulsory arbitration if he had coupled arbitration with a mandate for employers to recognize unions, as Australian reformers had done. King opposed compulsory arbitration as much as the AFL and TLC did, but for different reasons. He thought that the market, not the state, should set wage levels and that judges sitting as arbiters lacked the knowledge to set wage rates, that proponents of compulsory arbitration placed too much value on the short-term avoidance of strikes, and that strikes "may ... bring greater good than its prevention" (quoted in Craven 1980, 274). His views, which the Labour Department's Annual Report echoed, cited a preference for market-based wage determination and "difficulties besetting the enforcement of awards" as an additional objection to compulsory arbitration (Craven 1980, 278).

Collectively, the nature and timing of the crisis made both organized labour and the state feel less in need of compulsory arbitration, which of course reinforced the constraints imposed by the AFL's opposition to the idea. Labour did not need to cling to compulsory arbitration as a lifeline for organizational survival that way that Australasian unions did, and the timing of the crisis and the state's response to it came too late to avoid the AFL's influence on the Canadian unions. Mulock's tentative efforts aside, no champion of compulsory arbitration emerged within the Canadian state before or after organized labour defeated the Labour Department's trial balloon. Mulock did not possess the knowledge and long-term commitment to the idea of Pember Reeves or Charles Kingston (Webber 1991, 33).

Why No Voluntarism in Canada?

The key conditions that permitted Britain to consolidate a voluntarist regime during its critical juncture were an employer class that largely accepted unions and collective bargaining, the ability of the unions to bring effective political pressure upon the Liberals when the courts threatened them and the Liberal Party's decision to accede to the unions' demands for complete immunity from civil damages. These were not the only conditions that mattered, but they were the ones most immediate during the crisis. Conditions in Canada diverged from those in Britain at the turn of the century in all these respects.

EMPLOYERS' RESISTANCE TO UNIONS
Clearly, employer hostility to unions was an obstacle to voluntarism in Canada as it was in the United States. Describing the attitude of Canadian employers towards unions at the turn of the century, Heron wrote "few Canadian employers were prepared to have anything to do with this upstart labour movement" (Heron 1989, 38). Canadian employers did not take the accommodationist approach to labour that most of their British counterparts did. Undoubtedly, Canada's proximity to the United States had some effect. New management

theories like Taylorism and Fordism, which did not leave room for unions, developed in the United States and spread quickly to Canada. Employers' organizations often had close connections with American "open shop" organizations that existed to drive unions away, using scabs, blacklists, spies, and the court orders (Heron 1989, 33, 38). In a way very much reminiscent of American employers, even as late as the 1940s, many Canadian employers continued to resist unions and remained "blindly hostile" to them. Many of them looked upon the federal government's adoption of Wagner Act principles during the Second World War as an anomaly forced upon them that should not be continued during peacetime (McInnis 2001, 163–5).

We should not overstate the importance of employer opposition during the crisis. We saw that some British employers tried to use the courts to thwart unions and succeeded in a series of cases culminating in the *Taff Vale* decision and it was not employers' attitudes towards labour that resolved the crisis in labour's favour and removed the remaining legal impediments. It took the unions' political mobilization and pressure on the Liberal Party for the unions to get Parliament to pass the Labour Disputes Act.

THE UNIONS FIGHT IN THE COURTS AND LOSE

Canadian judges increasingly used criminal and civil law and injunctions to prevent unions from picketing and engaging in other strike-related activities. Canadian employers used criminal and civil law to stop unions from engaging in sympathy strikes or persuading other unions from doing so. Under civil law, employers invoked the injunction to counteract increasing solidarity across crafts and to preserve the open shop, particularly in Ontario where craft unions were strongest. These suits spread to unions in the West later in the crisis. Employers argued that by encouraging the breach of contracts, unions were engaged in conspiracies to injure. Employers also began suing unions for damages like the suits British employers brought at the turn of the twentieth century. In the wake of the British *Taff Vale* decision, Canadian courts grappled with the question of unions' legal liability for damages and the vulnerability of their strike funds. Although unions were unincorporated bodies, judges sometimes assessed them damages as if they were (Fudge and Tucker 2001, 18–34).

The critical juncture of the early twentieth century might have had as one of its outcomes moving Canada in the direction of voluntarism by removing legal obstacles to trade union activity that existed in Canada at the time, including the criminal and civil penalties that unions faced and court-ordered injunctions. Canada could have adopted these changes in place of, or perhaps even in addition to, the compulsory investigation and conciliation that Canadians ended up with. The issue was a top priority for Canadian labour starting in the first decade of the twentieth century (Craven 1980, 196–206). In the end, the labour movement was unable to remove the law and courts as impediments to union organizing and activities that the British movement accomplished through the Labour Disputes Act of 1906.

Canadian unions fought the legal restrictions on their activities imposed by the courts and common law in both judicial and legislative venues. In 1906, they turned to the courts in the Metallic Roofing Company case. The company had sought an injunction against the metal workers union to halt picketing and for damages. After some complicated litigation, the TLC decided to appeal to the Privy Council in London, the highest judicial authority of the Dominion. The Privy Council ordered a re-trial, and the case was settled out of court before any clear judicial determination on the larger issues that the case posed. A similar case arose in 1909 in Winnipeg involving a plumber's union and the TLC once again brought it before the Privy Council, but its appeal was denied (Craven 1981, 204–6).

KING'S LACK OF SUPPORT FOR REMOVING LEGAL RESTRICTIONS ON LABOUR
Given his domination of the government's response to the crisis of industrial unrest, the unions would have benefited greatly if King had sympathized with their demands, but King was not particularly concerned with protecting unions' organizational and legal interests or harmonizing those interests with his aim of reducing industrial unrest. One reason for this is that King's bureaucratic position as chief conciliator shaped his policy objectives. He placed primary emphasis upon bringing industrial disputes to an end as quickly and with as little disruption to the public as possible. He did not define his task as finding a final settlement or one that was equitable by some standard (Craven 1980, 221–2). The public would measure the Labour Department's success in industrial disputes in terms of whether it got workers back to work rather than "improving wages, working conditions or the long-term prospects for industrial relations in a particular industry" (Craven 1980, 233). Thus, for King, anything that might delay or impede bringing industrial disputes to a speedy conclusion posed a problem, especially labour's threshold demand for employer recognition. King's preferred policy tool for dealing with industrial conflict – conciliation – was not effective when confronted with demands for recognition (Fudge and Tucker 2001, 38–40). According to Craven (1980, 233), "King was extremely reluctant to grant legitimacy to some typical demands made by unions—in particular, recognition."

One reason for King's reluctance was practical – union recognition was a demand that defied compromise and so could easily make disputes intractable and prolong them, as King learned during the Lethbridge mining strike. Unlike the IDIA, labour law reform was not consistent with the state's goal of reducing unrest; strengthening labour by giving it a firmer legal foundation could work against the IDIA by strengthening labour's ability to challenge employers, worsening unrest.

The other reason King balked at using the state's power to restructure or rebalance capital and labour relations arose out of his belief in the importance of personal character in dispute resolution – that industrial disputes were mainly about whether people wanted and tried to get along with each other. Disputes continued and escalated, he believed, because of a lack of empathy on the part of employers and/or employees towards their adversary or because of poor interpersonal skills and relationships. He reasoned that some employers might be justified in refusing to recognize unions if the demands came from "agitators" and militants rather than "responsible" unionists (Craven 1980, 235). When King intervened to reach a settlement in the mining strike, it was his first experience with the socialist unions in the West (Cameron and Young 1960, 43). King not only had to negotiate between the miners and the mining companies, but also between the AFL's United Mine Workers of America and the syndicalist Western Federation of Miners, which were engaged in a jurisdictional clash (Craven 1980, 241; Heron 1989, 40–1). King was partial to the more "responsible" unions that fit the mold of the AFL – non-ideological, business-oriented, non-political, and controlled by moderate leaders. King did not embrace repression of organized labour, but he was no friend of unions that he considered "irresponsible" and made what he regarded as "unreasonable" demands.

These points help us sharpen the difference between King and his reformer counterparts in Australasia. While King, Reeves, and Kingston were all "new liberals," King was far less radical both in his vision of how much the state should intervene to reduce industrial unrest, whether it should use its powers to reshape the relationship between capital and labour. While all three reformers employed liberal rhetoric concerning the appropriateness of the state's "neutrality" in labour relations, the Australasians were much more willing to use the state to, as they saw it, "rebalance" class relations in favour of labour both for instrumental economic reasons and to promote a more just distribution of income. King would never describe himself, as Reeves and Kingston did, as a "state socialist." King was less sceptical than his Australasian reformers about the long-run viability of workable industrial relations under capitalism. Unlike his "state socialist" counterparts in other countries, King's philosophy was closer to the neutral liberalism that undergirded voluntarism, in which he viewed the state as "an impartial umpire" whose role was to interfere with the two parties as little as possible. Bolstering labour's institutional position by compelling employers to recognize unions would have put the state too much on the side of one of the parties and supplanting collective bargaining with compulsory arbitration awards would have violated the "mutual consent" of the two parties. Thus, King favoured a more coercive role for the state in regulating industrial relations than the British voluntarists did, and he did not display any willingness, as they did, to undertake the legal reforms necessary to allow labour to compete with employers on a more level playing field.

PARLIAMENTARY DEFERENCE TO COURTS AND OTHER INSTITUTIONAL
OBSTACLES

As important as he was, King was not the entire Liberal Party or the government in power. On the surface at least, it was not out of the question for the unions to appeal to the elected parts of the government. At the provincial level, the unions persuaded the British Columbia Parliament to pass a law barring the use of the labour injunction. The unions also had some victories in the Dominion Parliament unrelated to labour law. The Liberal Party, with whom the TLC was most closely aligned through patronage and Parliamentary representation, acceded to labour's demands by establishing the Labour Department and passing the Fair Wages Resolution and the Alien Labour Act, which constituted partial victories. On the issue of labour law reform, however, the Canadian legislatures honoured judicial independence and left much of the law in this area to judge-made common law (Craven 1980, 197). According to Craven (1980, 206, 196–7), the Liberal government refused the unions' demands for labour law reform, "taking refuge behind the civil law provisions of the BNA [British North America] Act" and "the constitutional safeguard of judicial independence." Sections 91 and 92 of the BNA enumerated the various powers of the federal ("Dominion") and provincial governments, but on the subject of labour relations they were ambiguous, which encouraged different opinions concerning the constitutionality of a national labour code and led to inertia (McInnis 2001, 158). The fact that the Privy Council in 1925 declared the IDIA *ultra vires* because it exceeded the powers of the federal government suggested that this was a real impediment, although it also served as a convenient excuse for the federal government's inaction. Second, as in Australasia, the upper chamber of Parliament was a bastion of anti-labour elites. The Senate blocked a law to give recognition rights that the Laurier Government passed in the House of Commons.

WEAK UNIONS AND COLLECTIVE BARGAINING

Trade union organization is a pre-condition for collective bargaining. We have seen that Britain established a large number of craft and operatives' unions and a network of voluntary joint boards of conciliation and arbitration long before the advent of major industrial relations crises and state intervention to settle disputes. Britain's early industrialization and its international lead for several crucial decades in the nineteenth century gave rise to the early emergence of unions and their gravitation to "responsible" unionism, which in turn, fostered a propensity for employers to cooperate with them. The accommodation was consolidated when employers realized the advantages of working with moderate unions and how getting rid of them would be more difficult. Growth in union and employer organizations, the foundation for widespread collective bargaining, gained further momentum.

Canadian industrialization was much slower, the emergence of unions took longer, and employer acceptance of unions was less widespread than in Britain or even the United States. Canadian labour organization was highly localized and divided, and we cannot speak of a Canadian labour movement with a national or regional presence until the 1870s. The Canadian movement was untouched by "the political experiments, the radicalism, and the various panaceas which successively challenged industrial methods in the United States" (Logan 1948, 38). By 1910, only 2 per cent of the Canadian labour force was unionized (Robin 1968, 280). Even if they had been unified, they "could not deliver the vote ..., [c]ontained only a tiny minority of Canada's non-agricultural labour force .... and were neither willing nor able to organize any sort of co-ordinated general strike action" (Bothwell, Drummond, and English 1987, 100).

It is hardly surprising, then, that collective bargaining and voluntary joint boards of conciliation and arbitration emerged late and very gradually in Canada (Webber 1991, 19). Throughout the nineteenth century, locally prominent government officials and other elites frequently volunteered their services and initiated mediation (Webber 1991, 20). The enactment of statutes to encourage conciliation and arbitration in three Canadian provinces in the late nineteenth century was tacit admission of the absence of effective collective bargaining machinery. The governments of Ontario (in 1873) and British Columbia (in 1894) passed laws providing for local boards for voluntary conciliation and arbitration, and Nova Scotia introduced compulsory arbitration (in 1888). All these experiments failed. The Ontario and British Columbia laws failed because they relied upon voluntary action. In Nova Scotia, labour lost the only dispute that came under the Act when the employers went to the federal (Dominion) government to get a settlement to their liking. Although compulsory, awards were not enforceable. According to Cameron and Young (1960, 35), "[h]ad that machinery been used to any extent, its very nature would have forced employers to recognize certain representatives of their employees and would almost surely have led rapidly to more extended collective bargaining. The decisions of councils and boards would then have provided precedents, which other parties could have used in turn to measure their own relationships."

Thus, dispute resolution machinery of any kind was weak in Canada until the eve of the industrial relations crises of 1903–11. With the onset of greater industrial conflict at the turn of the century, a number of Canadian unions and employers were involved in a "range of dispute settlement practices," but these were localized and apparently emerged late, in response to the growing industrial relations tension at the turn of the century (see Craven 1980, 149–56).

Voluntarism was very unlikely to emerge in Canada because the nation possessed few pre-crisis conditions that were conducive to such a system. Collective bargaining through the voluntary, self-initiated actions of employers and employee organizations had not become widespread. Canadian labour did not enjoy conditions that were especially hospitable to the organic development of a robust and widespread system of collective bargaining. Neither the establishment of the Labour Department nor the Conciliation Act could make up for these deficiencies, and Canadian unions failed to secure legal rights that would permit them to engage employers without the interference of the common law. To be sure, British labour did not completely secure its rights and free itself from judicial interference until 1906, but it had secured immunity from criminal prosecution for its strike activities before that time. The disunity of organized labour in Canadian industry and politics also diminished the prospects for voluntarism. Once Canada faced industrial relations crises, labour and industry could not resolve the disputes on their own. Although the state at this time was committed to a voluntarist approach, that approach was realistic only if disputes could be confined to the parties immediately affected.

LABOUR MOVEMENT FRAGMENTATION AND DISUNITY
Perhaps the central reason for the relative weakness of Canadian trade unions and collective bargaining was fragmentation and division within the movement's ranks (Cameron and Young 1960, 39). The movement was very divided along multiple, and often reinforcing, cleavages. Labour's disunity was especially acute just prior to and during the critical first decade of the twentieth century, when industrial unrest gave rise to the passage of the Railway Labour Disputes Act of 1903 and the Industrial Disputes and Investigation Act of 1907.

Labour's disunity is crucial to understanding labour's industrial weakness in these years (Cameron and Young 1960, 49–51). Labour's late development and internal disarray arose out of "differences in culture, immigration, geographic separation," and internal divisions within the labour movement prevented it from acting as a cohesive force and shaping public opinion to its advantage (Cameron and Young 1960, 33). Unlike both Britain and Australasia, Canada's early colonization meant that Canadian labour missed out on the intellectual support of English radicalism, and thus "there was none of that encouragement to organization which the English unionists received from the philosophic radicalism of upper and educated classes of 1825–50" (Coats 1913, 292). Cameron and Young (1960, 33) locate labour's disunity in "the scattered and predominantly agricultural population of the 19th and 20th Centuries.... Poor communications and the slow growth of industry hampered by severe depressions."

The sheer size of Canada gave rise to starkly different regional economies, which in turn, produced sharply different workers' interests. Eastern English Canada established a manufacturing economy, centred in Ontario, with relatively more politically moderate craft unions, while Western Canada's economy, centred in British Columbia, the nation's second most industrialized and unionized province, was based on mining, lumber, and other extractive resources and gave rise to more radical working-class organizations. Ethnic diversity, of course, was not unique to Canada. The other settler nations, Australia, New Zealand, and the United States, also had working classes divided along ethnic lines. French Canada, however, posed a much more daunting challenge to labour solidarity. "Ethnic heterogeneity of the electoral mass multiplied the number of cross pressures on the individual artisan and destroyed any possibilities of creating a homogeneous radical working-class subculture" (Robin 1968, 12). These divisions created a multitude of interests and a cacophony of positions on the goals and strategies that the movement should pursue. According to Bothwell, Drummond, and English (1987, 99), "[i]n truth, the Canadian unionists were never sure what they wanted.... This confusion created the atmosphere for weak legislation intermittent gains, rhetorical flourish, and a search for [immigrant] scapegoats.... [L]abour rode off in too many directions at once."

The Canadian government's policies also exacerbated the internal divisions of the labour movement. An important element of the Conservative Party's National Policy was high tariffs designed to nurture manufacturing industries in central Canada. Unions in Eastern Canada welcomed this policy, but workers in the West opposed it because of the differential impacts of protectionism on different sectors and the division between Catholic, Quebec-based unions and labour in the rest of Canada.

Another major source of disunity leading up to the crisis period of 1901–11 was the division between the Knights of Labor and the craft unions. The Knights began in the United States and made significant inroads in Canada in the 1880s. The Knights survived in Canada longer than in the United States, and their ideals and approach to industrial disputes shaped the Canadian labour movement until the mid-1890s, when Canadian trade unionists became more critical of the close connection with American labour organizations. The Knights believed in arbitration, not strikes, as the preferred remedy for settling industrial disputes (Logan 1928, 47, 77; Heron 1989, 25). They were about equally influential with the trade unions until the mid-1890s, but survived into the early 1900s (Logan 1928, 55). The division between the Knights and the craft unions helps to account for why Canada did not develop a permanent labour federation – the Trades and Labour Congress of Canada – until 1883, which was relatively late compared to the other Anglophone nations. The Knights of Labor also led an effort to disengage labour from politics (Logan 1928, 57). Canadian labour had reduced its involvement in politics in the 1890s when its attempts to win reforms though legislative means fell short. Finally, the Knights were a major impediment in movement towards developing a labour party until they died out after 1900, but by that time other divisions within the movement had surfaced and worsened (Logan 1928, 59). The conflict between the craft unions and the Knights culminated in 1902 when the TLC banished the Knights from the organization. The Knights and some national trade unions established the National Trades and Labor Congress, which became the Canadian Federation of Labour (CFL) in 1908. The Knights retreated to Quebec where local syndicates eventually replaced them.[5]

Labour's disunity impeded efforts to spread unionism and collective bargaining. The TLC was so absorbed in the late nineteenth and early twentieth centuries with "protecting itself from the onslaught of ... new dual unions" in western Canada, the Maritimes, and Quebec, that it "adopted a totally defensive posture, undertaking little new organization and offering no solace to the hundreds of thousands of unorganized workers in the country" (Abella 1975, 5). Second, "trade union leaders were so occupied with building an effective national organization and 'keeping the peace' within the organization, that they were unable to use the rudimentary statutory provisions to achieve collective bargaining and de facto recognition by employers" (Cameron and Young 1960, 39). Third, labour's divisions discouraged middle-class, progressive reformers from trying to help labour. Such reformers, as we have seen, were critical allies of the unions in Britain and Australasia. The internal conflicts and inability to coordinate a national movement drove Canadian reformers in other directions, such as making cities more livable and less corrupt (Bothwell Drumond, and English 1987, 102–3). Finally, disunity made it easier for employers to resist unions. Many employers refused to recognize unions, such as the mining magnate of British Columbia, James Dunsmuir (Bothwell, Drummond, and English 1987, 93; Karr 2003).

THE LEGAL INSECURITY OF TRADE UNIONS

Internal divisions and AFL influence were not the only forces that reduced the Canadian labour movement's strength. As in Britain and the United States, the common law tradition posed an obstacle to labour's ability to secure full legal rights. Unions were illegal entities – conspiracies in restraint of trade – during most of the nineteenth century. The arrest and imprisonment of twenty-four printers in Toronto in 1872, who had struck for a nine-hour working day, made it clear that Canadian workers were vulnerable to the same harsh legal penalties to which their British brethren had been subjected until passage of the enactment of the British Trade Union Acts of the 1870s. The British Acts had no force in Canada, so Canadian unions remained illegal combinations in the eyes of the law (reinforced by an amendment to the Canadian Criminal law in 1869) (Logan 1948, 38–41; Craven 1980, 168).

Canadian unions demanded legislation along British lines, pointing to the irony that workers enjoyed more rights in Britain than in Canada, despite in the mother country's greater class distinctions. Parliament passed the Canadian Trade Unions Act of 1872, a direct copy of the British Trade Unions Act of 1871, which repealed criminal penalties against unions as conspiracies in restraint of trade. Some historians view the adoption of the Act as driven by emulation. According to Coats (1913, 296), "British precedent," rather than trade union political strength, "was the sole argument which secured its support." Other historians have seen the 1872 Act as an effort by Conservatives to capture trade union votes that had usually gone to Liberal reformers (Creighton 1943). Still others argue that electoral incentives were not the main motivation for Conservatives because few workers possessed the vote at the time and the Liberals had alienated workers before the 1872 campaign began. Instead, the Trade Union Act was a necessary element in the Conservatives' "National Policy," which they launched around the same time, and which was directed at developing infant manufacturing industries in central Canada. As part of that effort, the Canadian government sought to attract skilled labour, particularly from Britain, and prevent those immigrants from migrating to the United States in search of higher wages (Craven 1980, 172). The government did not want British immigrant workers to be subject to restrictions to which they were not subject in Britain.

Passage of the 1872 Act did not settle the issue of labour's legal status in Canada, however. Canadian workers could join unions, but employers did not have to recognize them, could refuse to hire non-union workers, and could fire employees who became union members (Fudge and Tucker 2001, 2–3). The unions also continued to suffer from how the law treated picketing, boycotting, and injuries that resulted from unions persuading workers to break labour contracts (Logan 1928, 230–1; Kealey 1995, 420). Trade union organization was more akin to a legal privilege than a legal right. Workers were permitted to join unions, but the state did not protect them against employers who sought to subvert and impede them (Fudge and Tucker 2001, 10–11). The Canadian Act of 1872 included the same deficiencies as the 1871 British Act: at the same time that these nations adopted their Trade Unions Acts, they amended their Criminal Codes in ways that made picketing and other non-violent acts ("watching and besetting") illegal. The amendment to the Criminal Code "effectively, if unintentionally, repealed the Trade Union Act" by restating the common law prohibitions against conspiracies in restraint of trade" (Craven 1980, 199). The British Parliament remedied these deficiencies in British law in 1875, when it passed the Conspiracy and Protection of Property Act (and expanded them later in the Trade Disputes Act of 1906). The Canadian government approved no such remedies, however. Despite protests by the unions, the government refused to pass any new statutes, insisting that no new laws were needed because the 1872 Trade Unions Act did not list peaceful picketing as illegal (Logan 1928, 230). Thus, "[w]hile the legal right to freedom of association has existed since the 1870s, effective use of that right on a broad front was not achieved until the last years of World War II" (Cameron and Young 1960, 33). Thus, Canadian unions obtained full legal rights later than the unions in the other nations in this study.

The lack of effective legal rights was not as consequential before 1900 as it would become afterwards. The absence of such rights meant that employers had the opportunity to go to the courts to stifle unions. Yet, until the twentieth century, "employers infrequently resorted to legal institutions to deal with workers' collective action at the workplace and legal regimes designed specifically to deal with labour unrest were the exception rather than the rule" (Fudge and Tucker 2001, 2). Probably because labour was relatively unorganized in

Canada, employers were content to deal with workers simply through the workings of the labour market.

PARTY DIVISION AND CONTROL OVER THE LABOUR MOVEMENT
Canada was no different than other Anglophone democracies in the symbiotic relationship that developed between labour and the established parties. The unions sought access to the state to protect and promote their interests as organizations representing groups of workers, and the established bourgeois parties drew elected support from enfranchised workers. Whether the parties or the unions had greater leverage in the relationship depended, in part, on the coalition-building strategies of the political parties and, in part, on the strength and autonomy of labour.

The Liberal Party gained support nationwide in the late nineteenth century based upon its commitment to the maintenance of national unity. It positioned itself as a broad, inclusive, pan-Canadian party capable of appealing across the regional, class, and ethnic divisions of Canadian society. A key plank in the Liberals' program was the retention of provincial rights, which allowed them to appeal across regional and ethnic divisions. While national unity and provincial rights might seem at odds, Liberals believed that unity could be achieved by preserving a large measure of provincial autonomy, given Canada's beginnings as a confederation, its regionalism and the francophone minority centred in Quebec. Their electoral strategy in mid-twentieth century was rooted in this approach and it steered them away from bold efforts to confront or circumvent the obstacles to federal government expansion of labour rights and the welfare state that the courts and BNA had imposed. Liberals thus had more to gain electorally from resisting trade union demands than pursuing them.

The Liberal and Conservative parties of Canada acted as brokers for different groups and interests, which often cut across class lines. Commercial interests had greater influence than labour in both parties. This "imbalance of pressure" could not be counteracted by the election of labour friendly candidates. Some of these candidates abandoned labour once they took office, but even those that did not and succeeded to some degree in pushing the bourgeois parties for reforms, had to work within a system of party discipline in which it was the party's majority caucus, not individual members, that ultimately controlled what measures reached the agenda and were approved. "During the Laurier [Liberal] and Borden [Conservative] regimes there were too few labour friends to nearly fulfill the legislative aspirations of the TLC, central councils and provincial federations. Like the rural progressive revolt, the forays of labour into independent politics was inspired by the existence of elite dominated disciplined parties unable to satisfy the claims of competing pressure groups and conflicting classes" (Robin 1968, 291).

The Canadian labour movement's relationship with the party system was distinctive in a few ways. Canadian political parties had a stronger hold over the unions perhaps than in the other nations. According to Robin, "partyism" gained a strong grip on labour movement leaders and members. Both Liberal and Conservatives "had sunk their ideological and organizational roots into the new labour movement" by the 1880s (1968, 10). The ties between workers and unions and the parties were reinforced to an unusual degree by patronage. The parties maintained support by providing supporters with material incentives, including government jobs, as well as social and ideological incentives.

Second, workers did not have primary allegiance to a single bourgeois party but were split between the Liberals and Conservatives ("Grits and Tories"). Moreover, these loyalties reinforced other divisions within the labour movement. For example, the parties advanced policies that delivered benefits to some unions at the expense of others. The Conservative Party attracted many working-class votes with the threat that votes for the Liberals would bring an end to protectionist policies. Partyism itself reinforced regionally based working-class divisions – it was much weaker among the radical labour organizations of western Canada and stronger in Ontario. Some labour activists and intellectuals at the time, like Thomas Phillips Thompson, bemoaned these entrenched and divided loyalties and documented their impact on labour unity during labour conventions and other gatherings of union officials and members (Robin 1968, 8–10, 61).

Where labour was weak and divided, as in Canada, not only did it have less leverage over parties, but it bred a defensiveness that drove it to embrace patronage parties because they provided unions with a political and institutional anchor in a labour movement riven with factionalism and instability (Robin 1968, 281).

LABOUR'S INSUFFICIENT INFLUENCE IN THE CANADIAN PARTY SYSTEM
Some of these institutional obstacles were not unique. Pro-labour forces in Australia and New Zealand had overcome obstructionist behaviour of upper chambers dominated by propertied interests. Eventually, of course, these obstacles would yield and the Liberal Party would enact eventually a more far-reaching set of protections for labour and mandates upon employers than what labour demanded at the turn of the century. While the British North America Act was unique to Canada, an explanation resting purely on these factors begs the question as to why the Liberal Party lacked sufficient commitment to labour law reform to amend the BNA, if necessary, and in turn, why Canadian labour was unable to induce a different response from the Liberals on one of its top priorities.

Labour's strength in Parliament was weaker than it was in Britain and Australasia because of labour's deep political divisions and an inability to forge stronger union–party relationships. Much of the radicalism, syndicalism, and socialism that arose in western Canada originated in the western United States, which produced greater conflict in labour relations in western than in eastern Canada. Labour organizations in western Canada were more likely to resort to strikes and other forms of direct action rather than party politics and parliamentarism (Robin 1968, 273–5). The sheer size and proximity of the American economy and labour movement made American influence in Canada virtually inevitable. Many Canadian unions were branches of internationals headquartered in the United States.

The largest American labour organization, the American Federation of Labor (AFL) exerted the most influence in Canada. Most historians agree that the AFL's takeover of the TLC further weakened the Canadian labour movement (Abella 1975; Craven 1980, xxxx). The AFL's insistence on craft autonomy made it difficult to build the TLC into a truly nationwide, encompassing, and centralized labour organization. The TLC was no longer allowed to establish locals in trades where a union already existed, no national (Canadian) union could organize workers where an international union existed, and unions could not establish central labour councils in cities or towns unless they were chartered by the AFL-led TLC (Bothwell, Drummond and English, 1987, 95). The takeover also resulted in the creation of a set of labour organizations in French-speaking Quebec (which did not interest Gompers) and the Maritime provinces that were separate from those in the rest of English-speaking Canada (Abella 1975, 4).

More importantly, the AFL takeover exacerbated the pre-existing regional and ideological split between the conservative, business-oriented craft unions in the east, and the more radical industrial unions and encompassing worker organizations in the west (Abella 1975, 4–5). The AFL's takeover of the TLC came just when socialism was spreading in the west. The TLC's dominant craft unions distrusted particularly the American Labor Union (ALU), an American-born socialist organization that emerged in British Columbia in 1903 (Logan 1928, 79, 151). The Western Federation of Miners and the United Mine Workers in the United States also engaged in sharp jurisdictional disputes in 1903. "The strongly socialist philosophy of the Western Federation and its faith in direct action ran counter to the concentration on piecemeal improvement of wages and working conditions which was typical of craft unionism" (Cameron and Young 1960; Logan 1928, 152) (Eventually the radicals in the Western Federation migrated to the revolutionary Industrial Workers of the World in 1910 and the Federation joined the TLC).

As we have seen, trade unions may suffer from tremendous weakness and yet still remain important political forces. Australasian trade unions were decimated as an industrial force during the period when the state ushered in reforms, and unions in New Zealand were just getting off the ground when the crisis that would lead to reform occurred. It was the industrial defeats of the unions in those nations that led them to political mobilization. However, in Canada, a surge in political mobilization did not apparently occur because of the relative moderation of the crisis. Furthermore, the Canadian labour movement suffered from a level of internal division that was not present in the other countries that we have studied.

Labour's inability to change the law governing trade unions in Canada was due partly to its limited influence in the party system. Like their brethren in Australasia, Canadian workers enjoyed the early extension of the franchise, but Canadian labour was unable to convert that advantage into legal protections from the judiciary that British labour, without nearly as large a percentage of enfranchised workers, managed to secure. In Britain, the Conservative and

Liberal parties competed to correct the deficiencies in labour law in the run up to the 1875 election and trade union leaders worked closely with the Liberals in drafting major portions of the Trade Unions Act of 1875. Then, in the election campaign of 1906, the Liberals pledged to restore the unions' complete immunity from civil liability, which also accelerated the emergence of the British Labour Party (see chapter 4). British unions were helped by a cadre of middle-class radicals who held influential position within the state or had access to it.

Two possibilities existed for developing the kind of union–party relationship that would provide the unions with the political leverage they would need to produce a secure legal status. One was the creation of a Labour Party that would compete with the established parties. The other route was to become a key part of the Liberal Party's governing coalition. In Australia, a Labour Party emerged early to compete with liberal parties for labour's vote. In New Zealand, the labour party emerged later, but labour was a key part of a broad popular coalition put together by the Liberal Party. British unions first were an important constituency within the Liberal Party (the lib-labs), but then a Labour Party emerged in the midst of the industrial relations crisis.

The Liberals sought workers' votes and the TLC had a clientelistic relationship with the party. However, the Liberals' electoral strategy left its relationship with labour attenuated. The Liberals sought to appeal to a pan-Canadian identity that transcended the myriad regional, linguistic, and class divisions that existed across the great expanse of Canada. Therefore, it eschewed strong identification with specific classes, groups, and sectors of society in favour of an appeal that would reach across the many divisions of Canadian society. The Liberals gained support nationwide in the late nineteenth century based upon their commitment to the maintenance of national unity and the retention of provincial rights, which allowed them to appeal across regional and ethnic divisions. While national unity and provincial rights might seem at odds, Liberals believed that unity could be achieved by preserving a large measure of provincial autonomy, given Canada's beginnings as a confederation, its regionalism and francophone minority centred in Quebec. But provincial autonomy worked against labour's goal of a national labour code that insured labour rights.

A credible Canadian Labour Party would have given labour direct representation in Parliament and provided an incentive for the Liberal Party to be more responsive to workers' demands in order to retain their support. Even if a viable party that stood unequivocally for labour's public policy interests did not have immediate success in gaining control of the state, it could pose a competitive threat to the "bourgeois" parties that sought to attract and retain working-class support. Divisions within the labour movement did hinder its efforts to build an independent labour party. The monopoly that the established parties enjoyed in working-class politics made it much harder for workers to develop class consciousness and political solidarity, diminishing the prospects for the emergence of an electorally viable Labour or Socialist party. In addition, the division of different groups of workers' loyalties between the two established parties dissipated their impact, which did not happen in New Zealand where unions supported the Liberal Party overwhelmingly (Heron 1989, 48).

The issue of how labour should pursue the representation of its interests in Parliament began in 1899 and took about a dozen years to play out until it ended with the failure to launch a Canadian Labour Party (Robin 1967; Bothwell, Drummond and English 1987, 97). A struggle ensued among various elements in the labour movement that held different interests in representation, and different visions about how labour's interests should be pursued in Parliament (Heron 1989, 48). The leadership of the TLC included well-entrenched Liberal and Conservative politicians who received patronage jobs and payments from the established parties for their support and services, with the Liberals constituting the largest group. Starting in the late 1890s, sentiment for the establishment of direct working-class representation in Parliament through socialist and labour parties emerged to challenge the politicos in the TLC. One problem was simply the limited number of labour-supported candidates elected to Parliament. Only a small handful of Liberal MPs fell into that category (Fudge and Tucker 2001, 35). Moreover, throughout the early decades of the twentieth century, even MPs who had been explicitly elected as independent labour candidates, were coopted by the Liberals. They had little choice if they "were dedicated to the extraction of favorable bits of labour legislation" (Robin 1968, 270).

One group adopted the AFL's "labor pure and simple" approach of "rewarding friends and punishing enemies" who were affiliated with the major parties (Robin 1968, 69). They opposed allying the unions with any particular party or establishing a labour party and sought to strengthen the role of organized labour as a pressure group rather than affiliate with a party or sponsor a labour party (Robin 1968, 67). Another group, strongest with the industrial unions of British Columbia, supported the emerging Socialist Party. They favoured "dual unionism" (establishment of parallel radical and business labour organizations), opposed the AFL, and challenged the anti-socialist TLC. A third group of trade unionists rejected both socialism and the AFL's approach and favoured the formation of a Labour Party along British lines (Heron 1989, 48–9).

The dual unionism tactics of the Western Socialists posed a major risk to the TLC's political influence, by weakening its ability to claim that it represented the labour movement nationally in the nation's capital (Robin 1968, 69). It also adversely impacted the socialists in the west. According to Robin (1967, 201), "[b]y flirting with dual unionist tactics, the socialists isolated themselves from the mainstream of organized labour, minimized their effectiveness within the labour political movement, and by default, guaranteed the hegemony within the Congress of Liberal and Conservative politicians and supporters of 'independent labor representation.'" The TLC refused to endorse the Socialist Party or help launch a Labor Party and insisted instead upon maintaining "independent representation." Starting in 1906, a more auspicious moment to form a labour party arose when the divisive issue of dual unionism subsided in the west. However, unions in Alberta, and British Columbia (which was the second most populous unionized province), blocked efforts to establish a Labour Party in those provinces and established a Socialist Party instead, a move that aggravated the TLC's union leaders in the east (Robin 1967, 199–209). Visiting Canada at this time, British Labour Party leaders looked upon the divisions in the Canadian movement with dismay and criticized both the Socialists for insisting on a rigid dogma and the "old party opportunism" of the TLC establishment. In the end, the gap between the Socialists and the believers in "pure and simple" trade unionism were too large and the Canadian Labour Party withered on the vine (Robin 1967, 213–14).

The absence of a coherent political party strategy, and in particular, the inability to form a labour party was important because it inhibited the labour party from exerting political pressure upon the state to secure labour's rights. Had the Canadian labour movement been able to do so, it could have used the crisis to secure its rights.

Conclusion

We have seen that Canada's first answer to the labour question – compulsory investigation and conciliation without legal reforms – was the product of the peculiar set of antecedent, permissive, and productive conditions that existed during the late nineteenth and early twentieth centuries. Canadians adopted a unique answer to the labour question, but the institutional and political formula was familiar. It included employers hostile to unions, repressed but not decimated labour organizations, strong leadership from one or more progressive reformers (King) who occupied a strategic position within the state and a supportive labour movement. Party coalitions were less important in Canada than in the other Anglophone nations because of King's dominance of the process and because the limited nature of the crisis did not give rise to the change in party control of government that took place in the other cases of regime change.

A second level of explanation focuses on why Canadians were unable or unwilling to adopt one of the alternative answers to the labour question that the other Anglophone nations did. Voluntarism was a very unlikely outcome in Canada because antecedent conditions were not hospitable. Not only had trade unionism spread much less than it had in Britain, but they were deeply divided along regional and ethnic lines. A legacy of employer acceptance of trade unions across a number of sectors and rudimentary forms of collective bargaining, other critical building blocks of voluntarism, had not gotten very far either. Labour did not have enough influence to insist on the kind of legal reforms that would remove the courts and common law as impediments, the Liberal Party adhered to (or hid behind) judicial independence, the British North America Act, and a fictitious "neutrality" in industrial relations. King viewed legal reforms as risky changes that could enable unions to create more industrial unrest.

The timing and relatively constrained scope and severity of the industrial relations crisis that Canada experienced constrained bold actions of the kind that other nations undertook. The geographically and economically limited nature of the crisis led to less public disorder and concern, less perceived need for bold reforms among reformers and the state, and less desperation for state intervention among trade unions. While the unions lacked the main motivation for embracing compulsory arbitration that motivated their peers in Australasia – recovery from massive defeats at the hands of employers – their overall weaknesses led them to support it anyway. Judicial involvement in Canadian labour relations was relatively modest prior to the crisis period compared to Britain and the United States. Therefore, labour was not as inclined to oppose compulsory measures on the basis of judicial hostility towards unions as it did in Britain and the United States. Indeed, the leadership of the TLC favoured compulsory arbitration until the AFL takeover. That support disappeared abruptly when the AFL took over the movement. The timing of the crisis and the AFL's takeover meant that support for compulsory arbitration between the state and the movement were out of sync with each other.

Neither policymakers nor Canadian labour were fully constrained, however. Canadian unions' disunity and fragmentation, which the AFL's takeover of the TLC compounded, reduced labour's capacity to shape future policy responses, but did not destroy it. Despite the AFL's opposition to any form of compulsion, labour was eager to support some measure of compulsion and sought state support in its fight for the recognition of unions by employers. Labour fell short on the latter objective because it could not establish strong union ties to political parties and King's lack of support for including strong legal guarantees for unions with the regulation of industrial unrest. King dominated policymaking during the crisis, and he is responsible for crafting Canada's unique "middle way" of compulsory investigation and conciliation.

The Canadians' turn to a mild form of statism, whatever its merits, was not a viable long-term answer to the labour question. Canada's response to the first critical juncture addressed only the part of the labour question that dealt with reducing industrial unrest to maintain public order and convenience. It did not address labour's demands that employers recognize and bargain with unions, in stark contrast to the responses to the crises in Australasia and Britain that happened at around the same time. The unions' legal status and rights were no clearer and more secure at the end of the earlier crisis period than they were at the start of it. The IDIA was unaccompanied by significant legal reforms that would free labour organizations form restrictions that courts and the common law imposed. Although the unions at first thought that the IDIA would help spread collective bargaining, its prohibition of strikes during the investigatory phase impeded the unions' momentum by giving employers time to hire strikebreakers, stockpile inventory, and take punitive actions against strike organizers (Heron 1989, 47).

9 Canada Capitulates to Legalism

Canada's adoption of compulsory investigation and conciliation in 1907 did not establish a stable industrial relations regime because it left the issues of employer recognition of unions and other labour rights unresolved. This chapter examines the forces and conditions that led Canadians to adopt legalism. Many of the conditions were like those that led the United States to adopt legalism, but there were some differences in the causal paths that the two countries took to legalism.

Like their American and Australasian counterparts, Canadian employers were hostile to trade unions; labour rights and a measure of industrial peace could be achieved only with significant state regulation that went beyond the investigation and attempt to conciliate disputes. Second, again like the United States, and unlike the Australasian countries, employers managed to stifle the labour unions without endangering their survival. Indeed, during the second critical juncture, which occurred during the Second World War, Canadian unions grew stronger industrially and politically. Until almost the end of the war, the Liberal government in power resisted labour's demands, which marks as difference with the American New Deal. The state's own efforts to repress labour and defuse the crisis backfired, exacerbating the crisis to the point that its pretense of neutrality disappeared, and its legitimacy was called into question. The strong ties between Canadian and US labour movements as well as between its progressive reformers meant that the Canadian movement fell increasingly under more militant industrial unions and sought to duplicate the surge in the level of unionization in the United States after passage of the Wagner Act. The Liberal Party capitulated to the unions' demands their political mobilization once it became clear that the electoral threat posed by the Canadian Cooperative Federation (CCF) posed a credible threat to it remaining in power.

As in the United States, the process through which Canada went to produce legalism can best be described as a "breakdown and culmination," in which both a critical juncture and critical antecedent conditions carried a great deal of causal weight. The rapid and massive Second World War mobilization made employers and the state highly dependent upon workers in a tight labour market that magnified their bargaining power. The crisis broke out when the trade unions pressed their advantage by demanding employer recognition and other labour rights. When employers resisted and the state's pretense of neutrality became untenable, the regime's popularity suffered and the threat to the Liberal Party's power became apparent. Antecedent conditions were also important contributors to the outcome, however. American and Canadian unions and progressive reformers had grown increasingly close over the years leading up to the crisis, linked by geography and economic ties. Once they saw how the Wagner Act stimulated union organizing, Canadians sought to follow the American example by importing the Wagner Act. Some Canadian provinces adopted Wagner Act principles (though not enforcement machinery) prior to the crisis, which demonstrated that such changes were possible to legislate and added momentum to the campaign for a national Wagner Act. The IDIA was also an important antecedent, in a negative way, because it failed to mandate that employers recognize unions and bargain in good faith; and its prohibition against strikes gave employers great leverage over labour, making the inadequacy of the existing institutional arrangements clear. Others antecedent conditions include the emergence of the CCF in the 1930s, Canadian political institutions' receptivity to third parties like the CCF, and the emergence of industrial unions before the critical juncture (in contrast to the United States, where they emerged during the critical juncture).

Before exploring Canada's adoption of legalism, we first turn to the long interlude between the first and second critical junctures. Canada did not alter the basic contours of its industrial relations regime during this period; important changes occurred nonetheless that sustained the regime adopted in 1907 and had implications for the second critical juncture.

The Interlude between Critical Junctures

The IDIA became a fixture of Canadian labour relations soon after its enactment. The labour movement's support for the IDIA varied over time and across industries. During good economic times, when labour markets were tight, the unions viewed the law as a constraint. The law's prohibition on strikes during the investigation and conciliation phases produced lengthy delays that advantaged employers. During bad times, the unions appreciated the de facto recognition that the Act mandated from employers who came under it. Industries that had stronger unions and those in the West tended to oppose it; those with weaker unions and those in the East tended to support it. The government occasionally amended the Act to make it more suitable to labour. According to Cameron and Young (1960, 44, 52), the IDIA "often led to what was tantamount to collective bargaining ... which by its very nature required recognition of representatives of employees." For this reason, union density rates and collective bargaining in Canada surpassed levels in the United States until the implementation of the Wagner Act in the late 1930s. When the Privy Council declared the IDIA *ultra vires* in 1925 (because the Act exceeded the federal government's authority under the British North America Act), the TLC supported amending the BNA so that the IDA could apply throughout Canada (Logan 1928, 219–28).

The British North America (BNA) Act of 1867, which formed the core of the Canadian constitution, expressly reserved policies falling under "property and civil rights" to the provinces. The drafters of the BNA included this provision to ensure that Quebec would be able to preserve its system of French civil law (Mallory 1971, 322). A series of rulings by the Judicial Committee of the British Privy Council (JCPC) reinforced the principle that the BNA assigned primary responsibility for labour, social welfare, and civil rights to the provinces. In 1925, the JCPC ruled in the *Snider* case that the IDIA violated the BNA Act because labour contracts were governed by the BNA's "property and civil rights" section, and therefore, the IDIA could apply only to industries that fell under "federal jurisdiction," which amounted to 15 per cent of the workforce (Cameron and Young 1960, 43–7, 52; Woods 1973, 20–5). Some provincial governments in the late 1930s half-heartedly tried to fill the void left by *Snider* by permitting workers to organize and requiring employers to recognize unions, but these requirements were not enforced against recalcitrant employers (Woods 1973, 66–70; MacDowell 2006, 276; Cameron and Young 1960, 59). The JCPC's interpretations of the BNA in general seriously compromised the national government's ability to respond to the Depression by declaring most of Prime Minister Bennett's New Deal proposals beyond the scope of powers granted to the federal government under the BNA (Mallory 1971, 345–6; Simeon and Robinson 1990, 80). The rulings buttressed conservative provincial resistance to "federal encroachment" and made it impossible for the national government to assist those provinces that experienced the most severe economic and fiscal distress (see Anderson 1938; Mallory 1971, 361; Owram 1986, 221–3).

Snider posed a major obstacle to a national labour rights policy, but it was not insurmountable. Some suggest that the government used *Snider* as an excuse for inaction (McInnis 2001, 158; Simeon and Robinson 1990, 81). While amending the constitution was not an option because provincial governments had to approve changing federal-provincial powers under the BNA (Mallory 1971, 375–7),[1] the government could have declared the Supreme Court of Canada as the court of last resort and tried to overturn *Snider* by enlarging the Court, as Roosevelt did with the US Supreme Court, but without having to obtain the legislative approval that the US Senate denied him.[2] But it did not do these things. It also refused to legislate labour reform when it could have done so under the BNA's emergency wartime powers, and after the war, when it drafted permanent legislation to replace Order-in-Council PC 1003 and when several provinces supported extending federal jurisdiction over labour law (McInnis 2001, 158-72).

At the same time, the IDIA applied to only a limited number of industries, Canadian employers were not mandated to recognize unions or engage in collective bargaining and often thwarted strikes. Labour law remained unsettled and confusing, and as a result, Canadian unions were in a much less secure legal position than those in the other Anglophone countries, including the United States under the Clayton Act (Logan 1928, 241). Unions were permissible organizations under the law but lacked the legal security to acquire and deploy financial resources and bring leverage to bear upon employers through strike activities. Without freedom "of action," freedom "of association" was somewhat hollow (Hare 1958). Many courts continued to impose injunctions and rendered conflicting decisions on whether picketing and other strike activities were illegal. The government's Justice Department refused to go along with labour's demands during the post–First World War period arguing against their necessity. At the provincial level, as late as 1939, "collective bargaining was a tattered patchwork across the country; Ontario did not provide a statutory guarantee of workers' freedom of association or prohibit employer discrimination against trade unionists. And even where such legislation existed, as in British Columbia, it was apparent that the legislation did not amount to union recognition or require legally binding collective agreements to be signed" (Fudge and Tucker 2001, 234).

Divisions within the labour movement continued as well, between East and West, moderates and radicals, and the AFL and "all Canadian" organizations like the Canadian Federation of Labour, persisted throughout the 1920s (Cameron and Young 1960, 49-51). In the 1930s another division appeared that became dominant – between the older craft unions represented by the TLC and the emerging industrial unions represented by the Canadian Congress of Labour (CCL), the equivalent to the American Congress of Industrial Organizations (CIO). The unions were as weak and divided at the beginning of the Second World War as they were at the beginning of the First World War (Laskin 1944, 48). Canadians lagged far behind Britain and farther behind Australia in union density (Ross and Hartman 1960, 203).

The Great Depression followed. From 1929 to 1935, at first Liberal, and then Conservative-led governments, assumed that the Depression would go away without the need for bold policy innovations (Creighton 1970, 213-19). Labour began to develop greater industrial militancy and political mobilization in the 1930s, but unlike American unions under the New Deal, Canadian governments did nothing to promote unions' rights and repressed "radical" labour organizations like the Workers Unity League (WUL) (Fudge 1990, 84; Palmer 1992, 253). They jailed and deported large numbers of union organizers and political activists under criminal and immigration laws (Fudge 1990, 84-5; Palmer 1992, 262).

Ontario brutally repressed a non-violent strike by United Auto Workers at Oshawa in the same year (Creighton 1970, 229–31; Berton 1990, 439–46; Neatby 1972, 117, 133–4). Canadian relief camps, which were ostensibly modelled on the American Civilian Conservation Corps (CCC), treated the jobless harshly and were primarily meant to prevent them from being recruited into the ranks of "red agitators" (Struthers 1983 97–9, 102; Abella 1975, 17–18; Palmer 1992, 245–6). Protests against cuts in unemployment relief were met with repression, which in turn, fueled rioting (Neatby 1976, 264–5; Berton 1990, 446–59). The government also used the IDIA to dissipate unions' efforts to strike (Fudge 1990, 84).

No region presented a greater challenge than Quebec. Throughout the 1930s, and for years afterward, reactionary forces allied with the Liberal Party ruled Quebec (see Neatby 1972). When Quebec passed laws to which the Liberals strongly objected, such as its Padlock Law of 1937, the government declined to use its constitutional "disallowance" power to veto them (Simeon and Robinson 1990, 82; Berton 1990, 441). The Padlock Law of 1937 banned loosely defined "communists" and "Bolsheviks" from political action, threatened and evicted homeowners, confiscated literature, and jailed suspects. The Quebec Liberals forged a coalition between business, which gave them financial support, and a large, tradition-bound francophone rural constituency, which supplied them with votes. They fought any changes that threatened their autonomy from an English-speaking majority in Ottawa, Quebec business interests, and the French-Canadian rural way of life.

On the eve of the 1935 federal election, a desperate Conservative government endorsed Roosevelt's New Deal, but lost to the Liberals. Led by King, the Liberals clung to balanced budgets and free trade (Neatby 1976, 153–69). The Liberals were no more hospitable to labour' demands for the remainder of the Depression than the Conservatives had been.

Progressivism's development in Canada lagged behind the United States, but by the 1930s a group of reformers had emerged in Canada in the League for Social Reconstruction (Owram 1986, 78–9). Canadian progressives argued that federalism was a major impediment to dealing with the Depression and moving forward with building a modern welfare state, but they lacked direct access to the highest levels of the Canadian state until the Second World War, when they were brought in to plan the economy (Simeon and Robinson 1990, 83; Clarkson 2005, 10–11). King himself had evolved into a pragmatic and cautious politician who was convinced that policy intellectuals had no appreciation for the political constraints within a parliamentary party caucus and warmed up to newer economic theories like Keynesianism slowly and reluctantly (Owram 1986, 181–3, 193). Furthermore, Canada's parliamentary system did not afford labour and progressive reformers the institutional access that they would have needed to pressure the government to overcome these hurdles. Canadian prime ministers controlled Parliamentary majorities with strict party discipline and afforded no opportunity to someone like Senator Wagner, in the pivotal role of Congressional labour expert and New Deal adviser, to pressure a reluctant chief executive for reform. Indeed, Canadian reformers were much more hampered than their American cousins.

The Critical Juncture of the Second World War

At the outset of the Second World War, "the labour movement was as weak as it had been in 1914 and even more divided" and had made little progress since then in getting Canadian employers to recognize and bargain with independent unions (Fudge and Tucker 2001, 228). Although the law permitted unions to organize, employers could still discriminate against employees who joined unions and could seek relief from the courts to stop picketing and other actions by unions to pressure employers. Many Liberals in Parliament, including William Lyon Mackenzie King, who by this time had risen to prime minister, remained reluctant to help labour. Liberals also remained committed to voluntarism in industrial relations and were uncomfortable with the power wielded by the National Labor Relations Board in the United States. King still clung to the view that social welfare was mostly a provincial responsibility and made few efforts to reform a federal system that had come to hamstring the development of a modern, federal welfare state (Neatby 1976, 92–4, 242–57; Simeon and Robinson 1990, 83).[3] As a result, during this period "the Liberal regime of Mackenzie King ... did little to encourage unionist support" for the Liberals (Palmer 1992, 267). Even towards the end of the 1940s, when opposition to a Canadian Wagner Act had softened, the Labour Department was still badly split over the issue of labour rights and asserted that the American approach was "'too intrusive' and forced the state to play a decisive role in what must remain a consensual arrangement between labour and capital" (McInnis 2001, 159).

The Second World War produced an industrial relations crisis that created the conditions for Canadian labour to achieve rights and protections through the instalment of a legalist regime alongside the limited form of statism that Canada adopted early in the twentieth century. Following the example of a few provincial governments, Canada's federal government adopted Wagner Act principles. The construction of the Canadian legalist regime followed a pattern that resembled that which occurred in the United States during the transition from Section 7(a) of the NIRA of 1933 to the Wagner Act of 1935. The state, first a handful of provincial governments and then the federal government, adopted legislation that incorporated the goals of the Wagner Act, but they failed to provide adequate enforcement machinery to compel recalcitrant employers to comply with the new legal mandates. Driving these outcomes was a shifting political landscape. A growing threat from a third party – the Canadian

Commonwealth Federation (CCF) – of the Liberal government, until the latter finally capitulated to union demands by issuing Order-in-Council PC 1003 in 1944. Because the Order was a temporary emergency measure that the government issued during wartime and that it was scheduled to expire after the war ended, the unions had to re-fight the battle that they had waged during the war.

Permissive Conditions

Before the crisis, labour's demands for legal security and employer recognition was constrained by hostile employers, a judiciary that cooperated with employers, Liberal governments that were passively complicit, and labour's organizational weaknesses. The crisis engendered by the Second World War eventually loosened all of these constraints.

THE SECOND WORLD WAR INCREASES LABOUR'S BARGAINING POWER
The imperative of war mobilization created a severe labour shortage, increased labour's bargaining power and spurred organizing drives for higher wages and union recognition, particularly among industrial unions (Cameron and Young 1960, 59). As full employment returned, labour unions' membership and bargaining strength rose as did the level of conflict between unions and employers and the state. In the five years immediately before Canada adopted its version of the Wagner Act, which encompassed most of the war years, union membership in Canada rose by 365,000. This was about fifteen times greater than the growth in US union membership in the five years prior to the adoption of the Wagner Act (Ross and Hartman 1960, 200–1). Industrial unionism, which had spread from the United States to Canada in the late 1930s, made significant gains during the Second World War.

LABOUR MILITANCY DIRECTLY CONFRONTS THE GOVERNMENT
Predictably, union organizing drives met with resistance from employers, which in turn, led to increased worker militancy. But unlike union–employer clashes during peacetime, the need for uninterrupted war production and controlling inflation compelled the state to intervene to try to manage the unrest and control wages, which brought it into direct confrontation with labour over wage bargaining (MacDowell 2006, 273–4; Fudge and Tucker 2001, 230). This made it impossible for the government to maintain an official "neutrality" in labour relations and deny its responsibility for continuing to permit judicial and employer hostility towards trade unions. The government faced a full-blown legitimacy crisis.

State Actions Either Fail to Calm or Exacerbate the Unrest. The Canadian state's approach to labour during the war fuelled further labour militancy and conflict and undermined labour's trust in the state's willingness to come to a satisfactory resolution of the crisis. One of the state's responses to the crisis was repression. Convinced that the problem of industrial unrest was one of subversives and "agitators," Ontario and other provinces jailed labour leaders or threatened them with incarceration, especially if they were alleged to have ties to the Communist Party or similar organizations. Even when such individuals escaped conviction and jail, they were stigmatized (Fudge and Tucker 2001, 230-1). The courts also forced workers to end strikes and picketing by granting employers injunctions or finding that individual workers violated the criminal law in conducting pickets. Employers, on the other hand, were spared prosecution regularly if they violated laws intent to protect workers' rights to join unions (Fudge and Tucker 2001, 238-9).

At the same time, determined to maintain its decades-long policy of "neutrality" in labour–management relations, the federal government clung to its existing machinery for dealing with industrial disputes – the IDIA, which it extended during wartime to almost the entire economy. This decision had the support of the TLC and the Canadian Manufacturers Association (Fudge and Tucker 2001, 233-4). The IDIA forbade strikes during the mandatory "cooling off" period of fact-gathering and conciliation. The IDIA proved increasingly problematic as the war wore on. On the one hand, the IDIA did not require employers to recognize unions and bargain in good faith, which increasing numbers of them refused to do during the war. On the other, by delaying the time when unions could strike, the IDIA's mandatory investigation-conciliation period allowed employers to stall negotiations, recruit strikebreakers, promote employer-controlled unions, and relocate production. Labour no longer perceived the state as the "impartial umpire" that King had envisioned when he developed the IDIA forty years earlier (Craven 1980). According to Fudge and Tucker (2001, 237), "the legitimacy of the IDIA was undermined by delays, inconsistent board recommendations on the crucial issue of union recognition, and the government's increased reliance on the legislation's coercive elements to combat strikes. In an expanding economy, the delay imposed by the IDIA on unions' resort to the strike weapon tended to advantage employers, especially in situations in which the primary issue was union recognition."

The government took additional steps to stem the industrial conflict in 1940-4. None of these efforts induced employers to recognize unions and bargain faithfully. It announced a list of principles that it expected employers to follow, including union recognition, good faith bargaining, and conciliation. But it failed to enforce what were essentially voluntary principles or adhered to them in ways that mostly benefited employers. The government's own conciliation boards often failed to recommend recognition and Crown corporations refused to grant recognition (MacDowell 2006, 276; Fudge and Tucker 2001, 234-5, 242). The unions, in turn, increasingly resorted to strike activity and ignored the IDIA conciliation process (Fudge and Tucker 2001, 248).

Eventually, the government created an Industrial Disputes Inquiry Commission, a series of tripartite boards designed to speed up the conciliation process and address the backlog of IDIA cases. But the Commission ran aground when, to get around the problem of recognition, it proposed replacing trade union representation with "employee committees" (reminiscent of American "company unions") and imposed additional delays before unions could strike (Fudge and Tucker 2001, 247–50).

As workers turned increasingly to illegal strikes, the government responded by requiring that, before workers went on strike, unions had to secure the vote of a majority of those affected by the strike. The government would decide which workers would be allowed to vote. This policy added another layer of restrictions on unions but also had the unintended effects of raising the importance of strikes as a method for resolving disputes and legitimated them, since most strike votes received majority support (Fudge and Tucker 2001, 252–3).

The unions' discontent with the government increased further with the Kirkland Lake strike. This especially long and bitter strike ensued in 1942 after gold mine operators at Kirkland Lake refused to recognize the miners and smelters union and sought to break it (Fudge and Tucker 2001, 253–7). The miners' union lost, but the searing events at Kirkland Lake served as a focusing event that mobilized and unified the movement's two major labour federations, the TLC and CCL (MacDowell 2006, 280). After the mine operators refused to recognize the union, the miners applied for a conciliation board under the IDIA. The government undercut the unions by joining employers' efforts to establish an internal employee committee to negotiate with the mine operators instead. It finally agreed to appoint a conciliation board, which recommended union recognition on the basis that most workers supported it. When the mine operators still declined to recognize the union and the conflict dragged on, the government refused to support the conciliation board that it had appointed. It clung to its long-held view that requiring employers to bargain collectively would destroy the government's neutrality in industrial disputes and that it would worsen the adversary relationship between unions and employers.

Other strikes followed. Labour chafed under the government's strict wage controls since the state refused to guarantee trade union rights at the same time it demanded sacrifice (Fudge and Tucker 2001, 237). The most important strikes took place in critical wartime industries like steel, and it was these strikes that precipitated the government to issue PC 1003. Steel workers had a checkered history in their efforts to maintain strong trade unions. They gained the advantage in the context of wartime labour shortages and relations between the unions and the notoriously anti-union steel companies reached a crisis (Fudge and Tucker 2001, 258; Heron and Storey 1986, 230–1). After senior members of the government agreed to a pay raise for the workers, the War Labour Board reignited unrest when it rescinded the increase (MacDowell 2006, 281–2). Next,

King authorized Crown companies to bargain collectively with their employees. The unions grew angry, however, when the government procrastinated in implementing this change.

Thus, in one encounter after another, the government undermined its credibility and pretense of neutrality with the union movement. As Fudge and Tucker (2001, 245) summarize the government's quandary: "The government's choices were … stark and its constraints as complex. It had to ensure industrial peace while simultaneously combatting inflation. It needed employers' support for war production—and most employers were adamantly opposed to trade union recognition and collective bargaining. However, its labour policy was beginning to antagonize even the responsible leaders within the labour movement whose support it needed to contain the growing labour unrest."

Productive Conditions

LABOUR EXPERTS FORMULATE POLICY PROPOSALS, AND THE UNIONS PRESSURE FOR A CANADIAN WAGNER ACT

The TLC adopted a resolution at its 1940 annual convention calling for a Wagner Act at the federal level, and the CCL made adoption of a "Canadian Wagner Act" a legislative priority and cultivated a group of policy experts for the purpose of working with the government to develop a new labour policy (Woods 1973, 76–81). The CCL first turned to the energetic labour lawyer J.L. Cohen who had decades of experience working with the unions and served as labour's representative to the National War Labour Board (NWLB) in 1943. In his work for the Steelworkers Organizing Committee, Cohen argued in favour of making union recognition and collective bargaining compulsory. Like Robert Wagner in the United States, Cohen believed that collective bargaining was more than just a peaceable way to resolve labour disputes. Cohen viewed collective bargaining as a way in which workers could participate in industry and shape society. Cohen believed in strong national state intervention and helped push the CCL away from voluntarism and minimal state intervention. Cohen dominated the NWLB's public inquiry, which received a lot of media attention, through his understanding of the issues and sharp cross-examination of witnesses. Both the majority and minority reports of the NWLB's inquiry concluded that "inadequate federal laws had contributed significantly to union-management tensions" and recommended compulsory collective bargaining (McInnis 2001, 156).

Cohen's influence came to a halt, however, when he had a serious conflict with the chairman of the inquiry and then with the CCL leadership, the latter over suspicions that Cohen might have communist ties. The CCL turned next to Eugene Forsey, a trained academic and strong nationalist and social democrat, naming him as director of its Research Bureau. Forsey was a cautious pragmatist who valued established procedures, including Canada's strict division of federal and provincial powers (McInnis 2001, 150–4). Forsey was consulted closely by the government's drafters of the bill that became the Industrial Relations Disputes and Investigation Act (IRDIA) and presented a logical argument for "consistent, uniform labour legislation." According to McInnis (2001, 156), "the influence of Cohen and Forsey's legislative analyses may have led the [CCL] to direct its attention to state-centered settlements rather than to alternative society-centered actions."

LABOUR'S POLITICAL MOBILIZATION FOR A LEFT-WING PARTY THREATENS THE LIBERALS AND LEADS TO POLICY BREAKTHROUGHS

Labour responded to the state's intransigence and anti-union bias from 1939 to 1944 not only with industrial militancy, but also political mobilization. It eventually supplied the leverage sufficient to force the state to surrender on labour's terms.

Labour's role in the war effort reminded workers of how wages were kept down during the First World War and the Depression. They vowed not to accept a disproportionate share of the burden of wartime production and worried that, if they did not win their rights during the Second World War, they would lose them after it was concluded (MacDowell 2006, 273–4).

Just as American labour's support for the Democrats swelled in the 1930s, Canadian workers increasingly backed the CCF in the 1940s. The CCF was a socialist party that emerged during the Great Depression in western Canada. The CCF's support surged among workers dissatisfied with employers' and the state's treatment of them during the war. The CCF forged close ties with the CCL, the federation of industrial unions, and became increasingly popular with the growing industrial unions in Ontario, Canada's largest province. After the CCF won an important Ontario by-election in 1943, the province's anti-union Liberal government reversed course and adopted Canada's first legislation modelled on the Wagner Act with compulsory collective bargaining and with enforcement machinery (Laskin 1943; Creighton 1970, 255–6; Fudge and Tucker 2001, 257–61). The Ontario law allowed workers to join unions of their own choice without interference from employers and required both sides to bargain. The enforcement powers were put in the hands of a Labour Court under the Judicature Act, which served as the functional equivalent of the National Labor Relations Board in the United States. Like the NLRB, the Court had authority to conduct elections, certify unions as exclusive agents, and conduct investigations. The Court was empowered to hear complaints of legal violations and issue cease and desist orders, reinstate employees who had been dismissed, and award damages to them. The breakthrough in British Columbia was the establishment of administrative powers that would have the power to act on complaints from trade unions that employers had refused to recognize unions that most employees had designated as their representative (Woods 1973, 84–5).

The new law came too late for the Ontario Liberals, however, who were swept out of office, squeezed between the CCF on its left and an increasingly progressive Conservative Party occupying the centre (Fudge and Tucker 2001, 259). The CCF fell only four seats short of a majority and became the Official Opposition (MacDowell 2006, 284; Coates 1973). In 1943 the CCF was the official opposition in British Columbia and Saskatchewan (Lewis and Scott 1943, 126). To halt the CCF's electoral momentum, Liberal-led governments in British Columbia and Alberta followed Ontario with compulsory collective bargaining legislation of their own (Fudge and Tucker 2001, 261). Next, the CCF won two by-elections in Western provinces and gained control of the Saskatchewan Parliament in 1944, which the Liberals had controlled for years. (The insurgent party would go on to become the governing party in Saskatchewan and the official opposition in Ontario later in the decade [Hacker 1998, 99–100.])

With the CCF's growing popularity, Liberals worried about their chances of winning the next federal election. The CCF became a credible challenger for national power when public opinion shifted sharply pro-labour (Whitaker 1977, 137–50; Young 1969). Polls indicated not only that the CCF was leading as voters' top partisan preference in 1944, but that a majority of the public supported trade unions having greater influence over the government and in favour of collective bargaining legislation (Heron and Storey 1986, 21; Fudge and Tucker 2001, 264).

Prime Minister King attacked the CCF, swung the Liberals to the left, and appealed to the labour vote (MacDowell 2006, 285; Coates 1973; Heron and Storey 1986). A few months after Ontario acted, King directed the NWLB to conduct public hearings on labour unrest, which the unions used as a platform to make their case for a new labour policy. Following the NWLB report that recommended compulsory collective bargaining, the cabinet promulgated Order-in-Council PC 1003 in 1944 (MacDowell 2006, 285). PC 1003 included all of the essential elements of the Wagner Act plus the compulsory investigation and conciliation provisions of the IDIA. The combined Wagner principles and procedures and IDIA provisions were extended to all industries normally under the jurisdiction of the federal government, plus all industries normally under provincial jurisdiction that had a bearing upon war production (Woods 1973, 85–92).

ADAPTING LEGALISM TO PEACETIME REALITIES

PC 1003 became the prototype for the permanent IRDIA and the provincial laws that Canada adopted at the beginning of the post–Second World War era (Woods 1973, 93). PC 1003, like all wartime policies, had the force of law only during the emergency period while the war was being fought. Parliament extended PC 1003 through 1947 to provide time to decide upon a permanent policy. Many employers hoped that once PC 1003 expired, they could reestablish the employer-dominated, anti-union industrial relations system that existed prior to PC 1003. The unions responded by launching another wave of strikes and pressured the government for permanent, peacetime legislation (Heron and Storey 1986, 231). The doubling of the CCF's proportion of the vote in the 1945 election created "contagion from the left," helping to push the Liberal government to pass permanent legislation that replaced PC 1003.

The return to peacetime required adapting Wagner Act principles and machinery to changes in circumstances dictated by Canada's constitution and a changed political context. One issue was whether Canada should, following the American lead, adopt a uniform national labour code, or, whether it should follow Canadian tradition and constitutional interpretation of the BNA and allow for provincial autonomy and variation (McInnis 2001, 157–61). The other main issue was continued business resistance to Wagner Act principles, particularly unfair labour practices and prohibitions on employer interference with decisions to allow unions into enterprises and what they would be allowed to do, which many had thought had gone too far under the wartime policy. In the background was the fact that while labour and many experts expected that the federal government, having adopted a national labour policy during the war, could not and should not abandon its role, the political environment in Canada had turned more conservative in the wake of the outbreak of the Cold War (McInnis 2001).

In the end, the IRDIA that Parliament approved was considerably like PC 1003. Undoubtedly, the Liberals' loss of over sixty seats in the 1945 elections, labour's support for the legislation and the continued threat from the CCF contributed to the outcome. Given the years of labour unrest and struggle, the unions were willing to accept some provisions that it did not like in exchange for a system of protections and processes that promised to resolve disputes through bargaining more than sheer economic and organizational strength (McInnis 2001 171). The IRDIA incorporated the Wagner Act's basic provisions regarding compulsory recognition of unions by employers and collective bargaining and a Labour Relations Board, along with those of the IDIA regarding compulsory conciliation. Organized labour objected to a couple of new provisions, including one that permitted decertification of union representation and another that prohibited strike votes to be taken until seven days after the conciliation process had been completed. Nevertheless, "essentially, the federal government re-enacted the war time labour-relations policy as it existed after 1944" (Woods 1973, 95–8; McInnis 2001, 172). The Supreme Court of Canada (successor to the Privy Council) ruled in 1950 that each province had to legislate its own labour laws. Industries that did not fall under federal jurisdiction came under separate provincial laws and labour relations boards. These laws largely followed the example of federal legislation, although as the post-war period wore on, provincial laws became less uniform (Woods 1973, 98–9).

Critical Antecedent Conditions

Several conditions that pre-dated the crisis facilitated the adoption of the Canadian Wagner Act. To these conditions we now turn.

The Adoption of the IDIA of 1907

The IDIA's ban on strikes and lockouts during the mandatory investigation and conciliation phases of industrial disputes constrained labour's ability to bring pressure on employers and, in effect, facilitated employers' ability to avoid granting unions recognition and negotiations with them. As a result, it indirectly led labour to the realization that they needed further state intervention to end employers' resistance to recognition and negotiation (Woods 1973, 81).

Canadian Federalism: The Criminal Code Amendment of 1939, Labour's Pre-crisis Push for Provincial Experiments with Wagner Act Principles, and the "Dual" Federalist System

In 1939, Canada made an important change in its criminal code (Section 502A) which recognized for the first time that workers' rights to join unions could only be assured if employers were prevented from taking actions to restrain them from doing so. Parliament adopted a new section of the Criminal Code that "made it an indictable offence for an employer or his agent to refuse to employ or to dismiss any person for the sole reason that he was a member of a lawful trade union ... [and] to use intimidation or threat of loss of position or to impose any pecuniary penalty with thebjectt of compelling workmen or employees to abstain from belonging to a trade union" (Woods 1973, 42). Of course, making employer actions unlawful did not mean that employers would comply in the absence of enforcement tools, but establishing this commitment in law was an important part of the foundation leading up to a full-fledged legalist regime.

At the urging of organized labour, certain provinces legislated Wagner Act principles once they had been legislated and approved by the US Supreme Court. As in the case of the Criminal Code amendments, these changes were not accompanied by effective enforcement machinery. Yet, they demonstrated that such changes were possible in Canada and added to the momentum for broader changes at the federal level once the war crisis occurred. The Nova Scotia Parliament approved legislation in 1937 that made it legal for workers to form and join unions and for those organizations to engage in collective bargaining with employers. Employers could be fined or imprisoned for failing to bargain with a union designated by a majority of employers or if employers sought to restrain employees from joining unions or exercising their other rights or using yellow dog contracts. British Columbia passed a law in the same year that combined Wagner Act principles with the IDIA's approach to compulsory dispute settlement. Manitoba in 1937 and New Brunswick in 1938 passed similar laws (Woods 1973, 66–9). These changes were important not only for their substantive innovations for Canadian labour law, but they could be used as a basis for stronger laws that included enforcement machinery once it could be pointed out that employers were failing to comply with the legal requirements.

Canadian federalism also shaped which levels of government had jurisdiction for implementing the IRDIA, which differed substantially from the Wagner Act in the United States. Canadian federalism is much more decentralized than American federalism, with fewer concurrent or shared powers (Bakvis, Baier, and Brown 2009, 250–1). The British North America (BNA) Act of 1867, which formed the core of the Canadian constitution, expressly reserved policies falling under "property and civil rights" to the provinces. The drafters of the BNA included this provision to ensure that Quebec would be able to preserve its system of French civil law (Mallory 1971, 332). A series of rulings by the Judicial Committee of the British Privy Council (JCPC) reinforced the principle that the BNA assigned primary responsibility for labour, social welfare, and civil rights to the provinces. In 1925, the JCPC ruled in the *Snider* case that the IDIA violated the BNA Act. As a result, the IRDIA provided for a much larger role for Canadian provinces in labour law than the American states had. The Wagner Act federalized most labour law in the United States.

The Rise of Industrial Unions

The spread of mass production industries like steel, autos, and shipbuilding changed the complexion of unionism. Industrial unions added to organized labour's ranks significantly, offsetting the weakness of a divided Canadian labour movement in the Second World War. The CCL's membership was almost as large in 1939 as the TLC's. Industrial unions encountered employers who were more highly organized and more adamantly opposed to unionization than those that dealt with craft unions (Fudge and Tucker 2001, 245). As a result, industrial unions were more militant and more firmly committed to a broader role for the state in industrial relations.

Industrial unions in Canada emerged before the adoption of Canada's Wagner Act, unlike the United States, where they emerged as a major political force *after* passage of the National Industrial Recovery Act and Wagner Act (Cameron and Young 1960, 56–9; Abella 1975, 19). The level of unionization in Canada *before* Canadian workers had won their rights was almost as high as the level in the United States *after* the Americans had won theirs.

Labour's Political Mobilization under the CCF

The role of the CCF, as we saw, was crucial for inducing the Liberal Party to capitulate finally to labour's demands for legal reform. The CCF did not simply appear on the scene during the Second World War crisis, however. Workers made a major advance in political organization in the 1930s, in no small measure because the Depression tarnished the image of capitalism and because of the Canadian government's continued hostility towards organized labour (Lewis and Scott 1943, 78, 116–17). The lack of responsiveness of the two established parties induced the working class to channel much of its discontent during the Great Depression into protest parties, particularly the Cooperative Commonwealth Federation (CCF) and the Social Credit Party. The percentage of the vote that these parties garnered dwarfed those of similar third and fourth parties in the United States.[4] Established in 1932 at the height of the Great Depression, the CCF brought together the labour and farmer political activities that had been scattered up until that time. It was begun by university-based intellectuals and a handful of members of Parliament who represented labour interests. Its mission, according to its manifesto, was "to promote through political action and other appropriate means, the establishment in Canada of a Cooperative Commonwealth in which the principle regulating production, distribution and exchange will be the supplying of human needs and not the making of profits" (quoted in McHenry 1950, 29; see also Lewis and Scott 1943, 113–22).

Although smaller than the CCF and Social Credit, more radical political organizations also emerged in the 1930s. The Canadian Communist Party was larger than its American counterpart, with 40,000 members in 1932 (Lipton 1966, 255; Palmer 1992, 253), more than twice as many as the American Communist Party even though Canada's population was much smaller (Klehr 1984, 88–9, 91).[5]

Third Parties as Innovators in Canada

Seen in a broader context, Canadian political institutions provided fertile ground for the cultivation of viable third and fourth parties. Part of the credit goes to the parliamentary system and the lack of institutions that represent regional and state-based interests at the national level. According to Hacker (1998, 73; see also his cite), "Strict party discipline in parliament hinders the major parties from absorbing regional factions, and the Canadian federal government lacks a territorially organized legislative body such as the U.S. Senate. Regionally based parties are thus viewed as important defenders of provincial interests in both interprovincial deliberations and national politics."

Adoption of the Wagner Act in the United States

It would be difficult to over-emphasize the importance of the adoption of the Wagner Act in the United States for Canadian unions. We have seen that Canadian labour insisted on adopting a Canadian version of the Wagner Act during the crisis and Ontario and the federal government of Canada ultimately acceded to this demand (Woods 1973, 80–1, 84–6). The American law was obviously a critical antecedent condition because it pre-dated the Canadian critical juncture of the 1940s and served as the root for all legalist regimes that followed its adoption in the United States. Since PC 1003 and the Canadian provincial acts legislated before and during the crisis borrowed heavily from the Wagner Act, it owed a large debt to American progressive reformers like Senator Wagner. As we have seen, the Wagner Act provided a legal framework and a detailed body of case law governing labour rights. It presented a practical, concrete template for legislating a Canadian labour rights policy and a goal to which labour could aspire and rally. Progressive reformers in and out of the American federal government created the Act, in part by borrowing and learning from earlier progressive legislation (i.e., the Railway Labor Act, Erdman Act, and Norris–LaGuardia Act), experience with the First World War National War Labor Board, and investigations by various legislative committees and industrial commissions (Bernstein 1950, 18–19; Plotke 1990). Reformers also benefited from a two-year learning process in which the National Labor Board and the first National Labor Relations Board (NLRB) uncovered the legal and administrative deficiencies with labour protections under the NIRA's Section 7(a) and developed a body of case law that would guide the NLRB under the Wagner Act (Gross 1974, 132; Gross 1981, 1–2; Bernstein 1950, 18).[6]

Once the effects of the Wagner Act on the growth of unions in the United States became apparent, the TLC dropped its long-held adherence to voluntarism in industrial relations policy. As late as 1932, the TLC explicitly opposed legislation guaranteeing the right to collective bargaining, just as the AFL had in the United States (Lipton 1966, 255). But the increase in union membership that occurred in the United States after the Supreme Court declared the Wagner Act constitutional in 1937 "had an electrifying effect," according to Jamieson (1973, 23), upon the Canadian movement, which ratcheted up the pressure for a Canadian version of the American law. Several provinces, as we saw, passed laws that contained Wagner Act principles in the late 1930s (but without enforcement mechanisms) based upon drafts submitted to them by the TLC (Cameron and Young 1960, 56; Woods 1973, 66–70; Logan 1956, 10).

Conclusion

Canadians and Americans turned in the direction of legalism in the twentieth century, but they did so by taking very different paths. The American labour movement and its progressive allies worked within a state structure that offered more opportunities to influence policymaking. First, federalism and the courts did not present the New Deal with the kind of obstacles that they did in Canada. No one argued that the Constitution left the regulation of labour relations only to the states and the New Deal did not face the divisions between levels of government and regions that challenged Canadian policymakers. Congress passed the NIRA, out of which the Wagner Act eventually sprang, *before* the Supreme Court invalidated New Deal legislation, and after considerable momentum had been building up for passage of the Wagner Act. The US Supreme Court declared the Wagner Act constitutional in 1937. In Canada, *Snider* came long before the push for labour rights in the 1930s and 1940s.

Second, unlike the major Canadian parties, the progressive wing of the Democratic Party was receptive to labour. As the most highly organized group within the urban, industrial working-class core of the New Deal coalition, unions and progressives forged a governing coalition. Clearly, progressive Congressional Democrats spearheaded the partnership with labour, but Roosevelt's reputation in 1932 was sufficiently progressive that he undercut the possibility of a serious challenge from the left. Though he offered few specific proposals during the campaign, FDR "struck a progressive tone" and had strong progressive credentials from his time as governor of New York (Sundquist 1983, 209–10). In office, Roosevelt and many of his advisers did not view promoting trade unionism as crucial to economic recovery, but they went along with Section 7(a) of the NIRA to appease labour (Bernstein 1950, 131). And FDR signed the Wagner Act into law, even though he opposed Wagner's efforts to strengthen the enforcement of collective bargaining rights in 1934 and did not endorse the Act. Roosevelt and progressive Democrats had much greater flexibility in constructing their coalition than King and the Canadian Liberals did. They held together a broad coalition that included labour and progressive liberals along with conservative sectional interests in the South. The South in those years did not have the leverage over the New Deal Democrats that Quebec had over King's Liberals (Simeon and Robinson 1990, 67).

Third, the separation of powers afforded progressive reformers, with Wagner as their leader, direct access to the New Deal state. Wagner operated within a system that afforded individual members of Congress ample opportunity to influence policy. He held a threefold position as a member of Roosevelt's brain trust, chair of the National Labor Board under the NIRA, and labour's best-known advocate in Congress (Bernstein 1950, 27–8). Wagner acted as a classic legislative entrepreneur, mobilizing support for his legislation as a member of the Senate labour committee (Bernstein 1950, 128). In the open, pluralistic advisory system that Roosevelt established, Wagner was labour's voice within the New Deal and perfectly positioned to insert labour rights into the NIRA, maintain them as a viable policy option, and pushed through the Wagner Act after the 1934 election delivered lopsided Democratic majorities. No Canadian backbencher could have exercised Wagner's level of influence.

Finally, unlike the United States, Canadian labour was solely responsible for securing its own rights because the state was opposed to its demands. Canadian labour was more organized and in a stronger bargaining position in the 1940s than they had ever been in the past. The Second World War afforded windows of opportunity for those seeking change and altered the balance of power between labour, business, and the state.

10 Conclusions

The role of the state in industrial relations that prevailed throughout most of the twentieth century varied dramatically across the Anglophone world. This chapter brings together the findings from the previous chapters to provide an explanation for why the Anglophone nations developed dramatically different industrial relations regimes. We saw how employers, trade unions, political parties, and reformers played the most active and influential roles in shaping the regimes. To understand why the Anglophone nations adopted such different regimes, we need to understand these four actors' behaviour and their preferences regarding the state's role. Structural constraints and transient economic conditions certainly played a role in shaping what they wanted and how they behaved, but I have also emphasized the importance of each actor's preferences and behaviour in shaping those of the others. Of particular importance in the causal stories of each nation were employers' actions and behaviour towards unions as well as how well unions fared during acute industrial relations crises. The outcomes in each case were not inevitable but were contingent on these actors' political choices and actions during crisis periods as well as the years leading up to them.

The second part of the chapter focuses on the processes of institutional emergence and development – how each nation arrived at its particular industrial relations regime. Critical junctures and critical antecedents influence institutional change, but each one's influence is contingent to a significant degree on the other. Expanding on the analysis presented in chapter 3 (see Table 3.1), I identify three patterns of institutional change that arise out of the impact of critical junctures on the scale and scope of change and critical antecedents' impact on institutional innovation.

Why the Anglophone Nation's Answers to the Labour Question Diverged

As previewed in chapter 2 (see Figure 2.1), the explanation for why the Anglophone nations adopted different industrial relations regimes begins by examining whether employers accepted trade unions as legitimate partners and whether industrial unrest posed an existential threat to the union movement (and to the community as a whole). These factors were critical because they influenced the calculations and behaviour of other key actors who played potentially important roles in designing each nation's distinctive answer to the labour question.

Voluntarism emerged only where, as in Britain, most employers accepted labour unions and collective bargaining. Without that acceptance, voluntarism could not exist. Employer acceptance made strong state intervention unlikely since it made it very unlikely that organized labour would suffer a defeat of such magnitude that it would disappear as a significant force in industrial relations (which explains the empty cell in the upper left quadrant of Figure 2.1). Neither labour unions nor public officials found it necessary to turn to compulsory state measures in industrial relations.

Where most employers refused to accept unions and collective bargaining in the absence of state compulsion, the labour movement, often reluctantly, had no choice but to accept strong state compulsion. *Statism* took hold in Australasia when employers defeated the labour movement and labour accepted a loss in its autonomy for the state's protection. *Legalism* developed where employers did not accept organized labour, but as in the United States and Canada, continued to stifle them for long periods of time without dealing them a decisive defeat. Most trade unions and public officials viewed statism as undesirable or unnecessary in these instances. Eventually, organized labour and its allies gained sufficient political leverage to compel the state to force employers to recognize unions and accept collective bargaining under legalist principles and institutional arrangements.

The explanation does not stop there, however, because we need to examine how these two variables shaped the calculations and behaviour of other critical actors in the process. Specifically, they influenced trade unions' preferences for particular regimes and what they were willing to accept, whether reformers had more or less latitude to craft and sell new institutional arrangements, and the preferences of party coalitions and key public officials on the state's role in industrial relations.

The Causal Impacts of Employer Accommodation or Rejection of Trade Unions

British employers' acceptance of unions and rudimentary forms of collective bargaining emerged early and developed over several decades in the context of Britain's early lead in industrialization. Most obviously, it enabled the unions to act as the key intermediaries between workers and their employers – in the dual role of representing workers' interests and in moderating and channeling workers' demands. Second, it shaped the unions' preferences concerning the state's role in industrial relations. In providing a hospitable environment for British unions to operate, it strengthened them, making it unnecessary for the unions to call upon the state to codify their rights and coerce employers to honour them and avoided the potential for state intervention to interfere with the unions' ability to represent their members as they saw fit. Third, labour could translate its growing organizational strength and role in industrial relations into an effective political capacity, including building ties with influential intellectuals and political parties. Leading English Positivists and political economists of the nineteenth century argued in favour of trade unions and helped remove legal barriers to their existence. The unions' political and intellectual ties to the Liberal Party ran deep and were forged over many decades, most notably with the Parliamentary Labor Committee, essentially a pressure group within the Party, and "lib-lab" parliamentarians. By the first decade of the twentieth century, labour gained added leverage by starting to organize its own Labour Party. Political engagement, in turn, made the unions formidable opponents to compulsory (and even voluntary) arbitration and a bulwark against employers and courts who threatened to derail voluntarism.

None of this prevented some employers and law courts from posing serious challenges to the unions. Indeed, the critical juncture in British industrial relations in the 1890s and at the turn of the twentieth century tested both labour's industrial and political strength and resilience. The most serious attack on the unions occurred in a series of court decisions, culminating in the *Taff Vale* case, where judges ruled that unions could be declared conspiracies to commit harm and that employers could sue them for damages incurred as the result of strike activities, a position that was supported by the Conservative government at the time and many of the most prominent social reformers. But the crisis never turned into a widespread defeat for labour much less an existential threat. The results of the many strikes and lockouts during the crisis period were mixed and labour scored a massive political victory with the adoption of the Trade Disputes Act of 1906, which neutralized the courts. It did so by mobilizing effectively to strengthen its alliance with radicals in the Liberal Party. As the cost of civil damages to the railway union in *Taff Vale* mounted, the hand of the most militant faction of the unions was strengthened. The movement to establish a Labour Party gained momentum, putting pressure on the Liberals to enact legislation essentially dictated by the unions. The Liberals' victory in the 1906 election and the willingness of radical liberal Prime Minister Campbell-Bannerman to back the unions' insistence on blanket immunity prevailed over the preferences of much of the cabinet and key social reformers to grant them a more limited form of immunity.

The crisis played out in such a way as to accelerate Britain's journey down the voluntarist path rather than taking it on to another. Most British employers, even during the crisis period, continued to recognize unions and remained accommodative towards them, in part because public sympathies were with the unions and in part because they calculated that they had more to gain through accommodation than confrontation.

Employer accommodation also shaped the state's response to industrial relations. The state chose to shore-up the voluntarist system instead of helping employers who sought to crush the unions. Investigatory commissions repeatedly endorsed voluntarism and the Labour Department eagerly encouraged it, mediating particularly intractable disputes, which it much preferred to managing class conflict in the industrial sphere broadly.

Within this context, British reformers who advocated a stronger role for the state on a continuous basis, particularly compulsory measures, could gain little traction to influence policy. Occasional recommendations for compulsory arbitration from civil servants, members of Parliament, and trade union officials fell mostly on deaf ears given the broad consensus among employers, unions, and royal commissions that voluntarism was feasible and preferable to state compulsion. Reformers had little direct role in shaping the Trade Disputes Act, which clarified that unions were to enjoy blanket immunity from civil liability and gave them broad latitude to engage in picketing and other forms of pressure. These reforms were straightforward applications of established principles and practices, not uncharted territory that demanded extensive study and thoughtful redesign or innovation of the kind that legalism and statism demanded. No elaborate criteria or procedures had to be developed for the registration or certification of unions as workers' legal representatives, for deciding what constituted an "unfair" labour practice, for the enforcement of rights and enforcement of decisions and awards.

Voluntarism was not a viable answer to the labour question in Australasia and North America because, as noted, employers in those nations did not accept trade unions. Major industrial disputes were less about wages and working conditions than were about whether employers were willing to grant independent labour organizations recognition as legitimate representatives of employees' interests. Up until the 1890s rural and mercantile elites dominated the Australian and New Zealand economies and imposed coercive labour laws. American employers were even more hostile towards unions and used the courts and military to suppress their activities. Efforts by accommodation-oriented groups like the National Civic Federation succeeded briefly in the early part of the century with the "Murray Hill Agreement," only to fall apart. In all four nations, not until the state, under political pressure from the unions and their allies, forced employers to recognize unions as rightful workers' representatives did employers' behaviour change. This occurred much earlier in Australasia than North America, but it only came about through bitter industrial confrontations, workers' political mobilization, and the election of labour friendly governments (or the threat of such in the case of Canada).

Employer hostility had several consequences for the trade union movements in the non-British cases. First, it constrained their ability to organize. Until they won their rights, the labour movements in these nations struggled to organize as workers' representatives in both industry and politics. In contrast to British employers, who came to appreciate the advantages of the unions and realized that there would be costs to rejecting them, employers in the other nations saw fewer and fewer advantages to working with unions and greater costs as time went on. Second, by calling upon the state to enforce their "property rights," anti-union employers made the labour movements suspicious of the state and turned them away from politics. Even after they realized that political mobilization was necessary, state repression in Australasia and North America bred labour's distrust of the state. Even when the American movement realized that it had to engage in politics, its prior negative experience with courts and elected bodies compelled them to reject any form of state compulsion. The suspicion of politics and the state meant that labour movements in these countries did not develop close ties to political parties until circumstances forced them to do so, as in Australasia after the unions were decimated in the 1890s. In the United States, strong ties to the Democrats took even longer to forge. Although they had enough political leverage to prevent compulsory measures from being instituted, they could not force employers to accept voluntarism and struggled fruitlessly for decades to create a viable voluntarist system by abolishing the labour injunction.

Canadian labour experienced the same political weakness, which was further exacerbated by its internal fragmentation and that contributed to a lack of strong ties to the party system before the early twentieth century. Canadian workers split their loyalties between the Liberal and Conservative parties and those parties brokered the interests of different group interests that cut across class lines. The unions were divided not only along regional and linguistic lines, but also the critical issue of how labour should be represented through the party system. The main labour federation (TLC), especially after its takeover by the American AFL, had a patronage relationship with the two established parties and adopted the AFL's non-partisan "reward friends and punish enemies" approach. A second, centred in western Canada, preferred the establishment of a Socialist Party and that favoured "dual" unions (radical organizations allied with the Socialists and business unions allied with the mainstream TLC). And a third, following the British and Australian examples, preferred the formation of a Labour Party. The Liberal Party, which positioned itself as a pan-Canadian party, sought to cultivate a reputation for not being too closely affiliated with any single interest and for being "neutral" in class relations. None of this bode well for labour (specifically the TLC) to play a leading role in the first critical juncture. It was not surprising, therefore, that labour was unable to leverage from the government legally enforced rights to organize and bargain collectively with employers and was the last nation in our group to achieve that outcome.

Simply put, employers' lack of acceptance of unions made it more challenging to find viable answers to the labour question and made the complicated state-building projects under legalism and statism more necessary. Reformers had more of a role to play in these nations because the non-viability of voluntarism made it necessary to craft new and more elaborate institutional arrangements that necessarily involved granting certain rights and powers to the state, employers, and unions. And the heightened industrial and political tensions that resulted from employer hostility created a higher level of risk to public order and convenience that required creative state intervention. Employer recalcitrance thus set in motion a series of industrial crises and political upheavals that forced the state to adopt significant new roles in managing the conflict between capital and labour.

The Causal Impacts of the Threat to Trade Union Survival or Its Absence

The other major variable – whether trade unions faced an existential threat or not – shaped labour's preferences for more state intervention or less. It also increased (or decreased) the role and influence of reformers and public officials in crafting and bringing institutional change to fruition.

The presence or absence of threat to the unions (and in some cases the community as well) helps to explain why statism emerged only in Australasia. Australasian unions were devastated in the economic and industrial relations crises of the 1890s, when employers took advantage of a deep depression to press their advantage on the unions. The devastation wrought by the Australasian strikes and depression convinced reformers and new governing coalitions governments that very strong state action would be necessary both to protect the unions and prevent industrial disputes from spiraling out of control and endangering social stability and prosperity. It also provided them with a golden opportunity to shape a radically different industrial relations regime. The exigency of the situation for the community more broadly suggests that nothing short of strong compulsory measures would prevent another industrial relations calamity. Reformers in those countries gravitated towards bold "state socialist" reforms that virtually guaranteed union survival, particularly for weaker unions, and severely constrained the resort to strikes and lockouts. Given the severity of the crisis and the public fear that it engendered, Australasian reformers enjoyed considerable latitude to devise a far-reaching statist approach that gave labour unions security in exchange for their loss in autonomy and prevented unrest by placing disputes in the hands of state officials. They undertook the creation of new adjudicatory institutions, the formulation of criteria and procedures for resolving disputes and for inducing employers and unions to honour awards and decisions that the new courts and boards were empowered to make.

British and North American unions escaped that fate. American and Canadian employers simply refused to recognize and bargain with unions and used the labour injunction and other tools to prevent them from operating effectively. But those unions never faced the imminent prospect of extinction. Employers made sure that the American and Canadian movements were stalemated, but they did not decimate them. When the United States and Canada adopted legalism in the 1930s and 1940s, respectively, the unions were on the offence and eventually prevailed after bitter struggles. Since the labour movements of North America never faced the threat of annihilation and industrial unrest never threatened the social order in general, they could afford to continue to oppose compulsory measures and persist in their ultimately fruitless quest to establish voluntarism.

The fact that American unions never faced an existential threat to their existence meant that they could reject compulsory arbitration and continue to hold out for voluntarism. Although some employers destroyed particular unions in bloody battles, they did not threaten the existence of the entire movement on a national scale. Most were content to use their influence with the courts and in legislative bodies to block the American Federation of Labor's efforts to remove the courts as impediments to their activities. As a result, at least until the 1930s, employers managed to escape the kind of political blame that Australasian employers experienced, which had opened the political space for statism. Trade union survival per se was not a concern of progressive reformers in America before or during the 1930s. Their aim, instead, was to put workers on an equal legal footing with employers and eventually to prevent industrial unrest from derailing the New Deal's recovery program. Attempts by some officials to move in the direction of compulsory arbitration never gained traction or were defeated in the Supreme Court, effectively placing that option off limits. Hence, employers' rejection of voluntarism and of their and labour's opposition to statism pushed American reformers to develop an alternative to statism that labour and the courts would accept. The unions wanted to be treated as purely voluntary, unincorporated bodies free of any legal liability, but the reformers concluded that the unions could end judicial attacks on their legitimacy and gain the leverage to force employers to negotiate collective bargaining agreements only if they became legally recognized agents. The foundations of legalism emerged gradually, but employer recalcitrance was not put to an end until the 1930s when leading progressives and the UMW took advantage of the opening provided by the Great Depression and New Deal recovery program to extend legalist principles throughout the economy and the NLRB developed a body of case law and effective enforcement mechanisms.

Because the Canadian labour movement was more fragmented on regional and economic lines than the American, Canadian employers had little need to try to destroy them unless they were on the geographic or ideological periphery. Acute episodes of unrest in the early part of the twentieth century were too localized to pose a major threat to the labour movement as a whole, but it did evoke a mild form of statism for a select group of "public utilities" in the form of compulsory investigation and conciliation. This reform proved ineffectual ultimately because it could not prevent large industrial unions from striking in the 1940s and most importantly because it never addressed the unions' demands for employer recognition. The fruits of American reformers' work was subsequently passed on to the Canadians who, in the 1940s, got their chance to adopt legalism.

Lest we assume that any of these outcomes were inevitable, they were not. They were genuine choices and were the result of a confluence of events and trends that were at least partly independent of one another. The crisis of the 1890s was a genuine challenge to the nascent voluntarist regime in Britain. Although *most* British employers were *relatively* accommodating towards trade unions *most* of the time, they still posed a significant challenge to the unions at key moments in which the survival of a voluntarist regime was in some doubt. Labour's leverage increased when the Liberals, under a radical prime minister, swept into power in 1906, a victory that had little to do with the party's stand on labour's demand to restore immunity from civil prosecution. But labour took advantage of the opportunity and won everything it asked for in the Trade Disputes Act. Most employers' acceptance of unions and their inability to deal them a devastating blow in the strikes and lockouts of the 1890s meant that Britain stood a good chance to stay on the voluntarist path, but it did not guarantee that outcome.

Neither were the development of statism and legalism in Australasia and North America, respectively, inevitable. Australasian workers decided to press their demands during a period of heightened global competition and depression. Employers chose to try to destroy the labour movement, which it very nearly succeeded in doing. The choices made in deciding when to strike, how to react to one another, and the resulting crisis convinced workers of the need to mobilize, instilled fear in the population, put employers on the defensive politically and induced the state to take bold actions under the leadership of new, broadly popular electoral coalitions and governments. Public sentiment could have instead come down on the side of employers and demanded a return to "normalcy." The state might have cooperated with employers in more harsh repression of the unions or may have encouraged both sides to embrace voluntarism. Labour's decision to go along with the statist solutions, where they did so, was also not pre-ordained, and many unions very reluctantly did so or remained opposed.

The confluence of events and political actors that came together in the United States in the 1930s was in many ways fortuitous. Economic recovery, not a crisis of labour relations initially, is what precipitated the reform process. Had the Depression never happened, with its resultant sweeping changes in governing coalitions, or had Roosevelt not recruited Senator Wagner (organized labour's most influential ally in Congress) to develop a recovery plan, the inclusion of labour rights in the legislation may have been in doubt. Several alternatives to the NIRA were seriously considered at the time and most of the labour movement preferred one of the others at the outset. The inclusion of Section 7(a) was almost an afterthought. And had the Democrats not enlarged their majorities in the 1934 elections, Wagner and labour would not have been afforded the political leverage that they enjoyed to resolve the stalemate between labour, the NLRB and employers, and the Roosevelt administration over the enforcement of labour rights. Finally, until a majority of members of the US Supreme Court decided to uphold the Wagner Act (the "switch in time that saved nine"), it was not certain that legalism would avoid the same demise that other New Deal legislation had met.

How the New Regimes Emerged

The second question that motivated this research focused on the historical processes that brought to fruition the new industrial relations regimes that emerged among the Anglophone nations. I have argued that institutional changes arise out of different combinations of critical junctures and critical antecedent conditions. The causal weight and role of each kind of historical process varies across cases, producing three different patterns: *breakdown and replacement, punctuated gradualism*, and *breakdown and culmination* (see Table 3.1). Breakdowns and replacements occur when an acute crisis sets in motion the conditions for a rapid dissolution of the existing regime and its replacement with a new one. Critical junctures play a dominant causal role in these cases. Punctuated gradualism occurs when a new regime gradually emerges over a long period of time. The changes are punctuated when crises occur that instead of reversing or cutting short the life of new regime, consolidates it or perhaps even accelerates its evolution and spread. Critical antecedent conditions have greater causal significance in these cases. Finally, in breakdown and culmination, critical junctures usher in a new regime in a rapid fashion, but critical antecedents also play a significant role in the outcome. Critical junctures and critical antecedents carry roughly equivalent causal weight.

Below, I summarize how each of the cases corresponding to statism (Australasia), voluntarism (Great Britain), and legalism (North America) illustrate the three patterns of institutional development. In the cases of breakdown and replacement, notice how the critical juncture played a leading role both in shaping the magnitude (size and scope) of change as well as in creating the institutional innovations that constitute the new industrial relations regime. Conversely, in cases of punctuated gradualism, critical antecedents had greater significance than critical junctures both as sources of institutional innovation and by limiting the magnitude of institutional change that was possible during the critical juncture. Finally, under breakdowns and culminations, critical junctures had a large impact in determining the magnitude of change, while antecedent conditions served as the major sources of innovation.

Breakdown and Replacement

In the Australasian cases, the process of breakdown and replacement produced change that was precipitous, comprehensive, and innovative. It is hard to imagine a critical juncture that so loosened political constraints as the one that occurred in Australia and New Zealand, allowing for sweeping and transformational changes in the conduct of industrial relations. And the lack of antecedent conditions that imposed constraints on innovation or provided relevant lessons and alternatives was a perfect environment for reformers during the 1890s to come up with their own bold "state socialist" innovations – compulsory arbitration and wages boards.

The crisis included crippling strikes in the maritime and pastoral industries that occurred during a long, deep depression. New, militant unions of semi-skilled and unskilled workers emerged in these and other industries while employers were threatened with heightened market competition. The strikes were extensive and spread from Australia to New Zealand. The issue quickly shifted from wages and working conditions to whether employers would accept unions, their determination to extinguish them, and their achievement of almost total victory over them. The unions insisted the employers recognize them as the legitimate representatives of workers and refused to work with non-union labour. Employers refused to accede to these demands. Employers took advantage of the weak economy to almost destroy the labour movements completely in these nations. Coupled with the depression, the labour crisis created unprecedented anxiety among investors and the public over the future of the economy.

The result was a sweeping away of the conditions that perpetuated the old regime of labour repression and insecurity – employers' control over labour relations, employers' access to the state, the state's pro-employer orientation, and labour's distance from political involvement. The crippling strikes, depressed economy, devastation of labour, and rising public fears about the future reduced employers' political influence, mobilized labour politically for the first time, and led to the victory of a broad, labour friendly governing coalition that supported a package of far-reaching reforms that placed state action at the centre.

The depth and breadth of the crisis convinced radical (progressive) reformers in the Liberal and newly founded Labour parties, first, of the need for bold innovations. It induced them to undertake sustained study and deliberation and craft concrete proposals. It also helped them frame their proposals in a way that would gain the active support or acquiescence of the labour movement and other constituencies for compulsory arbitration and other statist solutions beyond the realm of industrial relations. Because the class cleavage was so deep and the consequences of the crisis so devastating, reformers did not see voluntarism and mild interventions like voluntary arbitration and mediation, as effective options. Although they incorporated many of the legal guarantees and obligations on employers and unions that the Americans and Canadians would adopt much later, Kingston in Australia and Reeves in New Zealand placed compulsory arbitration at the centre of their answer to the labour question after a long period of studying of other countries, particularly the inadequacy of many approaches that rested on voluntary dispute resolution, which employers often undermined. They saw compulsory arbitration as the safest way to protect labour and to avoid the kind of social calamity that they had just experienced. The reformers framed the issue mostly in terms of widely shared values like "equity," "class harmony," and "social stability," rather than parochial interests. The ideas diffused throughout the Australian colonies and between the two nations. Organized labour, desperate for its survival, threw its support in favour of the idea (though reluctantly in some cases). The reformers' aims were to strengthen the unions as well as to avoid future industrial unrest, goals they believed were in harmony under institutional arrangements in which unions would facilitate orderly negotiations and workers would be less likely to go on strike if employers (in the face of strong unions) could not easily exploit workers.

The unprecedented political changes gave the reformers the opportunity to get their transformative solutions on the agenda and provided the political support for their adoption. Given their industrial weakness, organized labour came to accept compulsory arbitration, although not universally and in many cases reluctantly. The severity of the crisis induced labour to take a bigger risk on a statist solution than they would have if it were less so. Industrially weaker unions, in particular, saw it as their best hope for gaining the legal protections that would preserve their existence and secure economic gains. Reformers also convinced the public at large that bold measures were needed to protect society from the damages wrought by uncontrolled industrial unrest.

Critical antecedent conditions in these cases had limited intrinsic relevance to diagnosing the problem and addressing the crisis in terms of setting a new direction or translating it into novel and feasible institutional arrangements. The presence of a dire and unprecedented crisis motivated reformers and policymakers to create (or borrow) ground-breaking institutional solutions to social conflict that were not feasible typically but had a reasonable chance of adoption when the pre-existing political constraints were relaxed or swept away.

Although antecedent conditions in this case were not the source of the institutional innovations, they were not inconsequential. Four of them facilitated the reforms. First, the relative absence of judicial involvement historically in industrial relations lessened labour's concerns about investing so much control over dispute resolution with state tribunals and boards. The diminished reliance upon judge-made law meant that courts were less centrally involved in industrial relations, which in turn, coloured organized labour's views of state intervention that were less negative than they were in nations where the common law was more important. Second, the early establishment of universal male suffrage and the granting to unions of formal legal standing made it easier to transition to a regime in which the state would certify unions and regulate disputes.

Third, the geographic proximity between Australia and New Zealand facilitated the quick diffusion of the institutional innovations. New Zealand's William Reeves was aware of the deliberations over compulsory measures within some of the Australian states. Similarly, Charles Kingston and other Australian reformers closely monitored what was happening across the Tasman Sea once New Zealand adopted compulsory arbitration in 1894. Finally, the lack of union involvement in politics prior to the critical juncture made it much easier for the reformers to dominate the process of reform immediately following the crisis. Workers and their unions had not yet forged ties to parties that were rivals to the Liberals, had not begun to form their own Labour parties, and had not developed the experience and capability of developing proposals that would compete with those of the liberal reformers.

Another case that illustrates the breakdown and replacement pattern is Canada's adoption of compulsory investigation and conciliation in the early years of the twentieth century. Briefly, here again, a very acute crisis – prolonged strikes in vital industries like mining and transportation in Western Canada – induced the search for a significant and novel institutional innovation to address industrial strife. The crisis that arose during the critical juncture (sharp industrial conflict whose effects were felt in the community, but were localized), circumscribed the magnitude of change. The conception and adoption of the institutional innovation (compulsory investigation and conciliation) also largely took place during the critical juncture when William Mackenzie King formulated it and put it on the agenda.

Punctuated Gradualism

The historical process that led to Britain's adoption of voluntarism was very different from the one that led to statism in Australasia. It was marked by much more gradual change in which employers, workers, and reformers developed major building blocks of a new regime that were well in place before the critical juncture, but that the latter consolidated, elaborated, and accelerated. Antecedent conditions in Britain were so powerfully constraining that they precluded the introduction of innovations that ran contrary to the emerging institutional arrangements. Established political constraints reasserted themselves during the critical juncture and antecedent conditions were powerful. The result was a strengthening of institutional changes that were well underway prior to the critical juncture. The causal importance of the critical junctures and critical antecedents in this pattern are the reverse of what they were in Australasia. The crisis that triggered the critical juncture represented a palpable threat to the solution to social conflict that had been gradually emerging, but the constellation of forces in favour of preserving and enlarging the status quo asserted themselves effectively. The forces that gained the upper hand during the critical juncture did not merely maintain the historical legacy but strengthened their hold and quickened their spread.

Although some British employers and courts tried to cripple trade unions and at first succeeded, the unions survived the industrial conflict and triumphed in Parliament over the courts to consolidate the voluntarist regime that already had taken hold prior to the critical juncture of the 1890s. Strong union–party ties, employer acceptance of unions, and the gradual spread of collective bargaining were powerful antecedent conditions that kept the voluntarist regime on track.

The crisis that set off the critical juncture in Britain starting in the 1890s were an insurgent "new unionism" coupled with intensified international economic competition that challenged Britain's leading position among industrial nations. These pressures led to a two-pronged employer counterattack, first through employer resistance towards both the new unions and established craft unions and through judicial victories that culminated in the *Taff Vale* ruling that unions could be declared conspiracies to commit harm and that employers could sue them for damages incurred resulting from strikes. Combined, the industrial and judicial threats were real and significant enough that they conceivably could have led to an increase in class conflict that would have destabilized the emerging voluntarist regime and led to state regulation of industrial relations in ways that would have surely diminished the autonomy of the unions and employers. The Conservative government and many social reformers backed these restraints on the unions. Instead, the established unions held their own through most of the industrial strife and scored a decisive victory over the courts in Parliament. The spread of unionism and collective bargaining accelerated, and newly invigorated voluntarist institutions spread in both industry and government.

The immediate reasons for the outcome were the industrial resilience of the unions and the political mobilization and strength of the labour movement, the decision of a majority of employers to not destroy the unions, the incipient threat of a new political party – Labour – run by the labour movement, and the Liberal Party's sweeping victory in 1906 under the leadership of a radical prime minister.

However, most of these conditions did not suddenly emerge during the critical juncture, but grew out of the legacy of British industrial relations and labour politics that developed over several prior decades. First and foremost, employers developed a relatively accommodative stance towards unions that grew over time, which was based upon their calculation that union leaders and collective bargaining institutions included benefits for employers that at least for a time were worth the costs. One of the advantages, employers believed, was that union leaders could moderate the demands of their rank-in-file members, make the conduct of industrial relations more efficient and reliable, and preclude state interference in labour relations. In a typical path-dependent fashion, the costs of abandoning the system grew over time as trade unions came to expect employers to work with them. By the time of the critical juncture, employers were not in a position to eliminate the unions and learned that the state could not be enlisted to curb their industrial activities. They settled for stopping the new unions and harnessing the established unions more securely to voluntarist institutions.

Second, the intellectual and political ties between the unions and radical wing of the Liberal Party forged decades earlier gave the unions a powerful political tool to fight recalcitrant employers. The ties between the unions and the radical wing of the Liberal Party ran deep, beginning as early as the 1820s, and encompassed shared religious and political beliefs on a range of issues. Strong ties to middle-class allies through the Liberal Party helped compensate for the relatively slow and incomplete enfranchisement of the British working class compared to American and Australian workers. In 1868, the Trades Union Congress formed the Parliamentary Labour Committee, essentially a pressure group within the Liberal Party. The Liberals became labour's formal ally in Parliament and began fielding "lib-lab" candidates – working-class candidates, often unionists, who ran on the Liberal ticket. Long before the critical juncture of the late nineteenth century, this alliance rallied Parliament to defeat judicial decisions that declared unions to be criminal conspiracies. Hence, British labour was in a very strong position to stave off threats to their rights and autonomy, threats that could have led to a regime where employers had much greater power or where the state regulated industrial relations, or both.

Finally, the long-established principle of parliamentary supremacy over the courts proved decisive by guaranteeing that the legislative victory of the unions and their Liberal allies would not be overturned. Thus, critical antecedents like parliamentary supremacy facilitated the voluntarist outcome by removing a potentially serious obstacle, while others, like employer accommodation and the early development of collective bargaining fostered the development of voluntarism as a set of formal and informal institutional arrangements.

Breakdown and Culmination

Finally, in the North American cases, both critical junctures and antecedent conditions had far-reaching causal impacts. The critical juncture significantly loosened the established political constraints to make it possible to achieve comprehensive institutional change; but critical antecedents also significantly shaped and limited the kind of innovation that emerged. Antecedent conditions eliminated some alternatives of serious consideration and were a repository of solutions that reformers drew upon. The solutions were both foundational principles for the new regime that set it apart from what came earlier as well as specific prototypes and experiments that the reformers refashioned, refined, and borrowed from during the critical juncture beyond their initial applications. Developments prior to the critical juncture of the 1930s in the United States and the 1940s in Canada ruled out the possibility of adopting statism or voluntarism; Senator Robert F. Wagner and other New Deal reformers borrowed from the legalist prototypes that progressives developed in the First World War and in the Railway Labor Act. Their own contribution was making legalism enforceable throughout the US economy. A decade later, Canadian reformers borrowed heavily from the Americans.

The United States in the 1930s experienced an industrial relations crisis embedded in an economic crisis, like what occurred in Australasia several decades earlier. The economic and political impacts of the Depression and the initial New Deal response to it were profound. It vanquished the Republican Party, tamed the anti-labour impulses of the courts, and brought to power a new governing coalition in which organized labour and its progressive allies, led by Wagner, played a dominant role. The crisis of the Depression triggered the election of new progressive governing majorities in 1932 and 1934 (the Democratic New Deal coalition) whose leaders chose an innovative recovery plan (the NIRA), which included labour rights. Implementation of this nascent legalist regime added a further layer of crisis when fierce employer resistance and rising labour militancy threatened the economic recovery that the NIRA was intended to bring about, but it also induced a process of learning and further elaboration of legalist principles and practice, which eventually found their way into the Wagner Act of 1935 and strengthened the legalist regime.

Voters, many of them urban workers and newly enfranchised immigrants, increasingly turned to the Democratic Party in the 1930, 1932, and 1934 elections. Even before the New Deal, Democrats and progressive Republicans pushed through the Norris–LaGuardia Act of 1932, which once and for all did away with the labour injunction and yellow dog contracts and other potent anti-labour weapons that employers and judges had wielded for decades. After the 1932 election ushered in Roosevelt and Democratic Congressional majorities, the new administration and Congressional progressives like Wagner, cast about for a recovery policy. While the Roosevelt administration did not view industrial relations as critical to economic recovery, a small group of progressives surrounding Wagner, particularly United Mine Workers economist Jett Lauck, pressed for adding the labour provisions to the NIRA. Roosevelt acceded to the pressure because labour was part of his electoral coalition and progressives like Wagner argued that it would be unfair to labour to suspend the anti-trust laws for business without taking similar steps to protect labour's ability to organize and engage in collective bargaining.

Roosevelt and the NIRA favoured an interpretation of Section 7(a) that relied upon voluntary cooperation between business and labour and worried that forcing employers to comply with Section 7(a) would lead to the collapse of the NIRA and economic recovery. But when employers refused to permit employees to select representatives of their own choosing and workers responded with resistance, it became clear at last that voluntarism was not a viable answer to the labour question in the United States. It also strengthened the position of progressives like Wagner that employer compliance would have to be coerced through more effective statutory language and enforcement powers.

The critical juncture not only created the political space to adopt the Wagner Act, it also led to critical innovations that were necessary to make legalism viable administratively and constitutionally. Wagner and successive members of the National Labor Board (NLB), created to carry out Section 7(a) of the NIRA, spent three years building up a body of case law and developing appropriate statutory language and administrative procedures to shape legalism into an effective institutional remedy for persistent employer resistance to labour's rights to organize, strike, and engage in collective bargaining. Wagner and his aide Leon Keyserling drew heavily upon the lessons learned from implementation of Section 7(a) and the innovations that the labour boards charged with carrying out the law had developed in fashioning what would become the Wagner Act of 1935. The 1934 elections enlarged the number of progressive Democrats in Congress, paving the way for Wagner to prevail.

The Second World War triggered Canada's critical juncture that would result in its adoption of legalism. With war production leading to full employment and labour shortages, labour's bargaining power vis-à-vis employers gained strength. Influenced by the sharp rise in rates of unionization and the emergence of industrial unions in the United States prior to and during the war years, Canadian unions clamoured to attain the same rights that American workers enjoyed. A series of bitter strikes and lockouts ensued. Employers and the state resisted these organizing drives, through a mixture of repression and half-measures designed to maintain the state's time-honoured "neutrality" in labour relations. None of these efforts quelled the unrest, and the crisis intensified, ramping up the costs of the strikes, thus opening a window for a sharp break with the past. Two changes led the state to adopt PC 1003, which finally enshrined labour rights and the obligation of employers to bargain collectively. The first of these was that the social democratic Canadian Cooperative Commonwealth Federation (CCF) became a serious threat to the Liberal Party's hold on power. Once workers flocked to the CCF in key by-elections in 1943, the party was poised to displace the Liberals at the next national elections. Second, it was virtually inevitable that the recent adoption of the Wagner Act in the United States would have a large impact on Canada given the close geographic proximity and economic relations between the two nations. With the help of labour's representative on the National War Labor Board, J.L. Cohen, Canada imported the Wagner Act. Legalism afforded the labour movement all of the rights and obligations on employers with much less interference with the unions' ability to negotiate with employers.

Although the critical junctures in the United States and Canada created the conditions to make large-scale change possible and refined legalism to make it a practical, enforceable regime, reformers' choices during the critical junctures were profoundly affected by the legacies of past efforts to refashion the role of the state in labour relations. Antecedent events and developments had negative and positive effects by making the choice of some alternatives all but impossible as well as by providing progressive reformers with legalist principles and prototypes.

Legalism's path was cleared by the United States's earlier rejection of the two main alternatives in existence among industrialized Anglophone nations – statism and voluntarism. Wagner and other progressives never seriously considered a statist answer to the labour question during the critical juncture of the 1930s because compulsory conciliation and arbitration had been firmly rejected in the previous decades. Statism gained little traction in the United States given the opposition of organized labour and employers to it, and the Supreme Court declared it unconstitutional in the one state where it was viable for a short period of time. Before the 1920s, labour used the fragmented policy-making institutions at the federal and state level to block proposals for compulsory measures. In the 1920s, labour and its progressive allies did the same when Republicans sought to make compulsory arbitration a part of federal railroad regulation. For American labour, legalism provided critical, legally enforceable rights and obligations that employers were bound to honour, without giving up the unions' freedom of action in collective bargaining and without giving up the right to strike while disputes were under arbitration. A few years later, the Supreme Court declared the Kansas Industrial Courts unconstitutional, effectively rendering compulsory arbitration non-viable.

Voluntarism foundered repeatedly due to the hostility towards labour unions on the part of employers, who found powerful allies readily in the courts and Republican legislators. Even when the courts were denied the power to issue labour injunctions in 1932, with the passage of the Norris–LaGuardia Act, employers continued to refuse to recognize and bargain with the trade unions voluntarily. American labour leaders and some of their progressive allies assumed mistakenly for decades that a viable voluntarist regime could flourish if only the courts were stripped of their power to issue injunctions and the federal government stayed out of labour disputes. This ignored the fact that most segments of American business simply refused voluntarily to recognize independent labour unions and build collective bargaining institutions. Hostility to unions was nothing new to American employers, which had resisted voluntarism for several decades. Efforts by accommodation-oriented groups like the National Civic Federation succeeded briefly in the early part of the century with the Murray Hill Agreement, only to fall apart. In all of these cases, employer behaviour both served to hasten or worsen the crisis or constituted a prohibitive condition that foreclosed the possibility of developing voluntarism.

On the positive side, in the decades before the Great Depression, Americans had already started to develop and experiment with a legalist regime starting in the early part of the twentieth century when progressive jurists began developing common law reform that would change labour unions' legal standing. Unlike Australia and New Zealand, American unions remained totally voluntary organizations, unincorporated by the state. The doctrine of "responsible unionism" would replace the lack of legal rights and responsibilities that unions had under the regime of labour repression. The First World War War Labor Board and several pieces of railroad labour legislation, particularly the Transportation Act of 1920 and the Railway Labor Act of 1926, established for the first time that workers had the right to organize and that employers had the obligation to bargain with representatives of the workers' own choice. These ideas formed the core of the New Deal legalist regime.

By the 1930s, progressive reformers could draw upon a legacy of creative efforts that would establish legal rights and responsibilities for trade unions and compel employers to recognize unions and bargain with them collectively. The basic intellectual building blocks of the legalist regime were found in decades of development of the Progressive interpretations of the law of agency, in the labour regulations of the First World War Labor Board and the Railway Act of 1926. It was these breakthroughs and prototypes that Wagner and Lauck drew upon when they enshrined legalist principles in Section 7(a) and subsequently the Wagner Act.

In the United States, the early extension of the franchise meant that American workers already developed affiliations to the two parties well before the unions started to grow and engage in politics. Republicans attracted the support of many workers because of their political domination of Northern industrial states. Second, Gompers and the AFL shared the views of many progressives that political parties were corrupt. Their anti-partyism, along with fears that workers would shift their loyalties from unions to parties, was a key reason for their effective opposition to the formation of a labour or socialist party. Fear of a labour or socialist party did induce the unions to forge a close relationship with the Democratic Party during the Wilson administration. Of course, even if the unions' ties with the Democrats were stronger, that still left several formidable obstacles. The separation of powers and federal system of government in the United States made it difficult to impose party discipline on members. Presidents did not have the control of their majorities in Congress the way that prime ministers did in parliamentary systems. The Democratic Party remained a largely sectional party with its main strength confined to the South and the Democrats were out of power at the national level from 1895 to 1932, except for four years when they controlled Congress and the presidency. Shortly before the crisis, in the presidential election of 1928, working-class voters started supporting the Democrats in larger numbers, but closer ties between the Democrats and unions did not come until the New Deal realignment of the early 1930s during the crisis. By that time, progressive reformers had already developed the essential features of a legalist approach to industrial relations.

As in the United States, Canada turned to legalism in part because neither voluntarism nor statism had proved to be viable alternative regimes in the decades preceding the critical juncture. Like its neighbour to the south, Canada had a long history in which voluntarism failed to take hold given employers' hostility to unions and the state's willingness to go along with employer recalcitrance, sometimes actively imposing repressive conditions on labour organizing.

Statism had stood more of a chance in Canada at one point near the turn of the century, particularly given its adoption of compulsory investigation and conciliation in 1907, which could have served as a stepping-stone to compulsory arbitration. At one point, important voices in the labour movement seriously entertained compulsory arbitration, but that ended once the American Federation of Labor effectively penetrated the TLC in 1903. Shortly afterwards, some elements in the Canadian state raised the possibility of compulsory arbitration, but by that time labour had turned against it. The inadequacy of mandatory investigation and conciliation under the IDIA certainly did not help create an atmosphere conducive towards further movement in a statist direction. The IDIA did not deal effectively with industrial unrest in the long term because of its circumscribed sectoral reach, and more importantly, because it failed to satisfy organized labour's demand for rights and recognition and its effectiveness as a tool of national labour relations policy was put in jeopardy by the Privy Council in the 1920s when it ruled that it contravened provincial powers in industrial relations regulation.[1]

The most critical antecedent condition, of course, was the adoption of the Wagner Act in the United States in 1935 in the context, first, of the two nations' close geographic proximity and the inter-penetration of their economies and labour movements. Second, Canadian unions witnessed its immediate positive effects on union organizing and bargaining strength in the United States. It was inevitable that this event would have a large impact in mobilizing Canadian labour and their allies to demand that the government adopt a version of the Wagner Act.

Finally, the CCF emerged in the 1930s as a social democratic party expressly devoted to advancing working-class interests when the Liberal and Conservative parties were unresponsive to organized labour's demands during the Great Depression. By the time of the Second World War critical juncture, labour's ties with the CCF had grown; the third party became the political vehicle that the movement used to induce the Liberal government to adopt the legalist regime.

To summarize, the causal importance of critical junctures and critical antecedent conditions varied across our cases. Critical junctures were of overwhelming importance in the Australasian cases and critical antecedents were the same for Britain. In North America, both factors contributed in significant ways and roughly equally to the outcomes.

Evaluating the Regimes' Impacts

What difference did it make that the Anglophone nations developed such different industrial relations regimes? The focus of this study has been on why and how five Anglophone nations diverged dramatically in the industrial relations regimes that they developed in the late nineteenth and first half of the twentieth century. Whether the choice of one type of regime over another made any difference is a large subject unto itself that this volume cannot address in any comprehensive and systematic fashion. However, we can begin to think about ways in which the choice of regime made some difference. One way would simply be in terms of *durability*. Some regimes may have lasted longer than others.

We would also want to know how well each regime addressed the labour question by ascertaining their performance on the major goals of those who established them. The labour question was not simply an objective set of economic circumstances. It was also a social construct that meant different things to different people. The quotations presented at the beginning of chapter 1 are from two privileged Bostonians who shared little else in common; they illustrate the multiple meanings of "the labour question." For Wendell Phillips and other "agitators," the labour question was a profound moral issue akin to slavery that concerned social justice and workers' control over the workplace. For others, such as Richard Olney, the labour question was about maintaining social order and quelling class conflict.[2] The two parts of the labour question were inextricably linked. Disorder arose from the sense of social injustice that many workers experienced. As the Minority Report of the British Royal Commission on Labour stated in 1891, "[t]he fundamental causes of disputes between employers and employed is to be found ... in the unsatisfactory position occupied by the wage-earning class" (quoted in Hyman 1989, 5).

How well did these regimes seem to contribute to *social justice* and *social order*? These are very broad goals whose attainment might be measured in a variety of ways, but we will use only two. On the social justice dimension, the labour movement and their progressive or radical allies hoped that the establishment of the regimes would help protect and promote labour organization. Therefore, union density rates indicate how well each regime reached this goal (as well as indicating how much of the labour force was covered by the regime's rules.) On the social order dimension, many of the public officials and reformers who shaped the regimes hoped that they would lead to a lessening of industrial unrest and the resolution of industrial disputes without resorting to strikes, lockouts, and other means of industrial warfare. Days lost to strikes and lockouts per thousand employees per year is a standard measure of this variable.

Regime Durability

The durability of the regimes ranged from ninety-seven years for New Zealand to seventy-four years in Canada. The Canadian and US regimes have been in existence for the shortest period of time, but they are the only two that remain in existence (see the appendix). Merely looking at the number of years that these regimes have been in existence does not give a clear picture as to whether, in the end, one type will prove significantly more durable than the others. Rather than looking strictly at durability, perhaps the more pertinent question is regime survivability given the continued existence of legalism and the demise of statism and voluntarism. Statism proved to be too inflexible by the late twentieth century. The demise of compulsory arbitration and wages boards has been attributed to the effects of globalization on the economies of Australia and New Zealand and the rise of neoliberal governments determined to make those nations more competitive and adapted to international markets by making labour markets more flexible and market-directed (Bray and Walsh 1998). Voluntarism's free-wheeling adversarialism reached its limits when it ran into a similar neoliberal project, but one that sought to impose more restraints and controls on unions rather than to lift them. Its demise was hastened by a pervasive perception that labour unions had become too powerful and that Britain, under Thatcherite conservatism, needed to rein them in.

Legalism has occupied a middle ground between statism's tightly structured control over labour markets and voluntarism's potential for recurring industrial conflict, rendering the former more resilient and adaptable to changing political and economic circumstances that have swept over post-industrial nations. Legalism perhaps has survived because it provided a "middle ground" between the extremes of statism and voluntarism, offering enough regulation to maintain relative calm in industrial relations but not too much to control over the labour market that would interfere with an increasingly globalized capitalism. Legalism appears to be more adaptable to shifting political and economic circumstances, such as neoliberalism and globalization. Conservative and liberal or labour-oriented governments in the United States and Canada have been able to modify, through legislation and administrative and judicial rulings, whether their legalist regimes will bend more towards the interests of employers or unions. As a result, it has not been necessary for the United States and Canada to get off of the legalist path and engage in a wholesale reconstruction of a new regime type.

Promoting Social Justice by Enhancing Union Density

Undoubtedly an overriding goal of labour movements and many of their progressive liberal allies was to establish an industrial relations regime that would create conditions hospitable to union survival and growth.[3] The standard measure of union density is membership in trade unions as a percentage of the workforce. Union density rates may be influenced by several factors besides regime type, of course, such as short-term business cycle effects and long-term structural changes in the economy that make it easier or more difficult for unions to attract members and get employers to accept unions. Nations with a particular regime type may have quite different density rates due to policy choices that make it easier or more difficult for workers to join unions even when nations have adopted the same type of regime. Since the early 1990s Canadian union density rates have been more than twice as high as American rates, which have steadily declined (Visser 2006). These differences may, in turn, reflect differences in the political influence of labour and business. Thus, we should not expect regime type to have a significant impact on union density necessarily.

Nevertheless, the evidence suggests that not only did union density rates rise in all nations after they established one of the non-repressive regime types, but that they rose to higher levels for some regimes more than others. The peacetime period in which all three regimes were concurrently in existence was during the post–Second World War period, from 1950 to 1980. During these years at least, density rates were highest in the nations that adopted the statist regimes and lowest in those that adopted the legalist regime type, with Britain, the voluntarist nation, falling in between, but closer to the levels of the statist nations. For Australia, the union density rate ranged from 56 to 58 per cent in the 1950s, with a modest drop-off to about 50 per cent in the 1970s where it remained until 1990, when it dropped to 40 percent. For New Zealand, data could not be found for the 1950s or 1960s, but the rate rose in the 1970s from 56 per cent to 69 per cent in 1980. Britain's density rate ranged from the mid-40 per cent to 51 per cent over that period. We see lower rates in Canada, where it ranged from 33 to 36 per cent throughout the period, and especially in the United States where it ranged from about a third of the workforce (32–3 per cent) in the 1950s and then began a steady decline to about 20 per cent in 1980 (and has continued to decline up to the present).

Further evidence that these regimes had an impact on union density rates is what happened after Britain, Australia, and New Zealand dismantled their regimes and replaced them with ones that have been less conducive to union growth. The British density rate fell from 50 per cent in 1980 to 30 per cent in 2000, and the Australian and New Zealand rates dropped even more dramatically from 50 per cent and 69 per cent to 25 per cent and 23 per cent, respectively, over the same period (Visser 2006).

Voluntarism was conducive to union growth because employers accepted unions and the state had few opportunities to restrict their activities. The statist systems also were conducive for union growth because the number of members needed to form a union that was recognized by the state was very low and weaker, harder-to-organize unions were especially encouraged to register under the system because it gave them entry to the arbitration tribunals rather than having to rely exclusively upon their own bargaining power vis-à-vis employers. While the legalist regimes were established with an orientation towards making it easier for unions to emerge and grow, they were vulnerable to shifts in political power, such as when governments with conservative, anti-labour leanings came to power, modified labour laws, and made appointments to labour relations boards that rewrote regulations in ways more favourable to employer interests.

Finally, keep in mind that since all of the nations experienced union growth in the wake of whichever regime type they adopted, the nations that adopted regimes later delayed the benefits that accrued to the labour movement from adopting one of the regimes. Union growth in Canada and the United States suffered because their adoption of legalism came comparatively late.

Promoting Social Order by Stemming Industrial Unrest

The other overriding goal of industrial relations reform, especially for public officials, many reformers, as well as trade unionists, was to prevent or ameliorate high levels of industrial unrest. Here again, industrial relations regime type is only one among other possible influences on levels of industrial unrest, including tighter labour markets, employer resistance to union demands, and so forth. The most widely used measure of levels of industrial unrest is days lost due to strikes and lockouts per year per 1,000 workers, which standardizes the volume of work stoppages to take into account the size of each nation's workforce.

Just as none of the industrial relations regimes resulted in anything approaching 100 per cent union density rates, none of them banished industrial unrest. However, a clear pattern emerges more or less exactly as one would expect, with lower levels of strikes and lockouts in countries with higher levels of state regulation of industrial relations. Here again, we take the same 1950–80 peacetime period in which all three regime types were in existence (although the same pattern exists if we go back through the 1940s as well). Great Britain was by far the most prone to experience strikes and lockouts and represents an outlier among the five Anglophone nations. At the other end of the spectrum, Australia and New Zealand experienced the least amount of industrial unrest, until late in the period when the United States began to have even less than Australia (but not New Zealand), perhaps because of the weakened state of American unions by the 1980s. It stands to reason that Britain would be the most prone to strikes and lockouts given the maximum level of autonomy given to labour and capital in the conduct of industrial relations and that the Australasian countries would have the least given that strikes and lockouts were legally prohibited under the compulsory conciliation and arbitration processes to which most labour disputes were referred. The legalist systems of Canada and the United States experienced generally higher rates of industrial unrest than the Australasian nations, although much closer to their levels than to Britain's. Notable here is the consistently higher levels of unrest in Canada than the United States, which is surprising given the ban on strikes and lockouts during Canada's compulsory investigation and conciliation phases, but not given the steady erosion in union strength in the United States over the post–Second World War period and the stability in the union density rate for Canada.

Appendix: Major Reforms That Established Industrial Relations Regimes

Country	Year	Reform Measures Adopted	Regime Duration
Australia (Commonwealth and states)*	1895–1904	Conciliation and Arbitration Act	90 years
Canada	1907	Industrial Disputes Investigation Act (compulsory investigation and conciliation)	74 years +
	1944	PC 1003	
	1948	Industrial Relations and Disputes Investigation Act	
Great Britain	1871	Trade Union Act	76 years
	1875	Conspiracy and Protection of Property Act (same as 1871 Act)	
	1876	Trade Union Act Amendment Act (same as 1871 Act)	
	1906	Trade Disputes Act (immunity from civil liability for trade unions)	
New Zealand	1894	Industrial Conciliation and Arbitration Act (compulsory arbitration)	90 years
United States	1932	Norris–LaGuardia Act	83 years +
	1933	National Industrial Recovery Act (sec. 7)	
	1935	National Labor Relations Act ["Wagner Act"] (union certification and right to collective bargaining)	

* The Australian Commonwealth government and four of the six state governments adopted compulsory arbitration; two states adopted wages boards.

Notes

Chapter 1

1 They would also seek them in the development of modern welfare states, which is beyond the scope of this research. Industrial relations and the welfare state are related because the distribution of income, levels of poverty, and the like are partly a consequence of industrial relations – the share of income and levels of wages that workers can get from employers through trade unions and other organizations.
2 Much of the scholarship on the history of class conflict and industrial relations focuses on working-class politics rather than on the development of the role of the state. In these works, the development of the labour movement and its relationships with the state and capital serve as the dependent variable: How did the labour movement emerge and evolve as an industrial and political organization? Why were some movements more successful in attracting members and challenging employers? How was labour incorporated in national politics and what were the long-term political ramifications of incorporation? What were labour's political goals and strategies and why did they develop as they did? How did these fit into the interests of the working class broadly? A voluminous literature addresses these questions (see, for example, Archer 2007; Friedman 1998; Katznelson and Zolberg 1986; Marks 1989; Hyman 2001; Hattam 1993; Collier and Collier 1991). While social scientists and historians have written a great deal about the role of labour in politics and society, they have given less attention to the origins of the role of the state and public policy in industrial relations. Labour's role in politics and *its* answer to the labour question are important for our purposes only insofar as they had an impact on each nation's choice of industrial relations regime. Both labour and the state influenced (or sought to influence) each other; but this book is ultimately interested in knowing how their relationship shaped the institutional arrangements under which industrial relations was carried out.
3 By "Anglophone" I mean nations where the majority of the population is native speakers of English. The largest nations are the United States, Great Britain,

Canada, Australia, New Zealand, and Ireland. I have excluded Ireland from the study because it was part of Britain (or "United Kingdom") during the emergent and formative periods of British voluntarism (up to the First World War) and because Ireland inherited and retained the essential features of the British regime until the 1970s. According to Teague and McCartney (1999, 342), "Political independence in 1921 did not end British influence in the Republic of Ireland. For the most part, the new Free State inherited a British method of governance. Like many other parts of the administrative structure, little attempt was made to recast the established industrial relations arrangements by the early governments of the Free State. As a result, an ethos of voluntarism continued to govern relationships between labour and management. Indeed industrial relations in Britain and Ireland remained virtually indistinguishable until the mid-1970s."

4 The United States was a British colony until 1776 and Canada until 1867. Australia was a group of British colonies for part of the period we are examining, until 1901 when the former colonies became states that federated under the Commonwealth of Australia. New Zealand became a Dominion of the British Empire in 1907. It is important to point out that from early on Australia and New Zealand were self-governing (Archer 2001, 11).

5 The labour movements of these nations, particularly the United States, have been often described as pursuing "business unionism" or, in the language of American Federation of Labor president Samuel Gompers, "pure and simple unionism." Business unionism limited trade unions' goals and actions to economism, by treating labour as a commodity in which unions' goals were directed at the attainment of higher wages and benefits for particular segments of the workforce without regard to broader social, class, and political objectives. While this has undoubtedly been part of the ideology of many unions in the United States and other English-speaking nations, business unionism as a viable model has been undermined by the myriad ways in which state regulation and politics influence and are influenced by labour movements.

6 In referring to labour repression here I am referring only to wage labour, not slavery. Slavery was abolished in most of the British Empire in 1833 and in the United States in 1863.

7 As used in this book, "voluntarism" refers broadly to a type of industrial relations regime rather than to the philosophy that some labour movements adopt, which emphasizes a withdrawal from political action in favour of working within the economic sphere or eschewing political and welfare state reforms.

8 "Compulsory arbitration" here refers to measures that mandate that if two parties to a labour dispute cannot arrive at a settlement on their own, one or more arbitrators will resolve it. One party to the dispute may submit it to arbitration, thus forcing the other party into arbitration, or in some schemes, the state may initiate the process. The arbitrators' decisions are binding upon the parties

and backed by penalties for non-compliance. Thus, compulsion exists at the submission, decision, and enforcement stages of arbitration.
9 The typology developed in this book bears some resemblance to the one presented by Sydney and Beatrice Webb's (1897, 150) categorization of "Methods and Regulations actually practiced by British Trade Unionism" in the eighteenth and nineteenth centuries. The "Method of Collective Bargaining" is a critical part of what I describe as the voluntarist regime and the "Method of Legal Enactment," is remotely akin to the legalist and statist regimes. The Webbs' "methods" are more like strategies that trade unions used for promoting their interests rather than the broad institutional arrangements in which they operated, which is what I mean by "regimes." Regimes include the rules governing the state's role in industrial relations, its authority over the relationship between labour and employers and the legal rights and obligations that labour and employers are under. Furthermore, by the "method of legal enactment" the Webbs meant that unions sometimes sought legislation that regulated workplace conditions (mainly what we would call today labour standards and workplace safety standards) rather than the determination of wage and benefit levels and processes of dispute resolution.
10 Although the German industrial relations system may be thought of as a creation of the post–Second World War period when Germany emerged from defeat and its institutions had to be rebuilt, its architects borrowed heavily from "prewar institutions, practices and structures" of Imperial and Weimer Germany. Labour unions were recognized as legal bargaining agents in Imperial Germany, although employers and judges often failed to honour the law in practice. The country established its first non-repressive industrial relations regime during the Weimar period when business and social democratic unions leaders worked out the Stinnes-Legien agreement, which guaranteed workers the right to join unions and recognized independent unions as the sole legitimate representative of workers. The elements of this agreement were enshrined in the Weimer constitution (Silva 2013, 14–16). The regime put in place in the 1950s reflected the same principles and included "a full thicket of laws" that elaborated further upon them (Silva 2013, 4). The Basic Law included the strongest guarantees of workers' rights in German history and banned company unions. Similarly, the Collective Agreements Act of 1949 borrowed from a very similar Act of 1918 that made collective bargaining contracts legally binding and specified that the agreements were to be negotiated on a regional level.

Chapter 2

1 The scope and objectives of Plotke's and Finegold and Skocpol's research projects did not completely overlap. Finegold and Skocpol compared the NIRA with the AAA, seeking to answer why the former failed and the latter succeeded and they are interested in also explaining the implementation and consequences of the two programs.

276   Notes to pages 40–75

2 I have omitted Marxist treatments of the New Deal because they would require a separate chapter. For a review and critique of Marxist theory on this topic, see Finegold and Skocpol 1995, chapter 7.
3 As a caveat, we should keep in mind that none of these of actors – trade unionists, reformers, and state actors – constituted a monolithic group. They did not necessarily agree with their fellow trade unionists, reformers, and state actors and they did not have equal opportunities or capacities to influence decision-makers.
4 Finegold's and Skocpol's aims go beyond explaining policy adoption to show how the organizational capacities of the state were important for how well New Deal programs were implemented.
5 Plotke contends that many Democratic officeholders were not progressives and did not support unions; that many progressives were not public officials, and that their behaviour was shaped by their identity as reformers more than as public officials.

Chapter 3

1 Since the central focus of this book is the genesis of the new regimes, it does not apply all aspects of the critical juncture framework. While these regimes remained in place for many decades following the critical juncture, I do not describe those legacies in historical detail or trace out the "mechanisms of reproduction" that kept the regimes in place for so long.
2 The British Trade Disputes Act represents both a "near miss" – an opportunity to establish labour repression – as well as the emergence of a mechanism for reproducing the voluntarist regime that was gradually taking hold in Britain in the previous decades.
3 Leaving aside the fact that it is unclear that there was an actual "crisis" in existence.
4 Another potential candidate for a "near miss" would be when Congress nearly adopted compulsory arbitration for the railways in 1920. Here again, even if Congress and the president had approved the legislation, the Supreme Court would have been almost certain to have struck down because the Court nullified Kansas's compulsory arbitration statute a few years later.

Chapter 4

1 As in the United States, the Knights faded in the late 1890s, for reasons discussed in Sutch, p. 69.
2 In the same year, the name of the Congress was changed to the Trades and *Labour* Congress (Sutcliffe 1921, 48). The building support for compulsory arbitration in the Congress could be due to the fact that newer unions of industrial and general labourers had emerged and these unions tended to favour compulsory arbitration more than older unions.
3 Reeves chose a fellow progressive and a socialist sympathizer, Edward Tregear, to carry out the Arbitration Act, who in turn, chose two labour activists as his close assistants (Roth 1973, 19).

Chapter 5

1. In this case, British railway workers struck for union recognition and higher wages. The company brought suit against the union arguing that the strike violated the Conspiracy and Protection of Property Act of 1875. The railway workers countered that because it was neither a corporation nor an individual it could not be held liable. Justice Sir George Farwell decided against the union and the House of Lords upheld his decision in 1901.
2. These emphasized free trade, Chinese labour, and the taxation of land values (just like Australasia).
3. Another judicial attack on the unions came in the *Osborne* decision. The House of Lords affirmed an appeals court decision that had ruled that trade unions could not contribute to political parties. The case arose when a trade union member of the Liberal Party objected to being forced to contribute to the Labour Party. With the Liberal and Labour Parties losing seats to the Conservatives in 1910, the unions were unable to restore the status quo ante as they had done with the Trade Disputes Act of 1906. However, Parliament passed the Trade Union Act of 1913, which permitted unions to make political contributions as long as members could opt out of payment and required the unions to make contributions out of separate funds (Pelling 1987, 129–31).
4. Procedural norms included the equal rights of each side in a dispute to recognize each other, look after their own interests, and to observe and carry out agreements, and substantive norms included the establishment of minimum wages and conditions prior to others, agreement on criteria governing how often they are adjusted, and "productivity bargains," for example.
5. The state was most interventionist and had the greatest leverage over industrial relations in wartime. During the First World War, the "institutions of collective bargaining ... became greatly extended and centralized" (Fox 1985, 282). Industries that had collective bargaining fashioned national bargaining machinery; those that did not, like shipping, the railways, and the civil service, ended up creating it. Where they did not exist, the state pushed employers to develop associations and chambers of commerce, and for the first time, a peak association (the Federation of Business Industries). Labour union leaders and bureaucrats became ever more integrated into wartime planning and, through the Labour Party, the government. When these measures turned out to be inadequate for maintaining worker discipline, the government resorted to compulsory measures, including compulsory arbitration and limiting unions' restrictive practices (Fox 1985, 285–7). The government's actions during the war also spurred on the development of industry-wide employers' organizations and unions. Unions grew and the existence of full employment and the state's dependence upon workers for the war effort gave trade unions considerable leverage (Booth 1995, 19–21).
6. While a strategy of cooperation may have been beneficial to strong craft unions, it may not have been for workers who were harder to organize and who could bring

leverage to bear upon their employers as readily. Some historians have argued that while the union leadership and bureaucracy and the most well-paid workers may have gained from the unions' cooperation with management, many other workers did not gain and lost control over their work lives (see Cole 1973, 287; Burgess 1975, 306–8).

Chapter 6

1 Massachusetts, New York, and California all had boards that were formally not compulsory, but had extensive powers, particularly in the area of investigation. The Massachusetts board was the most powerful. If an employer or union petitioned the board, it would be authorized to make an inquiry and could publicize its findings. Failing efforts at mediation, and if the parties refused arbitration, the board could make an award that would be binding for six months, unless one party gave the other notice not to be bound by it within sixty days of the board's decision (Bliss 1897, 82; Witte 1952, 7–8).
2 Frank Walsh, the labour reformer and chair of the US Commission on Industrial Relations from 1913 to 1915 and the joint chair of the US War Labor Board, agreed with them (Gagliardo 1941, 25, 36–8, 47).
3 We are painting a somewhat broad brush here. There were a few industries in which industrial relations approaching the British model did emerge. There was one other, railroads, in which the state took active steps to foster voluntary cooperation.
4 American business also had to deal with policies like rate regulation and antitrust legislation that made collusion illegal. Instead, they squeezed profits by putting American business under competitive pressure, making it more difficult for businesses to pass along wage increases to consumers. Industries dominated by small firms in competitive markets were especially motivated to keep unions out partly based upon calculations of self-interest (Ernst 1991, 135). Thus, according to Robertson (2000, 87), "[i]n the absence of employer collusion, the battle over union power in the United States ... became a zero-sum game" as employers insisted on the open shop and unions on the closed shop (Greene 1998, 88–97).
5 At first, the AFL tried to define "conspiracy" in a way that would exclude unions from actions that if they were undertaken by individuals or businesses would be considered illegal. In 1912, it changed its strategy by proposing legislation that would declare that labour was not a commodity, thus exempting unions and agricultural organizations from the Sherman Act (Greene 1998, 85).
6 Business interests stoked fears that removing the restraints on labour imposed by the courts without placing other controls on labour could increase labour's potential to cause disruption and threaten public order and convenience. Progressives in both parties also professed concern that legislation that too heavily favoured labour would be perceived as "class legislation," which would call into question the liberal state's legitimacy, which rested on its perceived neutrality in class conflict.

Chapter 7

1. Although the AFL was abandoning voluntarism in practice in the early 1930s, its attachment to the ideology persisted. As late as early 1935, the AFL justified its support of the NIRA's encouragement of collective bargaining by arguing that it would forestall "arbitrary ... political control" of industrial relations (Tomlins 1985, 129–30).
2. According to the text of Section 7(a): *Every code of fair competition, agreement and license approved, prescribed or issues under this title shall contain the following conditions: 1) that employees shall have the right to organize and bargain collectively through representatives of their own choosing, and shall be free from the interference, restraint, or coercion of employers of labor, or their agents, in the designation of such representatives or in self-organization or in other concerted activities for the purpose of collective bargaining or other mutual aid or protection; 2) that no employee and no one seeking employment shall be required as a condition of employment to join any company union or to refrain from joining, organizing, or assisting a labor organization of his own choosing; and 3)that employers shall comply with the maximum hours of labor, minimum rates of pay, and other conditions of employment, approved or prescribed by the President.*
3. Congress replaced the Erdman Act with the Newlands Act in 1913. It established the first permanent federal agency devoted to industrial relations, the Board of Mediation and Conciliation, which provided federal mediators with a proactive role in dispute settlement (Zakson 1989, 339).
4. As with the NIRA, the labour movement preferred a significantly different policy than the one that Congress adopted in the cases of the Clayton Act, the Railway Labor Act, the Norris–LaGuardia Act, and the Wagner Act (O'Brien 1998, p. 149). The unions preferred the Pearre bill over the Clayton Act (Lovell 2003, 153). During the debate over Norris–LaGuardia, they preferred anti-injunction legislation that would give them immunity form equitable relief rather than make unions less vulnerable to the injunction (O'Brien 1998, 149). And they failed to get amendments to the proposed Wagner Act that they sought.

Chapter 8

1. The period culminated in long and intense strikes by street railway workers in cities across Canada, including London, Toronto, Hamilton, Winnipeg, and Saint John (Heron 1989, 36). Parliament's response was the Conciliation Act of 1900, which it patterned after the 1896 British Act by the same name. The Act created a Labour Department and directed it to collect statistics and investigate the causes of industrial disputes when they arose. The Act's approach to industrial relations was consistent with voluntarism. If both parties to a dispute agreed, the state could appoint a conciliator who would convene a meeting to try to resolve the two parties'

differences. The minister could also appoint an arbitrator if both parties approved (Cameron and Young 1960, 41).
2 The exception is Webber (1991), who argues that the core of King's approach to industrial relations – vigorous state efforts towards conciliation – was less his own invention than a continuation down a road that had begun a few years earlier when government-appointed conciliators like Roger Clute assumed an active role in working with both sides in industrial disputes in search of compromises. Clute's power to compel evidence and his status as a government agent led to success, which in turn, resulted in a large role in formulating the Conciliation Act of 1900. According to Webber (1991, 24), "it is clear that the practice of ad-hoc conciliation by governmental officers, using powers of investigation to explore avenues of compromise and invoking a public interest in settlement, was a product of the government's new-found commitment to industrial peace in certain key industries. It was not, as King was soon to claim, King's child."
3 Webber (1991, 27) challenged King's stated justification for compulsory investigation and conciliation – protecting the public – by pointing to evidence showing that the government saw industrial unrest as an impediment to economic development and the expansion of urban areas, particularly in the Western part of Canada.
4 In 1906, Parliament consolidated the Conciliation Act of 1900 and the RLDA into a single law in 1906 when it passed the Conciliation and Labour Act.
5 The syndicates came together in the 1920s as the Canadian and Catholic Confederation of Labour.

Chapter 9

1 After the Privy Council declared Bennett's New Deal proposals unconstitutional in 1937, King suggested amending the constitution to federalize unemployment insurance. It was his only effort to amend the constitution. The plan was shelved after three provinces objected, including Quebec (Neatby 1976, 243).
2 According to Simeon and Robinson (990, 67–8, 82), the government could have implemented the New Deal legislation, rally public opinion, and defend its constitutionality, as Roosevelt had done.
3 The main exception was his appointment of a Royal Commission on Dominion-Provincial Relations (Rowell Commission) of 1938.
4 The share of the vote of the Canadian parties rose from 6 per cent of votes cast in 1930 to 15 per cent in 1935; the share for the American parties fell from 3 per cent of the vote in 1932 to less than 1 per cent in 1936.
5 The Communists' share of the presidential vote in the United States dropped during the 1930s from 0.3 per cent in 1932 to 0.2 per cent in 1936; their share in Canada rose from 0.12 per cent in 1930 to 0.46 per cent in 1935. Party politics would have the greatest impact on labour's influence over public policy in the future, but it was

not the only form of working-class political engagement in the 1930s. Communists attracted workers to the Workers' Unity League (WUL) and engaged in "the ambitious campaign ... to organize the unemployed in the main cities and towns" into strikes and protests (Jamieson 1973, 87; Lipton 1966, 255–7; Palmer 1992, 252–7). Much larger proportions of the unemployed in Canada were single men and recent immigrants than in the United States, the larger pool of potential recruits for the Communists fostered fears in the government of insurrection (Struthers 1983, 97–9). The unemployed organized "across the country, to demonstrate for better relief, to fight evictions", and many of them caused "several major disturbances" (Jamieson 1968, 235, 242; Palmer 1992, 243–4).The WUL organized the Relief Camp Workers Union, which launched the "On to Ottawa trek." Two thousand men marched on the government to protest the meagre wages and unpleasant living conditions in the camps.
6 Senator Wagner and other progressives also framed their appeal in terms of widely cherished values like "democracy" (by giving labour a voice and bargaining power) and broad societal interests in advancing economic recovery (by increasing workers' purchasing power) and reducing industrial unrest (see Gross 1974, 64; Bernstein 1950, 90, 100, 115).

Chapter 10

1 In New Zealand and Australia, the problem of union security had been solved by making the state the guarantor of labour rights. In Britain union security was achieved through minimal state action, but more importantly by the development of a set of norms around collective bargaining (Charles 1973). In Canada neither the state nor labour (after it came under the influence of the AFL) thought that the strong version of statism adopted in Australasia was necessary.
2 Olney served as attorney general under President Grover Cleveland during the Pullman strike. He had the dubious distinction of ending the strike by obtaining an injunction against the strikers, which handed employers their most potent weapon against unions.
3 Several studies suggest that unions have a variety of positive impacts on workers' lives. They increase wages for both union and non-union employees, lead to more generous fringe benefits, and reduce income inequality (Freeman and Medoff 1984; Hirsch and Macpherson 2003; Pierce 1999; Card 1991; Blanchflower and Bryson 2002; Card et al. 2003; Buchmueller, DiNardo and Valletta 2001). The evidence linking union membership and job satisfaction is mixed, but controlling for conditions that can affect attitudes about one's job and that are also linked to "the need for and presence of a union," unions appear to have a positive impact on job satisfaction (Pfeffer and Davis-Blake 1990; Bender and Sloane 1998). Union membership at the individual level as well as higher membership across democratic countries is linked with significantly higher levels of subjective life satisfaction,

when controlling for other variables, and its effects compare favourably with other correlates of life satisfaction, such as marriage and employment (Keane, Pacek, and Radcliff 2012). Union contracts provide workers with greater job security, and due process procedures provide opportunities to overturn arbitrary and adverse employer actions. Unions appear to supply workers with social support and protection against job-related stress (Lowe and Northcott 1988; Brenner 1987). If unions have these salutary effects on individual workers' lives, then higher levels of union membership should increase those effects overall in a society.

Works Cited

Abella, Irving. 1975. "The Canadian Labour Movement, 1902–1960." *Canadian Historical Society Historical Booklet*, No. 28, Ottawa.

Abrams, Roger I., and Dennis R. Nolan. 1983. "American Labor Arbitration: The Early Years." *School of Law Faculty Publications*, Paper 202. http://hdlhandle.net/2047/d20002610.

Adams, T., 1997. "Market and Institutional Forces in Industrial Relations: The Development of National Collective Bargaining, 1910–1920." *Economic. History. Review* 50 (3): 506–30.

Akin, William E. 1967. "Arbitration and Labor Conflict: The Middle Class Panacea, 1886–1900." *The Historian* (August): 565–83. https://doi.org/10.1111/j.1540-6563.1967.tb01866.x.

Alderman, Geoffrey. 1971. "The Railway Companies and the Growth of Trade Unionism in the Late Nineteenth and Early Twentieth Centuries." *The Historical Journal* 14 (1) (March): 129–52. https://www-jstor-org.libproxy.temple.edu/stable/2637904?sid=primo.

Allen, Robert C. 1994. "Real Incomes in the English-Speaking World, 1879–1913." *Labour Market Evolution: The Economic History of Market Integration, Wage Flexibility and the Employment Relation*, edited by George Grantham and Mary MacKinnon, 107–38. London: Routledge.

Anderson, Violet, ed. 1938. *Problems in Canadian Unity: Lectures Given at the Canadian Institute on Economics and Politics, August 6 to 19*. Toronto: Thomas Nelson and Sons.

Archer, Robin. 2001. "Does Repression Help to Create Labor Parties? The Effect of Police and Military Intervention on Unions in the United States and Australia." *Studies in American Political Development* 15 (Fall): 189–219. https://doi.org/10.1017/S0898588X01000049.

Archer, Robin. 2007. *Why Is There No Labor Party in the United States?* Princeton: Princeton University Press.

Armstrong, E.G.A. 1984. "Employers Associations in Great Britain." In *Employers Associations and Industrial Relations: A Comparative Study*, edited by John P. Windmuller and Alan Gladstone, 24–42. Oxford: Clarendon Press.

Askwith, George R. 1974. *Industrial Problems and Disputes*. New York: Barnes and Noble Books.

Bagwell, Philip S. 1985. "The New Unionism in Britain: The Railway Industry." In *The Development of Trade Unionism in Great Britain and Germany, 1880–1914*, edited by Wolfgang J. Mommsen and Hans-Gerhard Husung, 185–200. London: Allen & Unwin.

Bain, G.S., and R. Price. 1980. *Profiles of Union Growth: A Comparative Statistical Portrait of Eight Countries*. Oxford: Basil Blackwell.

Baker, William M. 1983. "The Miners and the Mediator: The 1906 Lethbridge Strike and Mackenzie King." *Labour/Le Travailleur* 11(Spring): 89–117. https://www.jstor.org/stable/25140202.

Bakvis, Herman, Gerald Baier, and Douglas Brown. 2009. *Contested Federalism: Certainty and Ambiguity in the Canadian Federation*. Oxford: Oxford University Press.

Balke, N.S., and R.J. Gordon. 1989. "The Estimation of Prewar Gross National Product: Methodology and New Evidence." *Journal of Political Economy* 97 (1): 38–92. https://doi.org/10.1086/261593.

Bender, Keith A., and Peter J. Sloane. 1998. "Job Satisfaction, Trade Unions, and Exit-Voice Revisited." *Industrial and Labor Relations Review* 51 (2) (January): 222–40. https://doi.org/10.1177/001979399805100204.

Benson, John. 1982. "Coalmining." In *A History of British Industrial Relations 1875–1914*, edited by Chris Wrigley, 187–208. Amherst, MA: University of Massachusetts Press.

Berkowitz, Peter, Rebecca Gumbrell, Richard Hyman, Michel Pigenet, and Michael Schneider. 2004. "The Structure and Organisation of British, French and German Trade Unions before the First World War." In *The Emergence of European Trade Unions*, edited by Jean-Louis Robert, Antoine Prost, and Chris Wrigley, 215–32. Hampshire, UK: Ashgate.

Bernstein, Irving. 1950. *The New Deal Collective Bargaining Policy*. Berkeley: University of California Press.

Bernstein, Irving. 1970. *Turbulent Years: A History of the American Worker, 1933–1941*. Boston: Houghton Mifflin Company.

Brereton, David. 1989. "Theoretical Perspectives on Legislative Innovation: The Case of Compulsory Arbitration," in *Foundations of Arbitration: The Origins and Effects of State Compulsory Arbitration, 1890–1914*, edited by Stuart Macintyre and Richard Mitchell, 293–312.

Berton, Pierre. 1990. *The Great Depression, 1929–1939*. Toronto: McClelland and Stewart, Inc.

Biagini, Eugenio F., and Alastair J. Reid. 1991. *Currents of Radicalism: Popular Radicalism, Organised Laour and Party Politics in Britain, 1850–1914*. Cambridge: Cambridge University Press.

Blackburn, Sheila. 2007. *A Fair Day's Wage for a Fair Day's Work? Sweated Labour and the Origins of Minimum Wage Legislation in Britain*. Hampshire, UK: Ashgate.

Blanchflower, David G., and Alex Bryson. 2002. "Changes over Time in Union Relative Wage Effects in the U.K. and the U.S. Revisited." National Bureau of Economic Research, Working Paper No. 9395. Cambridge, MA: NBER. http://www.nber.org/papers/w9395.

Bliss, William D. 1897. "Arbitration and Conciliation in the United States." In *Encyclopedia of Social Reform*. New York: Funk and Wagnells.

Bonnett, Clarence E. 1922. *Employers' Associations in the United States: A Study of Typical Associations*. New York: Macmillan.

Booth, Alison L. 1995. *The Economics of the Trade Union*. Cambridge: Cambridge University Press.

Bothwell, Robert, Ian Drummond, and John English. 1987. *Canada, 1900–1945*. Toronto: University of Toronto Press.

Bray, Mark, and Malcolm Rimmer. 1989. "Voluntarism or Compulsion? Public Inquiries into Industrial Relations in New South Wales and Great Britain, 1890–94." In *Foundations of Arbitration: The Origins and Effects of State Compulsory Arbitration, 1890–1914*, edited by Stuart Macintyre and Richard Mitchell, 50–73. Melbourne: Oxford University Press.

Bray, Mark, and Pat Walsh. 1998. "Different Paths to Neo-Liberalism? Comparing Australia and New Zealand." *Industrial Relations* 37 (3): 358–86. https://doi.org/10.1111/0019-8676.00092.

Brenner, M. Harvey. 1987. "Relation of Economic Change to Swedish Health and Social Wellbeing." *Social Science and Medicine* 25: 183–95. https://doi.org/10.1016/0277-9536(87)90387-x.

Brookings Institution. 2016. "Vital Statistics on Congress." Accessed 4 February 2018. https://www.brookings.edu/wp-content/uploads/2016/06/Vital-Statistics-Chapter-2-Congressional-Elections.pdf.

Brosnan, Peter, David F. Smith, and Pat Walsh. 1990. *The Dynamics of New Zealand Industrial Relations*. Auckland, NZ: John Wiley & Sons.

Brown, E. Henry Phelps. 1959. *The Growth of British Industrial Relations: A Study from the Standpoint of 1906–14*. New York: Macmillan.

Brown, E. Henry Phelps. 1983. *The Origins of Trade Union Power*. Oxford: Clarendon Press.

Brown, Kenneth D. 1982. "Trade Unions and the Law." In *A History of British Industrial Relations, 1875–1914*, edited by Chris Wrigley, 116–34. Amherst, MA: University of Massachusetts Press.

Brugger, Bill, and Dean Jaensch. 1985. *Australian Politics: Theory and Practice*. Sydney: Allen & Unwin.

Buchmueller, Thomas C., John DiNardo, and Robert G Valletta. 2001. "Union Effects on Health Insurance Provision and Coverage in the United States." National Bureau of Economic Research, Working Paper No. 8238. Cambridge, MA: NBER.

Burgess, Keith. 1975. *The Origins of British Industrial Relations: The Nineteenth Century Experience*. London: Croom Helm.

Butlin, Noel G. 1962. *Australian Domestic Product, Investment and Foreign Borrowing, 1861–1938/39*. Cambridge: Cambridge University Press.
Cameron, James C., and Frederick J.L. Young. 1960. *The Status of Trade Unions in Canada*. Kingston, ON: Department of Industrial Relations, Queen's University.
Campbell, C., and W. Christian. 1996. *Parties, Leaders, and Ideologies in Canada*. Toronto: McGraw-Hill Ryerson.
Capoccia, G. 2015. "Critical Junctures and Institutional Change." In *Advances in Comparative-Historical Analysis*, edited by J. Mahoney and K. Thelen, 147–79. Cambridge: Cambridge University Press.
Capoccia, G. 2016. "Critical Junctures." In *The Oxford Handbook of Historical Institutionalism*, edited by O. Fioretos, T. Falleti, and A. Sheingate. 1–23. Oxford: Oxford University Press.
Capoccia, G., and R.D. Kelemen. 2007. "The Study of Critical Junctures: Theory, Narrative, and Counterfactuals in Institutional Analysis." *World Politics* 59 (3): 341–69.
Card, David. 1991. "The Effect of Unions on Distribution of Wages: Re-distribution or Relabelling? Princeton University, Department of Economics, Working Paper No. 287. Princeton: Princeton University.
Card, David, Thomas Lemieux, and W. Craig Riddell. 2003. "Unionization and Wage Inequality: A Comparative Study of the U.S., the U.K. and Canada." National Bureau of Economic Research, Working Paper No. 9473. Cambridge, MA: NBER. http://www.nber.org/papers/w9473.
Castles, Francis G. 1978. *The Social Democratic Image of Society*. London: Routledge and Keegan.
Castles, Francis G. 1985. *The Working Class and Welfare: Reflections on the Political Development of the Welfare State in Australia and New Zealand, 1890–1980*. Wellington: Allen & Unwin Port Nicholson Press.
Charles, Rodger. 1973. *The Development of Industrial Relations in Britain, 1911–1939*. London: Hutchinson.
Church, Roy. 1990. "Employers, Trade Unions and the State, 1889–1987: The Origins and Decline of Tripartism in the British Coal Industry." In *Workers, Owners and Politics in Coal Mining: An International Comparison of Industrial Relations*, edited by Gerald D. Feldman and Klaus Tenfelde. New York: St. Martin's Press.
Clark, Charles M.H. 1981. *A History of Australia, V, The People Make Laws, 1888–1915*. Melbourne: Melbourne University Press.
Clarkson, Stephen. 2005. *The Big Red Machine: How the Liberal Party Dominates Canadian Politics*. Vancouver: University of British Columbia Press.
Clegg, Hugh Armstrong. 1976. *Trade Unionism under Collective Bargaining: A Theory Based on Comparisons of Six Countries*. Oxford: Basil Blackwell.
Clegg, Hugh Armstrong. 1979. *The Changing System of Industrial Relations in Great Britain*. Oxford: Basil Blackwell.
Clegg, Hugh Armstrong, Alan Fox, and A.F. Thompson. 1964. *A History of British Trade Unions Since 1889*. Vol. 1. Oxford: Oxford University/Clarendon Press.

Coates, Daniel. 1973. "Organized Labor and Politics in Canada: The Development of a National Labor Code." PhD Thesis, Cornell University.
Coates, Daniel. 1975. *The Labour Party and the Struggle for Socialism*. London: Cambridge University Press.
Coates, Ken, and Tony Topham. 1991. *The Making of the Transport and General Workers' Union: The Emergence of the Labour Movement*. Oxford: Oxford University Press.
Coats, R.H. 1913. "The Labour Movement." In *Canada and Its Provinces: A History of the Canadian People and Their Institutions by One Hundred Associates*, edited by Adam Shortt and Arthur G. Doughty, 277–355. Toronto: Edinburgh University Press.
Coghlan, T.A. 1918. *Labour and Industry in Australia*. Vols. III and IV. Oxford: Oxford University Press.
Cole, G.D.H. 1965. *British Working Class Politics, 1832–1914*. London: Routledge & Kegan Paul.
Cole, G.D.H. 1973. *The World of Labour*. New York: Barnes and Noble.
Coleman, Peter J. 1987. *Progressivism and the World of Reform: New Zealand and the Origins of the American Welfare State*. Lawrence: University Press of Kansas.
Collier, Ruth B., and David Collier. 1991. *Shaping the Political Arena*. Princeton: Princeton University Press.
Cowley, J. 1967. "Idealist Tendencies in British Marxism." *Studies on the Left* 7 (2) (Spring).
Craven, Paul. 1980. *'An Impartial Umpire': Industrial Relations and the Canadian State, 1900–1911*. Toronto: University of Toronto Press.
Creighton, Donald G. 1943. "George Brown, Sir John MacDonald and the 'Workingman.'" *Canadian Historical Review* 24 (4): 362–76. https://doi.org/10.3138/chr-024-04-03.
Creighton, Donald G. 1970. *Canada's First Century: 1867–1967*. Toronto: Macmillan.
Crompton, Henry. 1876. *Industrial Conciliation*. London: Henry S. King.
Cronin, James E. 1985. "Strikes and the Struggle for Union Organization: Britain and Europe." In *The Development of Trade Unionism in Great Britain and Germany, 1880–1914*, edited by Wolfgang J. Mommsen and Hans-Gerhard Husung, 55–77. London: Allen & Unwin.
Crouch, Colin. 1979. *The Politics of Industrial Relations*. Manchester: Manchester University Press.
Crouch, Colin. 1993. *Industrial Relation and European State Traditions*. Oxford: Clarendon Press.
Crouch, Colin. 2005. *Capitalist Diversity and Change: Recombinant Governance and Institutional Entrepreneurs*, Oxford: Oxford University Press.
Crowley, F.K. 1954. "Master and Servant in Western Australia, 1851–1901." *Journal and Proceedings of the Western Australia Historical Society* 4 (6): 15–32. https://catalogue.nla.gov.au/Record/396481?lookfor=author:%22Western%20Australian%20Historical%20Society%22&offset=12&max=48.

Davidson, Roger. 1974. "Introduction." In *Industrial Problems and Disputes*, edited by George R. Askwith. New York: Barnes and Noble Books, vii–xiii.

Davidson, Roger. 1978. "The Board of Trade and Industrial Relations 1896–1914." *The Historical Journal* 31 (2) (1978): 571–91. https://doi.org/10.1017/S0018246X00019774.

Davidson, Roger. 1982. "Government Administration." In *A History of British Industrial Relations, 1875–1914*, edited by Chris Wrigley, 159–86. Amherst, MA: University of Massachusetts Press.

Derber, Milton. 1983. "Employers Associations in the United States." In *Employers Associations in Industrial Relations: A Comparative Study*, edited by John P. Windmuller and Alan Gladstone, 79–112. Oxford: Clarendon Press.

Dickey, Brian. 1966. "The Broken Hill Strike, 1892." *Labour History*, November, 40–53.

Dulles, Foster Rhea. 1966. *Labor in America: A History*. 3rd ed. New York: Crowell.

Dunlop, John T. 1958. *Industrial Relations Systems*. New York: Henry Holt.

Ebbels, R.N. 1965. *The Australian Labor Movement, 1850–1907*. Melbourne: Cheshire-Lansdowne.

Eggert, Gerald G. 1967. *Railroad Labor Disputes: The Beginnings of Federal Strike Policy*. Ann Arbor: The University of Michigan Press.

Ellingwood, A.R. 1928. "The Railway Labor Act of 1926." *Journal of Political Economy* 36 (1) (February): 53–82. https://doi.org/10.1086/253917.

Ernst, Daniel. 1991. "The Closed Shop, the Proprietary Capitalist and the Law, 1897–1915." In *Masters to Managers; Historical and Comparative Perspectives on American Employers*, edited by Sanford M. Jacoby, 132–48. New York: Columbia University Press.

Ernst, Daniel. 1995. *Lawyers against Labor: From Individual Rights to Corporate Liberalism*. Urbana: University of Illinois Press.

Eskridge, William N. 1994. *Dynamic Statutory Interpretation*. Cambridge: Harvard University Press.

Esping-Andersen, Gosta. 1985. *Politics against Markets: The Social Democratic Road to Power*. Princeton: Princeton University Press.

Finegold, Kenneth, and Theda Skocpol. 1995. *State and Party in America's New Deal*. Madison: University of Wisconsin Press.

Fink, Leon. 1997. *Progressive Intellectuals and the Dilemmas of Democratic Commitment*. Cambridge: Harvard University Press.

Fisher, Chay, and Christopher Kent. 1999. "Two Depressions, One Banking Collapse." Research Discussion Paper, June, Reserve Bank of Australia. Accessed July 4, 2016. www.rba.gov.au.

Fisher, Clyde Olin. 1922. "Use of Federal Power in Settlement of Railway Labor Disputes." Dissertation, Cornell University, printed as Bulletin of the United States Bureau of Labor Statistics, no. 303, March.

Foner, Philip S. 1980. *The History of the Labor Movement in the United States. Volume 5: The AFL in the Progressive Era, 1910–1915*. New York: International Publishers.

Forbath, William. 1989. "The Shaping of the American Labor Movement." *Harvard Law Review* 106 (April): 1111–256. https://doi.org/10.2307/1341293.
Forbath, William. 1991. *Law and the Shaping of the American Labor Movement*. Cambridge: Harvard University Press.
Fox, Alan. 1985. *History and Heritage: The Social Origins of the British Industrial Relations System*. London: Allen & Unwin.
Frankfurter, Felix, and Nathan Greene. 1930. *The Labor Injunction*. New York: Macmillan.
Fraser, W. Hamish. 1974. *Trade Unions and Society: The Struggle for Acceptance, 1850–1880*. Totowa, NJ: Rowman & Littlefield.
Fraser, W. Hamish. 1999. *A History of British Trade Unionism, 1700–1998*. New York: St. Martin's Press.
Freeman, Richard, and James Medoff. 1984. *What Do Unions Do?* New York: Basic Books.
French, Doris. 1962. *Faith, Sweat, and Politics: The Early Trade Union Years in Canada*. Toronto: McClelland and Stewart.
Friedman, Gerald. 1998. *State-Making and Labor Movements: France and the United States, 1876–1914*. Ithaca, NY: Cornell University Press.
Friedman, Gerald. 1999. "U.S. Historical Statistics: New Estimates of Union Membership in the United States, 1880–1914." *Historical Methods: A Journal of Quantitative and Interdisciplinary History* 32 (2) (Spring): 75–86. https://doi.org/10.1080/01615449909598928.
Fudge, Judy A. 1990. "Voluntarism, Compulsion and the 'Transformation' of Canadian Labour Law During World War II." In *Canadian and Australian Labour History Nathan*, edited by Gregory S. Kealey and Greg Patmore, 81–100. Australia: Australian-Canadian Studies.
Fudge, Judy A., and Eric Tucker. 2001. *Labour Before the Law: The Regulation of Workers' Collective Action in Canada, 1900–1948*. New York: Oxford University Press.
Gagliardo, Domenico. 1941. *The Kansas Industrial Court: An Experiment in Compulsory Arbitration*. Lawrence, KS: University of Kansas Publications Social Science Studies.
Galenson, Walter. 1968. *Comparative Labor Movements*. New York: Russell & Russell.
Garside, W.R., and Gospel, H.F. 1982. "Employers and Managers: Their Organizational Structure and Changing Industrial Strategies." In *A History of British Industrial Relations 1875–1914*, edited by Chris Wrigley, 99–115. Amherst, MA: University of Massachusetts Press.
Glass, Margaret. 1997. *Charles Cameron Kingston: Federation Father*. Melbourne: The Miegunyah Press at Melbourne University Press.
Goldfield, Michael. 1989. "Worker Insurgency, Radical Organization, and New Deal Labor Legislation." *American Political Science Review* 83: 1257–82. https://doi.org/10.2307/1961668.
Goldfield, Michael. 1990. "Explaining New Deal Labor Policy." *American Political Science Review* 85: 1304–15. https://doi.org/10.2307/1963265.

Gollan, Robin. 1960. *Radical and Working Class Politics: A Study of Eastern Australia, 1850–1910*. Melbourne: Melbourne University Press.

Gollan, Robin. 1963. *The Coalminers of New South Wales: A History of the Union, 1860–1960*. Melbourne: Melbourne University Press.

Gompers, Samuel. 1920. *Labor and the Employer*, compiled and edited by Hayes Robbins. New York: E.P. Dutton.

Gompers, Samuel. 1925. *Seventy Years of Life and Labor: An Autobiography*. Ithaca, NY: ILR Press New York State School of Industrial and Labor Relations, Cornell University.

Gospel, H.F. 1987. "Employers and Managers: Organization and Strategy." In *A History of British Industrial Relations, 1914–1939*, edited by Chris Wrigley. Brighton: Harvester Press.

Greene, Julie. 1998. *Pure and Simple Politics: The American Federation of Labor and Political Activism, 1881–1917*. New York: Cambridge University Press.

Greenstone, J. David. 1977. *Labor in American Politics*. Chicago: The University of Chicago Press.

Gregory, Charles O. 1958. *Labor and the Law*. New York: W.W. Norton. 2nd ed., with 1961 supplement.

Gross, James A. 1974. *The Making of the National Labor Relations Board: A Study in Economics, Politics and the Law*. Vol. 1 (1933–37). Albany: The State University of New York Press.

Gross, James A. 1981. *The Reshaping of the National Labor Relations Board: National Labor Policy in Transition, 1937–1947*. Albany: The State University of New York Press.

Guaranty Trust Company of New York. 1920. *Transportation Act of 1920*. New York: Guaranty Trust Company.

Hacker, Jacob S. 1998. "The Historical Logic of National Health Insurance: Structure and Sequence in the Development of British, Canadian and U.S. Medical Policy." *Studies in American Political Development* 12 (Spring): 57–130. https://doi.org/10.1017/S0898588X98001308.

Hall, Peter A., and Rosemary C.R. Taylor. 1996. "Political Science and the Three New Institutionalisms." *Political Studies* XLIV: 936–57. https://doi.org/10.1111/j.1467-9248.1996.tb00343.x.

Hamann, Kerstin, and John Kelly. 2017. "Varieties of Capitalism and Industrial Relations." In *The Sage Handbook of Industrial Relations: Varieties of Capitalism and Industrial Relations*, edited by Paul Blyton et al., 129–48. Thousand Oaks, CA: Sage.

Hansard (U.K.). 1893. "Remarks of Prime Minister W.E. Gladstone in debate," volume 11, May 2.

Hansard (U.K.). 1895. "House of Commons." March 5. http://hansard.millbanksystems.com/commons/1895/mar/05/conciliation-trade-disputes.

Hare, A.E.C. 1958. *The First Principles of Industrial Relations*. London: Macmillan.

Harris, Howell John. 1991. "Getting It Together: The Metal Manufacturers Association of Philadelphia, c. 1900–1930." In *Masters to Managers; Historical and Comparative*

Perspectives on American Employers, edited by Sanford M. Jacoby, 111–31. New York: Columbia University Press.

Harrison, Royden J. 1965. *Before the Socialists: Studies in Labour and Politics, 1861–1881*. London: Routledge and Keegan Paul.

Hartz, Louis. 1964. "Part One: A Theory of the Development of the New Societies." In *The Founding of New Societies: Studies in the History of the United States, Latin America, South Africa, Canada and Australia*, edited by Louis Hartz, 3–65. New York: Harcourt, Brace & World.

Hattam, Victoria. 1993. *Labor Visions and State Power: The Origins of Business Unionism in the United States*. Princeton: Princeton University Press.

Haydu, Jeffrey. 1988. "Employers, Unions and American Exceptionalism: Pre-World War I Open Shops in the Machine Trades in Comparative Perspective." *International Review of Social History* XXXIII: 25–41. https://doi.org/10.1017/S0020859000008622.

Heron, Craig. 1989. *The Canadian Labour Movement: A Short History*. Toronto: James Lorimer.

Heron, Craig, and Robert Storey. 1986. "On the Job in Canada." In *On the Job: Confronting the Labour Process in Canada*, edited by Craig Heron and Robert Storey. Kingston: McGill-Queen's University Press.

Hinton, James. 1973. *The First Shop Stewards' Movement*, Sydney: Allen & Unwin.

Hinton, James. 1983. *Labour and Socialism: A History of the British Labour Movement, 1867–1974*. Brighton, Sussex: Weatsheaf Books.

Hirsch, Barry T., and David A. Macpherson. 2003. *Union Membership and Earnings Data Book: Compilations from the Current Population Survey*. Washington, DC: Bureau of National Affairs.

Hobsbawm, Eric J. 1968. *Labouring Men: Studies in the History of Labour*. New York: Basic Books.

Hobsbawm, Eric J. 1985. "The 'New Unionism' Reconsidered." In *The Development of Trade Unionism in Great Britain and Germany, 1880–1914*, edited by Wolfgang J. Mommsen and Hans-Gerhard Husung, 13–31. London: Allen & Unwin.

Holt, James. 1976. "The Political Origins of Compulsory Arbitration in New Zealand." *Journal of New Zealand History* 10: 99–111. https://www.nzjh.auckland.ac.nz/document.php?wid=1387&action=null.

Holt, James. 1977. "Trade Unionism in the British and U.S. Steel Industries, 1880–1914." *Labor History* 18 (Winter): 5–35. https://doi.org/10.1080/00236567708584416.

Holt, James. 1986. *Compulsory Arbitration in New Zealand: The First Forty Years*. Auckland: Auckland University Press.

Horowitz, G. 1966. "Conservatism, Liberalism, and Socialism in Canada: An Interpretation." *The Canadian Journal of Economics and Political Science/Revue Canadienne d'Economique et de Science Politique* 5 (2) (May): 143–71. https://doi.org/10.2307/139794.

Howell, Chris. 2005. *Trade Unions and the State: The Construction of Industrial Relations Institutions in Britain, 1890–2000*. Oxford: Oxford University Press.

Hyman, Richard. 1979. "The Politics of Workplace Trade Unionism: Recent Tendencies and Some Problems for Theory." *Capital and Class* 8: 54–67. https://doi.org/10.1177/030981687900800104.

Hyman, Richard. 1989. *The Political Economy of Industrial Relations: Theory and Practice in a Cold Climate*. London: Macmillan.

Hyman, Richard. 2001. *Understanding European Trade Unionism: Between Market, Class and Society*. London: Sage.

Innis, Harold. 1956. *The Fur Trade in Canada: An Introduction to Canadian Economic History*. Toronto: University of Toronto Press.

Innis, Harold. 1954. *The Cod Fisheries: The History of an International Economy*. Toronto: University of Toronto Press.

Jacoby, Sanford M. 1991. "American Exceptionalism Revisited: The Importance of Management." In *Masters to Managers: Historical and Comparative Perspectives on American Employers*, edited by Sanford M. Jacoby. New York: Columbia University Press.

Jamieson, Stuart Marshall. 1973. *Industrial Relations in Canada*. 2nd ed. Toronto: Macmillan.

Jamieson, Stuart Marshall. 1968. *Times of Trouble: Labour Unrest and Industrial Conflict in Canada, 1900–66*. Ottawa: Task Force on Labour Relations, Study No. 22.

Johnson, James P. 1979. *The Politics of Soft Coal: The Bituminous Industry from World War I through the New Deal*. Urbana: University of Illinois Press.

Kahn-Freund, Otto. 1954. "Legal Framework." In *The System of Industrial Relations in Great Britain*, edited by Alan Flanders and H.A. Clegg, 42–127, Oxford: Basil Blackwell & Mott.

Karr, Clarence. 2003. "Dunsmuir, James." In *Dictionary of Canadian Biography*, vol. 14. University of Toronto/Université Laval. Accessed 30 November 2013. http://www.biographi.ca/en/bio/dunsmuir_james_14E.html.

Katznelson, Ira, and Aristide R. Zolberg, eds. 1986. *Working Class Formation: Nineteenth Century Patterns in Western Europe and the United States*. Princeton: Princeton University Press.

Kaufman, Bruce E. 2004. *The Global Evolution of Industrial Relations: Events, Ideas and the IIRA*. Geneva: International Labour Office.

Kealey, Gregory S. 1995. *Workers and Canadian History*. Montreal: McGill-Queen's University Press.

Kealey, Gregory S., and Bryan D. Palmer. 1982. *Dreaming of What Might Be: The Knights of Labour in Ontario*. Cambridge: Cambridge University Press.

Keane, Lauren, Alexander Pacek, and Benjamin Radcliff. 2012. "Organized Labor, Democracy, and Life Satisfaction: A Cross-National Analysis." *Labor Studies Journal* 37 (3): 253–70. https://doi.org/10.1177/0160449X12464396.

Kendrick, J.W. 1961. *Productivity Trends in the United States*. Princeton: Princeton University Press.

Kennedy, David M. 1999. *Freedom from Fear: The American People in Depression and War, 1929-1945*. New York: Oxford University Press.

Kerr, Clark, Frederick H. Harbison, John T. Dunlop, and Charles A. Meyers. 1955. "The Labour Problem in Economic Development: A Framework for a Reappraisal." *International Labor Review* 71 (3): 233-5. https://www.ilo.org/global/publications/journals/international-labour-review/lang--en/index.htm.

Kerr, Clark, Frederick H. Harbison, John T. Dunlop, and Charles A. Meyers. 1960. *Industrialism and Industrial Man; The Problems of Labor and Management in Economic Growth*. Cambridge: Harvard University Press.

King, William Lyon Mackenzie. 1918. *Industry and Humanity: A Study in the Principles Underlying Industrial Reconstruction* (reprinted in 1973 with introduction by David Jay Bercuson). Toronto: University of Toronto Press.

Kjellberg, Anders. 2009. "The Swedish Model of Industrial Relations: Self~Regulation and Combined Centralisation-Decentralisation." In *Trade Unionism Since 1945: Towards A Global History*, edited by Craig Phelan, vol. 1, 155-98. Oxford: Peter Lang.

Klehr, Harvey. 1984. *The Heyday of American Communism: The Depression Decade*. New York: Basic Books.

Korpi, Walter. 1983. *The Democratic Class Struggle*. London: Routledge and Keegan Paul.

Kuznets, S.S. 1961. *Capital in the American Economy: Its Formation and Financing*. Princeton: Princeton University Press.

Laskin, Bora. 1943. "Collective Bargaining in Ontario: A New Legislative Approach." *Canadian Bar Review* 21 (9) (November): 684-706. https://cbr.cba.org/index.php/cbr/article/view/1056.

Laskin, Bora. 1944. "Industrial Relations and Social Security." *Public Affairs* (Fall): 48-56.

Lecht, Leonard A. 1955. *Experience under Railway Labor Legislation*. New York: Columbia University Press.

Lewis, David, and Frank Scott. 1943. *Make This Your Canada: A Review of C.C.F. History and Policy*. Toronto: Central Canada Publishing Company.

Lichtenstein, Nelson. 1998. "Taft-Hartley: A Slave-Labor Law?" *Catholic University Law Review*, 47 (Spring): 763-89. https://scholarship.law.edu/lawreview.

Lipset, Seymour Martin. 1962. "Trade Unions and Social Structure: II." *Industrial Relations* (February), 1, 89-110. https://doi.org/10.1111/j.1468-232X.1962.tb00661.x.

Lipsitz, George. 1994. *Rainbow at Midnight: Labor and Culture in the 1940s*. Urbana: University of Illinois Press.

Lipson, Leslie. 1948. *The Politics of Equality: New Zealand's Adventures in Democracy*. Chicago: University of Chicago Press.

Lipton, Charles. 1966. *The Trade Union Movement of Canada, 1827-1959*. Montreal: Canadian Social Publications Limited.

Lloyd, Henry Demarest. 1900. *A Country without Strikes: A Visit to the Compulsory Arbitration Court of New Zealand*. New York: Doubleday, Page.

Logan, Harold A. 1928. *The History of Trade-Union Organization in Canada*. Chicago: University of Chicago Press.

Logan, Harold A. 1948. *Trade Unions in Canada: Their Development and Functioning*. Toronto: Macmillan.

Lorwin, Lewis. 1933. *The American Federation of Labor*. Washington: The Brookings Institution.

Lovell, George I. 2003. *Legislative Deferrals: Statutory Ambiguity, Judicial Power, and American Democracy*. Cambridge: Cambridge University Press.

Lowe, Graham S., and Herbert C. Northcott. 1988. "The Impact of Working Conditions, Social Roles, and Personal Characteristics on Gender Differences in Distress." *Work and Occupations* 15: 55–77. https://doi.org/10.1177/0730888488015001004.

Lubell, Samuel. 1965. *The Future of American Politics*. 3rd ed. Revised. New York: Harper and Row.

Luebbert, Gregory M. 1991. *Liberalism, Fascism, or Social Democracy: Social Classes and the Political Origins of Regimes in Interwar Europe*. New York: Oxford University Press.

Lyon, Leverett S., et al. 1935. *The National Recovery Administration: An Analysis and Appraisal*. Washington: The Brookings Institution.

Macarthy, Peter. 1967. "The Harvester Judgment: An Historical Assessment." PhD Thesis, Australian National University.

Macarthy, Peter. 1970. "Employers, the Tariff, and Legal Wage Determination in Australia—1890–1910." *Journal of Industrial Relations* 12 (1 June): 182–93. https://doi.org/10.1177/002218567001200205.

Macdonald, Donald F. 1960. *The State and the Trade Unions*. London: Macmillan.

MacDowell, Laurel Sefton. 2006. "The Formation of the Canadian Industrial Relations System during World War II." In *Canadian Working Class History*, edited by Laurel Sefton MacDowell and Ian Radforth, 273–89. Toronto: Canadian Scholars' Press.

Macintyre, Stuart. 1989. "Neither Capital nor Labour: The Politics of the Establishment of Arbitration." In *Foundations of Arbitration: The Origins and Effects of State Compulsory Arbitration, 1890–1914*, edited by Stuart Macintyre and Richard Mitchell, 178–200. Melbourne: Oxford University Press.

Macintyre, Stuart, and Richard Mitchell. 1989. "Introduction." In *Foundations of Arbitration: The Origins and Effects of State Compulsory Arbitration, 1890–1914*, edited by Stuart Macintyre and Richard Mitchell, 1–21. Melbourne: Oxford University Press.

Maddison, Angus. 2006. *The World Economy: Volume 1: A Billenial Perspective and Volume 2: Historical Statistics*. Paris: OECD Publishing.

Magnusson, Leifur, and Marguerite A. Gadsby. 1920. "Federal Intervention in Railroad Disputes." *Monthly Labor Review* 11 (1) (July): 26–43. https://fraser.stlouisfed.org

/title/monthly-labor-review-6130/july-1920-608034/federal-intervention-railroad-disputes-596412.

Mallory, J.R. 1971. *The Structure of Canadian Government*. Toronto: Macmillan.

Markey, Ray. 1989. "Trade Unions, the Labor Party and the Introduction of Arbitration in New South Wales and the Commonwealth." In *Foundations of Arbitration: The Origins and Effects of State Compulsory Arbitration, 1890–1914*, edited by Stuart Macintyre and Richard Mitchell, 156–77. Melbourne: Oxford University Press.

Marks, Gary. 1989. *Unions in Politics: Britain, Germany and the United States in the Nineteenth and Early Twentieth Centuries*. Princeton: Princeton University Press.

Marsh, David. 1991. "British Industrial Relations Policy Transformed: The Thatcher Legacy." *Journal of Public Policy* 11 (3): 291–313. https://doi.org/10.1017/S0143814X00005341.

McHenry, Dean E. 1950. *The Third Force in Canada: The Cooperative Commonwealth Federation, 1932–1948*. Berkeley: University of California Press.

McInnis, Peter S. 2001. *Harnessing Labour Confrontation: Shaping the Postwar Settlement in Canada, 1943–1950*. Toronto: University of Toronto Press.

McRae, Kenneth D. 1964. "The Structure of Canadian History." In *The Founding of New Societies: Studies in the History of the United States, Latin America, South Africa, Canada and Australia*, edited by Louis Hartz, 219–74. New York: Harcourt, Brace & World.

Merritt, A. 1981. "The Development and Application of Masters and Servants Legislation in New South Wales 1845-1930." PhD Thesis, Australian National University.

Mill, John Stuart. 1852. *Principles of Political Economy: With Some Applications to Social Philosophy*. London: J.W. Parker & Sons.

Millis, Harry A., and Emily Clark Brown. 1950. *From the Wagner Act to Taft-Hartley; A Study of National Labor Policy and Labor Relations*. Chicago: University of Chicago Press.

Mitchell, Richard. 1989. "State Systems of Conciliation and Arbitration: The Legal Origins of the Australasian Model." In *Foundations of Arbitration: The Origins and Effects of State Compulsory Arbitration, 1890–1914*, edited by Stuart Macintyre and Richard Mitchell, 74–103. Melbourne: Oxford University Press.

Mitchell, Richard, and Esther Stern. 1989. "The Compulsory Arbitration Model of Industrial Dispute Settlement: An Outline of Legal Developments." In *Foundations of Arbitration: The Origins and Effects of State Compulsory Arbitration, 1890–1914*, edited by Stuart Macintyre and Richard Mitchell, 104–34. Melbourne: Oxford University Press.

Morris, Charles J. 2005. *The Blue Eagle at Work: Reclaiming Democratic Rights in the American Workplace*. Ithaca, NY: ILR Press, an imprint of Cornell University Press.

Neatby, H. Blair. 1972. *The Politics of Chaos: Canada in the Thirties*. Toronto: Macmillan.

Neatby, H. Blair. 1976. *William Lyon Mackenzie King: The Prism of Unity, 1932–1939*. Toronto: University of Toronto Press.

New Zealand Parliamentary Debates, House. 1892. "Industrial Conciliation Bill." Second Reading, 12 August, 27–52.
New Zealand Parliamentary Debates, House. 1893. "Industrial Conciliation and Arbitration Bill." 30 June, 144–71.
New Zealand Royal Commission on Sweating. 1890. "Report of the Royal Commission Appointed to Inquire into Certain Relations between the Employers of Certain Kinds of Labour and the Persons Employed Therein."
Nolan, Dennis R., and Roger I. Abrams. 1983. "American Labor Arbitration: The Early Years." *University of Florida Law Review* 35 (3) (Summer): 373–421. https://scholarship.law.ufl.edu/flr/vol35/iss3/.
Norris, R. 1975. *The Emergent Commonwealth: Australian Federation: Expectations and Fulfillment, 1889–1910.* Melbourne: Melbourne University Press.
O'Brien, Ruth. 1998. *Workers' Paradise: The Republican Origins of New Deal Labor Policy, 1886–1935.* Chapel Hill: University of North Carolina Press.
Ostry, Bernard. 1960. "Conservatives, Liberals and Labour in the 1870s." *Canadian Historical Review* 41 (2): 93–127. https://www.utpjournals.press/toc/chr/41/2.
Owram, Doug. 1986. *The Government Generation: Canadian Intellectuals and the State, 1900–1945.* Toronto: University of Toronto Press.
Palmer, Bryan D. 1992. *Working Class Experience: Rethinking the History of Canadian Labor, 1800–1980.* Toronto: Butterworth.
Patmore, Greg. 1991. *Australian Labour History.* Melbourne: Longman Cheshire.
Pelling, Henry. 1987. *A History of British Trade Unionism.* 4th ed. London: Macmillan.
Pfeffer, Jeffrey, and Alison Davis-Blake. 1990. "Unions and Job Satisfaction: An Alternative View." *Work and Occupations* 17 (3) (August): 259–84. https://doi.org/10.1177/0730888490017003001.
Pierce, Brooks. 1999. "Compensation Inequality." Office of Compensation and Working Conditions, Department of Labor, Working Paper No. 323.
Piven, Frances Fox, and Richard A. Cloward. 1977. *Poor People's Movements: Why They Succeed, How They Fail.* New York: Pantheon Books.
Playford, John. "Kingston, Charles Cameron (1850–1908)." Australian Dictionary of Biography, National Centre of Biography, Australian National University. Accessed 23 February 2013. http://adb.anu.edu.au/biography/kingston-charles-cameron-6966/text12099.
Plotke, David. 1990. "The Wagner Act, Again: Politics and Labor, 1935–37." *Studies in American Political Development*: 105–56. https://www.cambridge.org/core/journals/studies-in-american-political-development/article/abs/wagner-act-again-politics-and-labor-193537/83682039CAA8CA34CB17E01C1A061619.
Plowman, David H. 1989. "Forced March: The Employers and Arbitration." In *Foundations of Arbitration: The Origins and Effects of State Compulsory Arbitration, 1890–1914*, edited by Stuart Macintyre and Richard Mitchell, 135–55. Melbourne: Oxford University Press.

Plowman, David H., and Genevieve Calkin. 2004. "The Origins of Compulsory Arbitration in Western Australia." *The Journal of Industrial Relations* 46 (1) (March): 53–83. https://doi.org/10.1111/j.0022-1856.2004.00126.x.

Pollard, Sidney. 1985. "The New Unionism in Britain: Its Economic Background." In *The Development of Trade Unionism in Great Britain and Germany, 1880–1914*, edited by Wolfgang J. Mommsen, and Hans-Gerhard Husung, 32–52. London: Allen & Unwin.

Pontusson, Jonas. 2005. *Inequality and Prosperity: Social Europe versus Liberal America*. Ithaca, NY: Cornell University Press.

Pontusson, Jonas. 2013. "Unionization, Inequality and Redistribution." *British Journal of Industrial Relations* 51 (4) (October). Accessed 15 March 2020. https://doi.org/10.1111/bjir.12045.

Porter, J.H. 1967. "Industrial Peace in the Cotton Trade, 1875–1913." *Bulletin of Economic Research* 19 (1) (May): 49–61. https://doi.org/10.1111/j.1467-8586.1967.tb00400.x.

Portus, J.H. 1958. *The Development of Australian Trade Union Law*. Melbourne: Melbourne University Press.

Price, Richard. 1980. *Masters, Unions and Men: Work Control in Building and the Rise of Labour, 1830–1914*. Cambridge: Cambridge University Press.

Price, Richard. 1985. "The New Unionism and the Labour Process." In *The Development of Trade Unionism in Great Britain and Germany, 1880–1914*, edited by Wolfgang J. Mommsen and Hans-Gerhard Husung, 133–65. London: Allen & Unwin.

Quinlan, Michael. 1989. "'Pre-arbitral' Labour Legislation in Australia and Its Implications for the Introduction of Compulsory Arbitration." In *Foundations of Arbitration: The Origins and Effects of State Compulsory Arbitration, 1890–1914*, edited by Stuart Macintyre and Richard Mitchell, 25–49. Melbourne: Oxford University Press.

Reed, Louis S. 1930. *The Labor Philosophy of Samuel Gompers*. New York: Columbia University Press.

Reeves, W.P. 1902a. *State Experiments in Australia and New Zealand*. Vol. I. London: Grant Richards.

Reeves, W.P. 1902b. *State Experiments in Australia and New Zealand*. Vol. II. London: Grant Richards.

Reid, Alastair. 1991. "Employers' Strategies and Craft Production: The British Shipbuilding Industry 1870–1950." In *The Power to Manage? Employers and Industrial Relations in Comparative-Historical Perspective*, edited by Steven Tolliday and Jonathan Zeitlin, 35–51. London: Routledge.

Report of the Royal Commission on Strikes. 1891. New South Wales, Appointed November 25, 1890, Presented to Parliament, Sydney: G.S. Chapman, Acting Government Printer.

Rickard, John. 1976. *Class and Politics: New South Wales, Victoria and the Early Commonwealth, 1890-1910*. Canberra: Australian National University Press.

Robertson, David Brian. 2000. *Capital, Labor and State: The Battle for American Labor Markets from the Civil War to the New Deal*. New York: Rowman & Littlefield.

Robin, Martin. 1967. "The Trades and Labor Congress of Canada and Political Action, 1898-1908." *Industrial Relations/Relations Industrielles* 22 (2): 187-215. https://doi.org/10.7202/027780ar.

Robin, Martin. 1968. *Radical Politics and Canadian Labour, 1880-1930*. Kingston, Ontario: Industrial Relations Centre, Queen's University.

Rodgers, Daniel T. 1998. *Atlantic Crossings: Social Politics in a Progressive Age*. Cambridge: The Belknap Press of Harvard University Press.

Rosecrance, Richard N. 1964. "The Radical Culture of Australia." In *The Founding of New Societies: Studies in the History of the United States, Latin America, South Africa, Canada and Australia*, edited by Louis Hartz, 275-317. New York: Harcourt, Brace & World.

Ross, Arthur M., and Paul T. Hartman. 1960. *Changing Patterns of Industrial Conflict*. New York: John Wiley & Sons.

Roth, H. 1973. *Trade Unions in New Zealand: Past and Present*. Wellington, NZ: Reed.

Royal Commission on Strikes. 1891. *Report*. New South Wales, G.S. Chapman Printer.

Rubinstein, David. 1982. "Trade Unions, Politicians and Public Opinion, 1906-1914." In *Trade Unions in British Politics*, edited by Ben Pilott and Chris Cook, 58-78. London: Longman.

Salvatore, Nick. 1984. "Introduction." In *Seventy Years of Life and Labor: An Autobiography*, edited by Samuel Gompers (orig. pub. 1925). Ithaca, NY: ILR Press New York State School of Industrial and Labor Relations, Cornell University.

Saville, John. 1985. "The British State, the Business Community and the Trade Unions." In *The Development of Trade Unionism in Great Britain and Germany, 1880-1914*, edited by Wolfgang J. Mommsen and Hans-Gerhard Husung, 315-24. London: Allen & Unwin.

Schmitter, Phillipe. 1974. "Still the Century of Corporatism?" *The Review of Politics* 36 (1): 85-131. https://doi.org/10.1017/S0034670500022178.

Scotton, Clifford A. 1956. *A Brief History of Canadian Labour*. Ottawa: Woodsworth House.

Shadwell, Arthur. 1913. *Industrial Efficiency: A Comparative Study of Industrial Life in England, Germany and America*. London: Longmans, Green.

Shepherd, John. 1991. "Labour and Parliament: The Lib.-Labs. As the First Working Class MPs, 1885-1906." In *Currents of Radicalism: Popular Radicalism, Organized Labour and Party Politics in Britain, 1850-1914*, edited by Eugenio F. Biagini and Alastair J. Reid, 187-213. Cambridge: Cambridge University Press.

Silva, Stephen J. 2013. *Holding the Shop Together: German Industrial Relations in the Postwar Era*. Ithaca, NY: Cornell University Press.
Simeon, Richard, and Ian Robinson. 1990. *State, Society, and the Development of Canadian Federalism*. Toronto: University of Toronto Press.
Sinclair, Keith. 1965. *William Pember Reeves: New Zealand Fabian*. Oxford: Clarendon Press.
Sinclair, Keith. 1970. *A History of New Zealand*. Harmondsworth, UK: Penguin.
Skowronek, Stephen. 1982. *Building a New American State: The Expansion of National Administrative Capacities, 1877–1922*. New York: Cambridge University Press.
Slater, Dan, and Erica Simmons. 2010. "Informative Regress: Critical Antecedents in Comparative Politics." *Comparative Political Studies* 43 (7): 886–917. https://doi.org/10.1177/0010414010361343.
Soifer, Hillel David. 2012. "The Causal Logic of Critical Junctures." *Comparative Political Studies* 45 (12): 1572–97.
South Australian Chronicle. 1894a. "Conciliation in Industrial Disputes." Adelaide, SA, 17 November, 5. Accessed 11 February 2013. http://nla.gov.au/nla.news-title290.
South Australian Chronicle. 1894b. "Industrial Conciliation and Arbitration: The New Zealand Act." Adelaide, SA, 6 October, 8. Accessed 11 February 2013. http://nla.gov.au/nla.news-title290.
South Australian Register. 1890. "Summary of Remarks of Charles C. Kingston before the South Australian House Assembly on the Second Reading of the Industrial Disputes Settlement Bill." Adelaide, SA, 17–18 December, 6–7. Accessed 10 February 2013. https://trove.nla.gov.au/newspaper/title/41#:~:text=http%3A//nla.gov.au/nla.news%2Dtitle41.
South Australian Register. 1894. "Industrial Disputes and Conciliation." Adelaide, SA, July 3, 4. Accessed 10 February 2013. https://trove.nla.gov.au/newspaper/title/41#:~:text=http%3A//nla.gov.au/nla.news%2Dtitle41.
Spain, Jonathan. 1991. "Trade Unionists, Gladstonian Liberals and the Labour Law Reforms of 1875." In *Currents of Radicalism: Popular Radicalism, Organized Labour and Party Politics in Britain, 1850–1914*, edited by Eugenio F. Biagini, and Alastair J. Reid, 109–33. Cambridge: Cambridge University Press.
Spence, William G. 1909. *Australia's Awakening: Thirty Years in the Life of an Australian Agitator*. Sydney: The Worker Trustees.
Stephens, John D. 1980. *The Transition from Capitalism to Socialism*. Atlantic Highlands, NJ: Humanities Press.
Stephenson, W. Tetley. 1911. "The Railway Conciliation Scheme." *The Economic Journal* 21 (84) (December): 503–12. https://doi.org/10.2307/2221735.
Streek, Wolfgang, and Kathleen Thelen. 2005. "Introduction: Institutional Change in Advanced Political Economies." In *Beyond Continuity: Institutional Change in Advanced Political Economies*, edited by Wolfgang Streek and Kathleen Thelen. Oxford: Oxford University Press.

Stromquist, Shelton. 1987. *A Generation of Boomers: The Pattern of Railroad Labor Conflict in Nineteenth-Century America*. Urbana: University of Illinois Press.
Struthers, James. 1983. *No Fault of Their Own: Unemployment and the Canadian Welfare State, 1914–1941*. Toronto: University of Toronto Press.
Sundquist, James L. 1983. *Dynamics of the Party System: Alignment and Realignment of Political Parties in the United States*. Washington: The Brookings Institution.
Sutch, William B. 1966. *The Quest for Security in New Zealand, 1840 to 1966*. Wellington: Oxford University Press.
Sutcliffe, J.T. 1921. *A History of Trade Unionism in Australia*. London: Macmillan.
Sydney Morning Herald. 1900a. "Recognition of Trades-Unionism." 28 April, 5.
Sydney Morning Herald. 1900b. "Conciliation and Arbitration in New Zealand." 1 July, 7.
Sydney Morning Herald. 1901a. "Mr. See and the Labour Party." 10 June, 7.
Sydney Morning Herald. 1901b. "Compulsory Arbitration." 25 July, 6.
Sydney Morning Herald. 1901c. "Legislative Assembly." 30 August, 8.
Taft, Philip. 1957. *The A.F. of L. in the Time of Gompers*. New York: Harper & Brothers.
Teague, Paul, and John McCartney. 1999. "Industrial Relations in the Two Irish Economies." In *Proceedings of the British Academy*, vol. 98, 341–68. Oxford: Oxford University Press.
Thelen, Kathleen. 2001. "Varieties of Labor Politics in the Developed Democracies." In *Varieties of Capitalism: The Institutional Foundations of Comparative Advantage*, edited by Peter A. Hall and David Soskice. Oxford: Oxford Scholarship Online, November 2003. https://doi.org/10.1093/oxfordhb/9780199646135.013.31.
Tomlins, Christopher L. 1985. *The State and the Unions: Labor Relations, Law and the Organized Labor Movement in America, 1880–1960*. New York: Cambridge University Press.
Tuck, J. Hugh. 1983. "The United Brotherhood of Railway Employees in Western Canada, 1898–1905." *Labour/Le Travailleur* 11 (Spring): 63–88. https://doi.org/10.2307/25140201.
Turner, Herbert A. 1962. *Trade Union Growth, Structure and Policy: A Comparative Study of the Cotton Unions*. London: Allen & Unwin.
Turner, Ian. 1965. *Industrial Labour and Politics: The Dynamics of the Labour Movement in Eastern Australia, 1900–1921*. Canberra: The Australian National University.
Typographical Journal. 1911. "Even Numbered Arbitration Boards." Indianapolis, IN, May, 520.
United States Strike Commission. 1895. *Report on the Chicago Strike of June–July 1894*. Washington, DC: Government Printing Office.
United States Congress. 1935. Congressional Record, Senator Robert F. Wagner, Speech on the National Labor Relations Act (February 21), 74th Cong., 1st Sess., Vol 79: 2371–2.

Visser, Jelle. 2006. "Union Membership Statistics in 24 Countries." *Monthly Labor Review*, January: 38–49.
Voss, Kim. 1993. *The Making of American Exceptionalism: The Knights of Labor and Class Formation in the Nineteenth Century*. Ithaca, NY: Cornell University Press.
Watkins, Mel. "A Staples Theory of Economic Growth." In *Approaches to Canadian Economic History*, edited by William Thomas Easterbrook and Mel Watkins. Toronto: McClelland and Stewart.
Webb, Sydney, and Beatrice Webb. 1897. *Industrial Democracy*. New York: Augustus M. Kelley, Bookseller, Reprints of Economic Classics, Reprinted from the 1920 Edition in 1965.
Webber, Jeremy. 1991. "Compelling Compromise: Canada Chooses Conciliation Over Arbitration 1900–1907." *Labour/Le Travailleur* (Fall): 15–57. https://doi.org/10.2307/25143506.
Whitaker, Reginald. 1977. *The Governing Party: Organizing and Financing the Liberal Party of Canada, 1930–58*. Toronto: University of Toronto Press.
Whitten, David O. "The Depression of 1893." Accessed 4 July 2016. www.EH.net.
Wigham, Eric. 1982. *Strikes and the Government, 1893–1981*. London: Macmillan.
Witte, Edwin E. *Historical Survey of Labor Arbitration, Labor Relations Council of the Wharton School of Finance and Commerce*. Philadelphia: University of Pennsylvania Press.
Woods, H. D. 1973. *Labour Policy in Canada. Vol. 1 of Labour Policy and Labour Economics in Canada*. 2nd ed. Toronto: Macmillan.
Woods, Noel S. 1963. *Industrial Conciliation and Arbitration in New Zealand*. Wellington, NZ: R. E. Owen, Government Printer.
Wrigley, Chris. 1982. "The Government and Industrial Relations." In *A History of British Industrial Relations 1875–1914*, edited by Chris Wrigley, 135–58. Amherst, MA: University of Massachusetts Press.
Yellowitz, Irwin. 1965. *Labor and the Progressive Movement in New York State, 1897–1916*. Ithaca, NY: Cornell University Press.
Young, Walter. 1969. *The Anatomy of a Party: The National CCF, 1936–61*. Toronto: University of Toronto Press.
Zakson, Laurence Scott. 1989. "Railway Labor Legislation 1888 to 1930: A Legal History of Congressional Railway Labor Relations Policy." *Rutgers Law Journal* 20 (Winter): 317–91. https://leeds.primo.exlibrisgroup.com/discovery/search?query=creator,equals,Zakson,%20Laurence%20Scott,AND&tab=AlmostEverything&search_scope=My_Inst_CI_not_ebsco&sortby=rank&vid=44LEE_INST:VU1&lang=en&mode=advanced&offset=0.
Zammit, Nick. 2011. "Expectations Reconsidered: Canada in Another Context." Unpublished Manuscript, University of Warwick, 11 May.
Zeitlin, Jonathan. 1987. "From Labour History to the History of Industrial Relations." *Economic History Review*, 2nd ser. XL (2): 159–84. https://doi.org/10.2307/2596686.

Zeitlin, Jonathan. 1991. "The Internal Politics of Employer Organization: The Engineering Employers' Federation 1896–1939." In *The Power to Manage? Employers and Industrial Relations in Comparative-historical Perspective*, edited by Steven Tolliday and Jonathan Zeitlin, 52–80. London: Routledge.

Zieger, Robert H. 1969. *Republicans and Labor: 1919–1929*. Lexington: University of Kentucky Press.

Zolberg, Aristide R. 1986. "How Many Exceptionalisms?" In *Working Class Formation: Nineteenth Century Patterns in Western Europe and the United States*, edited by Katznelson, Ira and Aristide R. Zolberg, 397–455. Princeton: Princeton University Press.

Index

Amalgamated Society of Engineers, 91, 107, 119
Amalgamated Society of Railway Servants, 92–4
American Federation of Labor (AFL): abandonment of voluntarism in 1930s, 175; alignment with Democratic Party after 1908, 163, 167; and anti-partyism, 163–5; and avoidance of politics, 163; and depression of 1893, 136; embrace of voluntarism, 137–42; failure to eliminate labour injunctions, 160; opposition to compulsion, 138–42, 203; political mobilization after 1890, 163; and rejection of Morgan program, 164–5; rejects creation of a labour party, 164; takeover of Canadian labour movement, 208, 222, 250; weakened Canadian labour movement, 222–3, 227, 231. *See also* Gompers, Samuel; trade unions (US)
American Labour Union, 223
American Political Development (APD) explanations: problems with, 40–3, 196; state and party, 42; union and reformer, 42–3; working-class mobilization, 40–1
American progressives: as architects of legalism, 172, 176–7, 195, 260; attitudes towards trade unions, 144; and passage of Norris-LaGuardia Act, 175; and support for arbitration, 145; ties with Canadian trade unions and progressives, 229
American Railway Union, 147
Anglophone nations, 5–8, 273nn3–4. *See also* "most similar systems design"
Anti-Combination Acts, 119
Applegarth, Robert, 128
arbitration. *See* compulsory arbitration; voluntary arbitration
Arbitration Act of 1888 (US), 135, 147, 191, 207
Arbitration Act of 1894 (New Zealand), 75
Asquith, Prime Minister George, 95, 97, 100, 102, 114, 116–17
Australian Commonwealth, 71, 73
Aves, Ernest, 95

Balance, Prime Minister John, 67
Barnes, George, 95, 99
Bellamy, Edward, 76
Bell, Richard, 95, 99
Bennett, Prime Minister R. B., 230
Black Bill, 177
Board of Trade, 99, 101–2, 116
breakdown and culmination: in Canada, 229; critical antecedents and critical junctures as both important in, 259–60;

304   Index

breakdown and culmination: (*continued*) defined, 56–7, 254; in the US., 172
breakdown and replacement: in Australasia, 59, 255–7; in Canada, 198; critical junctures as dominant in, 255–6; defined, 56–7, 254
British North America Act, 215, 221, 226, 230, 242. See also *Toronto Electric Commissioners v. Snider*
Brooklands Agreement, 106
Buck's Stove & Range, Co. v. AFL, Lowe & Lawlor, 158
"business unions", 102, 139, 274n5
Buxton, Sydney, 102, 116

Campbell-Bannerman, Prime Minister Henry, 97, 114, 131, 162
Canadian Congress of Labor (CCL), 231, 237–8, 242
Canadian Cooperative Commonwealth Federation (CCF): as social democratic party, 26, 238–9, 242, 265; as threat to established parties, 228–9, 234, 261
Canadian Federation of Labour, 218, 231
Canadian Manufacturers Association, 235
Canadian Trades and Labour Congress. See Trades and Labour Congress (Canada)
Canadian "Wagner Act". See Industrial Relations and Disputes Investigation Act of 1948 (Canada); National Labor Relations Act of 1935 (US)
Cannon, Speaker Joseph, 160, 167
Chamberlain, Joseph, 100–1
Charnock v. Court, 93
Chartism, 35, 121–2
Chas. Wolff Packing Company v. Court of Industrial Relations of the State of Kansas, 151
Churchill, Sir Winston, 98, 100, 102, 104, 116–17

"class legislation", 192, 278n6
class origins and dominant ideology explanation. See Fragment theory
Clayton Act of 1914: as a "near miss", 51; interpreted by US courts, 158–9; and political party-union ties, 166; and political weakness of American labor, 160–1
Cleveland, President Grover, 147
Coal Commission, 194
Cohen, J.L., 23, 26, 45, 237–8, 262
collective bargaining: advantages of for employers, 121; as alternative to repression and compulsory arbitration, 193; in Australasia, 58, 84; as benefiting union leaders and well-paid employees, 277–8n6; as contributing to development of trade unions, 121; emerges late in Canada, 215–6; in Ontario, 238; in the US, 136, 193; and voluntarism, 10; weak in Canada during inter-war period, 231
collective bargaining (Great Britain): acceleration during critical juncture, 258; favoured by employers, 120, 124, 129; spread and formalization of, 106–12, 119–21, 129; state support for, 117–18; in voluntarism, 86–7; during wartime, 277n5
Combination Acts (Britain), 16, 87
Combination Laws Repeal Amendment Act of 1825 (Britain), 126–7
common law versus statutory law: in Australasia, 81–2, 257; in Canada, 219; in Great Britain, 126. See also courts
Commonwealth Supreme Court, 80
Communist Parties, 235, 243, 280n5
compulsory arbitration: acceptance by trade unions in Australasia, 69–72, 251, 256; accepted by some labour organizations in US, 138; adopted in Australasia, 30, 58–9, 74–9, 83, 256;

Index   305

embraced by American conservatives, 143–4, 146, 262; embraced by weaker trade unions, 24, 102, 138, 251, 256, 268; in Great Britain during wartime, 277n5; in Kansas (*see* Kansas): linked to union recognition in Australasia, 77; and railway labour disputes in US, 147–9, 276n4; rejected by Canadian railway union, 210; rejected in Great Britain, 89, 100–2, 109, 129, 249; rejected in US, 133–5, 147, 150–2, 151–2, 194, 262; repression as an alternative to in US, 137; result of learning and diffusion in Australasia, 78–9; in statist industrial relations regimes, 12–13; support among US progressives, 144–5; support and opposition from Canadian Trades and Labour Congress, 207, 209–10; support within the Canadian state, 205–11
compulsory conciliation and investigation: as a "middle way" between voluntarism and statism, 197, 202; Canada as a hybrid regime, 197; and its failure to address labour rights and recognition, 228. *See also* industrial relations regimes
Conciliation Act of 1896 (Great Britain), 114–15, 118, 132
Conciliation Act of 1900 (Canada), 199–202, 206, 209, 279n1
Conciliation and Arbitration Act of 1904 (Australia), 16, 80
Conference in Industrial Reorganization and Industrial Relations, 118
Congress of Industrial Organizations, 231
Conservative Party (Canada), 217, 219, 221, 232, 238
Conservative Party (Great Britain), 95–6, 128
Conspiracy and Protection of Property Act of 1875 (Great Britain), 16, 128
Coolidge, Calvin, 150

Council on Industrial Reorganization and Industrial Relations, 119
Court of Conciliation and Arbitration Act of 1904 (Australia), 80
courts: in Australasia, 45–6, 59, 80, 256; in Canada, 212–3, 227, 233; as explanation for trade unions' embrace of voluntarism, 140; in Great Britain, 45, 93–4, 128–31, 248; and hostility to trade unions, 9, 126–31, 141, 158–9; judicial versus parliamentary supremacy, 54–5; problems with as explanation for absence of voluntarism in US, 46, 159–60; as shaping unions' perceptions of the state, 80, 140–1; in the US, 45, 141. *See also* common law versus statutory law; "freedom of contract"; labour injunctions; parliamentary supremacy
Criminal Code Amendment of 1939 (Canada), 241
Criminal Law Amendment Act of 1871 (Great Britain), 122, 128
crises: accelerating voluntarism in Great Britain, 248; American "crisis within a crisis" in the 1930s, 174, 260; Australasia and US compared, 135–6; in breakdown and replacement pattern, 254; in Canada, 198, 205, 229, 233–7; defined, 48; economic, 29, 61–4, 81; impacts of, 135; Kansas miners strike, 150; scope, severity, and timing of, 31, 49, 135. *See also* critical junctures; economic downturns/crises; First World War; Second World War; strikes and lockouts
crisis as existential threat to trade unions: in Australasia, 59, 65, 83, 251; avoided in Canada, 198, 206; avoided in Great Britain, 104–8, 130–1; avoided in US, 135–7, 169, 172, 178–9; causal implications of, 247, 251–2; impact on outcomes, 27–9, 247, 251–4

critical antecedent conditions: in Australasia, 61–3, 81–3, 256–7; in Canada, 204, 229, 260; causal importance of vis-à-vis critical junctures, 57, 257; combining with critical junctures, 56; defined, 48, 53; geographic proximity of nations, 55, 257, 264; in Great Britain, 88, 119–29; as neglected in APD accounts of Wagner Act, 196; in the US, 188–94, 260; and varieties of causal impacts, 54. *See also* courts, judicial versus parliamentary supremacy; employer rejection or acceptance of trade unions

critical junctures: in Australasia, 60–1, 80–3, 255–6; in Canada, 198–204, 233–40; causal importance of vis-à-vis critical antecedent conditions, 57, 254–5; combining with critical antecedents, 56; defined, 18–19, 47–8; elements of, 48–52; fluidity and contingency in, 49; in Great Britain, 88–119; and lasting effects, 49; and "near misses", 51; in reconciling different APD explanations, 195; and the role of crises in, 47–9; in US, 173–88. *See also* critical antecedent conditions; permissive conditions; productive conditions; trade union-party relationships

Crompton, Henry, 101, 122
Cummins, Senator Albert, 148

Davis-Kelly bill. *See* National Industrial Recovery Act of 1933, Section 7(a) (US)
Deakin, Prime Minister Alfred, 68, 75
Deering v. Duplex Printing Co., 159
Delano, F. A., 146
Democratic Party (US): and adoption of National Labor Relations Act, 194; compared to Liberal Party in Canada, 244–5; and electoral gains in 1930s, 42, 174, 254, 260–1; and New Deal coalition, 26, 172, 260; start of New Deal realignment before 1930, 189, 264

Disraeli, Prime Minister Benjamin, 128
"dual unionism" (Canada), 225
Dyer, Colonel Reginald, 110

economic downturns/crises: accompanied by industrial unrest, 135; in Australasia, 59, 63–4; Australasia and US compared, 136; in Canada, 205; in general, 29; in Great Britain, 88; Great Britain and Australasia compared, 105, 114, 131; in the US, 135–6, 173. *See also* critical junctures

economic structure: as a rival explanation, 29–34

employers: attitude toward state intervention in labour relations, 25, 137; impact on reformers and state preferences, 28; impact on trade union preferences for state intervention, 28, 103; importance of, neglected in APD explanations for the Wagner Act, 196; opposition to compulsory arbitration, 79, 101, 137; organizations of, 108, 277n5; political weakness in 1930s, 172, 174; recognition of trade unions, 28, 43, 62, 134; rejection of voluntarism in US, 159–60, 170; strategies towards trade unions, 27–9, 109–10; victory over Australasian trade unions, 63. *See also* employers' accommodation of trade unions in Great Britain

employers' accommodation of trade unions in Great Britain: in general, 25, 55, 87, 109–13, 116, 119–20, 170, 247–8, 258–9; impact on the state, 247–9; impact on trade unions, 103,

247–8; reasons for, 111–13, 123, 125, 259; as reducing the impacts of reformers, 249
Employers' Federation of Engineering Associations, 110
employers' hostility towards trade unions: in Australasia, 59, 61–3, 65–6, 70, 249, 255; in Canada, 198, 204, 211–2, 215, 234–6; causing trade unions to be cautious, 154–5; causing trade unions to distrust the state and parties, 250; in Great Britain, 87, 90–2, 105; impeding trade union organization, 249–50; making legalism or statism necessary, 189, 247, 262; in New Zealand, 59, 61–3; reasons for, 88, 90–1, 154–9, 278n4; state support of, 154, 158–9; tactics used to repress/discourage unionism, 154; in US, 25, 137, 152–60, 172, 179, 189, 249, 260; and US – British comparison, 120, 153–9, 169; use of violence towards unions, 154
Engineering Employers Federation, 91, 107
equifinality, 18
Erdman Act of 1898 (US), 135, 139, 142–3, 146–8, 191–2
Esch, Rep. John J., 148

Fabians, 76, 95, 99, 104
federalism: in Australia, 58, 67, 69, 71, 79; in Canada, 232, 241–2; Canada and US compared, 244; as explanation for outcomes, 44–5
First World War, 136, 139, 191, 238
Flett, John, 208
Forsey, Eugene, 45, 237–8
Fragment theory, 34–8
Frankfurter, Justice Felix, 158, 190
freedom of contract, 60, 62, 158–9
Free Labour Association, 110

General Federation of Trade Unions, 95
geographic proximity of nations. *See* critical antecedent conditions
George, Henry, 76
George, Lloyd, 99, 116–17
Germany, 9, 15, 88, 113, 153
Gladstone, Prime Minister William, 90, 104, 116, 123, 128
Gompers, Samuel: belief in trade unions as "natural" organizations, 168; and Canadian labour movement, 208; control over American Federation of Labor, 138–9; embrace of "pure and simple" business unionism, 139, 167, 274n5; embrace of voluntarism as ideology, 141–2; fear of union competition with labour party, 167–8, 263; negative views of unions' political involvement, 140–2; opposition to compulsory measures, 139, 142, 152, 203; and opposition to labour party creation, 165–8. *See also* American Federation of Labor; trade unions (US)
Great Depression of the 1930s: as catalyst for New Deal and legalism, 172; impact on Canadian politics and labor relations, 231–2; impact on US industrial relations, 139

Harding, President Warren, 149–50
Harrison, Frederic, 122, 128
Higgins, Henry, 74
Hitchman Coal & Coke Co., v. Mitchell, 159
Homestead strike, 49, 136, 154
Hooper, Ben, 150
Hoover, President Herbert, 193
Hornby v. Close, 126, 128
House of Lords, 93
Howell, George, 128
Huggins, William, 151
Hughes, Thomas, 122, 128

ideology. *See* Fragment theory
Industrial Conciliation and Arbitration Act, (New Zealand), 16
industrial conflict. *See* strikes and lockouts
industrial conflict: crises of, 49, 61–3; defeat as an existential threat to trade unions, 27, 65–6, 134–6, 248; impact on of size of US labour market, 136; and impact on reformers, 29; impact on unions' political decisions/involvement, 29, 66–9; kept in check by repression in US, 136–7; in Western Canada, 199–200. *See also* strikes and lockouts
industrial conflict, rates of across regime types: explanation for variation, 268–9; highest under voluntarism, 268; lowest under statism, 268. *See also* strikes and lockouts
Industrial Council, 104, 118
Industrial Disputes Inquiry Commission, 235
Industrial Disputes Investigation Act of 1907 (Canada): adopted, 17, 50, 52, 100, 127, 203, 217; as antecedent condition for legalism in Canada, 229, 240–1; as an unsatisfactory answer to the labour question, 264; applied to "public utilities", 198; based upon Railway and Labour Disputes Act (RLDA) of 1903, 197, 203; created by William Mackenzie King, 200; declared *ultra vires*, 215; described, 197–8; labour movement support for varied, 203, 229; legitimacy undermined during Second World War, 235. *See also* industrial relations regimes, Canada as a hybrid
industrialization: and early British lead in, 123–4, 157, 247; impact on growth of British trade unions, 124; as intensifying class conflict, 3; as slow in Canada, 215

industrial relations: defined, 4, 8; and the state's interest in, 4–5
Industrial Relations and Disputes Investigation Act of 1948 (Canada): approved by Parliament, 240; described, 17; drafted, 237–8; embodying Wagner Act principles, 243; provincial prototypes of, 241; as successor to Order-in-Council PC 1003, 240, 243
industrial relations regimes: Canada as a hybrid, 5–6, 197; Colin Crouch's typology, 13–15; compared, 5–6, 9–13; criteria for evaluating success, 265; defined, 5, 8; durability of, 265–7; in promoting union density, 267–8; in stemming industrial unrest, 268–9; types of, 5–6. *See also* breakdown and culmination; breakdown and replacement; legalism; punctuated gradualism; repression; statism; voluntarism
injunction. *See* labour injunction
institutional explanations: bureaucratic organization and capacity, 45; judicial and legal, 45–6; separation of powers v. parliamentary systems, 44; unitary v. federal systems, 44–5
Interstate Commerce Act (US), 146
Interstate Commerce Commission (US), 142

Johnson, Gen. Hugh, 181
joint control. *See* collective bargaining
judicial review, 159
judiciary. *See* courts

Kansas: experiment with compulsory arbitration, 134–5, 150–2; Industrial Court, 151; US Supreme Court invalidates Industrial Court, 194, 262. *See also* strikes and lockouts

Kettle, Rupert, 121, 123, 125
Keyserling, Leon, 23, 186, 195, 261
Kingston, Charles Cameron, 23, 26, 74–5, 78, 104, 256–7
King, William Lyon Mackenzie: as author, 201; belief that voluntary measures were insufficient, 202; creator of RLDA and IDIA, 199–204, 226; labour mediator, 201–3; Labour Minister, 206; liberal reformer, 23, 26, 199–204, 280n2; opposition to compulsory arbitration, 210–1; philosophy of industrial relations, 201, 213; Prime Minister of Canada, 232–3, 236; protecting the public as justification for compulsion, 201, 280n3; pushed to the left by CCF, 239; reasons for lack of support for labor rights, 213; and "responsible" unions, 214; view of state as "impartial umpire", 213
Knights of Labour: in Australasia, 67, 70; in Canada, 205, 207, 218, 276n1; support for compulsory arbitration, 208; in US, 138–9, 154–5

Labor Disputes bill of 1934 (US), 184, 186
labour injunctions: expanded use in 1920s, 189; failure to curtail in US, 160, 165; loss of support for in US, 189, 260; US-British comparison, 159; used in Canada, 212–13; used in US, 140, 158
labour movements. *See* trade unions
Labour Party (Canada): failure to organize before 1930s, 224–6
Labour Party (Australia): emergence of, 67; varied importance of for passage of arbitration across states and Commonwealth, 68–9, 80
Labour Party (Great Britain), 26, 96, 248
Labour Party (New Zealand), late emergence of, 67–8

"labour question", alternative explanations for answers to, 29–46; as a misnomer, 201; answers to (*see* industrial relations regimes): defined, 3–5; explanation for answers adopted, 27–8, 246–54; multiple meanings of, 4, 265–6
Labour Representation Committee (LRC), 95–6
labour unions. *See* trade unions
land reform, 73
Lansdowne, Lord Henry, 111
Lassalle, Ferdinand, 140
Lauck, Jett, 177, 193, 195, 260
League for Social Reconstruction, 232
legalism: arising out of rejection of voluntarism and statism, 133–4, 168, 173, 188–9; Canada's importation of Wagner Act priniples from US, 229, 240, 243–4, 262, 264; conditions leading to the emergence of, 28, 172, 247; culminating in the NLRA, 186; and declining support for labour injunctions, 189–90; described, 5–6, 11–12, 171–2; durability of, 266–7; emerging from implementation of Section 7(a) of NIRA, 182–6; emerging from pre-New Deal legal and policy innovations, 190–3; as grafted on to compulsory investigation and conciliation in Canada, 197; hastened by Great Depression and New Deal coalition, 182–7; hastened by trade union abandonment of voluntarism, 175, 193–4; as malleable to changing political and economic conditions, 266; outcome that was not inevitable in Canada and the US, 253–4; paths taken in Canada and US compared, 241–2, 244; resisted by Liberal government in Canada, 233; in the US, 19

310   Index

Legislative Councils, 60, 69, 79–80
Leiserson, William M., 185
Lemieux Act. *See* Industrial Disputes Investigation Act
Lethbridge mining strike. *See* strikes and lockouts
Lewis, John L., 177, 194
liberal ideology, 4, 34–5, 74–6, 214
Liberal Party (Canada): adoption of compulsory investigation and conciliation, 199; allied with Quebec reactionaries, 232; allied with Trades and Labour Congress, 215, 224; attenuated relationship with labour movement, 221, 224; capitulation to labour in 1940s, 228–9, 242; challenged by CCF, 238–9, 261; committed to voluntarism in 1940s, 233; continuity in government, 207; as dominant at turn of 20th Century, 220; as pan-Canadian, 221, 250; support for judicial independence, 226
Liberal Party (Great Britain): debate over immunity from damages, 95–8; favouring blanket immunity, 97–8; legislates labour rights, 26; and passage of protections from criminal prosecution, 128; responsive to trade union demands, 131, 162; strong historical ties to trade unions, 259; victory in 1906 elections, 258. *See also* "lib-lab" coalitions
Liberal Party (New Zealand), 26, 66–9, 80. *See also* "lib-lab" coalitions
Liberal Party (Australia), 67–8, 72–4, 82. *See also* "lib-lab" coalitions
"lib-lab" coalitions: in Australasia, 59, 66–9; in Canada, 203; in Great Britain, 96, 98–9, 248, 259
"logic of industrialism", 33–4
London Dock Strike, 90
Lyons v. Wilkins, 93

Maritime Council, 62, 70
Marshall, Alfred, 123
Master and Servant Laws, 126, 129
McBride, John, 139, 165
Millar, Andrew J., 70
Mill, John Stuart, 76, 123
Miners Federation, 90, 106
Minimum Wage Act, 107
Morgan program. *See* American Federation of Labor
"most similar systems design", 6–7, 18
Mulock, William, 206, 210
Mundella, A. J., 115, 121–3, 125, 128
Murray Hill Agreement, 156–7, 249, 263

National Association of Manufacturers, 153, 163
National Civic Federation, 157, 249, 263
National Industrial Conference, 118
National Industrial Recovery Act (NIRA) of 1933, Section 7(a) (US): as a concession to organized labour, 178, 261; as almost an after-thought, 254; arising out of crisis, 50; a blend of legalism and voluntarism, 178, 180–1; as borrowed from Kelly-Davis bill, 193–4; as catalyst for trade union organization and militancy, 174, 178–9; containing labour rights, 173, 177, 260, 279n2; *Denver Tramway* case, 185; embodying legalist principles, 173, 178; employer resistance to, 179–82; as example of failed voluntarism, 181–3, 194; failure of, leading to National Labor Relations Act of 1935, 175; *Houde Engineering Company* case, 185; as including restraints on employers, 178–9; intended to redress imbalance of power between employers and employees, 187; invalidated by Supreme Court, 184, 187; lessons from implementation of, 23, 182–6;

moving from mediating disputes to enforcing rights, 186; problems with implementation and enforcement, 180–3; shaped by reformers and trade unions, 23, 195
National Labor Board, 178, 180–6, 261
National Labor Relations Act (NLRB) of 1935, (US): and American Political Development explanations, 41–2, 195; arising out of learning from NIRA failures, 184–5, 261; Canadian trade unions demand for, 237, 243; continuity with pre–New Deal legislation, 173; as culmination of legalism, 16–17, 171; differences with Railway Act of 1926, 191; drafted to increase constitutionality, 187; goals of, 193; impact on Canada, 229, 233, 243–4; rooted in National War Labor Board policies, 191, 260; rooted in railway labour legislation, 191–2; rooted in the "law of agency" and "responsible unionism", 190, 263; as shaped by Progressive reformers, 23; Supreme Court upholds, 172, 187–8, 254
National Labor Relations Board (NLRB), 183–6, 233
"National Policy" (Canada). *See* Conservative Party (Canada)
National Recovery Administration (NRA), 181, 183
National Union of Railwaymen, 92
National War Labor Board, 45, 191, 237, 239
New Deal coalition, 174–5
New Deal recovery program, 176–86
Newlands Act of 1913, 135, 147
New Protectionist Policy, 73
New South Wales Royal Commission on Strikes, 75, 78
"new" unions: in Australasia, 83; in Canada as industrial unions in the West, 199; in Great Britain, 88–90, 105, 258; as spurring the creation of labour parties, 166
NLRB v. Jones and Laughlin Steel Corp., 187
Norris-LaGuardia Act of 1932: as a pre–New Deal response to Great Depression, 50, 260; and declining support for labour injunctions, 189–90; and employer rejection of voluntarism, 160; helpful for labour organizing, 188–9; mixture of voluntarism and legalism, 175; National War Labour Board reliance upon, 191; outlaws labour injunction, 152, 170; railway legislation as a precursor to, 193; resulting from 1930 election, 174
Norris, Sen. George, 190

Olney, Richard, 147
Order-in-Council PC 1003 (Canada): based upon Wagner Act, 17, 243; issued during 1944 strikes, 50, 234, 236, 261; replaced by IRDIA, 231, 239
Owen, Robert, 121, 127

Padlock Law of 1937 (Quebec), 232
parliamentary supremacy: absent in US, 152, 159; in Australia, 81–2; in Great Britain, 87, 129, 259. *See also* courts
party realignment, 189
pastoralists, 62
People's Party, 164
permissive conditions: in Australasia, 61–6; in Canada, 199–200, 234–7; in general, 52–3; in Great Britain, 89–94; in US, 173–4
Phillips, Wendell, 265
Pickard, Ben, 95
policy feedback, 195
political coalitions: as explanation for outcomes, 38–43

312 Index

political parties, 25
Positivists, 101, 122, 248
Privy Council, 215, 230
productive conditions: in Australasia, 66–81; in Canada, 200–3, 237–40; in general, 52–3; in Great Britain, 94–119; in US, 174–88
progressivism: in Canada, 200, 232; in the Anglophone world, 74, 144–5. *See also* American progressives
Protectionist Party, 73
Provincial Workmen's Association (Nova Scotia), 207
Public Resolution Number 44, 184
Pullman strike. *See* strikes
punctuated gradualism: antecedent conditions as dominant in, 257–9; defined, 56–7; in Great Britain, 87, 254, 257–9

Quinn v. Leatham, 93

R. v Duffield, 126
R. v. Rowlands, 126
radicalism: in Great Britain, 127–8, 248. *See also* radical liberals; reformers, role of
radical liberals, 7, 23, 63, 73, 127, 129. *See also* Liberal Party (Great Britain)
Railway Labor Act of 1926 (US), 52, 135, 173, 260, 263
Railway Labor Board (US), 148–50
Railway Labour Disputes Act of 1903 (Canada): as a precursor to IDIA, 197, 202; passage of, 217
railway labour policy: in Canada (*see* Railroad Labour Disputes Act): in Great Britain, 91–2, 107, 117; in US, 138, 144, 147–50
Railway Regulation Act of 1844, 92
Reeves, William Pember, 23, 26, 74–5, 77, 104, 201, 256–7

Reform Act of 1867, 128, 130
reformers: antipathy to strikes and lockouts, 75, 99; in Australasia, 73–80; in Canada, 233, 260; in Great Britain, 87, 99, 121–8, 249; greater impact where employers refused to accept unions, 251, 256; greater impact with more severe crises, 251, 256; impact of, 23, 200–1; in learning and diffusion of innovations, 78; role of, 22–3; and support for unions, 76–7. *See also* American progressives; radical liberals; state socialists
regimes. *See* industrial relations regimes
repression of trade unions: in Australia, 16; in Canada, 16, 208; in Great Britain, 16; in New Zealand, 16; as regime type, 9; as shaping unions' ideology, membership and agenda in US, 141; in US, 16, 133, 136, 140–1, 166. *See also* courts
Republican Party (US), 146, 148, 151–2, 260
Richberg, Donald, 181
"right of contract", 9
Ritchie, Lord Charles, 100
Robson, Sir William, 97
Roosevelt, Franklin: plan to enlarge Supreme Court, 230; position on the Wagner Act, 245; and the NIRA, 180, 183, 245, 261
Roosevelt, Theodore, 146
Rosebery, Lord Archibald, 90–1, 116
Royal Commission of 1868, 125
Royal Commission on Labour of 1891, 94, 101, 104, 114
Royal Commission on the Relations of Capital and Labour, 209
Royal Commission on Trade Disputes of 1906, 94

Scheckter Poultry Corp. v. United States, 187
Second World War: as Canada's second critical juncture, 229, 261; catalyst for Canadian trade union demands, 238; employers' refusal to recognize trade unions, 235; forces state intervention in industrial relations, 234; increases Canadian unions' size and power, 233–4; legitimacy crisis for Canadian government, 234–7; and War Labor Board, 236
self-regulation. *See* voluntarism
Shackleton, David, 98
Shadwell, Arthur, 153
shearers, 62
"Sheffield Outrages", 122
Sherman Act (US), 140, 158
Shipowners Association, 62
single case studies: limitations of, 18
Smith, Llewllyn, 100
Smith, Ralph, 203, 207–9
Social Credit Party, 242
Social democratic model, 38–40
Socialist Party (Canada), 225–6
Spence, W. G., 70
State socialism/socialists, 28, 76, 99, 213, 255
statism: arising out of existential threat to unions, 251; conditions disfavouring in US, 168–9, 247; conditions favouring the emergence of, 28, 247; described, 5–6, 12–13; dismantled in late Twentieth Century, 266; embraced by Australasian reformers, 75–6, 144; limited version adopted in Canada, 197–8; as not inevitable in Australasia, 253; rejected in Great Britain, 89, 100–2, 109, 129, 249; rejected in US, 28, 134–52, 188, 262; strong version rejected in Canada, 28, 227, 262, 264

strikes and lockouts: in Australia, 61–3, 255; on British railways, 91–2, 107, 116–17; in British textiles, 106; in Canada, 198, 205, 234–6, 261; in Canadian mining, 200; and Canadian Northern Railway, 199; and Canadian Pacific Railway, 199, 205; in coal mining, 90, 107, 115–16, 206; in cotton, 91; Dock strike, 90; Engineering lockout, 9, 106; in general, 3; Grand Trunk Railway, 205; in Great Britain, 19, 88–94, 108; Homestead, 49, 135–6, 154; jeopardizing fuel supplies in Western Canada, 200; in Kansas, 150; Kirkland Lake, 236; as leading to collective bargaining, 109; Lethbridge, 203, 205–6, 213; Maritime, 50, 62–3, 67; national strike, 89, 91; in New Zealand, 62–3; Pullman, 49, 135–7, 143, 147, 150, 154, 192; shearers, 62; in the US, 136, 179; on US railways, 136, 147–9
Sweden, 15, 38

Taff Vale, 93–6, 108, 110–12, 126, 158, 159, 248, 277n1
Taft-Hartley Act, 19
Taft, President William, 160, 167
Temperton v. Russell, 93
Terms of Agreement, 106, 156
Terms of Settlement of 1898, 106–7
Tillett, Ben, 99, 102
Toronto Electric Commissioners v. Snider: as obstacle to labor rights in Canada, 230. *See also* British North America Act
Toronto Trades and Labour Council, 207
Trade Disputes Act of 1906 (Great Britain), 16, 51, 87, 92, 96–8, 108, 111, 131, 159, 162, 212, 248, 253

Trades and Labor Congress, TLC (Canada), embrace of IDIA, 203; abandonment of voluntarism, 244; and CCL, 231; and Knights of Labour, 218; position on compulsory arbitration, 207–10; reflecting fragmentation, 250; support for amending BNA, 230; support for Canadian Wagner Act, 237; weakened by AFL takeover, 222, 250

Trades and Labour Council (New Zealand), 70

Trades Union Congress, TUC (Great Britain), 95–7, 100, 102, 110, 128, 259

Trade Union Act of 1871 (Great Britain), 16, 83, 123, 128

Trade Union Act of 1875 (Great Britain), 93, 122, 223

Trade Union Act of 1878 (New Zealand), 83

Trade Union Amendment Act of 1876 (Great Britain), 16, 83

trade union density: benefits of higher density for workers, 282n3; decreasing after demise of statism and voluntarism, 267–8; highest under statism, 267; increasing after adoption of regimes, 267; lowest under legalism, 267; reasons for union density rate variation, 267–8

trade union militancy: in Australasia, 61–3, 255; in Canada, 198, 216, 228, 235, 279n1; in general, 24; in Great Britain, 88, 105, 123; making legalism more likely, 189; rising with unpopularity of labor injunctions, 190; in US, 148, 178–80, 184, 189–90

trade union-party relationships: in Australasia, 66–70, 72–3, 250, 257; in Canada, 220–1, 221–6, 238–9, 250; in general, 24, 26, 55, 162; in Great Britain, 95–7, 127–9, 131, 162, 248, 258–9

trade unions: contributing to the growth of collective bargaining, 108; density rate as poor predictor of political success, 161; distrust of courts, 126; having positive impacts on workers' lives, 281n3; impact of organizing on political capacity, 248; industrial unions, 229, 234, 242; influence (or lack of) in legislative bodies, 24, 161, 279n4; legalization of, 82–3, 198; political mobilization of, 66–9, 128–9, 248; preference for voluntarism, 23, 137; "pure and simple" unionism, 138; recognition of, 9, 119, 180. *See also* crisis as existential threat to trade unions; employers' hostility towards unions; "new unions"; trade unions' legal insecurity; trade union militancy; trade union-party relationships; trade unions (Australia; Canada; Great Britain; New Zealand; US)

trade unions (Australia): defeat, 62–3; disengagement from politics before crisis, 60–1; early enfranchisement of workers, 82; low density at turn of 20th Century, 71; part of broad coalitions, 72–3; political mobilization, 66–9; spread of unionism, 83

trade unions (Canada): growing strength in Second World War, 228, 230, 242, 261; impact of Wagner Act, 244; repression, 231–2; ties with US unions, 227; weakness and fragmentation of, 198, 204, 207, 215–7, 222, 231, 233

trade unions (Great Britain): efforts to make acceptable, 121–3; and immunity from damages, 94–8; resilience of, 105–8, 129, 258; survival and membership growth after *Taff Vale* and Trade Disputes Act, 92, 104, 108, 112, 129; during wartime, 277n5 trade unions (New Zealand): compared with Australia, 62; low density at turn of 20th Century, 71; political mobilization, 66–9; spread of unionism, 83

trade unions (US): company unions, 180, 182–5; embrace of legalism in 1930s, 174–5, 262; failure to achieve voluntarism, 133–4; frustration with courts, 140; frustration with political action and elected branches of government, 140–1; political weakness prior to 1930s, 169; railway brotherhoods in US, 191; reject creation of a labour party, 164; rejection of compulsory measures, 137–42, 145, 148, 151, 210; repression of by courts and police, 140, 169; role in bringing about National Industrial Recovery Act, Section 7(a), 195; surge in political participation during New Deal, 174; ties to Democratic Party, 134, 144, 163–4, 174; use of fragmented government to veto legislation, 143–4

Trade Unions Act of 1872 (Canada), 219–20

Trade Unions Act of 1881 (Australia), 83

trade unions' legal insecurity: in Canada, 219–20, 231; in Great Britain, 92–4, 122, 126, 128; in US, 133. *See also* American Federation of Labor; trade unions' legal insecurity; trade union militancy; trade union-party relationships

trade unions' positions on compulsory measures: in Australasia, 60–1, 69–72, 83; in Canada, 203, 207–9; Canada and US compared, 206; in general, 23–4; in Great Britain, 100, 103, 126, 131; in US, 137–8, 148, 168–9

Transportation Act of 1920 (US), 135, 144, 148–9, 263

Trollope v. London Building Trades Federation, 93

unfair labour practices, 172, 185, 186
unionization. *See* trade unions; trade union density
unions. *See* trade unions
Union Steam Ship Company, 62
United Mine Workers (Canada), 206
United Mine Workers (US), 24, 139, 159, 177, 193, 214, 260; in US, 144, 152–3, 250; in US and Great Britain compared, 162–6
US Strike Commission, 143, 147

"varieties of capitalism", 14
voluntarism: abandoned by Canadian labour movement, 244; abandoned by US labour movement, 193, 261; as a quixotic goal of American labour movement, 170, 262–3; conditions favoring the development of, 27–8, 211–12, 247–9; described/defined, 5–6, 10–11, 55, 114; dismantled in late Twentieth Century, 266; embraced in Great Britain, 86, 104, 114–5, 118–25, 129–31, 170; as infeasible in Canada, 28, 198, 211–24, 226, 264; as infeasible in the US, 28, 133–4, 152–68, 188–9, 194, 261–2; an outcome that was not inevitable in Great Britain, 253; reasons for trade union support in US, 140–3; role of state in, 87, 114–19; status of trade unions in, 137–8; in US railway legislation, 191; wartime as exceptional, 118

voluntary conciliation and arbitration: in Australasia, 72, 78; in Canada, 199, 202, 209, 216; in Great Britain, 101, 117, 120, 129; in US, 135, 139, 142–3, 147 voting franchise: early extension in Australasia, 60, 81–3; slow extension of in Great Britain, 12

wages boards. *See* compulsory arbitration; statism
Wagner, Sen. Robert: arguments in favor of NLRA, 171, 187, 281n6; author of NLRA, 187, 195; as key state actor, 26, 196, 245; and NIRA Section 7(a), 177–8; as NLB Chairman, 181, 187, 245, 261; as progressive reformer and leader, 23, 172, 260
Wagner Act. *See* National Labor Relations Act of 1935
Wakefieldism, 30
Walton, Sir John, 97

War Labor Board (US), 173
Webb, Beatrice, 1–4, 99
Webb, Sydney, 95, 99, 104
Western Federation of Miners, 214
Whitley Councils, 118
Wilkie, Alexander, 99
Wilson v. New, 151
Wilson, Woodrow, 51, 160, 165–6, 190–1
Wise, Bernhard Ringrose, 74
Workers Unity League, 231, 281n5
World War I. *See* First World War
World War II. *See* Second World War

yellow dog contracts: expanded use of in 1920s, 190; made illegal under Norris-LaGuardia Act, 179, 260; prohibition of, 192; as tool of employers, 147, 154, 159

Milton Keynes UK
Ingram Content Group UK Ltd.
UKHW022243130624
444101UK00006BA/217